THE ENGLISH
CIVIL WARS

LOCAL ASPECTS

Books by R.C. Richardson

Puritanism in North-West England. A Regional Study of the Diocese of Chester to 1642, Manchester University Press, 1972.

British Economic and Social History. A Bibliographical Guide, with W.H. Chaloner, Manchester University Press, 1st edn 1976, 2nd edn 1984, 3rd edn 1996.

The Debate on the English Revolution, Methuen, 1977.

The Urban Experience. English, Scottish and Welsh Towns, 1450–1700, with T.B. James, Manchester University Press, 1983.

Freedom and the English Revolution, with G.M. Ridden, Manchester University Press, 1986.

The Debate on the English Revolution Revisited, Routledge, 1988.

The Study of History. A Bibliographical Guide, Manchester University Press, 1988.

Town and Countryside in the English Revolution, Manchester University Press, 1992.

Images of Oliver Cromwell, Manchester University Press, 1993.

THE ENGLISH CIVIL WARS

LOCAL ASPECTS

EDITED BY
R.C. RICHARDSON

SUTTON PUBLISHING

First published in 1997 by
Sutton Publishing Limited · Phoenix Mill
Thrupp · Stroud · Gloucestershire · GL5 2BU

British Library Cataloguing in Publication Data
A catalogue record for this book is available from the British Library

ISBN 0 7509 1240 5 (case)
ISBN 0 7509 1241 3 (paper)

Cover illustration: contemporary engraving showing Colonel Lunsford assaulting the Londoners at Westminster Hall (History Today *archives*)

ALAN SUTTON™ and SUTTON™ are the
trade marks of Sutton Publishing Limited

Typeset in 10/12 pt Baskerville.
Typesetting and origination by
Sutton Publishing Limited.
Printed in Great Britain
by WBC Limited, Bridgend.

CONTENTS

NOTES ON CONTRIBUTORS

B.G. Blackwood was Head of History at Felixstowe College until his retirement. He is the author of *The Lancashire Gentry and the Great Rebellion, 1640–60*, Chetham Society, 3rd series 25, (Manchester, 1978), and more than twenty articles in historical journals. He is currently completing a book on Tudor and Stuart Suffolk.

Joan A. Dils is a part-time tutor for the Extra Mural departments of the Universities of Reading and Oxford. Her research interests lie in the social and economic development of the Middle Thames area in the early modern period. Her publications include *Redding, 1540–1640* (1980), based on the work of a research group, and a chapter in *The Growth of Reading*, ed. M. Petyt (1993).

Alan Everitt is Hatton Professor Emeritus of English Local History in the University of Leicester; he was elected a Fellow of the British Academy in 1989. His publications include *Suffolk and the Great Rebellion, 1640–1660* (Ipswich, 1960); *The Community of Kent and the Great Rebellion, 1640–1660* (Leicester, 1966); *Change in the Provinces: the Seventeenth Century* (Leicester, 1969); *The Pattern of Rural Dissent: the Nineteenth Century* (Leicester, 1972); *Perspectives in English Urban History* (London, 1973); *Landscape and Community in England* (London, 1985); *Continuity and Colonization: the Evolution of Kentish Settlement* (Leicester, 1986). He is at present writing a book on *The Common Lands of England: an Inquiry into their History and Extent*.

P.G. Holiday obtained his BA and Ph.D. degrees from the University of Leeds. On graduating he entered university administration, and after a varied career involving posts on both sides of the former binary line, is now Academic Registrar of Queen Mary and Westfield College, University of London.

Roger Howell, Jr. (1936–89) spent twenty-five years at Bowdoin College, Maine, and was President of the College for a ten-year period from 1968. His principal publications were *Newcastle upon Tyne and the Puritan Revolution* (Oxford, 1967); *Cromwell* (London, 1977); *Puritans and Radicals in North England. Essays on the English Revolution* (Washington DC, 1984). See also *Images of Oliver Cromwell. Essays by and for Roger Howell*, ed. R.C. Richardson (Manchester, 1993).

Tai Liu was born in Nanyang, Honan, China in 1930 and was brought up in traditional Chinese culture. He was uprooted by a destructive civil war and eventually sought refuge in the West. He studied for his MA and Ph.D. at Indiana University and taught at the University of Delaware from 1967 until his retirement in 1993. His chief publications are *Discord in Zion. The Puritan Divines and the Puritan Revolution, 1640–1660* (The Hague, 1973) and *Puritan London. A Study of Religion and Society in the City Parishes* (Newark, Delaware, 1986).

Patrick McGrath (1914–91) taught at the University of Bristol from 1946. He became Reader in History in 1963 and was appointed Professor in 1975. His publications include *The Marchants Avizo* (Boston, Mass., 1957); *Papists and Puritans under Elizabeth I* (London, 1967) and *The Merchant Venturers of Bristol* (Bristol, 1975). He edited for the Bristol Record Society volumes of *Records relating to the Society of Merchant Venturers of the City of Bristol in the Seventeenth Century* (1952), and *Merchants and Merchandise in Seventeenth-Century Bristol* (1955), and also served as general editor for the Society.

C.B. Phillips is Senior Lecturer in Economic History at the University of Manchester where he has taught since 1969. He has published various articles on the Civil War period, the landed gentry, the iron industry, urban history, and on the use of computers in historical research and in history teaching. His edition of the Lowther Family Estate Books 1617–75 appeared in 1979 and he contributed to *Town and Countryside in the English Revolution*, ed. R.C. Richardson (Manchester, 1992).

R.C. Richardson has been Head of History at King Alfred's College since 1977 and before that was Senior Lecturer in History at Thames Polytechnic, London. He has held visiting professorships at the University of Southern Maine in 1982 and 1988 and at Southern Oregon University in 1993 and from 1995–7. His principal publications are *Puritanism in North-West England* (Manchester, 1972); *The Debate on the English Revolution* (London, 1977, 1988, 3rd edn 1997); *The Urban Experience. English, Scottish and Welsh Towns, 1450–1700* with T.B. James (Manchester, 1983); *Freedom and the English Revolution*, with G.M. Ridden (Manchester, 1986); *Town and Countryside in the English Revolution* (Manchester, 1992); *Images of Oliver Cromwell* (Manchester, 1993). He is general editor of two series of books published by Manchester University Press – *Historical Bibliographies* and *Issues in Historiography* and has been co-editor of the journal *Literature & History* since 1975.

M.J. Stoyle is Lecturer in History at the University of Southampton. He is the author of *Loyalty and Locality: Popular Allegiance in Devon during the English Civil War* (Exeter, 1994) and *From Deliverance to Destruction: Rebellion and Civil War in an English City* (Exeter, 1996). He is currently working on the place of the Civil War in folklore, memory and myth.

Philip Styles (1905–76) had an academic career at the University of Birmingham first as Special Lecturer in Local History from 1932 and then as Reader from 1948 until his retirement in 1970. He contributed a number of papers to the Dugdale Society many of which were collected together in *Studies in Seventeenth-Century West Midlands History* (Kineton, 1978). For many years he edited the *University of Birmingham Historical Journal.*

Philip Tennant is a former university lecturer specializing in nineteenth-century French poetry and painting who in early retirement switched to local history, particularly that of South Warwickshire from which his family originated. The result was to add to his study of *Theophile Gautier* (London, 1975); *Edgehill and Beyond: the People's War in the South Midlands* (Stroud, 1992) and *The Civil War in Stratford-upon-Avon: Conflict and Community in South Warwickshire 1642–1646* (Stroud, 1996), both considerably expanding the subject of his article, originally published in *Warwickshire History*, 1989/90.

John Webb was formerly Head of the History Department at Portsmouth College of Education and a principal lecturer at Portsmouth Polytechnic. He has written extensively on the local history of Hampshire and Suffolk, his special interest being urban history during the early modern period. His publications include *The City of Portsmouth and the Royal Navy* (London, 1984); *The Spirit of Portsmouth – A History* (Chichester, 1989), of which he was joint author; *Great Tooley of Ipswich: Portrait of an Early Tudor Merchant* (Ipswich, 1962). He also edited two volumes of sixteenth-century documents in the Suffolk Records Society series (1966, 1996), and has made numerous contributions, on a wide variety of historical topics, to learned journals and symposia.

ACKNOWLEDGEMENTS

Permissions to reprint the various articles contained in this collection have been granted as follows:

Chapter 2, originally published as a Historical Association (General Series) pamphlet in 1969 is reprinted with the kind permission of the author and of the Historical Association.

Chapter 3 is reprinted with the kind permission of the author and publisher of *Guildhall Studies in London History* III:2, 1978, in which the article first appeared.

Chapter 4 – originally published in the *Portsmouth Papers* series in 1969 and in a revised form in 1977 – appears here with the permission of the author and of Portsmouth City Council.

Chapter 5 was originally published as a pamphlet by the Bristol branch of the Historical Association and appears by the permission of the copyright owner, Mrs Sheila McGrath, the author's widow.

Chapters 6 and 7 appear by kind permission of their respective authors and of the editor of *Southern History*, the journal in which they were first published (in 1994 and 1989).

Chapter 8 appears by kind permission of the author and of the editor of *Warwickshire History*.

Chapter 9 appears by kind permission of the Dugdale Society.

Chapters 10, 11 and 12 appear by kind permission of their respective authors and of the editor of *Northern History* in which journal they were first published (in 1978, 1993 and 1970).

Chapter 13 appears by kind permission of the author's literary executor, Professor Paul Nyhus of Bowdoin College, Maine, and of the Society of Antiquaries of Newcastle upon Tyne which first published the article in *Archaeologia Aeliana*, 5th ser., VIII, 1980.

INTRODUCTION: LOCAL HISTORIANS AND THE ENGLISH CIVIL WARS

R.C. Richardson

Few subjects in English history have attracted more attention and disagreement than the causes, course and consequences of the Civil Wars. The debate began in the seventeenth century while blood was still being spilt in battle and sieges, and quartering, requisitioning, plundering and dispossession were being experienced. In different ways the confrontations and controversies still continue towards the end of the last decade of the twentieth century.[1] For generations of commentators Civil War politics was the centre of interest and historians like Clarendon, Hume, Macaulay and S.R. Gardiner devoted themselves to resolving its complexities and to establishing the precise sequence of events.[2] History, indeed, as a field of study in the later nineteenth century when Gardiner was writing his large-scale, multi-volume narrative history of the early Stuarts was largely defined as 'past politics' and it was the chronologies of kings, parliaments, and the events related to their doings, which were deemed most important.

It was within this kind of narrative framework that the earliest local and regional histories of the English Civil Wars were firmly placed. Written largely by amateurs, it should be noted, such histories were designed to have one overriding primary function: to illustrate the national picture by means of local detail. With this object in mind J.R. Phillips offered his *Memoirs of the Civil War in Wales and the Marches 1642–1646* (London, 1874). G.N. Godwin followed suit with his study of the *Great Civil War in Hampshire* (London, 1882), 'a useful aid', so he said in its preface, 'to the recorders of the great events of English history'.[3] Alfred Kingston brought out his two like-minded books on *Hertfordshire during the Great Civil War* (London, 1894), and *East Anglia and the Civil War* (London, 1897).

A new crop of local studies of the Civil War period came out in the early years of the twentieth century and their authors were able to place them securely within the detailed picture of events outlined by Gardiner's *History* and its continuation by Sir Charles Firth, Regius Professor of History at the University of Oxford. A second edition of Godwin's book on Hampshire, which appeared in 1904, made abundant and deferential use of these secondary sources as did J.W. Willis-Bund's account of *The Civil War in Worcestershire, 1642–1646 and the Scottish Invasion of 1651* (Birmingham, 1905). Ernest Broxap's *The Great Civil War in Lancashire 1642–51* (Manchester, 1910), and A.R. Bayley's *The Great Civil War in*

Dorset 1642–1660 (Taunton, 1910), were written at Firth's suggestion and were both published in the same year. Sir Charles Thomas-Stanford's *Sussex in the Great Civil War and the Interregnum 1642–1660* (London, 1910), was issued at the same time and again deferentially acknowledged Firth's help. These local historians knew their subordinate place in the Edwardian academic order and never challenged the primacy of the professional historians and their outline of national politics.

Total war in the years 1914–18 brought home the harsh realities of conflict in ways never felt before in England and helped condition a new outlook on warfare in the past and its intrusions on nation, locality and home. A noticeable historiographical wind of change began to be felt in the interwar period. W.J. Farrow's book, *The Great Civil War in Shropshire 1642–49* (Shrewsbury, 1926), offered more than a political and military narrative, finding space for a discussion of the growth of parties and – unusually for its time – of neutralism and of the social aspects of the struggles in the county. Studies by Mary Coate and A.C. Wood of Cornwall and Nottinghamshire published in 1933 and 1937 respectively went even further in recognizing the depth and intensity of localism in these two counties. In the first of these books Mary Coate left the reader in no doubt that she saw Cornwall's history as that of:

> a county with a strong personality, priding itself on its peculiarities and alive with a local patriotism rooted in racial differences and fed by geographical isolation . . . Again and again this local patriotism . . . knit together in a common unity men of differing political and religious opinions.

Alfred Wood took a similar line in offering a predominantly social approach to Nottinghamshire in the Civil War, setting out the distinctive features of his county, examining Royalist and Parliamentarian organization, and the religious developments of the time:

> The war in Nottinghamshire was predominantly local in character and it can be isolated for separate treatment without distortion or omission of the facts. I have endeavoured throughout to keep the parish pump linked up to the main street, but my primary object has been to narrate the fortunes of this county during the twenty most febrile and dramatic years of its history.[5]

After 1945 with another wartime experience behind them, with private collections of landed families' estate and other records increasingly available and with the new county record offices in operation, another generation of local and regional historians was well placed to develop the credentials of their subject and move out in a number of new directions. And increasingly these historians were professionals not amateurs. Local history became firmly established in higher education, a favourite field for doctoral dissertations, and a laboratory for new, pathfinding research.

One direction in which a number of local and regional historians moved was in that of the 'gentry controversy' initiated by R.H. Tawney and H.R. Trevor Roper. Conducted in its earliest stages at the level of generalization and giving off more heat than was comfortable for anyone, the next phase of the debate proceeded by means of detailed case studies of particular counties; the microscope rather than the wide-angled lens was summoned into use. Mary Finch was one of the first to grasp its value. In her painstaking monograph, *The Wealth of Five Northamptonshire Families 1540–1640* (Northants. Record Society, XIX, 1956), she lent support to Tawney's interpretation of the gentry's fortunes in the early modern period by showing the steady profits that could be obtained from landowning. Alan Simpson's work, *The Wealth of the Gentry 1540–1660. East Anglian Studies* (Cambridge, Mass., 1961), had broadly similar conclusions.

> Apart from a few Bacons that rose, a few Heydons that crashed, and rather more who disappeared through lack of male heirs, it is an interesting possibility, after all the talk of rise and fall, that the rest may just have endured. If so, it would be something of an anti-climax; but to one student, at least, the agrarian history of this century has turned out to be far more prosaic than he ever expected.

A stream of further county studies of the gentry followed. H.A. Lloyd dealt with *The Gentry of South West Wales 1540–1640* (Cardiff, 1968), while J.T. Cliffe provided a weighty volume, *The Yorkshire Gentry from the Reformation to the Civil War* (London, 1969), which explored the economic fortunes, religious affiliations and political allegiances of the social elite of that county. B.G. Blackwood's heavily quantitative examination of *The Lancashire Gentry and the Great Rebellion, 1640–1660* (Manchester, 1978), is one of the latest in a very distinguished line of historical research.

The unit of investigation in all these gentry studies was the county and no historian did more to vindicate the value of this research focus than Alan Everitt in a stream of publications in the 1960s. First came his book *Suffolk and the Great Rebellion, 1640–1660* (Suffolk Record Society, III for 1960, Ipswich, 1960), then – more influentially – *The Community of Kent and the Great Rebellion, 1640–1660* (Leicester, 1966), and two complementary essays both published in 1969, *Change in the Provinces: the Seventeenth Century* and *The Local Community and the Great Rebellion*.[7] The last of these, which originally appeared as a Historical Association pamphlet, is reprinted in this volume (pp. 15–36).

Everitt's primary emphasis, as the title of his book on Kent made absolutely clear, was on county communities, each of which had a unique set of defining features:

In many respects, despite its ancient centralized government, the England of 1640 resembled a union of partially independent county-states of communities, each with its own distinct ethos and loyalty . . . One important aspect of the history of the Great Rebellion is certainly the gradual merging or submerging of these communities, under the stress of revolution, in the national community of the New Model Army and the Protectorate.

Everitt's book on Kent in some ways took its cue from the earlier study of Cornwall by Mary Coate in its insistence that the historian's task was to uncover the local determinants of local issues and circumstances, and not to illustrate through local evidence the familiar sequence of national events. Despite its proximity to London 'the most striking political feature of Kent during 1640–1660', he wrote, 'was its insularity'. Active Royalists and Parliamentarians in the county were at first militant minorities of extremists. The moderate majority preferred to remain neutral for as long as possible, and in the 1650s resisted the intrusions of the Protectorate no less strongly than they had opposed King Charles I. The county community reunited and, though not unchanging in its actual composition, was no less in evidence in 1660 than it had been in 1640. The backbone of Everitt's 'community' of Kent was its gentry. They were its embodiment and its spokesmen. Almost three quarters of them were indigenous to the county and by and large they were men 'whose connections were confined to the circle of neighbours and cousins whom they met in their manorhouses day by day'. Caught up in the continuities and complex fabric of everyday social and economic life they endured the dramatic but temporary impact of Civil War.[7]

Other historians followed where Everitt had led, Anthony Fletcher for example in his substantial study *A County Community in Peace and War. Sussex 1600–1660* (London, 1975). His title no less than Everitt's proclaimed the same assumptions and definitions; the gentry again occupied centre stage. A more noticeable trend, however, since the mid-1970s has been for Everitt's model of the county community to be re-evaluated and modified. Even Fletcher by the time he published his book, *The Outbreak of the English Civil War* (London, 1981), had had second thoughts about the introversion of county communities, about the nature of localism and neutralism, and the relationship between them.[8] Others went further in their criticisms. Clive Holmes, for example, in an influential article published in 1980 insisted that in many ways Everitt's model relied too heavily on the very untypical county of Kent.[9] Moreover he brought Everitt to task for over-stressing the importance of both localism and of counties, for minimizing the gentry's awareness of, and involvement in, a wider world, for playing down the significance of deep-seated ideological divisions, for neglecting the importance of popular politics, and for presenting the central government as some kind of monolithic external 'Other'. The stress on the internal features of Everitt's local world of the county meant that too little attention had been paid to what was happening outside at the national centre. The collapse of Ship Money collection in 1639/40, for example, needed to be explained not just in terms of the strength of local opposition to it but of the growing inability of the central government – distracted by the Scottish war and its attendant problems – to crush its opponents. Everitt's prioritizing of the gentry was also criticized, as was his stress on the administrative unity of the county. JPs functioned for the most part within sub-divisions of counties. Full gatherings of all the JPs of a shire were infrequent and when whole county events did take place – at the Assizes or in county elections – they provided forceful reminders of the national, and not simply local, context. Internally counties were far more multi-layered and disunited than Everitt's model allowed.[10] Ann Hughes agreed and set out her case in an essay published in 1989. Counties, she argued, were not homogenous and settlement patterns, economic activity, social and religious networks, and administrative arrangements were not determined by county boundaries. Even in politics, she insisted, the importance of counties as units could easily be exaggerated as tense relations between corporate towns and their surrounding shires amply demonstrated. 'Communities' in seventeenth-century England and the outlooks that accompanied them were plural and overlapping. No county was coterminous with a single, coherent, all-important 'community'.[11]

Ann Hughes had earlier published an important monograph, *Politics, Society and Civil War in Warwickshire, 1620–1660* (Cambridge, 1987), in which she had challenged many of Everitt's findings in more detail. This county, economically diverse and with no major urban centre, had boundaries which were quite irrelevant to many of its inhabitants. Agriculture, landholding, trade and industry all had more complex and geographically extended patterns. Lawyers had practices which extended in range beyond the limits of the shire. The gentry as a group were lacking in county coherence; they were as likely to marry outside Warwickshire as within it, and indulged in an antiquarianism which, above all, displayed their heraldic interests. They were not torn by conflicting loyalties to the nation and the county, and though neutralism was in evidence in and after 1642 it took different, disunited forms. The lack of 'county-mindedness', not the strength of it, in Hughes's view, provided the key to Warwickshire's experience of Civil War.[12]

John Morrill's earlier study, *Cheshire 1630–1660. County Government and Society during the 'English Revolution'* (Oxford, 1974), had also reached different conclusions from those of Everitt about the nature of his 'county community' and its upheavals. Cheshire's 'crisis' in the 1640s was not a gentry monopoly. Nor was it even the same kind of crisis for both 'county gentry' and 'parochial gentry'. It went deeper than Everitt had allowed and its different forms corresponded to the varied experience and growing self-confidence of different social groups. Morrill found signs at least of stirrings of a grassroots social revolution at village level which, unsurprisingly, the gentry on both sides found unwelcome.[13]

The particular strength of county community studies lay in their detailed exposure of the subtleties and distinctive texture of provincial life. For some historians, however, this strength, paradoxically, produced their greatest weakness – a kind of 'island' approach to the history of individual shires. To counteract this tendency David Underdown, for instance, in his account, *Somerset in the Civil War and Interregnum* (Newton Abbot, 1973), was careful to explore the interconnections between local and national politics and demonstrated, for instance, the ways in which MPs' attitudes and actions were responses to local conditions.

A similar concern with the dialectical relationships between the centre and the provinces underpinned Clive Holmes's study, *The Eastern Association in the English Civil War* (Cambridge, 1974). Holmes took pains to show that the rise and fall of the Eastern Association could not be satisfactorily explained in regional terms; it was not the 'natural' outcome of regional conditions. 'The Association was formed in spite of, rather than because of, the socio-economic substructure of the region'. Puritan unity was not the explanation either. And in politics it was not choice but necessity which brought the eastern counties together. Local and regional forces, therefore, in Holmes's scenario were simply not strong enough to bring the Association into being in the first place nor to keep it together later. Rather it was a 'complex and tension ridden dialogue' between politicians in London and those in the counties which conditioned each stage of the Eastern Association's existence. Ultimately it was the Parliamentarian leaders who first created and then dismantled this instrument of aggression.[14]

The very title of John Morrill's book, *The Revolt of the Provinces: Conservatives and Radicals in the English Civil War 1630–1650* (London, 1976), proclaimed its major concern with the interactions between London and the counties. What Morrill dealt with was both resistance to Charles I's policies before 1640 and resistance to aspects of the impact of the Civil Wars themselves, the physical destruction which came in their wake and the increased, unremitting burdens of taxation. Morrill had much to say about the provinces' perceptions of outside events and policies and he underlined the importance of both neutralism and radical conservatism as elements in the range of provincial responses to the shifting scene in the two decades after 1630.[15]

Everitt's own studies of county communities and most of those written by the historians who followed him had relatively little to say about the specifically urban experience of the mid-century crisis. This neglect has been countered both at a general and specific level. Roger Howell produced two important articles dealing with urban elites in the provinces and the ways in which their conservatism was translated into neutralism or political alignment when the crisis burst after 1640. R.C. Richardson's edited volume, *Town and Countryside in the English Revolution* (Manchester, 1992), explored the numerous points of contact between towns and their rural hinterlands, their shared and separate interests, and asked questions about the extent to which the English Revolution could be considered to have been urban led and about its 'winners' and 'losers'. Case studies of the experience of five urban communities in the Civil War period and its aftermath were provided.[16]

One of these case studies was London and it joined a growing collection of investigations of the Civil War capital. Occupying pride of place in these studies was Valerie Pearl's account of *London and the Outbreak of the Puritan Revolution. City Government and National Politics, 1625–43* (Oxford, 1961). In it she challenged simplistic accounts of London's alignment with the Parliamentarian cause, demonstrating conclusively that it was only in 1642 that a puritan coup took place which captured control of the city government and trained bands. She took the story forward in a later article, 'London's Counter Revolution', and her earlier account was amplified and in some respects modified in a book by Robert Ashton, *The City and the Court, 1603–1643* (Cambridge, 1980). Keith Lindley carefully scrutinized the political attitudes and activity of London citizens in the 1640s in two important essays. Tai Liu provided a full-length study of London Puritanism. An essay by him dealing with the city's part in the 1640s Presbyterian experiment is included in this collection.[17]

The provincial capitals in the mid-century decades have also found their historians. John T. Evans in his examination, *Seventeenth-Century Norwich. Politics, Religion and Government 1620–1690* (Oxford, 1980), demonstrated the stability of the city's political elite, the enduring economic links with London based on the textile trades, and the absence of profound social change or revolution. Roger Howell's major study, *Newcastle upon Tyne and the Puritan Revolution* (Oxford, 1967), examined the political as well as economic implications of Newcastle's coal supply link with London (its main customer), and the ways in which the experience of Civil War provided new opportunities within Newcastle to attempt to prise open the grip of the ruling oligarchy on the corporation and the coal trade. (An article by Roger Howell on Newcastle is reprinted in this collection, pp. 309–29). David Harris Sacks placed Bristol's Civil War years within the context of a longer time span in his impressive book, *The Widening Gate. Bristol and the Atlantic Economy, 1450–1700* (Berkeley and Los Angeles, 1991). York and Exeter, other provincial capitals, have had their Civil War histories addressed by David Scott and Mark Stoyle.[18]

Ports in the Civil War period have also found their historians. A.M. Johnson examined the intricacies of 'Politics in Chester during the Civil Wars and the Interregnum, 1640–1662'. John Webb wrote on the siege of Portsmouth, an essay reprinted in this volume, (pp. 63–90). Inland provincial towns during the mid-century decades have also received attention. David Underdown's absorbing study, *Fire from Heaven. Life in an English Town in the Seventeenth Century* (London, 1992), dealt at length with Dorchester, tracing the establishment of a puritan ascendancy in the town in the aftermath of the great fire of 1613 and the vicissitudes of Civil War and its aftermath. Adrienne Rosen surveyed Winchester's Civil War history and showed that despite extensive destruction and economic dislocation recovery and reorientation were relatively rapid. Most recently Philip Tennant – a contributor to this volume – has provided a useful study of *The Civil War in Stratford-upon-Avon* (Stroud, 1996).[19]

Religious developments in the localities have also attracted attention. R.A. Marchant examined *The Puritans and the Church Courts in the Diocese of York 1560–1642* (London, 1960), while R.C. Richardson analyzed the structural components of *Puritanism in North-West England. A Regional Study of the Diocese of Chester to 1642* (Manchester, 1972). In a study of Essex William Hunt looked at *The Puritan Moment. The Coming of Revolution in an English County* (Cambridge, Mass., 1983). Essex also received attention from Alan Macfarlane who, marrying history with sociology and psychology, produced a fascinating reconstruction of *The Family Life of Ralph Josselin, a Seventeenth-Century Clergyman* (Cambridge, 1970). A similar painstaking reconstruction, *Wallington's World. A Puritan Artisan in Seventeenth-Century London* (London, 1985), was attempted by Paul Seaver and revealed the complex, multi-layered, paradoxical, and tension-laden relations between religion and capitalism in the early modern capital city. With the aid of churchwardens' accounts John Morrill documented the survival of Anglicanism at parish level in the 1640s and '50s. John Bossy, Keith Lindley, M.J. Harvan, Hugh Aveling and P.R. Newman wrote on different aspects of the Roman Catholic community in the provinces and in London.[20]

All of these studies of towns and of religious developments in the English Revolution had something to say about the varied experiences of groups below the gentry. 'History from below', indeed, has become a thriving branch of Civil War studies no less than in many other fields. A key contribution, which relied heavily on local evidence such as corporation records and voting lists to make its case, was Derek Hirst's *The Representative of the People? Voters and Voting in England under the Early Stuarts* (Cambridge, 1975). Hirst demonstrated the increasing frequency of contested constituency elections and the exertion of pressure on elected MPs from an electorate growing in size, political knowledge and experience. Riots and disturbances – which clearly formed part of the pre-Civil War scene in the provinces – have been examined in a number of important local studies. Buchanan Sharp's *In Contempt of All Authority, Rural Artisans and Riot in the West of England, 1586–1660* (Berkeley and Los Angeles, 1980), was joined by Keith Lindley's investigation of *Fenland Riots and the English Revolution* (London, 1982), which portrayed the political ramifications and consequences of drainage schemes, enclosure and the loss of common rights. David Underdown's highly original and pathfinding book, *Revel, Riot and Rebellion. Popular Politics and Culture* (Oxford, 1985), was concerned with patterns of popular allegiance in the Civil Wars. Concentrating his research on the western counties, Underdown attempted to show how long-term trends involving population growth, inflation, enclosure,

Puritanism and regional culture were integrated with the politicizing effects of Civil War. Given the difficulties and intractability of his sources Underdown's achievement in portraying rank-and-file Parliamentarians and Royalists and their settings was astonishing and it is little wonder that the publication of his book was hailed as one of the major events of the decade in Civil War studies.[21]

That a book of his kind could achieve such high-ranking status is indicative of what has happened to local history in England in the post-Second World War decades. Though it is still a flourishing branch of historical studies in its own right with professionals leading it and with a larger than ever army of amateur followers the impact of the local approach on Civil War studies now extends beyond its immediate boundaries. Local history research has become so firmly integrated into the general practices of history that books which on the face of it seem only tangentially related to the parish pump in fact, in varying degrees, rely on it. In political history Kevin Sharpe's monumental study, *The Personal Rule of Charles I* (New Haven and London, 1992), presented a revisionist case for the absence of royal tyranny in the years 1629 to 1640 which depended partly on the careful marshalling of local sources. Robert Ashton's book on *Counter Revolution. The Second Civil War and its Origins, 1646–48* (New Haven and London, 1994), its title notwithstanding, is partly a local study. Social History, however, has come to have a special relationship with Local History, so much so that the dividing line between them often becomes almost invisible. The book by Felicity Heal and Clive Holmes, *The Gentry in England and Wales, 1500–1700* (London, 1994), is a good example. In socio-military history Charles Carlton's *Going to the Wars. The Experience of the British Civil Wars, 1638–1651* (London, 1992), would have been inconceivable without the elaborate piecing together of a vast assortment of local material. So would Stephen Porter's recent examination of *Destruction in the English Civil Wars* (Stroud, 1994). Finally historians studying the social and cultural identities and ramifications of Puritanism have made unmistakably clear their reliance on the sources and strategies of the local historian. How else could Christopher Durston's and Jacqueline Eales's collection of essays, *The Culture of English Puritanism, 1560–1700* (London, 1996), have made any headway with its investigation of Puritanism as a form of popular religious culture, of puritans and the church courts, of puritans and iconoclasm, of the puritan death-bed, of opposition to Puritans, of the continuities in Puritanism, and of puritan rule in the late 1640s and '50s and the failure of cultural revolution? Such books, like the present volume, provide further proof of the absolute necessity of the local approach and are indications that Local History in England is emphatically not the poor relation of historical studies.

The essays reprinted in this collection range in date from 1969 to 1994 and bear witness to the historiographical changes that have occurred in these years and to the very considerable amount of research and writing that have been devoted to the local and regional history of the English Civil War period. They draw on a wide range of source material housed in county and urban record offices, in two cases make use of archaeological evidence, they pose and attempt to answer a large number of questions, and they employ a significant variety of research and presentational strategies.

Quite deliberately the book begins with its most general and wide-ranging component – Alan Everitt's famous essay on 'The Local Community and the Great Rebellion'. First published in 1969 this was one of the chief statements Everitt made about his 'county community' model of England's mid-seventeenth-century experience. Using the two case studies of Leicestershire and Northamptonshire the author examined the ways in which Civil War entered the dense and unique fabric of two very different localities and the networks of gentry families they contained.

Tai Liu's essay, reprinted here as chapter 3, dates from 1978 and takes us away from the Midlands, from 'county communities', and from the world of politics and of the gentry to London. His subject is the capital's experience of the mid-1640s Presbyterian experiment and he relates it to the complexities of city government, to London factions, to the Scottish presence, and to the role of vocal and influential clergymen such as William Gouge and Edmund Calamy.

The remainder of the volume follows a geographical pattern, moving from the southern counties to the North. Chapters 4, 5 and 6 deal, in different ways, with three sieges. In the first – published in a revised form in 1977 – John Webb examines the siege of Portsmouth, one of the early encounters of the first Civil War. He shows why the port and dockyard mattered to both sides, why and how they vied for control of it, and how it fell to the Parliamentarian general Sir William Waller. Patrick McGrath's siege – a later one – is that of Bristol. He makes clear the city's preference for neutrality and self-determination and shows how the pressures of external forces, far more than factions within, made such a posture impossible to sustain. A longer lasting siege than that which Portsmouth experienced, it had correspondingly greater implications for the civilian population, not least for the women of the city. Their activism comes under review and in the course of it we catch significant glimpses of the redoubtable Mrs Dorothy Hazard whose defiance of the Royalist intruders became legendary. Mark Stoyle's subject is Exeter and the impact of the prolonged siege which it endured in the course of the first Civil War. The importance of 'defensive destruction' is stressed and the extent of it is partly explored with the aid of newly-acquired archaeological evidence. The repairing and revival of the city form the author's postscript.

Joan Dils's essay in chapter 7, which first appeared in *Southern History* in 1989, is an 'impact study' of a different kind. Chiefly using parish registers and reinforced with archaeological evidence, she looks at the consequences for the civilian population of Berkshire of the movement of disease-ridden rival armies.

Philip Tennant's study in chapter 8, originally published in *Warwickshire History* for 1989/90, is again concerned with the impact of the criss-crossing of troops of the rival armies, of the presence of the Royalist garrision at Banbury and that of the Parliamentarians at Warwick, and of the attendant requisitioning, quartering, plundering and other forms of lawlessness which went on.

In chapter 9 Philip Styles offers a rounded, long-span study of Worcester, the largest city in the West Midlands, through the middle decades of the seventeenth century which stresses its deep-seated provincialism and the corporation's determination to defend its chartered privileges. Tensions, factions and side-taking are examined as well as the damage and pillaging incurred when the city changed hands in the 1640s. Unpleasant though they were, however, they were nothing in comparison with the destruction and carnage which took place in 1651 when Worcester became the scene of the last and crushingly unsuccessful Royalist attempt – led by the future Charles II – to reverse the military outcome of the Civil Wars.

C.B. Phillips in chapter 10 surveys the implications of the coming of Civil War for the gentry of Cumberland and Westmorland. He shows that a reputation for Royalism notwithstanding it is more accurate to view these two counties as a primarily neutral area in which Royalists attempted to recruit support. He also demonstrates that Parliamentarian convictions that Royalism and Popery here went hand in hand rested on prejudice rather than evidence.

In chapter 11, reprinted from *Northern History* of 1993, B.G. Blackwood offers a characteristically ambitious statistical approach to the geographical and social patterns of Civil War allegiance in Lancashire, Norfolk and Suffolk, calling into question as he proceeds some aspects of localist interpretations of this period.

P.G. Holiday in chapter 12 takes as his starting point Joan Thirsk's work on Royalist estates in S.E. England which showed conclusively that the vast majority of those temporarily dispossessed regained their lands by 1660. Yorkshire, it seems, witnessed the same process with 87% of Royalist estates coming back to their original owners, often with the aid of agents or friends acting as intermediaries.

Finally in chapter 13 Roger Howell looks at the interaction between local and national politics in the period between the reign of James I and the Glorious Revolution taking Newcastle, 'the eye of the North' as his example. He examines the dominance of the town's inner ring, the 'lords of coal', and the intrusion of outside forces, as in 1645 when a Parliamentarian corporation was installed and in 1662 when, in a very different set of political conditions, the corporation was again remodelled.

The essays chosen for inclusion in this volume thus range very widely – geographically, thematically, socially, and historiographically. They demonstrate first that the experience of Civil War in England was essentially plural and lacking in uniformity and second, since this is the case, that local historians of the English Civil Wars have placed all others in their debt. As late as the 1970s in opening his essay on 'The City of Worcester during the Civil Wars' the late Philip Styles could diffidently state that 'local studies of the Civil War tell us more about its effects than about its causes'. Today's local historians are more bold. Mark Stoyle's final judgement in his newly published book on Civil War Exeter is that many of the mid-century tensions and divisions were evident in the city in earlier decades. Exeter's inhabitants, therefore, 'were not mere witnesses to the political strife of the 1640s – uncomprehending victims of an imported conflict – but were rather committed players in a politico-religious game which possessed local, as well as national, dimensions'.[22] Stoyle's study of Exeter and others of its kind make clear that local histories of this diverse and troubled period are both fundamental and indispensable.

Notes

1. For a general survey of the historiography of this subject see R.C. Richardson, *The Long Debate on the English Revolution Revisited* (London, 1988)

2. W.D. Macray, ed., *Clarendon. History of the Rebellion and Civil Wars in England* (6 vols, Oxford, 1888). See also B.H.G. Wormald, *Clarendon. Politics, Historiography and Religion, 1640–1660* (Cambridge, 1964), and R. Hutton, 'Clarendon's History of the Rebellion', *English Historical Review*, xcvii, 1982, pp. 70–88; D. Hume, *History of Great Britain. The Reigns of James I and Charles I*, D. Forbes, ed. (Harmondsworth, 1970); T.B. Macaulay, *History of England*, Everyman edn (London, 1953). See also C.H. Firth, *A Commentary on Macaulay's History of England* (London, 1938), and J.W. Burrow, *A Liberal Descent. Victorian Historians and the English Past* (Cambridge, 1981); S.R. Gardiner, *History of the Great Civil War, 1642–1649* 4 vols (London, 1893). See also T. Lang, *The Victorians and the Stuart Heritage. Interpretations of a Discordant Past* (Cambridge, 1995).

3. On Godwin see R.C. Richardson, 'Winchester and the Civil War', in S. Barker and C. Haydon, eds, *Winchester in History and Literature* (York, 1992), pp. 63–5.

4. These were Kingston's two major works. In addition he published *A History of Royston, Hertfordshire, with Biographical Notes of Royston Worthies* (Royston, 1906).

5. Mary Coate, *Cornwall in the Great Civil War and Interregnum, 1642–1660* (Oxford, 1933), pp. 1, 351. Mary Coate taught history at Oxford from 1918 to 1947 and was subsequently connected with the Extra Mural Department at the University of Exeter. A.C. Wood, *Nottinghamshire in the Civil War* (Oxford, 1937), p. ix. Alfred Wood (1896–1968) spent his whole career at the University of Nottingham, becoming Professor in 1951.

6. Simpson, *op. cit.*, p. 2. Jacqueline Eales, by contrast, focussed on the fortunes of an individual gentry family in *Puritans and Roundheads. The Harleys of Brampton Bryan and the Outbreak of the English Civil War* (Cambridge, 1990). Other county studies of the Civil War include: E.A. Andriette, *Devon and Exeter in the Civil War* (Newton Abbot, 1971); M. Atkin, *The Civil War in Worcestershire* (Stroud, 1995); A.M. Coleby, *Central Government and the Localities. Hampshire, 1649–1689* (Cambridge, 1987); D. Eddershaw, *The Civil War in Oxfordshire* (Stroud, 1995); C. Holmes, *Seventeenth-Century Lincolnshire*(Lincoln, 1980); R.W. Ketton-Cremer, *Norfolk in the Civil War* (London, 1969); S.K. Roberts, *Recovery and Restoration in an English County. Devon Local Administration, 1646–1670* (Exeter, 1985).

7. Everitt, *Community of Kent*, pp. 13, 23, 33.

8. Fletcher, *Outbreak*, pp. 374, 379–81.

9. C. Holmes, 'The County Community in Stuart Historiography', *Journal of British Studies*, xix, 1980, pp. 54–73. Note, however, that Peter Clark in his *English Provincial Society from the Reformation to the Revolution. Religion, Politics and Society in Kent, 1500–1640* (Brighton, 1977), took issue even with Everitt's interpretation of the nature and chronology of Kentish society.

10. Holmes, article *cit.*, pp. 61, 72.

11. Ann Hughes, 'Local History and the Origins of the English Civil War', in R. Cust and Ann Hughes, eds, *Conflict in Early Stuart England. Studies in Religion and Politics, 1603–42* (London, 1989), pp. 224–53.

12. Hughes, *Warwickshire*, pp. 20, 39–41, 43, 87, 167–8, 220, 163–5, 336.

13. Morrill, *Cheshire, passim.*

14. Holmes, *Eastern Association*, pp. 15, 20, 34.

15. Morrill, *Revolt, passim.* For Morrill's later reflections on this book see J. Morrill, 'County Communities and the Problem of Allegiance in the English Civil War' in Morrill, *The Nature of the English Revolution* (London, 1993), p. 183.

16. The five case studies were of London, York, Bristol, Coventry and Oxford.

17. Pearl, 'London's Counter Revolution', G.E. Aylmer, ed., *The Interregnum. The Quest for Settlement, 1646–1660* (London, 1972), pp. 29–56; K.J. Lindley, 'London and Popular Freedom in the 1640s', in R.C. Richardson and G.M. Ridden, eds, *Freedom and the English Revolution* (Manchester, 1986), pp. 111–50 and 'London's Citizenry in the English Revolution', in R.C. Richardson, ed., *Town and Countryside in the English Revolution* (Manchester, 1992), pp. 19–45; Tai Liu, *Puritan London* (Newark, Delaware, 1986). See also S. Porter, ed., *London and the Civil War* (London, 1996).

18. D. Scott, 'Politics and Government in York, 1640–1662', in R.C. Richardson, ed., *Town and Countryside in the English Revolution* (Manchester, 1992), pp. 46–68; M. Stoyle, *From Deliverance to Destruction. Rebellion and Civil War in an English City* (Exeter, 1996).

19. Johnson's essay formed part of P. Clark and P. Slack, eds, *Crisis and Order in English Towns, 1500–1700* (London, 1972), pp. 204–36; Adrienne Rosen, 'Winchester in Transition, 1580–1700', in P. Clark, ed., *Country Towns in Preindustrial England* (Leicester, 1981), pp. 143–95.

20. J. Morrill, 'The Church in England, 1642–9', in J. Morrill, ed., *Reactions to the English Civil War* (London, 1982), pp. 89–114; J. Bossy, *The English Catholic Community* (London, 1976); K.J. Lindley, 'The Lay Catholics of England in the Reign of Charles I', *Journal of Ecclesiastical History*, xxii, 1971, pp. 199–221, and 'The Part played by the Catholics', in B.S. Manning, ed., *Politics, Religion and the English Civil War* (London, 1973), pp. 127–76; M.J. Havran, *The Catholics in Caroline England*, (London, 1962); H. Aveling, *Post Reformation Catholicism in East Yorkshire, 1558–1790* (York, 1960), 'The Catholic Recusants of the West Riding of Yorkshire, 1558–1790', *Proceedings Leeds Literary and Philosophical Society*, X, pt. vi, Leeds, 1963, and *Northern Catholics. The Catholic Recusants of the North Riding of Yorkshire, 1558–1790* (London, 1966); P.R. Newman, 'Catholic Royalist Activists in the North', *Recusant History*, xiv, 1977, pp. 26–38.

21. See, for example, J. Morrill, 'The Ecology of Allegiance in the English Civil War', *Journal of British Studies*, 26, 1987, C. Hill, 'The Cakes and Ale Revolution', *The Guardian*, 12 December 1985, and R.C. Richardson in *Times Higher Education Supplement*, 21 February 1986.

22. For Styles see p. 187; Stoyle, *Exeter*, p. 141.

2

THE LOCAL COMMUNITY
AND THE GREAT REBELLION

Alan Everitt

The local history of the Great Rebellion cannot be described as a neglected branch of English historiography. Many towns and most counties have produced some kind of account of their part in the Civil War: Staffordshire, Nottinghamshire, Hampshire, Lancashire, Dorset, Suffolk, Cornwall and Kent, to name but a few.[1] Almost before the war was over, indeed, it began to throw up a crop of local histories, principally of the more startling kind and about the more dramatic events, such as the relief of Gloucester or the siege of Colchester. Quite a number of the 20,000 or so tracts in the famous Thomason Collection in the British Library are in fact local history of a kind. The great bulk of them are purely ephemeral, of course; but some, like Matthew Carter's *Most True and Exact Relation of that as Honourable as Unfortunate Expedition of Kent, Essex, and Colchester* (1650), are serious works of history in their own right, based on manuscript sources and eye-witness accounts. A few, like *L'Estrange his Vindication to Kent. And the Justification of Kent to the World* (1649) are still immensely good reading, sharp, vivid, observant, and not a little scandalous.

After 1660 the Great Rebellion became a sensitive and embarrassing subject in most local communities. If you were a country squire and had not actively supported the king, or at least been sequestrated, it was usually best to keep as quiet about it as possible, and leave it to your descendants to invent a loyalist grandfather. Everywhere Cavalier legends were spawning themselves, like mushrooms in the dark, even in such unlikely counties as Suffolk and Northamptonshire. For this reason the Restoration era was no more conducive to scholarship in the field of local history than to common sense in the field of politics. And despite a mass of local information in the great county historians of the next century, such as Edward Hasted and John Nichols, there was little serious re-examination of the local history of the Civil War period until the reign of Queen Victoria.

During the nineteenth century, however, the Great Rebellion once again became a popular subject of study. Local histories abounded, and edited texts were published with increasing frequency. The first four volumes of *Archaeologia Cantiana*, for example, printed the complete journal of Sir Roger Twysden of Roydon Hall, in the Kentish Weald: one of the most graphic of all Civil War diaries, a perfect mine of information on what it really felt like to live through that traumatic period. Later volumes of *Archaeologia Cantiana* printed a valuable series of letters of Thomas Stanley of West Peckham, also in the Weald; a very detailed account book of his neighbour James Master of Yotes Court, and several other important manuscript sources for the history of Kent in the seventeenth century. About the same time, one of the early volumes of the Camden Society was devoted to an edition of Sir Roger Twysden's *Government of England*, another to a manuscript collection entitled *Proceedings, principally in the County of Kent . . . in 1640*, and part of a third to the Civil War papers of Thomas Weller of Tonbridge Castle.[2] The county of Kent, it is true, was probably better served than most by nineteenth-century editors interested in the Great Rebellion; but its fortunes in this respect were certainly not altogether untypical.

Generally speaking, the Victorians performed a more valuable service to the local historian in printing original sources than in writing full scale accounts of this period. Twysden's journal gives a far more revealing picture of life in Kent at this time than H.F. Abell's rather superficial and unscholarly sketch of *Kent and the Great Civil War* (1901). The weaknesses of the straight Victorian histories of the time are not far to seek. In the first place they paid far too much attention to local sieges and skirmishes. The cynic's remark that the only battle that matters in any war is the last is no doubt an oversimplification: the sack of Leicester, after all, was a decisive and disastrous event for Leicester itself, even if its consequences for the nation at large were reversed a few days later at Naseby. But it must be confessed that the average tale of local skirmishes usually makes rather dreary reading for all but the specialist military historian or the dedicated antiquary.

The second defect of most of the older local histories is that they make very little attempt to relate political events to the development of local society. They often tell us about the fortunes of a few particular families; but they rarely envisage the local community as a whole. They do not see the people of the town or county they purport to describe as a self-conscious and coherent society with a distinct life of its own, developing at a different pace and in different ways from the economy of the country at large. The tensions set up between the local and national community, if perceived at all, are explained simply in personal terms or in terms of one or two well-known local leaders, instead of as a conflict between two distinct organisms, each with its own independent existence. Perhaps the first local history to avoid these pitfalls with complete success was Mary Coate's *Cornwall in the Great Civil War and Interregnum*, which was published in 1933 and is still one of the best local studies of the period.

THE CONFLICT OF ALLEGIANCE

It would be absurd to blame the Victorians too severely for their limited conceptions of Civil War historiography. Our own are no doubt more limited than we realize, and in any case we all stand upon our predecessors' shoulders. Nevertheless, their historical ideas were limited, and if we are to improve upon them it is important to start from a new standpoint. The point I wish to set out from is the recurring problem that faced so many provincial people in this period, the conflict between loyalty to the local community and loyalty to the state. The conflict is evident in urban communities as well as rural, as important recent studies of Newcastle-upon-Tyne and the parliamentary boroughs of Kent have shown.[3] But for reasons of space and simplicity I shall confine myself principally to county society and to its leaders, the local gentry.

The allegiance of the provincial gentry to the community of their native shire is one of the basic facts of English history in the seventeenth and eighteenth centuries. Though the sense of national identity had been increasing since the early Tudors, so too had the sense of county identity. There were many factors in the development of regional loyalty: the growth of county administration, the development of county institutions, the expanding wealth of the local gentry, their increasing tendency to intermarriage, their growing interest in local history and legal custom, the rise of the county towns as social, cultural, and administrative centres: these and many other elements entered into the rise of what Namier once called the 'county commonwealths' of England.

In some respects the Civil War period, by greatly adding to the complexity and volume of local government, increased this sense of county awareness. Certainly the inevitable collision between local and national loyalties implicit in the social development of the sixteenth and seventeenth centuries was precipitated by the political events of 1640–60. Quite apart from the politics of the Civil War, however, there was much in the development of English society that fostered the sense of county cohesion. Despite the well-known fact that many gentry attended the universities and some of the wealthier families spent part of the year in London, the vast majority of country gentry passed most of their lives within a few miles of their native manor-house, in a circle often as limited as that of their tenants and labourers. The brief years at the university and the Inns of Court were no more than an interlude, principally designed to fit them out for their functions as justices, squires, and landlords in their own county. After the time spent at Oxford or in London, most of them quickly settled back into the old routine of country life. Henry Oxinden of Maydeacon in East Kent, for example, apparently visited London only once in his life: and when he was there he told his wife that, if he could only get clear of it, he desired never to come thither again.[4] The mother of Edward Hyde, the great minister of Charles I and Charles II, is said to have spent the whole of her life in the county of Wiltshire, and never once to have stepped over its borders into the neighbouring shires. Not surprisingly, when people like Mary Hyde and Henry Oxinden spoke of their 'country', they did not mean England, but Wiltshire or Kent, Leicestershire or Northamptonshire, Cumberland or Durham.

The basis of this intense attachment of most provincial gentry to their native soil, despite the social changes of the previous century, is not difficult to understand in the context of the time. In speaking of the gentry of the mid-seventeenth century one has to think oneself back into a world which was very different, not only from that of Victorian England, but in many ways from that of George III as well. In 1640 armigerous families were far thicker on the ground than in, say, 1800, perhaps twice as numerous in counties like Devonshire, Suffolk, and Kent. In Suffolk there were 700–750 gentry in 1640, and in Kent about 850. While I am not aware of any late eighteenth-century figures, the decline is clear both from county histories like Hasted, from genealogical sources, and also from the number of manor-houses which, by 1800, had declined to the status of farms.[5] As a consequence the average landed estate was probably far smaller in 1640, too small to enable these families to maintain a second household in London, and too small to let them pay a merely casual attention to its prosperity. The average Caroline estate in Suffolk, Kent, and Leicestershire cannot have been more than about 1,000 acres, and in most counties there were probably hundreds of parochial squires like Henry Oxinden of Maydeacon whose property extended to no more than six or seven hundred. Such people had of necessity to be much 'taken up with the business of farming', as one of them later described it.[6] Every manor-house, except a few of the very largest, was quite as much a farmhouse as a hall, and the centre of a local agrarian commonwealth. On the rare occasions when Henry Oxinden was away from home, his letters were full of inquiries about his harvests and his labourers. His countryman Sir Edward Dering evidently spent a great deal of time and thought upon his famous orchards at Surrenden Dering, where he cultivated more than 150 varieties of fruit-tree, and kept a very detailed orchard-book recording their prosperity from year to year.[7]

The simple fact was that in 1640 farming in England was not yet always looked down upon as the dismal occupation of yeomen and boors. The change of attitude towards it seems to have come with the latter-day cavaliers, who spoke of the older generation of men like Oxinden and Dering as 'the female gentry of the smock'.[8] In some counties at least the change of attitude was furthered, from 1660 onwards, by the gradual amalgamation of smaller properties, partly due to intermarriage, and partly because many Cavalier gentry who had failed to pay detailed attention to husbandry were forced to sell out.[9] Only local research would show whether this kind of development was universal; but the very large number of Caroline manor-houses in counties like Norfolk, Suffolk, Kent, and Devon which, during the eighteenth and nineteenth centuries, declined to the status of mere farmhouses suggests that it was a widespread phenomenon. As a result of amalgamation, and the general increase in the national wealth, the margin of prosperity for the landed family increased: there was not the same urge to pay scrupulous attention to every detail of one's property, and it often became possible to maintain a second household in the county town or in London. The deep local roots of the gentry, though certainly not yet severed, were in some cases beginning to be sapped.

In 1640, however, local attachments were, if anything, becoming deeper rather than more superficial. For this reason the Civil War was not simply a struggle between gallant Cavaliers and psalm-singing Roundheads. If one studies the history of any particular county community in this period, particularly if one is fortunate enough to find an extensive *corpus* of family correspondence, one finds that only a small minority of provincial gentry can be exactly classified in either of these conventional categories. This does not mean that most English people were indifferent to the political problems of the time, but that their loyalties were polarized around different ideals. For them, bounded as they so often were by local horizons, a more urgent problem was the conflict between loyalty to the nation and loyalty to the county community. This division cut across the conventional divisions, like a geological fault. The unwillingness of most people to forgo the independence of their shire and to admit that allegiance to the kingdom as a whole must override it was certainly one of the reasons why the Civil War was so long drawn out. In some respects the England of 1640 resembled a union of partially independent county-states, rather as Canada today is a union of self-governing provinces, or America of federated states: and that union, as we all know, is not always a very simple or easy relationship.

During the Civil War , there were three periods of peculiarly intense crisis, and on each occasion the conflict between loyalty to county and to state was one of the basic issues. In the winter of 1643–4 a crisis occurred over the attempt to form various groups of counties into regional associations. As is well known, these associations were set on foot specifically in order to counteract the tendency of each shire to confine its activities to raising and paying troops for its own defence alone, to the neglect of the safety of neighbouring shires. The effort to associate the counties often provoked intense opposition, and the only thoroughly successful amalgamation – though even there not without difficulties – was the famous Eastern Association under the earl of Manchester.[10] The South-Eastern Association, which comprised Hampshire, Sussex, Surrey, and Kent, never really held together and was little more than a name. The Midland Association, which included such counties as Northamptonshire, Buckinghamshire and Leicestershire, was also rent assunder by disturbing feuds.

The second time of crisis came a year later in 1644–5, when the abler and more forceful leaders on the parliamentarian side, such as Fairfax and Cromwell, realized that these county associations themselves were inadequate to solve the problem of local allegiance. The only solution was the formation of a newly-modelled, nationally-organized army. Hitherto the parliamentary regiments had been raised, paid and officered by each county independently, so that they were regarded as existing primarily for local defence, and as being responsible to the counties who raised them rather than to parliament. Even in the loyal Eastern Association, local leaders were of the opinion that the 'safety of the kingdom . . . was not our work'.[11] In the New Model Army of 1645, however, though the regiments were still raised locally, they were commissioned by parliament, paid by the Treasurers at War in London, and controlled far more completely by the Committee of Both Kingdoms than by the counties. At the same time, and for similar reasons, the King's armies themselves underwent a good deal of reorganization.[12] The consequence was to provoke the final, decisive battle for which the more militant leaders on both sides had been pressing for years, and the moderate majority, by and large, had been endeavouring to avoid. Naseby was the triumph of the state over the county community as much as of parliament over the king.

The third crisis came with the Second Civil War in 1648. Naseby had been a great military victory; but it had been the triumph of organization rather than the effect of a widespread change of feeling in provincial society. In 1648, therefore, in Kent and elsewhere the county community rose once again in an effort to curb the authority of the central government. The Cavaliers made a desperate bid to convert what was essentially regional loyalty into thoroughgoing support for the king. But they were unable to form any sort of union between the rebellious shires. The Kentish leaders refused to enter into negotiations with Surrey, Sussex, Essex, or Suffolk, and, with the storming of Maidstone and the siege of Colchester, the movement was overwhelmed by the victorious New Model Army. Paradoxically the cause of county independence was a victim once again of the obstinacy of local allegiance.[13] Not until 1660, after years of frustration, interference, and insecurity, were the counties willing for a time to forgo a measure of independence and join with the real royalists, the Cavaliers, in an effort to restore the monarchy. Even then it was only a few months before Charles II began to find himself up against the same problem of provincial intransigence as his father and his usurper before him.

THE WAR IN THE EAST MIDLANDS: TWO CASE-STUDIES

I have endeavoured elsewhere to delineate this conflict of loyalties in the two counties of Suffolk and Kent. In Cornwall the same phenomenon has been described with a wealth of detail by Miss Mary Coate. In Staffordshire, Nottinghamshire, Wales, and other districts similar developments have been noted by other scholars.[14] There is no point in repeating here what has already been better said elsewhere. Instead, in the limited space available, I should like to trace the story of two Midland shires in this period – Leicestershire and Northamptonshire – where somewhat similar problems were at issue. In some ways these two counties form an especially interesting and perhaps rather surprising illustration of my theme. Since they are both small inland counties, surrounded on all sides by other shires, one would expect local allegiance within them to be less pronounced than in counties like Cornwall or Kent, which are larger in area and geographically more isolated from other regions. But though Leicestershire and Northamptonshire undoubtedly were less isolated, they were nevertheless remarkably independent in their reactions. Moreover, despite the fact that they adjoined one another, and the fact that both were subject to the ebb and flow of warfare, their fortunes in this period were remarkably dissimilar. First I shall outline some of these differences, and then explore some of the reasons for them and some of their consequences.

The salient fact in both Leicestershire and Northamptonshire in this period, when compared with the counties of the east, the south-east or the far north, is that they were always in the front line of fighting. Both counties were equally unfortunate in this respect. The tide of warfare was continually flowing to and fro across them, whereas counties like Suffolk, Kent, and Cumberland experienced little of the horrors of civil strife. In fact the final issues of the war were decided in these two counties, with the sack of Leicester by Prince Rupert in May 1645, and the defeat of the king at Naseby, fifteen miles away in Northamptonshire, a few days later. Throughout the war, the people of Leicestershire and Northamptonshire were subject to raiding and plundering, and in both counties there were several well-known garrisons. The two county-towns were held for parliament, and a number of the great country houses of the region, such as Belvoir and Ashby de la Zouch, for the king. Apart from Northampton, none of these garrisons was very powerful, but from the point of view of the local population they had almost unlimited nuisance value. Yet despite the superficial resemblance between them, the two counties of Leicestershire and Northamptonshire responded to their common situation in very different ways.

The reactions of Leicestershire were remarkable for their hesitancy and indecision. At the risk of some rather tedious detail, we must outline the principal military events in the county during this period.[15] Like other English shires, when war broke out in 1642, Leicestershire endeavoured to maintain its neutrality and join neither side in the dispute. But the attitude of indecision lasted much longer there than elsewhere, in fact right up to the eve of the Battle of Naseby in 1645: a period of more than three years since the first tentative efforts to secure the county magazine and the militia in the spring of 1642.

In March of the latter year the House of Commons had nominated the earl of Stamford Lord Lieutenant, and when he arrived in Leicester he was, to all appearance, enthusiastically received by the townsmen. The king, who alone had legal power to appoint to this office, retaliated by forbidding the raising of troops in the county under Stamford, and the local royalist leader, Henry Hastings, successfully prevented many people from obeying Stamford's summons to appear for parliament. Stamford, however, was successful in removing a large part of the county magazine from Leicester to his own mansion at Bradgate Park, a few miles from the town, and in holding recruiting meetings at Melton Mowbray, Copt Oak, Kibworth, Broughton Astley and Queniborough. Henry Hastings replied by making a series of raids against Bradgate Park itself and these forays achieved a fair measure of success. When the king visited Leicester on 22nd July 1642, he is said to have been warmly received by a crowd of 10,000 people. Though the reports of this welcome were probably exaggerated, there was no doubt some truth in them. According to Edward Hyde, however, 'if the king were loved [in Leicester] as he ought to be, the Parliament was more feared than he'.[16] As a consequence, despite the apparent welcome, Charles I was asked by the county to leave the magazine in the hands of Stamford, whom he had already declared a traitor. In fact the Leicestershire magazine was never secured for the king; but, despite this rebuff, Charles I did not give up his attempts to win over the county. When Prince Rupert, after Charles I had left Leicestershire to set up his standard at Nottingham, demanded a levy of £2,000 from the townsmen of Leicester, the king indignantly repudiated his high-handed action. Unfortunately for the town, it seems that Rupert never forgot this incident, and it may have influenced his decision to sack it in 1645, when once again the violence of his supporters was deplored by the king.[17]

During the following winter of 1642–3, Leicester was finally secured for parliament by Lord Grey of Groby, the active puritan heir of the old earl of Stamford.[18] This gain, however, was offset by the seizure of Belvoir Castle for the king, at the other end of the county, by the sheriff of Lincolnshire. Throughout Leicestershire conditions of near anarchy obtained, and for two years there were frequent raids on the countryside by the royalist garrisons at Belvoir and Ashby de la Zouch. Indeed, the riotous Cavaliers of Ashby rapidly became infamous for their depredations. Needless to say, contemporary accounts of their pillage lost nothing in the telling. According to one parliamentarian they were 'as debased wicked wretches there as if they had been raked out of hell . . . ' They 'have three malignant priests there,' this writer continued, 'such as will drink and roar . . . and swear and domineer so as it would make one's heart ache to hear the country people to relate what they heard of them.'[19]

It was partly in an effort to provide more effective defence against these conditions that Parliament re-formed its County Committee in Leicestershire – that is its local governing body – in July 1644. A new Committee for the Militia was set up, with special powers to raise and pay local forces and suppress revolts. This arrangement, however, led to further local friction and even accentuated the indecision in the county, because it was complained that the best men were left out of the new Committee, and that Lord Grey had not been given adequate forces to restrain the royalists.[20] Attempts were then made to reduce the garrisons at Ashby and Belvoir; but the temporary success of these efforts was reversed by Sir Marmaduke Langdale's victory, in March 1645, at Melton Mowbray in East Leicestershire. This victory was followed by the storming and capture of Leicester itself, in May 1645, by Prince Rupert.

The infamous and disastrous sack of the town that followed was the price that Leicester had to pay for its lack of decision in supporting either party during the previous three years. This is the essential lesson of all the rather confused events of 1642–5 in Leicestershire. If the town had unequivocally supported parliament, its defences would have been more capable of withstanding Rupert's attack.[21] Indeed, he might never have ventured on making it. If, on the other hand, the town had firmly and consistently supported the king, it would have avoided a sack. Then, after Naseby, it would probably have been able to make advantageous terms of surrender with Fairfax, for as a rule Fairfax preferred to offer generous terms of surrender rather than engage in a wasteful and lengthy siege.

Quite different was the response of Northamptonshire to the similar decision with which it was faced in 1642. It is not necessary to enter into another detailed account of the local military events of the period. Suffice it to say that Northampton town, from the outset, was decisively on the side of parliament. There was little of the shilly-shallying of Leicester about it, and within a few months of the beginning of the war, it had become the most powerful garrison in the South Midlands. Resolutely controlled by both corporation and county committee, it retained this position throughout the war. In the borough records of the time it is possible to trace how its proximity to attack only served to intensify its sense of somewhat grim and puritanical self-discipline. Not that by any means the majority of the inhabitants of town and county were in fact puritans; but, after the manner of their kind, the more puritanical amongst them soon managed to secure leading positions on the corporation and the committee. In the corporation's right of presentation to the living of All Saints, moreover, a source of influence of unique importance was available to them. With its pulpit in their hands, the great church in the centre of the town virtually became the cathedral of puritanism in Northamptonshire, both for the borough and for the surrounding countryside. Almost twice as large as its present successor, it provided the party with a splendid propaganda-hall.

LOCAL LEADERSHIP IN LEICESTERSHIRE AND NORTHAMPTONSHIRE

Such were the differences between the two provincial towns and counties in their response to the Great Rebellion. How do we account for their differing reactions? In the case of Northampton there can be no doubt that there was a certain economic basis for its allegiance to parliament. That interesting mixture of holiness and hard-headedness which seems the peculiar prerogative of puritanism was not altogether absent from this Midland entrepôt. The first major rendezvous of the earl of Essex's armies was held just outside Northampton, and the town benefited greatly, both then and later, from the fact that orders for thousands of pairs of shoes for the army were from time to time placed with its cordwainers.[22] This was, indeed, the beginning of the great shoe-industry of Northampton. The town's prosperity as the chief horse-market of England was also stimulated by its ability to supply the armies of the Eastern Association under the earl of Manchester.[23] Every subsequent war in English history, until Queen Victoria's reign, exerted precisely the same kind of stimulus upon the two basic trades of the borough. Northampton had a vested interest in other people's misfortunes.

These economic advantages were a contributory factor in the differing response of the two towns and counties; but they cannot have been the decisive one. Leicester, one might expect, would have been equally subject to commercial interests, and scarcely less addicted to puritanism. The ultimate explanation is of a different kind, and seems, in fact, to have been a twofold one. Partly it lies in a difference in the quality of leadership in the two shires; and partly, at a deeper level, in the inherent dissimilarities in their social structure.

In Leicestershire leadership was implacably divided between two evenly-balanced rivals: on one hand Henry Hastings, later created Lord Loughborough, a younger son but the most forceful member of the ancient Leicestershire dynasty seated at Castle Donington and Ashby de la Zouch: and on the other hand Lord Grey of Groby, the puritan heir of the old earl of Stamford at Bradgate Park. This division was much more than a rivalry between puritan and Cavalier, however. Traditionally, indeed almost until the outbreak of the Civil War, the Hastings family had been as notoriously puritan as the Greys, though Loughborough himself, of course, was no adherent of that persuasion. But the division between the two families went back to personal feuds of far longer standing than the Civil War, in fact to their rivalry for the control of the county since the mid-sixteenth century. For these two families the Rebellion was, at one level, simply a further stage in the long drawn-out battle for local dominion.

Leicestershire had long been notorious for this family feud. According to Clarendon the whole county was violently divided between the Greys and the Hastingses, 'a notable animosity', he said, without the addition of any other quarrel. According to another contemporary the county was 'like a cockpit, one spurring against another.'[24] Further research shows the truth of these assertions. Behind the Grey family one finds aligned, during the Rebellion, such local families as the Ashbys of Quenby, the Babingtons of Rothley, the Caves of Stanford, the Faunts of Foston, the Hartopps of Buckminster, the Heselriges of Noseley, the Herricks of Beaumanor, and the Villierses of Brooksby. Ranged behind the Hastingses, on the other hand, were families like the Shirleys of Staunton Harold, the Turvilles of Aston Flamville, the Turpins of Knaptoft, the Poulteneys of Lubbenham, the Beaumonts of Gracedieu, and the Nevills of Nevill Holt. The division between the two parties in Leicestershire was in this manner remarkably evenly balanced.[25]

The even division of parties had several far-reaching consequences in the history of the county at this time. It explains, on the one hand, why the struggle for control was so indecisive. It also explains the long drawn-out contest for the control of Leicester town, and the almost morbid reluctance of the corporation to support either of the leading families so far as to antagonize the other. Finally it explains why Leicestershire people were so fully engaged with purely local issues that they seem to have had little interest in concerns of more far-reaching import. In marked contrast with the gentry of Suffolk, Northamptonshire and Kent, few local families left the county to join the king at Oxford or the parliamentarian armies under Fairfax. Events in Leicestershire were quite sufficiently exciting and animosities quite sufficiently intense to confine their interests to the county itself. Most of the parliamentarians were fully preoccupied with their work for the County Committee, though their frequent divisions seriously impaired the efficiency of that body. Most of the royalists were either engaged in defending their estates from attack by the parliamentarians, or themselves became members of one of the predatory Cavalier garrisons of the county.

The consequent insularity of the Leicestershire community, though in the very heart of England, comes to light in the reasons given for the sequestration of royalist estates in the county. These reasons are often mentioned in the records of the Committee for Compounding, and from them we learn that most Leicestershire 'delinquents' were sequestrated either because they were papists or because they had joined one of the local garrisons. Altogether there were about 150 'delinquents' in the county, and the majority for whom relevant details survive confessed to some kind of connection with Belvoir Castle or Ashby de la Zouch. Edward Farnham of Quorndon, for example, was sequestrated because he had joined the garrison at Ashby Castle. William Roberts of Sutton Cheney had also joined the garrison there, partly in order to visit his kindred and partly to secure himself from his creditors. Antony Allen of Ilston had joined the royalists at Ashby when still a mere boy, no more than fifteen years of age. His case graphically illustrates the tragic political and military pressures to which even the most innocent Leicestershire people were subjected.[26]

Most of these Leicestershire royalists came of quite minor local families, and probably many of them were very moderate in their adhesion to the king's cause. Local circumstances forced them to take sides; but, in contrast with the Cavaliers of Suffolk and Northamptonshire, few of them were sufficiently dedicated to Charles I to join his forces at Oxford. Some had spent only a few weeks in one of the local royalist strongholds. Not a few, like John Butler of Bilstone, confessed that they had joined the king's garrison at Ashby merely because their homes were under the power of the Cavaliers and they had no alternative but to submit. Such pleas may sometimes have been mere excuses; but they were accepted by the parliamentarian Committee, and they suggest that many delinquents, if royalists at all, were only so by force of circumstance.[27] In times of political pressure the moderate majority are always driven into positions they scarcely agree with by doctrinaire minorities and angry partisans. They are often the victims, of course, of their own lack of organization.

In Northamptonshire, in the early days of the war, leadership was for a short time divided very much as it was in Leicestershire and other counties. But here the parliamentarian caucus had relatively little difficulty in securing the county-town and most of the shire for their party. Their success was principally due to the fact that the most powerful royalist, the earl of Northampton, together with many other local families, left the county in order to join the king. This migration of local royalists was partly occasioned by the relative proximity of Oxford – barely 40 miles from Northampton – and the consequent magnetism of the Court. It was also due, however, to the fact that Northamptonshire seems to have been a more politically-minded county than Leicestershire, and one where family divisions ran more naturally along lines of religious division, instead of cutting across them. As a consequence, out of a total of 103 Northamptonshire families who supported the king and whose activities can be traced, three-quarters were sequestrated, not for local rebellion, but for leaving the county to join the king's forces elsewhere. Of the rest, a number were recusants, and a mere 7 per cent were sequestrated for taking part in raids or revolts within the county.[28] In striking contrast with the Cavaliers of Leicestershire, Northamptonshire royalists made remarkably little organized effort to challenge the dominance of the County Committee. There was a good deal of raiding and plundering in the shire, but relatively little of it was inspired by local royalists. Much of it emanated from the garrison at Banbury, across the border in Oxfordshire. Most of the Northamptonshire Cavaliers were far away at the time, in other parts of England, many of them at Oxford or Newark.

THE PATTERN OF SOCIETY IN LEICESTERSHIRE AND NORTHAMPTONSHIRE

Underlying these differences in the quality of leadership were deeper differences in the social structure of the two counties. In some ways Leicestershire was still a curiously 'feudal' shire, dominated as it was by the age-old rivalry of its two great families. Between the Greys and the Hastingses, it was divided not only personally but geographically.[29] Altogether, it is possible to trace the allegiance of about 220 Leicestershire families, or probably about two-thirds of the gentry in the shire. About 75 of the gentry became at some date members of the County Committee under Lord Grey; and of these 75 the great majority were seated in the south and east of the county. About 140 became 'delinquents'; and of these more than two-thirds, or almost exactly 100, came from the north and west of the county, from the three hundreds of East Goscote, West Goscote, and Sparkenhoe. As these figures show, there were nearly twice as many nominal 'royalists' as parliamentarians in Leicestershire; but the two parties were evenly balanced because most of the former came of rather obscure minor families.

In Leicestershire, as in several other counties, there was also a marked tendency for the older, more deeply-rooted families to support the king, and the newer gentry to side with parliament. At least 57 per cent of the royalist supporters came of families settled in Leicestershire for more than 150 years, and only 13 per cent of them had arrived in the county since 1603. The history of the Leicestershire parliamentarians is less easy to trace, chiefly because many of them stemmed from mercantile or yeoman stock of rather uncertain origin. But it is safe to say that about one-third of the committee men came of families with a lengthy local lineage of more than 150 years' standing. Of course we must be careful not to exaggerate these social distinctions between the two parties. Some of the oldest Leicestershire families, like the Greys themselves, were convinced parliamentarians. Nevertheless, the contrast cannot be altogether ignored, and it is not, after all, very surprising. It was natural that the more deeply rooted and often smaller gentry should tend to support what seemed, in the 1640s, the more conservative side. It was equally natural for the brisker, newer and more dynamic to support political innovations which might be expected to extend their power. Many of the former, of course, had themselves opposed the king in the 1620s and 1630s, when *he* had appeared to be the innovator, and parliament – whether rightly or wrongly – the bulwark of traditional rights. Perhaps it would be more accurate to call these provincial gentry traditionalists rather than royalists.[30]

It should perhaps be remarked at this point that, in endeavouring to trace the social origins of any county community, it is essential to cover every armigerous family in the shire concerned, or at least a very large representative sample. Estimates based on subjective impressions, or on selected examples for which documentary material happens to be abundant, are usually misleading and often quite valueless. The point is obvious, but it needs to be stressed, because so much nonsense has been written about the rise and decline of the gentry by historians who base their remarks on selected examples, instead of studying the local community *as a whole*. The tendency to notice the striking and dramatic instead of the typical is the besetting sin of most of us; but in elucidating the causes of historical development it is the typical and not the exceptional that we need to study.

Quite as significant as the social differences within the county of Leicester were the contrasts between it and its southern neighbour. Even today the most casual observer of the Midland countryside is struck by the fact that Northamptonshire is a county of superb country houses, usually dating from the sixteenth and seventeenth centuries: whereas Leicestershire, despite a few great mansions like Nevill Holt and Bradgate, is essentially a county of village manor-houses, sometimes little larger than farmhouses. In the seventeenth century the contrast between the two shires was at least equally striking. Kirby, Holdenby, Burghley, Drayton, Milton, Apethorpe, Althorp, Rushton, Deene, and Castle Ashby: Leicestershire had little to compare with these Northamptonshire palaces.

This is how Daniel Defoe described the contrast at the end of the seventeenth century. Northamptonshire, he said, is 'not so full of antiquities, large towns, and gentlemen's seats but this county of Leicester is as empty. The whole county seems to be taken up in country business . . . particularly in breeding and feeding cattle; . . . even most of the gentlemen are graziers, and in some places the graziers are so rich that they grow gentlemen'. Two or three generations earlier William Camden had made much the same observation, remarking that Northamptonshire was 'everywhere adorned with noblemen's and gentlemen['s] houses'.[31] And two or three generations later, largely because of its lack of imposing and pretentious buildings, Leicestershire was looked down upon as one of the most 'impolite' counties in England. The grandiose and somewhat limited mind of the eighteenth century could not appreciate the intimate, friendly charm of a house like the Palmers' at Carlton Curlieu, lost among the lark-haunted pastures of East Leicestershire. It was the same kind of mental limitation that made sophisticated persons of an earlier generation, like John Evelyn, speak disparagingly of the old manor-houses of the Kentish Weald, set in their wooded, moated, romantic hollows. Happily for us, a great many people in both counties kept to the old ways, and were no doubt unaware how unfashionable they were. Perhaps this is one reason why Leicestershire in the eighteenth century was one of the earliest centres of the Gothic Revival. The old Gothic, indeed, virtually never died out.

These differences in the architectural legacy of Leicestershire and Northamptonshire express, of course, a profound difference in their social structure. The basis of this difference is hinted at in the comments of Defoe. The roots of the Leicestershire gentry, like their manor-houses, were for the most part local rather than alien. Their interests were agrarian rather than courtly. Many of them in fact were graziers. The phalanx of Tudor and Stuart *nouveaux-riches* who dominated Northamptonshire had no real parallel in the adjoining county. Not that by any means all the Leicestershire gentry stemmed from medieval squires. In fact no more than about 41 per cent of them came of really ancient armigerous stock in the county, a figure which may be compared with nearly 75 per cent in Kent. Nevertheless, many of them undoubtedly stemmed from local roots of some kind. For the most part their ancestors seem to have been small Leicestershire yeomen, who had gradually pushed their way up into gentility, largely through successful stock-farming. And, as Defoe implies, many of them retained these grazing interests throughout the seventeenth century. This interest in grazing was indeed equally apparent in Leicester town. In striking contrast with Northampton, most of the townsmen still invested a good deal of their capital in stock-farming, and in the seventeenth century some of the wealthiest inhabitants were grazing butchers.[32] These facts certainly go some way to explain the introversion of the Leicestershire community during the seventeenth century. Where their treasure was, their heart was also.

In Northamptonshire the picture was very different.[33] More than almost any other English county, this shire had undgergone a remarkable social transformation in the Tudor and early Stuart period, a transformation which seems to have been just about complete by the beginning of the Civil War. Out of a total of some 300 families whose history is traceable with fair certainty, only 27 per cent were genuinely indigenous to the county. As many as 40 per cent had settled in Northamptonshire under the Tudors, principally under Queen Elizabeth, and another 33 per cent since 1603. Moreover, most of the 80 or so indigenous families had only risen to the status of gentry quite late in the Tudor period. In other words, in 1640, at least three-quarters of the leading families of Northamptonshire, and perhaps more than four-fifths, were of very recent social origin. Through trade, or the law, or office under the crown, or simply by marrying a succession of heiresses, they had managed to purchase estates in the county and build or rebuild the splendid mansions we still marvel at today. If any county furnishes a classic example of the Rise of the Gentry, that county is Northamptonshire.

What is the explanation of this revolutionary change in the composition of society in Northamptonshire? Why was it possible for so many newcomers, often extremely wealthy newcomers like the Cecils, Spencers, and Hattons, to settle in the county? Partly it was because the open-field areas of the county offered adventurers admirable scope for enclosure and for large-scale investment in sheep- and corn-farming. Judging from the findings of the Enclosure Commissioners (though admittedly these are not very reliable evidence) the acreage of land enclosed in Northamptonshire seems to have been greater than in any other Midland county, possibly more than twice as much.[34] Partly, too, the change seems to have been facilitated by the fact that large tracts of royal forest were still available to be granted out to favourites of the Court, or disposed of to ambitious merchants by an impecunious crown. There were almost certainly other reasons, however, which at present we can only guess at until we know more about the basic economy of the county.

Whatever the reasons, by the year 1640 a more or less united phalanx of new and wealthy gentry had come into existence in Northamptonshire, with relatively few connections as yet with the indigenous gentry. Like families of similar origin elsewhere, they were often strongly parliamentarian in sympathy, and more than able, as a group, to challenge the local power of the older, royalist magnates like the earl of Northampton. Within a few generations, it is true, the new families were destined to come to terms with the old, and during the eighteenth century, through frequent intermarriage, to become completely merged with them. But in 1640 they were still distinct. Cartwrights, Cleypooles, Crews, Danverses, Drydens, Harbys, Knightleys, Norwiches, Pickerings, Samwells, Thorntons, Yelvertons: all of these were relative newcomers to Northamptonshire, and it was they who formed the backbone of county society and provided the leadership in the County Committee. During the Civil War some of them went so far as to move house into the county town, partly of course for the sake of protection, but also specifically to reinforce the rule of the godly in the area. The consequent combination of urban puritanism and landed authoritarianism was a phenomenon to which there was no real parallel in Leicestershire. It was, however, the overwhelming fact in both the economic fortunes and the political allegiance of Northamptonshire.

THE TEXTURE OF PROVINCIAL LIFE

Earlier in this paper it was remarked that the basic defect of the older local histories of the Civil War was their failure to relate the narrative of events to the development of local society. It was also stated that the lives of most provincial people were not simply polarized around the ideals of Cavalier and Roundhead, but rather around local rivalries and loyalties, and the common facts of daily life. In a world with poor communications and no country newspapers it was inevitable that most people should be chiefly concerned with the fortunes of their local community. It was not that they never heard any national news, but that they were not *continuously* preoccupied with it as we are today. There were other matters of more immediate concern, and most people lived too near the bone to spare much time for political speculation.

For these reasons few political actions in the seventeenth century could be determined by unfettered idealism, or by abstract principle alone. They had to work themselves out in a complex and intractable provincial world. Every decision, every loyalty was shaped, not so much by a fiat of government, as by the whole network of local society: by all the pressures of personal influence, family connection, ancient amity, local pride, religious sentiment, economic necessity, and a dozen other matters, now often very difficult to track down. In describing social conditions at this time, even in confining oneself to a couple of Midland counties, it is easy to invest one's story with a deceptive air of simplicity, and to forget the underlying diversity, the extraordinary density of this web of provincial life.

This density in the fabric of local life, this elaborate network of family loyalties and personal necessities that shaped the pattern of politics in the countryside, was, of course, neither a novel feature of the county community of the seventeenth century nor a merely ephemeral one. It had existed at least as early as Henry VIII's reign – no doubt a good deal earlier – and it continued to influence the pattern of county society until the days of Queen Victoria. In the sixteenth century, for example, the evolution of the Reformation in the north was shaped, not only by religious developments affecting the whole of Europe, but by many confused influences peculiar to the society of the region itself. In elucidating the motives behind Sir Francis Bigod's protestant revolt in Yorkshire,

Professor Dickens has unravelled a whole tangle of personal and temperamental factors, problems of debts and land, and many other notions inextricably intertwined with them, 'not merely family affection and ancestral loyalty, but credit in the county and the very prestige of the Reformation movement upon the dubious soil of the north'.[35]

At the end of the nineteenth century, in a revealing passage, Richard Jefferies depicted strikingly similar conditions in Wiltshire, in his description of county society in *Hodge and his Masters*. 'Now the business of the county,' he said, 'was not very intricate; the details were innumerable, but the general drift was easy to acquire. Much more complicated to see through were all the little personal likings, dislikings, petty spites, foibles, hobbies, secret misunderstandings, family jars and so forth, which *really decide a man's vote* or the scale into which he throws his influence. There were scores of squires dotted over the county, each of whom possessed local power more or less considerable . . . Every family had its history and its archives containing records of negotiations with other families. People who met with all outward friendliness, and belonged to the same party, might have grudges half a century old but not forgotten. If you made friends with one you might mortally offend the other . . . Those who would attain to power must *study the inner social life*, and learn the secret motives that animate men. But to get at the secret behind the speech, the private thought behind the vote, *would occupy one for years* . . . '[36] In these phrases Richard Jefferies might well have been describing the community of Leicestershire or Kent at the time of the Great Rebellion. The matrix of local society in which political opinion in the provinces was formed was essentially similar in both periods, though of course there were important differences as well.

Now and again the local historian lights upon some past event that momentarily illuminates these tracts of ordinary human life during the Civil War. The texture of provincial society and the pattern of politics woven into it suddenly begin to focus. The question forces itself upon one's attention: How much were ordinary people really affected by the events of the Great Rebellion? The present writer is gradually coming to the conclusion that we may have exaggerated the impact of the war itself upon daily life in the provinces. In the Midlands, of course, country people could not fail at times to be conscious of the fighting, and for some of them – the people of Leicester, for instance, on a May evening in 1645 – it brought horror and tragedy. Yet it would be misleading to suppose that daily life was *continuously* disrupted by fighting, even in the Midlands. The Great Rebellion was far from being a total war as we understand that term.[37]

When we read of the uproar occasioned in 1643 by Lord Northampton's seizure of a train of carriers' waggons at Daventry, drawn by fifty-seven horses on their journey from Cheshire to London, we need to remember, not only the outrage itself, but the fact that normally speaking these carriers' trains must have continued to reach their destination, otherwise there would have been no occasion for the outcry. When Sir Samuel Luke tells us how, after the king's astonishing victory at Leicester in 1645, the country people of Buckinghamshire and Bedfordshire suddenly refused to supply any further provisions for the local parliamentary garrisons, we need to envisage, first the fact that farming life in the Midland counties had evidently continued, and secondly that for farming folk there were clearly more pressing matters than political allegiance. And when one finds the supposedly puritan inhabitants of Hampden's county suddenly becoming 'so malignant, that neither the power of the army nor of the Committees could be sufficient to force in provisions' for the troops at Newport Pagnell, one need not suppose that all these country people were astute political cynics, but that, in a subsistence society, allegiance was unavoidably dictated chiefly by economic necessity.[38]

The suspicion that we may have exaggerated the impact of the Civil War upon provincial society is often confirmed if one isolates the experience of a single community in the seventeenth century, and studies its life-cycle as a whole. The town of Northampton need not be taken as a typical instance, and in fact the Great Rebellion probably played a larger part in its development than in most provincial boroughs. As we have seen, it not only stimulated the horse-trade and shoe-industry, but also encouraged the town's propensity towards puritanism. Yet the impact of the Civil War also needs to be seen in perspective. Quite as decisive in the economic and religious development of Northampton were the effects of harvest-failure, disease, and fire. In 1605, for example, largely as a result of plague, one person in every six in Northampton died: a total of more than 600 people, or the equivalent, size for size, of more than 20,000 in the town of today. In 1638, barely a generation later, nearly 700 of the inhabitants perished, principally through a second visitation of the same disease.[39] Less than forty years later, in 1675, four-fifths of the town was destroyed by fire, including its whole business centre. More than 700 families were rendered homeless, and the wealth that it had taken many tradesmen upwards of twenty years to accumulate disappeared in the space of three hours.[40] Important though the impact of the Civil War was, it was certainly not as catastrophic, for the people of Northampton, as these overwhelming local disasters. We may argue that such occurrences were merely local; but of course most towns and villages were from time to time smitten by very similar tragedies.

There is, of course, no need to minimize the impact of the Civil War upon seventeenth-century England. Its consequences for provincial society were obviously far-reaching. But we also need to see the Rebellion as one of a succession of problems to which society at the time was peculiarly vulnerable. The recurrent problems of harvest failure, and the malnutrition and disease that often followed in its wake, were, for most English people, more serious and more persistent than the tragic but temporary upheaval of the Civil War. As Professor

Hoskins has remarked, the economy of Stuart England worked on a very fine margin between sufficiency and shortage. Probably at least one-third of the population lived so close to the poverty-line that every poor harvest plunged them far beneath it. Even when vigorous action was taken locally to remedy the shortage, unrest and hardship remained acute. During the seventeenth century as a whole every fourth harvest, on the average, fell seriously short of basic requirements, and in some decades several successive years showed a marked deficiency. Those who lived through the Civil War and Commonwealth period, for example, suffered no fewer than ten harvest failures within the space of fifteen or sixteen years, and in two years (1649–50 and 1661–2) the general price-level of food-stuffs was more than 50 per cent above normal.[41] This kind of situation affected every class in the country, and for hundreds of thousands of labourers, yeomen, craftsmen, and traders it might well mean ruin.

For us in the twentieth century it is hard to recapture how far provincial life under the Stuarts centred on the annual yield of the harvest. But in an agrarian society it was, of course, the basic fact of existence. It was the common talk of every market town, far more so than affairs of state. Perhaps we need to view the whole early modern period more frequently in this connotation. We need to study both the tragic consequences of harvest failure and disease, and the remarkable stimulus of abundance upon the life of the local community. The stubbornness and the resilience of country people, over the generations, in the face of this alternating harshness and generosity of nature were equally remarkable. Their experiences certainly go some way to explain that latent intransigence of the provincial world which, in the last resort, was one of the principal factors in the failure of both Charles I and Cromwell. For if you have been engaged for centuries in hand-to-hand warfare with the forces of nature, you naturally develop a certain dumb obstinacy towards the world at large – and not least towards the strange doings of princes and protectors.

POSTSCRIPT

Forty years have passed since my first publication on the Civil War period and thirty since *The Community of Kent and the Great Rebellion, 1640–1660* appeared. Shortly afterwards the Historical Association asked me to write the pamphlet reprinted here, and I have written nothing on the subject since. When the Hambledon Press issued some of my essays under the title *Landscape and Community in England* (1985), I did not include the pamphlet. My interests and teaching duties had taken me in other directions and I was trying to complete a book on English settlement-history. Study of the Civil War period and Interregnum had developed into a massive industry; the misrepresentation to which my work had been subjected discouraged me; and I did not feel equal to grappling with the problem once again.

On re-reading this paper there is not much I wish to alter in the light of what I have read since, apart from the deletion of two over-positive statements in the sixth and seventh paragraphs. It is not one of my favourite essays, but I still think the 'county community' has a place in English history. It was only one of many forms of community, as I have frequently indicated elsewhere, and I have never claimed that it was the only factor behind the events of 1640–60. Despite what some have said, I have nowhere denied the importance of idealism behind those events. But we also need, I am certain, to try and recreate the kind of deeply-rooted provincial society through which idealism had to work itself out in this country, and in which it often took its unexpected rise.

There is no need here to reply to others, however, or to review the relevant literature. The obvious place to begin is Dr John Morrill's survey, *The Revolt of the Provinces: Conservatives and Radicals in the English Civil War, 1630–1650*, now in its third (revised) edition, and a work far beyond my own capacity to emulate. For myself, it has often been publications on earlier periods that have proved most interesting. If it is not invidious, I should like to mention two in particular: Professor Hassell Smith's book, *County and Court: Government and Politics in Norfolk, 1558–1603* (1974), and Dr J.R. Maddicott's article, 'The County Community and the Making of Public Opinion in Fourteenth-Century England', in the *Transactions of the Royal Historical Society* (Fifth Series, 28, 1978). It is clear that the basic idea discussed in my pamphlet and in *The Community of Kent and the Great Rebellion* may be pressed further back than I used to suppose. The title of my book was in fact suggested by a phrase in the Eyre of Kent of 6 & 7 Edward II: 'And then came the community of the whole county to the bar, and prayed the Justices that they might be allowed their customs which they had ever been used to have . . . ' But as I pointed out at the time, neither Kent nor any other county can be taken as typical of the kingdom as a whole. The present reprint re-emphasizes that essential qualification in relation to other areas. There are more things in heaven and earth, indeed, than are dreamt of in our philosophy.

Alan Everitt, July 1996.

Notes

1. D.H. Pennington and I.A. Roots, eds., *The Committee at Stafford, 1643–45* (1957); D.A. Johnson and D.G. Vaisey, *Staffordshire and the Great Rebellion* (1964); A.C. Wood, *Nottinghamshire in the Civil War* (1937); G.N. Godwin, *The Civil War in Hampshire (1642–45) and the Story of Basing House* (1904); E. Broxap, *The Great Civil War in Lancashire, 1642–1651* (1910); A.R. Bayley, *The Great Civil War in Dorset, 1642–1660* (1910); C.H. Mayo, ed., *The Minute Books of the Dorset Standing Committee . . .* (1902); Alan Everitt, *Suffolk and the Great Rebellion, 1640–1660*, Suffolk Records Society, iii (1960); Mary Coate, *Cornwall in the Great Civil War and Interregnum, 1642–60* (1933); Alan Everitt, *The Community of Kent and the Great Rebellion, 1640–1660* (1966).

2. 'Dalison Documents: Letters of Thomas Stanley of Hamptons', *Archaeologia Cantiana*, xvii (1887);

'The Expense Book of James Master, Esq.', *Archaeologia Cantiana*, xv–xviii (1883, 1886, 1887, 1889); Sir Roger Twysden, *Certaine Considerations upon the Government of England*, J.M. Kemble, ed., Camden Soc., 1st Ser., xlv (1849); *Proceedings, principally in the County of Kent, in connexion with the Parliaments called in 1640 . . .* , L.B. Larking, ed., Camden Soc., 1st Ser., lxxx (1862); 'Papers relating to Proceedings in the County of Kent, A.D. 1642–A.D. 1646', R. Almack, ed., *Camden Miscellany*, iii (1854).

3. Roger Howell, *Newcastle upon Tyne and the Puritan Revolution* (1967); Madeline Jones, *The Political History of the Parliamentary Boroughs of Kent, 1642–1662*, London Ph.D. thesis (1967).

4. Cf. Everitt, *Community of Kent*, p. 44.

5. Sabine Baring-Gould noted the same decline in Devon in *Old Country Life*, 1890, Chapter 1, 'Old County Families'.

6. Quoted in Everitt, *Community of Kent*, p. 277.

7. The manuscript was originally in the Phillipps Collection and was sold at Messrs Sotheby's in 1967.

8. The phrase occurs in British Museum, Harleian MS 6918, f.34.

9. Cf. Everitt, *Community of Kent*, pp. 323–4.

10. Everitt, *Suffolk and the Great Rebellion*, pp. 28–34.

11. *Ibid.*, p. 34.

12. For the military reorganization of this period generally see C.V. Wedgwood, *The King's War, 1641–1647* (1958), Book 2, Chapter iv.

13. Everitt, *Community of Kent*, Chapter vii.

14. For Wales, see A.H. Dodd, *Studies in Stuart Wales* (1952); J.R. Phillips, *Memoirs of the Civil War in Wales and the Marches, 1642–1649* (1874).

15. There is a valuable narrative of political events in Leicestershire in these years by Sir John Plumb in V.C.H., *Leics*, ii, pp. 109–18. The following pages are based on this account and on further research, chiefly in the Thomason Tracts, contemporary newspapers, records of the Committee for Compounding, Lords' and Commons' Journals, State Papers, and John Nichols, *The History and Antiquities of the County of Leicester*, iii, Pt. ii, App. iv. See also J.F. Hollings, *The History of Leicester during the Great Civil War* (1840).

16. Edward Hyde, earl of Clarendon, *The History of the Rebellion and Civil Wars in England*, W.D. Macray, ed., ii, p. 241.

17. *Ibid.*, iv, p. 39.

18. Clarendon, however, described him as 'a young man of no eminent parts' (*ibid.*, ii, p. 473). This view does not entirely square with his activities in Leicestershire.

19. Nichols, *Leics.*, iii, Pt. ii, App. iv., p. 39.

20. V.C.H., *Leics.*, ii, p. 114.

21. One of the best of the numerous accounts of the storming and sack is *A Perfect Relation of the Taking of Leicester . . .* , June 1645 (Thomason Tracts, E.288.4). This parliamentarian tract shows both the weakness of the defences and the fact that the carnage attributed to the Royalists was exaggerated at the time. There are other detailed accounts in *Perfect Passages of each Day's Proceedings in Parliament*, No. 32; *Perfect Occurrences of Parliament*, No. 23; *A Perfect Diurnal of some Passages in Parliament*, No. 97.

22. E.g., in 1642 thirteen Northampton shoemakers supplied the Treasurers at War with 4,000 pairs of shoes and 600 pairs of boots for troops in Ireland. – V.C.H., *Northants.*, ii, pp. 318–9.

23. Lt. Russell was paid £500 to buy horses at Northampton Fair for Manchester in April 1644,

probably for about 80 horses. A further £1,256 was paid to him to buy horses during the following seven weeks, probably at Northampton, though he also purchased at Cambridge. – Everitt, *Suffolk and the Great Rebellion*, pp. 90, 91.

24. Clarendon, *op. cit.*, ii, p. 473; V.C.H., *Leics.*, ii, p. 109, quoting *Terrible News from Leicester* (Thomason Tracts, E.108.16).

25. Facts about Leicestershire and Northamptonshire family allegiance are based primarily on committee lists in C.H. Firth and R.S. Rait, *Acts and Ordinances of the Interregnum, 1642–1660* (1911); *Calendar of the Committee for Compounding*, Leics. and Northants. cases; and miscellaneous references, chiefly in State Papers and numerous contemporary tracts in the British Museum. There seem to be few large local collections of family letters at present available for either county during this period.

26. *Calendar of the Committee for Compounding*, pp. 941, 962, 2290.

27. Cf. *ibid.*, pp. 1121, 1133, 1166–7, 1987, 2615.

28. *Ibid., passim.*

29. This was first pointed out by Sir John Plumb in V.C.H., *Leics.*, ii, pp. 109–10.

30. For Leicestershire family history I have relied chiefly on John Nichols's *Leicestershire* (one of the most reliable of the great county histories), the usual printed genealogical sources, and in some cases the relevant sections of V.C.H., *Leics.*, topographical volumes.

31. Daniel Defoe, *A Tour through England and Wales*, (Everyman edn, 1959), ii, p. 89; William Camden, *Britannia, or a Chorographical Description of Great Britain and Ireland*, Edmund Gibson, ed., (1753), i, col. 511.

32. V.C.H., *Leics.*, iv, pp. 99–104. By the mid-seventeenth century, few Northampton townsmen had any considerable agricultural wealth, to judge from their wills and probate inventories.

33. For the Northamptonshire gentry, see my article, 'Social Mobility in Early Modern England', *Past and Present*, xxxiii (1966), pp. 63–8.

34. Joan Thirsk, ed., *The Agrarian History of England*, iv, *1500–1640* (1967), pp. 241–2. With a total of 41,416 acres returned by the Commissioners of 1517–19 and 1607, the Northants. figure was more than twice that of any other county.

35. See A.G. Dickens, *Lollards and Protestants in the Diocese of York, 1509–1558* (1959), p. 69 and Chapter iii as a whole.

36. Richard Jefferies, *Hodge and his Masters*, (1946 edn), pp. 278–9. The italics are mine.

37. A superficial reading of contemporary tract literature sometimes gives the impression that it was a total war. But tracts, by their nature, do not usually record the *ordinary* facts of daily life, but its disruptions. It is the background of common existence that we need to visualize.

38. *Special Passages and Certain Informations*, No. 24; Hist. MSS Commission, *The Letter Books of Sir Samuel Luke, 1644–45*, H.G. Tibbutt, ed., (1963), pp. 304, 306.

39. *The Records of the Borough of Northampton*, ii, (1898), J.C. Cox, ed., p. 238. The average annual mortality about 1605 was 139, and about 1638, 122. Deaths from plague alone were probably, therefore, about 500 in each of these two years, the total number of deaths being 625 in 1605 and 665 in 1638.

40. C.H. Hartshorne, *Historical Memorials of Northampton* (1848), p. 245; *A True and Faithful Relation of the late Dreadful Fire at Northampton* . . . (1675).

41. W.G. Hoskins, 'Harvest Fluctuations and English Economic History, 1620–1759', *The Agricultural History Review*, xvi, i (1968), pp. 15–21.

3

THE FOUNDING OF THE LONDON PROVINCIAL ASSEMBLY, 1645–47

Tai Liu

Modern historians seldom give serious consideration to Presbyterianism as a viable religious force during the English Revolution. Unlike the Independents, the Baptists, the Fifth Monarchy Men, or even the Laudians, the Presbyterians of this period have yet to have their history written.[1] It has usually been assumed that English Presbyterianism in this period was a product of military necessity during the Civil War, a price leaders of the Long Parliament had to pay for the Scottish alliance. As a new form of church government and discipline, as W.A. Shaw observed, it did not represent 'the expression of the constant element of Puritanism', but rather 'an abrupt and startling and illogical' departure from the English Puritan tradition. In short, it was a 'mere accident' of the years 1645–47.[2]

This interpretation, however, does not reveal the entire story of English Presbyterianism. During the years of the Civil War, a clerical Presbyterian faction gradually took shape, especially in the City of London, where its influence in Puritan politics was probably far greater than has been recognized. In the crucial years 1645–47, it almost succeeded in capturing the government of the municipality by winning the support of the City fathers, thus bringing London to a dangerous confrontation with the Army.[3] Furthermore, London was one of the places where the Presbyterian church government was established by ordinances of Parliament. In spite of the triumph of the Independents in 1648 and subsequent changes of government at Westminster, the London Provincial Assembly did, in fact, continue to exist until 1660.[4] Admittedly, the London Presbyterian clergy failed in their attempts in 1645–47 to force a rigid Presbyterianism upon Parliament, and their religious experiment in the City was anything but a success. Yet English Presbyterianism was by no means a historical nonentity during the English Revolution. A study of the London Presbyterians, lay as well as clerical, and the founding of their Provincial Assembly may shed some new light upon the real strength and weakness of English Presbyterianism during the Interregnum.

It is not intended in this essay to trace in detail the gradual formation of a Presbyterian faction in the City of London. A few general observations, however, may be made regarding its beginnings before 1645. The Scottish divines came to London long before the arrival of the Scottish army on the battlefield.[5] Although it is difficult to measure the total impact of these Scottish divines in London, their propaganda would certainly not be without effect. In the City, they were conveniently lodged in the parish of St. Antholin's, 'a place', as Clarendon put it, 'in all times made famous by some seditious lecturers'. They were allowed to have free use of the pulpit of St. Antholin's, where their preaching soon became so popular that, to quote Clarendon again, 'from the first appearance of the day in the morning on every Sunday to the shutting in of the light the church was never empty'.[6] Nor, we may be sure, did they come to London, as one of the Scottish divines wrote, to 'live any of us here to be idle'. They were in close touch with the 'Root-and-Branch' movement in the City; they were deeply concerned about the possible success of Archbishop Ussher's plan for a reduced episcopacy; and they were negotiating with the Independents, hoping that the latter 'will join to overthrow Episcopacy, erect Presbyterian government and Assemblies, and in any difference they have to be silent upon hope either of satisfaction when we get leisure, or of toleration on their good and peaceable behaviour'.[7]

To be sure, there had been no Presbyterian faction as such in pre-revolutionary London. In the early years of the Revolution, the English Puritan divines, whose voices more and more dominated the pulpits in the City and at Westminster, consciously avoided using factional language in their sermons and tracts. But there can be little doubt that the idea of some sort of Presbyterianism was soon developed; the presbyter was now publicly proposed to Parliament by the Puritan clergy to replace the bishop in future reformation of the Church.[8] In fact, the future London Presbyterian divines seem to have become well aware of the fundamental differences between their church polity, however undefined as yet, and Independency. They, too, came to an agreement with the Independents that '(for advancing of the publike cause of a happy Reformation) neither side should preach, print, or dispute, or otherwise act against the other's way'.[9] In the meantime, with the Laudians in London sequestered, the benefices of the City fell largely into the hands of future Presbyterian ministers.[10] In mid-1642, a number of ministers in London sent a letter to the General Assembly of the Scottish Kirk, in which they openly expressed their desire for a Presbyterian church government.[11] During the following two years, the London clergy acted more and more as a collective body in petitioning for the establishment of Presbyterian church government and discipline.[12] A clerical Presbyterian faction had taken shape in the City.

In 1645, the London Presbyterian clergy and the lay Presbyterian leaders in the City began to coalesce. Again, signs of such coalescence had appeared in the previous year. On January 22, 1644, for instance, the Court of Common Council ordered the consideration of a petition to be presented in the name of the City to both Houses of Parliament.[13] In all probability, this petition had been drafted by the London Presbyterian divines.[14] In it, the City was to plead with Parliament for a speedy settlement of the question of church government so that private men 'may bee prohibited . . . [from] assembling themselves together and Exercising of

Church discipline without the warr^t of Civile pow^{er}, which tendeth much to the dishono^r of the Parliament, and disturbance of the Peace of the Church City and Kingdome'.[15] Later in the year, the Court of Aldermen ordered four silver vessels, 'with the Cittie Armes engraven there upon', to be presented to the four Scottish divines in London: Alexander Henderson, Robert Baillie, Samuel Rutherford and George Gillespie, who, 'out of their love and good respect', had lately preached before the Lord Mayor and Aldermen of the City.[16]

The situation in 1645 was different. On August 19, the first parliamentary ordinance for the establishment of Presbyterian church government was passed. For all practical purposes, it was for the constitution of the church government in the Province of London.[17] The ordinance fell far short of what the London Presbyterian clergy had wanted. They at once sent a petition to the House of Commons, obliquely criticizing the ordinance for its restrictions on the presbytery. Shortly afterwards, another petition was presented by lay Presbyterians in the City, calling for the erection of a church government 'with a compleat measure of power and authoritie upon the Presbyteries'.[18] The action of the London Presbyterians failed to change the attitude of the members of the House of Commons, who on September 23 adopted a further resolution for immediate election of the classical elderships of the London Province, and on October 8 the Lord Mayor of London was instructed by the House to give notice of the order to all the ministers of the City.[19] It was under such circumstances that the London Presbyterian clergy appealed to the City authorities for support.

In response to this appeal by the London clergy, the Common Council set up a special committee to hold conferences with them as to what was to be done.[20] This special committee, which included the Lord Mayor, five Aldermen and twelve Common Councilmen, gives us the first glimpse of the political Presbyterian leadership in the City government during the English Revolution.[21] What followed was a well-coordinated Presbyterian campaign in London. Early in November, a petition of 'divers citizens' was produced, with a list of sixty signatories.[22] Roger Drake, whose name heads the list, was himself a future prominent Presbyterian divine in the City.[23] In all probability he drafted the petition. More important, eighty-eight City ministers were recruited within four or five days to subscribe a document called 'Desires and reasons of the Ministers'.[24]

The 'Desires and reasons' is a highly important document in the history of London Presbyterianism during the Revolution. First, it expresses clearly and unmistakably the fundamental beliefs of the London Presbyterian clergy in regard to church policy at a time when they thought they were able to put their beliefs into effect. Second, it speaks collectively for the largest group of London Presbyterian ministers who ever gathered together to enunciate their church policy. Third, it signifies the support the London Presbyterian clergy received from the leaders of the City government, for the document could not have been drawn up without the knowledge or even the approval of the City committee on church government. Indeed, it was to be included as part of the City's petition. And, finally, this entire Presbyterian campaign amounted to nothing less than an open challenge by the lay as well as the clerical Presbyterian leaders of the City of London to the authority of Parliament in the settlement of the Church.

The foremost desire of the London Presbyterian divines was to establish their claim to *jus divinum* for the church government and discipline they wanted to create, although they must have known that this was a highly controversial issue. In fact, it was a point of which the Westminster Assembly of Divines was never able to convince Parliament.[25] Yet how could the London ministers, true Presbyterians as they now were, fail to make this claim? In the ordinances and the directions that Parliament had passed for the creation of a Presbyterian church government, the London ministers observed, there was 'noe notice at all of any intrinsicall power in the Ministers or Elders derived unto them from Christ', particularly in such matters as 'the substantialls in Governem[t] and discipline'. On the contrary, they continued, the parliamentary ordinances concerning church government all 'run in such a straine as if all of it were onley of Politicall institution, and merely to be derived from the Civile Magistrate'.[26]

In addition to this fundamental claim, the London ministers also contended, probably quite correctly, that for practical reasons the authority of the ministers and the lay ruling elders under the Presbyterian church government had to be established upon the strongest foundation, if only because Presbyterian elderships were something 'soe newe to this Kingdome'. Without statutory sanction, the elderships would hardly command respect or obedience, if they could function at all. In actuality, an Elizabethan statute, as yet unrepealed, condemned 'the Exercise of all Ecclesiasticall Jurisdiction not established by authority under severest penalties'.[27] Furthermore, the London ministers argued, the parliamentary ordinances for constituting Presbyterian elderships had omitted from their jurisdiction many 'notorious scandalls' – scandals such as 'heresy', 'preaching publiquely or privately by such as neither ordeyned nor Probation[rs], and common frequenting of such', and 'Mens renounceing their Baptisme or ministry'.[28] In the light of these arguments, one can perhaps better understand the central item among the London ministers' desires: 'That a sufficient power may bee setled uppon all the aforesaid (that is, Congregational, Classical, Provincial and National) Eldersh[pps] that they may fully and faithfully put in Execuccon the said Presbyteriall governem[t] according to the severall Subordinaccons respectivelie'.[29]

The City's petition was not favourably received by Parliament. In fact, in the House of Commons it aroused much displeasure and indignation. It was thought that the whole thing was contrived by some Presbyterians in the City; and, of course, the House was right in this judgment. More important, the petition was considered an improper encroachment upon the privileges of Parliament. In its answer to the City's delegation, the House declared that the proceedings of Parliament on this matter of church government had been 'misrepresented and mistaken' by the City, and that 'in things depending in Parliament, their proceedings may neither bee prejudged, nor precipitated nor any sense put uppon them, other than the Parliam^t itself shall declare'.[30] So far as the City's clerical delegates themselves were concerned, the House rather contemptuously decided to ignore them completely. They were simply told not to attend the House any longer but to go home to look after their pastoral charges in their own parishes.[31]

This rebuff from the House of Commons did not deter the London Presbyterians. In the following month, when the wardmotes were held for the annual election of Common Councilmen, the City Presbyterians used this occasion to agitate for further action by the citizens. The extent of this campaign to arouse popular support is unknown, but it is clear that fresh petitions were drawn up in several wards.[32] On January 8, 1646, these petitions were presented to the Court of Common Council, which, 'att the humble and earnest desires of the inhabitants of several wards within this Citty', revived the old committee on church government.[33] Furthermore, the Common Council ordered a day of humiliation to be held on the following Wednesday, January 14. Two of the leading Presbyterian divines of the city, Edmund Calamy and Simeon Ashe, were invited to preach before the Lord Mayor, the Aldermen and the Common Councilmen on this occasion. The Court of Common Council also resolved that after the sermons were delivered, the two divines 'be desired to minister the oath of Covenant to the Lord Mayor, Aldermen and the Common Council; & then every one of them to subscribe their names in a booke to bee appointed for that purpose'.[34] It is obvious that the day of humiliation was meant to be a day of political demonstration, and the resolution to renew the Covenant was not only to reassure those who might be in doubt but also to intimidate those who were in opposition in the City.[35]

The day of humiliation was duly celebrated. On the same day, another petition was introduced into the Court of Common Council by the revived committee for church government. Unlike the petition of the year before, which incurred an unsympathetic reaction from the House of Commons, the new petition avoided explicit criticism of parliamentary legislation on religion, directing the attack against toleration and its evil consequences.[36] Nevertheless, no answer was returned immediately to the City.[37] In the meantime, the House of Commons attempted to resolve the issue by creating an independent parliamentary commission for scandalous offences in the Province of London, to be both outside the jurisdiction of the City and beyond the control of the London Presbyterians.[38] And the two burgesses who communicated the order to the City government, Alderman Isaac Pennington and Colonel John Venn, were both political Independents in the City.[39]

These developments were undoubtedly disconcerting for the Presbyterian faction in London. When further negotiations failed, the Common Council took action in retaliation against not only Independent preachers in the City but also the Independent members of the Common Council.[40] This latter action, it is

worth noting, was an unmistakable sign of the increasing militancy of the
Presbyterian leaders in the City, foreshadowing their attempt to seize the London
militia in the following year.[41] Frustrated and embittered, the City Presbyterian
fathers were to become reckless.

In the middle of February, 1646, the Scottish Commissioners in London paid a
visit to the Common Council and delivered a letter from the Scottish
Parliament.[42] This moral support from their Scottish brethren, though
questioned by the House of Commons, must have strengthened the spirit of the
London Presbyterian faction. Early in the following month, they once more took
action, openly and imprudently challenging the Parliament's plan for an
independent commission concerning scandalous offences *above* the new church
government. Such a commission, the City Presbyterian fathers categorically
asserted, 'tendeth much to the discouragement of such as are willing to submit to
the Presbyteriall Government established by both houses of Parliament'.[43] They
acknowledged that the intention of the Parliament in constituting an independent
commission was 'for prevenccon of an arbitrary power', but, they argued, the
rules to be prescribed for the commission would 'produce the like effect' if they
were given 'to the Parochiall, Classicall, Provinciall and nationall assemblies'. In
fact, they contended, the erection of such a commission was only 'well pleasing to
those that have opposed the Establishm^t of Presbyteriall Government'.[44]

There can be no doubt that this petition from the City government was
contemptuous in nature and arrogant in language. It reflected, directly and explicitly,
upon the wisdom and intention of Parliament in its legislation for future religious
settlement. It is a clear indication of the desperation of the high Presbyterian faction
in the City of London. However, the petition must have aroused such wrath in the
House of Commons that the City leaders took fright and asked that it be withdrawn
and expunged from the Commons' journal. Their request was granted only on the
condition that the petition be expunged from the City's records as well.[45]

Surprisingly, the London Presbyterian leaders renewed their agitation early in
April. It seems that at first the foremost concern of the City Presbyterian leaders
was still exclusively over the matter of church government.[46] This religious issue,
however, was soon to be lost in a gathering storm of larger political questions.
The Civil War was now coming to an end, and Charles I surrendered himself to
the Scots on April 27. On May 19, the King's address to the City arrived, in
which he declared that he was ready to concur in settling truth and peace in the
nation, that he desired to have all things speedily brought to that end, and that he
hoped to return to his ancient city to the satisfaction both of the Parliament and
his people.[47] On the very next day, the Court of Common Council adopted a
'Remonstrance and Petition' to be presented to the House of Commons.[48]

The 'Remonstrance and Petition' was a product of the new political
circumstances. It was primarily a political document, and as such the
Presbyterian claim to *jus divinum* for a rigid, hierarchical church government was

not raised.[49] Perhaps, as Dr. Valerie Pearl has suggested, this fundamental principle of high Presbyterianism was consciously sacrificed by the City fathers in order to create a broader base of political alliance with the peace party in Parliament. In any case, with the 'Remonstrance and Petition' the London Presbyterian movement embarked upon a new and highly perilous road which eventually led to what Dr. Pearl calls London's counter-revolution in 1647.[50]

The future developments in the forthcoming confrontation between the City of London and the Army lie beyond the scope of this essay. The agitation of the City's Presbyterian leaders for a strong Presbyterian church government and discipline was over. On June 5, 1646, a new national parliamentary commission was created by ordinance.[51] Four days later, the House of Commons issued an order, 'requiring and injoyning all Ministers of the Province of *London* forthwith to put [into] execution the Ordinances concerning Church Government'.[52] On June 19, the London Presbyterian divines met at Sion College and with 'certain considerations and cautions' resolved at long last to act in accordance with the parliamentary order.[53] After almost a whole year of preparation in the election of ruling elders and in the organization of individual classes, the first session of the London Provincial Assembly was convened at the Convocation House of St. Paul's Cathedral on May 3, 1647.[54]

It will appear to be mere tautology to say that the Presbyterian church government in the City of London was a creation of the London Presbyterians. Yet, perhaps, only such a tautological observation may help to make clear the paradox that as a religious ideology, Presbyterianism had, indeed, a strong following in the City not only among the Puritan ministers but also among its civil leaders; whereas, as an ecclesiastical institution, the Presbyterian church government was but an artificial superstructure without true socio-historical roots in the City's parishes. The success of Presbyterianism in London, therefore, depended upon the presence of lay as well as clerical leaders in the individual parish communities of the City. Consequently, out of the twelve classes which composed the London Province, only eight had succeeded in constituting their classical governments and sending two ministerial representatives and four lay ruling elders to the first assembly.[55] The other four classes, as we shall see, were never able to form their governments at all.[56] More surprisingly, in a comprehensive examination of the London parish records for the entire period of the Interregnum, few institutional ties can be discerned between the various parishes and the new church government.[57] In short, the strength of Presbyterianism in London lay in its ministerial and civic leadership; its weakness came from the artificiality of its institution without either deep historical or broad social foundation. It will be illuminating to have a closer look at these different aspects of the London Provincial Assembly. Let us first turn to its clerical and civic composition.

From the First Classis, the two ministerial delegates were William Gouge and Lazarus Seaman, both of whom were leading Puritan divines in seventeenth-century England. Gouge, perhaps the most renowned and respected Puritan minister in the City, had been rector of St. Anne's, Blackfriars, since 1621. A clerical feoffee himself, he had been closely associated with the Puritan scheme of purchasing impropriations during the early 1630s. Now a member of the Westminster Assembly, he was elected one of its assessors in 1647. The esteem he commanded among his London brethren was clearly expressed by the fact that he was chosen Moderator of this First London Provincial Assembly. It is to be noted, however, that Gouge was a man more of the Puritan tradition of the old generation than of the revolutionary Puritanism of the English Civil War. He seems to have stood conspicuously aloof from the high Presbyterian agitation in the City during the previous two years.[58] Seaman, on the other hand, who was rector of All Hallows, Bread Street, was deeply involved in Puritan politics throughout the Interregnum. He had been one of the Puritan divines who testified at the trial of Archbishop Laud, giving evidence concerning the illegal proceedings of the Archbishop in the Court of High Commission. An outspoken opponent of the Army in 1647, Seaman was undoubtedly for rigid Presbyterianism and religious conformity. Also a member of the Westminster Assembly, he was considered by Robert Baillie to be one of those who supported the Scottish position. Although a man politically too astute to commit himself uncompromisingly in Puritan politics, Seaman was the only founding member to attend the very last session of the London Provincial Assembly in 1660.[59]

The lay ruling elders from the First Classis were Dr. John Clarke, Christopher Meredith, William Kendall and Thomas Gillibrand. Clarke, a leading parishioner of St. Martin, Ludgate, was president of the Royal College of Physicians in 1645–49. He had been appointed by the Parliament as one of the Triers for the First Classis in 1645.[60] Meredith, a ruling elder in the parish of St. Faith, was one of the leading Presbyterian publishers in the City. Also appointed Trier in 1645, he was active in the Assembly and probably involved in the plot of Christopher Love in 1651.[61] Kendall's delegacy was a significant one. He was a Common Councilman and had been one of the members of the City committee for the establishment of a strong Presbyterian church government. He, too, had been appointed Trier in 1645.[62] In comparison, Gillibrand was the least well-known of the lay ruling elders from the First Classis. A parishioner of St. Augustine's, Watling Street, he appears to have played no important role in parish affairs during the years of the Civil War – at least, insofar as we can see from the records of the parish. His name first appeared as one of the assessors for the poor in 1650 and he was not elected churchwarden until 1656 and 1657. But there can be no doubt that he was a strong, active Presbyterian in the City and had twice signed the citizens' petitions to the Common Council in 1645 and 1646 for the establishment of rigid Presbyterianism.[63]

Of the two ministerial delegates from the Third Classis, Ralph Robinson was an able young man and a strong Presbyterian both in personal sentiment and in political association. Educated at St. Catherine's Hall, Cambridge, Robinson received his B.A. in 1638 and M.A. in 1642. But he had become widely known for his preaching and was invited to St. Mary Woolnoth, Lombard Street, where he received Presbyterian ordination. Actively involved in the London Presbyterian agitation during these years, Robinson was to be implicated in Christopher Love's plot.[64] In contrast to Robinson, John Cardell, the other ministerial delegate from the Third Classis, appears to be a rather odd choice. All Hallows, Lombard Street, where Cardell was lecturer and minister in 1647, had had a long radical tradition. John Archer, one of the former St. Antholin lecturers, had been preacher in this parish. And Archer was the author of an influential millenarian tract, *The Personal Reigne of Christ upon Earth*, and had been associated with the Independents in exile in the Netherlands. Cardell himself probably was, or soon turned out to be, an Independent. If he was known to have had Independent leanings, his selection as a delegate was certainly meant to be a gesture on the part of the Presbyterians to include men of different persuasion within the Presbyterian system. In any case, Cardell was soon to disappear from the Third Classis's delegation. It was reported in 1652 that the minister and the ruling elders of All Hallows had long ceased to join in the classical government.[65]

The lay ruling elders from the Third Classis included one of the most important civic leaders in the City, John Warner, Alderman, who had been a member of the City committee for a strong Presbyterian church government. A prominent Puritan, he was reported to have been a signatory of the Root and Branch petition in December, 1640, and in November, 1642, he alone contributed £200 for the parliamentary cause. Although he was soon to change his political allegiance and be instituted as Lord Mayor by the victorious Army later in the year, his delegacy for the time being certainly added much prestige to the First London Provincial Assembly.[66] The other three lay elders from the Third Classis were William Ashwell, Thomas Eyres and Robert English. Ashwell, too, was a prominent civic leader in the City, though it seems that he was far less involved in Puritan politics than Warner. He was Deputy in 1642 and Alderman from 1643 to 1644. An important East India Company merchant and a committee member from 1639 to 1655, Ashwell was nominated for the Company's Deputy-Governorship in 1642 and for its Governorship in 1643, though he was not elected to either office.[67] Little is known about Thomas Eyres, a lay ruling elder of the parish of St. Mary Woolnoth, the records of which for this period have been lost.[68] Of the four lay elders from the Third Classis, Robert English was probably the most active Presbyterian both in parish affairs and in the assembly. He was a leading vestryman in the parish of St. Swithin, London Wall, in 1647, when John Sheffield was chosen minister. Later in the year, he presented to the assembly various books and the Solemn League and Covenant in a frame. In 1651, he was appointed custodian of the reports concerning the state of the ministry and elderships in the various classes of the Province of London. After all, English was a merchant whose trade activities were primarily with Scotland.[69]

The ministerial delegates from the Fourth Classis were John Wall and John Ley. Wall, otherwise a man of slight significance in Puritan politics during the period of Revolution, was minister of St. Michael, Cornhill, one of the strongly Presbyterian parishes in the City. Having been chosen minister by the parish early in 1647, Wall must have been a known Presbyterian, and according to John Price in *The Pulpit Incendiary*, Wall was one of the London Presbyterian ministers who publicly denounced the Army and the Independents in the pulpit early in 1648 after the Army had triumphantly entered the City.[70] Ley, on the other hand, was a renowned Presbyterian divine. In the words of Anthony Wood, Ley was 'esteemed in his time a man of note, especially by those of the Presbyterian persuasion, well vers'd in various authors, and a ready preacher'. In fact, Ley was one of the ablest polemicists in Puritan politics. He had been engaged in a long and strenuous debate with John Saltmarsh, a radical army chaplain, in defence of high Presbyterianism in 1645 and 1646, and in 1653 he was to write again in defence of the national ministry when it was in danger of total destruction by the radicals in the Barebones Parliament. Also a member of the Westminster Assembly, Ley had been elected in 1645 President of Sion College, the centre of the Presbyterian movement in the City of London.[71]

The lay ruling elders from the Fourth Classis were Colonel Edward Hooker, Colonel John Bellamy, John Gase and William Bromwich, all of whom were pronounced Presbyterian leaders in the City and had been appointed Triers for the Fourth Classis in 1645.[72] Little is known of William Bromwich's involvement in the Presbyterian agitation in the City except that he was a ruling elder of the parish of St. Peter, Cornhill, and active in parish and classical affairs. Apparently not a very wealthy man, he contributed only £5 for the advance of money to the Parliament in 1642, though his rent in 1638 was estimated at £35, a respectable figure. He was elected master of the Company of Armourers and Brasiers in 1652.[73] Unlike Bromwich, the other three lay elders from this classis had all been deeply engaged in Puritan politics in the City throughout the years of the Civil War. All three had been appointed assessors for the advance of money in the City to the Parliament in 1642; all three had been members on the City committee for the settlement of a strong Presbyterian church government; and, as indicated by the military titles, two had been high officers in London's Trained Bands.[74] More important, all three played a decisive role in their own respective parishes. Hooker was a leading vestryman in the parish of St. Mary at Hill.[75] In the parish of St. Michael Cornhill, Bellamy diligently attended to all the issues of the parish.[76] At St. Andrew Hubbard, John Gase's influence continued to rise until the middle of the 1650s when he was elected Common Councilman between 1654 and 1657.[77]

From the Fifth Classis the two ministerial delegates were Anthony Tuckney and

Nicholas Proffett, both prominent figures among the London Presbyterian brethren. Tuckney, rector of St. Michael le Querne, was to become a leading Puritan scholar in the University of Cambridge. As master of Emmanuel College from 1645 to 1653, he was twice elected Vice-Chancellor of the University. From 1653 to his ejection in 1661, he was Master of St. John's College, and in 1650 he became the Regius Professor of Divinity at the University. A celebrated member of the Westminster Assembly, Tuckney helped to prepare the Assembly's Directory of Worship and the Confession of Faith.[78] Proffett, likewise, was a leading member of the Westminster Assembly, sitting on several committees and frequently making reports to the Assembly. As minister of St. Vedast, Foster Lane, he represented the Fifth Classis in all the first four assemblies of the Province of London.[79]

The lay ruling elders from the Fifth Classis, too, were active civic leaders in London during the years of the Civil War. Among the four, William Greenhill, a ruling elder of the parish of Christ Church, was probably the least known, and we have no records of the parish for this period to see his role in parish affairs. But he was appointed as one of the assessors of Farringdon Ward Within for the advance of money to the Parliament in November, 1642, and early in the following month, when the Common Council set up a committee for 'all malignant scandalous and seditious ministers in and about the City', Greenhill was also selected as one of its members. In April, 1645, he was again chosen by the Common Council as a member of the Committee for Arms. Undoubtedly a zealous Puritan, he was condemned by Edward Finch, the old vicar of Christ Church, as 'the arch-incendiary of Christ Church parish'.[80] The other three lay delegates, Richard Glyde, John Johnson and James Russell, all seem to have been important figures in the City. Johnson and Russell had been appointed Triers in 1645, and both Russell and Glyde had been on the City committee for church government.[81] Johnson, Deputy of Aldersgate Ward, was the most prominent figure in the parish affairs of St. Botolph, Aldersgate. Indeed, the churchwardens' accounts of St. Botolph begin with beautifully illuminated arms of Deputy John Johnson.[82] Glyde was appointed to many important committees of the Common Council, and he served as Deputy of Farringdon Within in 1649 and 1660.[83] James Russell, perhaps the best known of the four in London politics during the Interregnum, was Common Councilman in 1642, sat on various important committees from 1642 to 1649, and played an active role both in the parish of St. Botolph Aldersgate and later in the parish of St. Stephen Coleman Street.[84]

It was from the Sixth Classis that one of the truly prominent and important Presbyterian divines of the city came. Edmund Calamy, Minister of St. Mary Aldermanbury and one of the *Smectymnuans*, may be justifiably considered the moving spirit of the London Presbyterian movement. During the Civil War, his home in Aldermanbury became the meeting place of the leaders of the City Presbyterian clergy to discuss ways of propagating the godly cause in Parliament and in the City. It was in these meetings, as one contemporary pamphleteer openly asserted, that the Westminster Assembly had its origin. It was in these meetings, too, that an alliance had been worked out with the Independents for a concerted campaign against the bishops in the early years of the Revolution. An active member himself in the Westminster Assembly and a popular preacher before Parliament and the authorities of the City, Calamy's position among the London Presbyterian divines was unparalleled.[85] Calamy's fellow delegate from the Sixth Classis was Arthur Jackson, another eminent Puritan divine who had had long ties with the City. Since 1619, Jackson had been lecturer and subsequently rector of St. Michael's, Wood Street, and also served as chaplain to the Clothworkers' Company. Although a 'quiet and peaceable man', Jackson was possibly involved in Love's plot in 1651.[86]

With Calamy and Jackson from their respective parishes came two equally prominent lay ruling elders to the first assembly of the London Province: John Bastwick and Walter Boothby. Bastwick, together with William Prynne and Henry Burton, had been the famous Puritan sufferers in London in the 1630s under Archbishop Laud. It is interesting to observe that while Burton had become an Independent minister and Prynne turned to Erastianism, Bastwick had become a strong Presbyterian. To be sure, all three remained as polemical and controversial as ever during the years of the Civil War. Bastwick published a number of tracts against Independency and was to be implicated in the plot of Christopher Love in 1651.[87] Boothby was an important civic leader both in the parish of St. Mary Aldermanbury and in the City. Elected Common Councilman in 1642, Boothby was appointed a member of the committee for church government in 1645, and he also sat on a number of other committees of the Common Council. A faithful supporter of Calamy in all parish affairs, Boothby, like his respected parish minister, was undoubtedly a genuine Presbyterian.[88] The other two lay delegates from the Sixth Classis, William Webb and Lawrence Brinley, were comparatively lesser men, but both had been appointed Triers for the Sixth Classis in the parliamentary ordinance of 1645. We have no records for the parish of St. Martin, Ironmonger Lane, for this date, and it is difficult to identify Webb. A number of men with the same name were active in London politics during this period.[89] Brinley, a ruling elder of St. Mary Magdalen, Milk Street, was certainly a zealous Presbyterian. He had signed both of the citizens' petitions to the Common Council for strong Presbyterianism in 1645 and 1646.[90]

The ministerial delegates from the Seventh Classis were James Cranford and Samuel Clarke. Cranford, as Anthony Wood correctly observed, was 'a zealous presbyterian'. As a licenser of books of divinity, Cranford approved of and wrote prefatory epistles for Thomas Edwards's notorious book, *Gangraena*, in which, he said, readers might see the evil consequences of toleration. Of course, Cranford was himself an able polemicist, and he was one of the City Presbyterians who had worked closely and ill-advisedly with the Scottish divines in London. In 1645, goaded by Robert Baillie, he involved himself in a plot to defame and destroy the

Independent leaders in Parliament.[91] Clarke, rector of St. Benet Fink, was a prominent scholar and twice elected President of Sion College. A protégé of Lord Brook, one of the leading figures of the Puritan faction in the nation, Clarke had been deputed in 1640 to visit Charles I at York to protest against the 'etcetera' oath. He supported the Covenant and had signed the London ministers' petition in 1645. Yet it is worth noting that Clarke was a moderate man and later to be closely associated with Richard Baxter.[92]

The lay ruling elders from the Seventh Classis were John Everett, James Story, Joseph Vaughan and Robert Lant. Lant was from the parish of St. Peter le Poer, of which no records for this period are available. He had been appointed assessor for the advance of money in Broad Street Ward in 1642 and Trier in 1645. It is not known whether he is the same Lant who was to be elected master of the Company of Merchant Taylors, in 1658.[93] On the other hand, the other three lay delegates from this classis were all known figures in London politics during the years of the Civil War. Everett, churchwarden for the parish of St. Botolph, Bishopsgate, 1640–41, was elected Common Councilman in 1642. He sat on the committee for the fortification of the City in 1643 and also on several parliamentary commissions during the years of the Civil War. He had been active in parish affairs, too, during these years.[94] Story was probably the zealous Puritan in pre-revolutionary London who paid £50 in 1642 for the parliamentary cause – a rather large sum in view of the fact that his rent in 1638 was estimated at £10 only. Having been churchwarden in 1632–33, Story was now a leading parishioner in the parish of St. Benet Fink and a friendly supporter of the minister. During the years of the Civil War, he seems to have been active in Puritan politics in the City as well, being both on the committee for the fortification of London in 1642 and on the committee for the maintenance of the City ministers in 1646. He had been appointed as Trier for this classis in 1645.[95] Vaughan was from the parish of St. Christopher le Stocks. Although by no means a very prominent parishioner there, Vaughan's delegacy was an important one. He was a member of the Honourable Artillery Company, and a colonel in the London militia. He had been churchwarden in the parish in 1643–44, and must have been a strong supporter of Cranford, minister of this parish. Both Cranford and Vaughan were to be implicated in the plot of Christopher Love in 1651.[96]

From the Eighth Classis the ministerial delegates were William Spurstow and Thomas Manton. Spurstow, like Edmund Calamy, was one of the *Smectymnuans* and had been involved in Puritan politics from the beginning of the Revolution. In the early days of the Civil War, he served as chaplain to John Hampden's regiment in the parliamentary army. Also a member of the Westminster Assembly, he preached frequently before the Parliament. He had been appointed to the mastership of St. Catherine's Hall, Cambridge, a position he was to lose in 1650 because of his refusal to take the Engagement for the Commonwealth. Although Spurstow appears to have been a moderate man, his fear of religious anarchy and his support for a strong Presbyterianism are both unmistakable.[97] Manton was a younger man but soon to become a recognized leader among his London Presbyterian brethren. A man favouring broader latitude in ecclesiastical polity, he appears to have developed a more sympathetic understanding towards the Independents. Nonetheless, Manton was a Presbyterian. He served as one of the scribes to the Westminster Assembly, signed the London ministers' *Vindication* in 1649, attended Christopher Love at the scaffold and preached Love's funeral sermon.[98]

The lay ruling elders from the Eighth Classis were Sir David Watkins, Colonel Edward Popham, Isaac Legay and John Bence. Watkins had been one of the radicals in the City in the early days of the Civil War and, in alliance with such Independents as John Goodwin and Hugh Peters, in opposition to any peace treaty with the King. Unfortunately, the relevant records of St. Andrew Undershaft, of which he was ruling elder, have been lost, and there is no way of observing his role in the establishment of Presbyterianism in his own parish. His support for Presbyterianism can be inferred, perhaps, from the fact that he was elected as a leading member on the Grand Committee in the first assembly.[99] Colonel Popham's parish cannot be identified, but his choice was a significant one. His father, Sir Francis Popham, was a member of the Long Parliament, and Popham was now a leading officer in the parliamentary army. A future admiral and general at sea, he was soon to leave his London residence.[100] Bence, too, was the son of a member of the Long Parliament, Alexander Bence, who had been appointed Trier for this classis. It is doubtful, however, whether the Bences were regular inhabitants in the parish of St. Botolph Aldgate, with which his father was associated when appointed Trier. The parish records of St. Botoloph for this period do not provide any evidence of their residence or activities in the parish. However, Bence was to become a leading figure in the City. He was to be elected Alderman in 1664–65 and master of the Grocers' Company in 1668. He was also to sit in Parliament in 1659 and 1669–87.[101] Efforts have failed to identify the parish of Isaac Legay, and nothing has been learned about his activities in religious affairs during this period. Legay was apparently a London merchant engaged in tobacco trade with the Spanish West Indies. One of his relatives, Peter Legay, was Alderman in the city of Southampton in 1649 and a commissioner of trade in the 1650s.[102]

The ministerial delegates from the Tenth Classis were Jeremiah Whitaker and John Rawlinson. Whitaker, like William Gouge, was another renowned Puritan divine of the older generation. He was one of the morning lecturers chosen by the Parliament in the early years of the Revolution to preach in the Abbey Church of Westminster for the edification of the members of the House of Commons. Also a prominent member in the Westminster Assembly, he was elected its Moderator in 1647. As rector of St. Mary Magdalen, Bermondsey, from 1644 to his death in 1654, Whitaker preached frequently before both the

Parliament and the authorities of the City.[103] Rawlinson was a younger man but seems to have had close ties in the City. He lectured at St. Anne and St. Agnes, Aldersgate, in 1642, and later became minister of St. Mary Abchurch. Early in 1647, he was instituted as rector of Lambeth, where he had probably officiated since 1644. Undoubtedly a strong Presbyterian, Rawlinson was Moderator of the Tenth Classis in 1647.[104]

The lay ruling elders from the Tenth Classis were Robert Houghton, Daniel Sowton, Jeremiah Baines and Andrew Dandy. No biographical information of Dandy has been found to enable us either to identify his parish or to see his role in religious affairs. But he represented the Tenth Classis in all the first five assemblies of the London Province and afterwards intermittently until 1659. He was also frequently elected a member of the Grand Committee in the assembly.[105] The other three delegates, on the other hand, were all important choices. Houghton had been a radical leader in the parish of St. Olave, Southwark, where the radical Puritans caused great disturbances in June, 1641. As churchwarden of St. Olave, Houghton had torn down the rails around the altar and was temporarily imprisoned. He had been appointed Trier for the Tenth Classis in 1645 and was to play an active role in Puritan politics throughout the years of the Civil War.[106] Both Sowton and Baines were militant Presbyterians, and both were high officers in the Southwark militia. They were soon to be involved in the riots in London and the intimidation of the Parliament. In August, 1647, the House of Commons resolved to bring in an impeachment of high treason against Lieutenant-Colonel Baines, though action against Colonel Sowton was put off. In the future, they were again to be involved in the plot of Christopher Love in 1651.[107]

From the preceding analysis of the ministerial and lay composition of the first London Provincial Assembly, it is clear that the leadership of English Presbyterianism, at least in the City of London, was, indeed, strong and influential in 1647, when the new Presbyterian church government was established. Among the sixteen ministerial delegates, nine were members of the Westminster Assembly and two were serving at that very juncture as its assessor and moderator. Three had been elected presidents of Sion College in London, and two had been appointed to masterships in the University of Cambridge. Two of the *Smectymnuans* were included, and the majority of the ministerial delegates were popular preachers and able polemicists. The lay ruling elders were equally prominent. Of the thirty-two lay delegates, eight had been members on the committee of the Common Council for the settlement of a strong Presbyterian church government and discipline in the City. Many had been on a variety of other committees as well. More importantly, six were high ranking officers either of the Trained Bands of London or of the militia in Southwark, and six were appointed to the Militia Committee of the City on May 4, 1647, the very day

after the attempt by the London Presbyterian leaders to control the City's
military forces. In addition, they included the President of the Royal College of
Physicians, the Postmaster of England for foreign countries, one leading
committee member of the East India Company, probably three future masters of
livery companies in the City, two prominent publishers and stationers, and, last
but not the least important, one of the famous Puritan martyrs of the City under
Archbishop Laud. It may not be an exaggeration to say, therefore, that English
Presbyterianism was probably never to have such strong leadership again in the
City of London.

This strength of English Presbyterianism in its leadership in the City, however,
must not conceal the weakness of the London Provincial Assembly as a new
ecclesiastical institution. Unlike the old episcopacy, it had no traditional and
customary relationship with the individual London parishes. And, perhaps even
more importantly, after a century of rapid growth and social change in and about
the old City of London, the parish communities of the City had become much
diversified in their demographic structure and in their general climate of religious
and political life. Consequently this new Presbyterian church government and
discipline had neither the historical tradition nor the social foundation to claim
or command general acceptance by a London parish community. As has been
previously indicated, the conspicuous absence from the London parish records of
this period of direct references to the jurisdiction or existence of the London
Provincial Assembly is simply unmistakable and arresting.[108] It seems that even in
parishes where lay or clerical Presbyterian leadership was strong, the
Presbyterians acted virtually outside the institutional framework of the parish.
The election of ruling elders, for instance, which was considered by all sides the
most essential part of the constitution of the Presbyterian church government and
discipline, was seldom officially acknowledged in the vestries of London parishes.
In fact, among all extant parish records of the period, only nine parishes in 1646
recorded the names of the lay ruling elders elected for that year. Almost no such
elections were ever recorded again.[109] And, after all, four of the twelve classes of
the London Province were not even formed in 1646–47, when the Presbyterian
movement in London was at its strongest. The reasons why these classes failed to
constitute their classical governments were many, and they varied from classis to
classis. The scope of this essay does not permit a full analysis of the whole
situation, but a few general observations may be in place.

One of the reasons was obviously geographical: three of the four unformed
classes lay largely outside the Wall of the City and thus were further removed
from the direct influence of the Presbyterian City leaders. The Ninth Classis
covered a large area from the parishes in the east end of the City within the Wall
to the eastern suburbs of Stepney and Wapping. These eastern suburbs were
especially diverse in their social components and had been unusually radical in

religion and politics.[110] The Eleventh Classis, on the other hand, comprised the western suburbs of the City. Stretching from Drury Lane on the east to Knightsbridge on the west, from St. Giles's Fields on the north to Tothill Fields on the south, it corresponded in general to the political as well as the geographical contours of the City of Westminster. As the centre of national government and politics, the City of Westminster was an arena of political forces far too powerful to be contained within the classical structure.[111] Again, the Twelfth Classis was composed of eight parish churches outside the Wall to the northwest of the City. The core of this classis was obviously the Ward of Farringdon Without, which, in fact, appears to have been strongly Presbyterian. Yet the inclusion of parishes far to the north and outside the boundary of the Ward made the classis unwieldy in size and utterly lacking in unity.[112]

The failure of the Second Classis to form its classical government is in every sense a surprise. Geographically, it lay in the heart of the City. Furthermore, among the fifteen parishes which made up the Second Classis was that of St. Antholin's, which had for almost a century served as the centre of the Puritan movement in the City of London. In 1559, at the very beginning of the reign of Queen Elizabeth I, the famous St. Antholin lectureship was founded. For generations to come, the bells of this parish church would ring at five o'clock in the morning to summon the parishioners to the new morning prayer, psalm singing and the lecture at six, all after the Genevan pattern, as a contemporary diarist had observed. Richly endowed and continuously augmented, St. Antholin's, unique even in the City of London, had a lecture every weekday. And it had attracted some of the most celebrated Puritan preachers.[113]

The role played by St. Antholin's in the history of Puritanism was by no means confined to its parish boundaries. In 1617, Charles Offspring became the rector of the parish and through him St. Antholin's was to be closely associated with the work of the feoffees for the purchase of impropriations in the nation. A clerical feoffee himself, Offspring was to turn St. Antholin's into a sort of Puritan seminary in the City. And it was at St. Antholin's, we may recall, that the Scottish divines preached to the London citizens in the early days of the Revolution. Moreover, unlike William Gouge, Offspring was actively engaged in the Presbyterian movement in the City throughout the years of the Civil War. He had signed the London minister's petition for the establishment of a strong Presbyterian church government.[114]

An examination of the individual parish churches within the Second Classis would reveal another cause of the London Assembly's failure. Out of the fifteen parishes of this classis, nine were reported in October, 1648, to be without a minister because of the poverty of these benefices, and of these nine benefices, four are identified by a modern historian as among economically impoverished or decayed parishes of the City. In fact, in few of the nine parishes was the ministry ever settled on a firm and perpetual basis during the entire period of the

Interregnum.[115] This lack of settled ministry in London, as a result of the
economic problems of individual parish churches, was a predicament which the
Presbyterians inherited from the past and which they were never able to
overcome when they were in power. This is another revealing example of the
weakness of the London Province as a new ecclesiastical institution.

At this point, we may return to the civic Presbyterian leaders in London, who
did try to solve this problem. On August 13, 1646, the Court of Common
Council was informed that 'divers Parishes within the Citie and Liberties thereof
have noe ministers, and that of late some godly ministers have left the Citie and
gone into the Countrie and that others alsoe intend to goe away likewise'. If no
action was to be taken to amend the situation, the City, the Common Council
was warned, 'will be destitute of Godly and faithful ministers to instruct the
people'.[116] Although the blame was placed mainly upon those who refused to pay
tithes, the truth was that the economic predicament of many City parishes went
beyond the denial of tithes by certain parishioners.

It seems that the City fathers clearly understood the real issue; and, for a time,
they attempted a noble solution. The Common Council created a special
committee for a competent maintenance of the City ministry. To be sure, this
committee was composed mostly of the leaders of the civic Presbyterian faction
in the City. It took the committee almost two months to design a solution, but the
plan the committee eventually introduced into Common Council on October 2
was a most significant attempt on the part of the civic Presbyterian leaders in
London to lay a firm foundation for the new church government. First, the
committee recommended that, in lieu of tithes, an annual City tax be levied on
all the houses within the City and the suburban precincts. Second, all former
ecclesiastical estates in the City were to be procured from the Parliament. Third,
the committee advised that a comprehensive survey be conducted of the true
annual value of every house in the City. And, finally, during the debate in the
Common Council, the survey was extended to cover all other categories of
property as well: 'all halls, shops, warehouses, store houses, Die houses, Brew
houses, Sellars, Stables, Keyes or Wharfes with Cranes belonging to the same,
Tymber yards and gardens'.[117]

There can be no doubt that this plan, if successfully executed, would have
changed completely the economic life of the London parishes, and, incidentally,
would also have provided modern historians with invaluable information, in
tabular form, about the wealth of mid-seventeenth-century London. In fact, a
precept was issued by the Lord Mayor to the Alderman, Deputy and Common
Councilmen of every Ward, commanding them to make the survey and to certify
the returns of the results to the Lord Mayor by October 12. Obviously, the task
involved in such a survey was too complicated to be accomplished within the
prescribed time of ten days. Furthermore, such a survey could hardly expect to
receive the cooperation of the inhabitants of the City in general. Not surprisingly,

therefore, several weeks were to elapse without any sign of the returns being rendered. On November 3, another order was issued by the Common Council, once more commanding that 'returnes be made by all the several Wards of this Cittie to the Lord Maior, according to the true intent & meaneing of the said Precept' within a week.[118] Again, nothing was heard of the survey in the following three months until March 1, 1647, when it was ordered that 'the bookes already brought in to the Lord Maior from severall Wards of the value of the houses &c.' be delivered to the committee for the maintenance of the City ministers.[119] With this reference, we see the last trace of this project in the records of the City. It is unknown to what extent this survey was actually carried out, but it is very doubtful that it was a complete survey. In any case, the London Provincial Assembly itself had no legal power to change the economic conditions of the City parish churches. When the political Presbyterian faction in the City government was destroyed in the forthcoming contest of strength between the Army and the City, this noble attempt was doomed.

In conclusion, it may be emphasized that, contrary to the views of former historians, Presbyterianism was clearly a significant force during the years of the English Civil War – at least, in the City of London. The London Presbyterian clergy, in particular, almost evolved into something like a modern party with an ideology and a platform. Their agitation in the years 1645–47 reminds one of the familiar pattern of many revolutionary groups in modern history. Furthermore, they succeeded, for a time, in winning over the civic leaders in London. The support of the City fathers in 1645–47 for a strong Presbyterian church government and discipline does not seem to have been motivated merely by political expediency. Although the triumph of the radical Army made the establishment of a rigid, hierarchical church government an impossible dream, the London Provincial Assembly survived. The Presbyterian divines continued to play an important part in the religious life of the City until their ejection in 1662.

This study also raises certain important questions. Why was Presbyterianism an ideology which appealed to a large number of the civic leaders in London? In what parishes of the City was Presbyterianism firmly established? In what parishes did Presbyterianism fail to establish itself? Was there any co-relation between the social and economic conditions of the individual parishes and their religious associations? And, finally, to what extent and in what ways did the Puritan experiment in London change the religious and social life of the London citizens? To answer all such questions, we shall have to look beyond the Presbyterian movement in the City in 1645–47 and to engage in a comprehensive study and analysis of the society and religion of Puritan London.[120]

Notes

1. I wish to take this opportunity to express my deep appreciation and gratitude to the staff of

Guildhall Library for all their unfailing courtesy and assistance during the long summers of my research at the Library. Professor George Frick, my senior colleague at the University of Delaware, has kindly read the manuscript of this essay, made valuable suggestions for improvement and shared with me his rich knowledge about the history of the City of London.

For the Independents, see Geoffrey F. Nuttall, *Visible Saints: The Congregational Way, 1640–1660* (Oxford, 1957) and George Yule, *The Independents in the Civil War* (Cambridge, 1958). For the Baptists, see A.C. Underwood, *A History of English Baptists* (London, 1947) and W.T. Whitley, *History of the British Baptists* (London, 1932). For the Fifth Monarchy Men, see L.F. Brown, *The Political Activities of the Baptists and Fifth Monarchy Men* (New York, 1912) and B.S. Capp, *The Fifth Monarchy Men: A Study of Seventeenth-Century English Millenarianism* (London, 1972). For the Laudians, see R.S. Bosher, *The Making of the Restoration Settlement: The Influence of the Laudians, 1649–1662* (London, 1951) and J.W. Packer, *The Transformation of Anglicanism, 1643–1660* (Manchester, 1969). For the Presbyterians, both A.H. Drysdale, *History of the Presbyterians in England* (London, 1889) and C.G. Bolam and others, *The English Presbyterians: From Elizabethan Puritanism to Modern Unitarianism* (London, 1968) cover the period of the Interregnum in one chapter. Neither touches upon the high Presbyterian movement in the City of London during the mid-1640s. G.R. Abernathy, Jr., 'The English Presbyterians and the Stuart Restoration, 1648–1663', *Transactions of the American Philosophical Society*, new series, LV, Part 2 (1965), deals with the concluding rather than the first phase of the Presbyterian movement in the English Revolution. In fact, W.A. Shaw, *A History of the English Church during the Civil Wars and under the Commonwealth*, 2 vols. (London, 1900) still is, in many ways, the most comprehensive treatment of English Presbyterianism of this period, but to Shaw, the Presbyterian church polity was merely an accidental episode of the Puritan Revolution.

2. *Ibid.*, I, pp. 6–7.

3. See pp. 43–3 and footnote 50.

4. See Charles E. Surman, ed., 'The Records of the Provincial Assembly of London, 1647–1660', a typescript in 2 vols. held at Dr. Williams Library, London, from the original manuscript, which is now in the possession of Sion College, London. The 'Records', which contain the official activities of twenty-seven assemblies of the London Province from May 3, 1647, to August 15, 1660, are essential for a study of the Presbyterian experiment in the City of London during the revolutionary era. Mr. Surman's biographical notes, although far from complete, are useful.

5. The Scottish divines arrived in London on November 15, 1640. It is also worth noting that the four divines from Scotland were deliberately chosen in such a way as to deal with the various issues confronting their English Puritan brotherhood: Alexander Henderson and Robert Blair 'to satisfy the minds of many in England who love the way of New England better than that of Presbyteries used in our Church' [that is, the Scottish Kirk], Robert Baillie, 'for the convincing of that prevalent faction [that is, the 'Canterburians'] against which I have written', and George Gillespie 'for the crying down of the English ceremonies for which he has written'. See Robert Baillie, *Letters and Journals*, 3 vols., edited by David Laing (Edinburgh, 1841–42), I, p. 269; Shaw, *loc. cit.*, I, p. 127.

6. Clarendon, Edward Hyde, Earl of, *The History of the Rebellion and Civil Wars in England*, 6 vols., edited by W.D. Macray (Oxford, 1969), I, p. 251. See also Valerie Pearl, *London and the Outbreak of the Puritan Revolution* (London, 1961), p. 231.

7. Baillie, *loc. cit.*, I, pp. 286–87.

8. Some years later Edmund Calamy wrote: 'After my coming to London at the beginning of this

Parliament I was one of those that joyn in making *Smectymnuans*, which was the first deadly blow to *Episcopacy* in England of late years . . . I was the first that openly before a *Committee of Parliament* did defend that our *Bishops* were not only not an *Order* distinct from *Presbyters*, but that in Scripture a Bishop and Presbyter were all one'. See Calamy, *A Just and necessary Apology* (London, 1646), p. 9.

9. John Vicars, *The Schismatick Shifted. Or, The Picture of Independents* (London, 1646), pp. 15–16; W.R. [i.e. William Rathband], *A Briefe Narration of Some Church Courses* (London, 1644), 'Preface to the Reader'; Thomas Edwards, *Antapologia: Or A Full Answer to the Apologeticall Narration* (London, 1644), pp. 240–243. For further discussion on the background of this agreement, see Tai Liu, *Discord in Zion: The Puritan Divines and the Puritan Revolution, 1640–1660* (The Hague, 1973), p. 9.

10. See A.G. Matthews, *Walker Revised* (Oxford, 1948), pp. 42–63.

11. Shaw, *loc. cit.*, I, p. 136.

12. See, for instances, S.W. Carruthers, *The Everyday Work of the Westminster Assembly* (Philadelphia, 1943), p. 91; *To the Honourable the Commons House of Parliament: The Humble Petition of the Ministers of the City of London* (London, 1644); The Royal Commission on Historical Manuscripts [hereafter cited as Hist. MSS. Comm.], *Sixth Report* (London, 1877), p. 50.

13. C(orporation of) L(ondon) R(ecords) O(ffice) J(ournals of the) Co(mmon) Co(uncil), Vol. 40, ff. 86–86b; Letter Books, QQ, f. 101b.

14. Both the language of the resolution and the procedure of the Common Council on this matter suggest such an interpretation. It is also interesting to note that at this very juncture the City authorities had appointed a committee to address the Westminster Assembly and to invite the divines to join the City fathers in the service for a day of public thanksgiving in London. And, at the same time, a letter from the Westminster Assembly had arrived, in which the divines said that they had 'received very great incouragem^t from that famous and loyall Citty to goe on with cheerfullnesse in the great service to which wee are called', CLRO J.Co.Co, Vol. 40, f. 86; Letter Books, QQ, f. 101.

15. CLRO J.Co.Co., Vol. 40, f. 86b; Letter Books, QQ, f. 101b.

16. CLRO, Repertories, Vol. 57, f. 167b.

17. House of Lords, *Journals* (hereafter cited as *L.J.*), VII, pp. 544–545; C.H. Firth and R.S. Rait, eds., *Acts and Ordinances of the Interregnum*, 3 vols. (London, 1911), I, pp. 749–754. In this ordinance, only the Province of London was divided into classical assemblies.

18. House of Commons, *Journals* (hereafter cited as *C.J.*), IV, pp. 253, 280; *L.J.*, VII, p. 558; *To the right Honourable the Lords and Commons assembled in Parliament* (London, 1645); *The True Informer*, September 23, 1645. See also Shaw, *loc. cit.*, I, p. 273; W.K. Jordan, *The Development of Religious Toleration in England*, 4 vols. (London, 1932–40), III, p. 71.

19. *C.J.*, IV, pp. 282, 300.

20. CLRO J.Co.Co, Vol. 40, f. 148; Letter Books, QQ, f. 180.

21. Lord Mayor Thomas Atkins, Aldermen Sir John Wollaston, John Warner, John Langham, James Bunce, Samuel Avery, and Common Councilmen William Kendall, James Russell, Christopher Pack, Walter Boothby, Lawrence Bromfield, Edward Hooker, Alexander Jones, Richard Venner, Richard Glyde, John Gase, Richard Young and Thomas Arnold. Later in November, Alderman John Fowke, Alderman William Gibbs, and Common Councilmen John Bellamy, Edward Dobson, Francis Allen and Michael Herring were added to this committee. See CLRO J.Co.Co., Vol. 40, ff. 148, 151; Letter Books, QQ, ff. 180, 183b. To be sure, not all these men were strong

Presbyterians, and some of them would change their religious affiliations with the changing course of the Puritan Revolution. This is not the place to describe the role played by these men in Puritan politics in the City during the Revolution. It may be pointed out, however, that eight of them were to serve as lay ruling elders in the first London Provincial Assembly. See below, Section II of this essay.

22. CLRO J.Co.Co., Vol. 40, ff. 153–153b; Letter Books, QQ, ff. 187–187b.

23. For Drake, see *D(ictionary of) N(ational) B(iography), s.v.*; A.G. Matthews, *Calamy Revised* (Oxford, 1934) (Hereafter cited as *C.R.*), *s.v.*

24. CLRO J.Co.Co., Vol. 40, ff. 151–153b; Letter Books, QQ, ff. 184b–187; Hist. MSS. Comm., *Sixth Report*, p. 85.

25. See Shaw, *loc. cit.*, I, pp. 303–18; Carruthers, *loc. cit.*, pp. 12–17.

26. CLRO Letter Books, QQ, f. 185.

27. *Ibid.*, f. 185b.

28. *Ibid.*, f. 186.

29. *Ibid.*, f. 185.

30. *C.J.*, IV, p. 348; CLRO Letter Books, QQ, f. 188b; Bulstrode Whitelock, *Memorials of the English Affairs from the Beginning of the Reign of Charles the First to the Happy Restoration of King Charles the Second*, 4 vols. (London, 1853), I, p. 537; Reginald R. Sharpe, *London and the Kingdom*, 3 vols. (London, 1894), II, pp. 223–24.

31. Whitelock, *loc. cit.*, I, p. 538.

32. CLRO J.Co.Co., Vol. 40, f. 160; Letter Books, QQ, f. 195. Later the petition from the Ward of Farringdon Within was attached to the petition of the Common Council. See CLRO J.Co.Co., Vol. 40, f. 161; Letter Books, QQ, f. 196b.

33. CLRO J.Co.Co., Vol. 40, f. 160; Letter Books, QQ, f. 195.

34. *Ibid.*; Sharpe, *loc. cit.*, II, p. 226.

35. It should be pointed out that the Long Parliament had passed, on December 20, 1643, 'An Ordinance to disable any person within the City and Liberties thereof, to be of the Common-Councell, or in any Office of trust within the said City, that shall not take the late Solemne League and Covenant'. See Firth and Rait, eds., *Acts and Ordinances*, I, p. 395. If the ordinance was originally meant to purge the City government of men in favour of the old episcopacy on the right, it could be used now against those in opposition to Presbyterianism on the left. Afterwards the Common Council did take action against those of the Common Council, who had either stayed away from the service or openly declined to take the oath. See below, footnote 40.

36. CLRO J.Co.Co., Vol. 40, ff. 160b–161; Letter Books, QQ, ff. 195b–196b; Hist. MSS. Comm., *Sixth Report*, p. 93.

37. The House of Commons made several resolutions on the petition on January 15, but no answer was returned to the Common Council of the City until February 9. The reason for the delay was that the House referred the petition to the Grand Committee for Church Government, which did not act on it until January 23 and 30. See *C.J.*, IV, pp. 407, 412, 422; Letter Books, QQ, ff. 197, 203.

38. The Grand Committee of the House of Commons ordered that this committee was to be composed of such members as were nominated by the members of the House of Commons who

represented the City of London, the City of Westminster, the Borough of Southwark, the Counties of Middlesex and Surrey, as well as the Inns of Court and the Serjeant Inns.

39. For Pennington and Venn, see *D.N.B.*, *s.vv.* See also Pearl, *loc. cit.*, pp. 176–84, 187–89.

40. CLRO J.Co.Co., Vol. 40, ff. 166–166b; Letter Books, QQ, ff. 204–204b.

41. CLRO J.Co.Co., Vol. 40, ff. 215b; Letter Books, QQ, ff. 268b–269b, 274–274b; Sharpe, *loc. cit.*, II, pp. 239–261.

42. CLRO J.Co.Co., Vol. 40, f. 170; Letter Books, QQ, ff. 209b–210b; Sharpe, *loc. cit.*, pp. 228–230.

43. CLRO J.Co.Co., Vol. 40, ff. 174–174b; Letter Books, QQ, ff. 213b–215b. Quotation from *ibid.*, f. 214.

44. *Ibid.*, ff. 214–214b. See also Hist. MSS. Comm., *Sixth Report*, pp. 104–105.

45. *C.J.*, IV, p. 479; Sharpe, *loc. cit.*, II, p. 233.

46. CLRO J.Co.Co., Vol. 40, f. 176; Letter Books, QQ, f. 216b.

47. Sharpe, *loc. cit.*, II, p. 234.

48. CLRO J.Co.Co., Vol. 40, ff. 178b–182b; Letter Books, QQ, ff. 218–221; *C.J.*, IV, p. 555; Hist. MSS. Comm., *Sixth Report*, pp. 118, 213.

49. It should be noted, however, that the City fathers continued to attack toleration and Independency very strongly.

50. Valerie Pearl, 'London and the Counter-Revolution', in G.E. Aylmer, ed., *The Interregnum: The Quest for Settlement 1646–1660* (London, 1972), pp. 29–56.

51. Firth and Rait, eds., *Acts and Ordinances*, I, pp. 852–855.

52. *C.J.*, IV, p. 569.

53. See *Certain Considerations and Cautions agreed upon by the Ministers of London* (London, 1646).

54. Surman, ed., 'Records of the Provincial Assembly of London', II., p. 6.

55. *Ibid.*, pp. 3–5.

56. For further discussion on these four classes, see below, Section III of this essay.

57. Only very rarely do we find a parish where the lay Presbyterians exercised strong leadership, voluntarily consulting the classical assembly on certain particular issues. See, for instance, G(uildhall) L(ibrary) MS 4072/1, f. 179. For further discussion on this subject, see Section III below.

58. For Gouge, see *D.N.B.*, *s.v.* Cf. also Isabel M. Calder, ed., *Activities of the Puritan Faction of the Church of England* (London, 1957); Paul S. Seaver, *The Puritan Lectureships: The Politics of Religious Dissent, 1560–1662* (Stanford, Calif., 1970); Alexander F. Mitchell and John Struthers, eds., *Minutes of the Sessions of the Westminster Assembly of Divines* (London, 1874).

59. For Seaman, see *D.N.B.*, *s.v.; C.R.*, *s.v.*; for his testimony, see C(alendar of the) S(tate) P(apers) D(omestic), 1644, p. 4.

60. GLMS 1311/1, ff. 134b, 138; *D.N.B.*, *s.v.*; Shaw, *loc. cit.*, II, p. 400.

61. Surman, ed., 'Records of the Provincial Assembly of London', I, p. 259, *s.v.*

62. CLRO J.Co.Co., Vol. 40, ff. 148, 193; Letter Books, QQ, ff. 180, 237b.

63. GLMS 635/1, no. fol., see vestry minutes under those years; CLRO J.Co.Co., Vol. 40, ff. 153b, 174b; Letter Books, QQ, ff. 187b, 215.

64. For Robinson, see *D.N.B.*, *s.v.*

65. Cardell preached, along with John Owen, on January 31, 1649, the day following the execution of

Charles I, before the House of Commons justifying the act. See his sermon, *Gods Wisdom Justified and Mans Folly condemned* (London, 1649). But Cardell, who had been curate in this parish, might have turned himself into a Presbyterian during the 1640s, when two leading parishioners at Allhallows, Alderman Thomas Cullum and Richard Young, were strong Presbyterian leaders in the City. See GLMS 4049/1, ff. 21–26; CLRO J.Co.Co., Vol. 40, f. 148; Letter Books, QQ, f. 180. It is clear that Cardell must have changed his position to Independency by October 17, 1648, when the vestry of Allhallows resolved that 'Mr Thomas Goodwynn minister of God's word shall be thankfully accepted to preach each other Lord's day the afternoon in our church and to administer the sacrament to his own congregation at such times as his soe doinge may not preiudice us nor wee him'. GLMS 4049/1, f. 27 (originally f. 13).

66. The records of the parish of St. Stephen, Walbrook, for the mid-1640s are lost so that we cannot observe John Warner's activities in parish affairs. In the vestry minutes for April 24, 1648, his brother, Samuel Warner, was the leading signatory. See GLMS 594/2, no fol.; CLRO J.Co.Co., Vol. 40, f. 148 and *passim*; Letter Books, QQ, f. 180 and *passim*; P(ublic) R(ecord) O(ffice), State Papers, 16/492, f. 75; Pearl, *loc. cit.*, pp. 325–327.

67. In the parish of St. Nicholas Acons, of which Ashwell was one of the ruling elders, John Babington, Common Councilman, seems to have been more actively involved in Puritan politics in the City during the 1640s. But Ashwell was one of the leading men on the vestry. GLMS 4060/1, ff. 59, 105 and *passim*; Pearl, *loc. cit.*, p. 311.

68. Eyres was delegate to the first three assemblies of the London Province. See Surman, ed., 'Records of the Provincial Assembly of London', I, p. 220.

69. GLMS 560/1, see vestry minutes under July 27, November 7, and November 10, 1647; Surman, ed., 'Records of the Provincial Assembly of London', I, p. 218.

70. GLMS 4072/1, ff. 179b–180, 180b–181. St. Michael Cornhill is one of the few London parishes which recorded the election of lay ruling elders in 1646. After all, John Bellamy was a leading parishioner and one of the ruling elders at St. Michael's. *Ibid.*, f. 178. See also John Price, *The Pulpit Incendiary* (London, 1648), p. 14.

71. For Ley, see *D.N.B.*, *s.v.* For his polemical writings in this period, see *A Comparison of the Parliamentary Protestation with the late Canonical Oath, and the Difference betwixt them* (London, 1641); *The New Quere, and Determination upon it, by Mr. Saltmarsh, published to retard the establishment of the Presbyteriall Government, examined and shewed to be unseasonable* (London, 1645); *Light for Smoke: or a cleare Reply by John Ley to a Darke Book intituled The Smoke in the Temple, by John Saltmarsh* (London, 1646); *Learned Defence for the Legality of Tithes for, and towards, the Maintenance of Gospel Ministers* (Oxford, 1653). In his parish, St. Mary at Hill, Ley had the support of Colonel Edward Hooker, a strong Presbyterian leader in the City and ruling elder of St. Mary's. GLMS 1240/1, ff. 46–51.

72. Shaw, *loc. cit.*, II, p. 401.

73. GLMS 4165/1, ff. 260, 268, 287; P.R.O., State Papers, 19/78, f. 1; T.C. Dale, ed., *The Inhabitants of London in 1638* (London, 1931), p. 177 (where his name is spelled as Brumidge); S.H. Pitt, *Some Notes on the History of the Worshipful Company of Armourers and Braisiers* (London, 1930), p. 42.

74. CLRO J.Co.Co., Vol. 40, ff. 148, 151, 215; Letter Books, QQ, ff. 180, 213, 269–270.

75. GLMS 1240/1, ff. 46–51b.

76. GLMS 4072/1, ff. 169–199.

77. GLMS 1278/1, *passim*.

78. For Tuckney, see *D.N.B.*, *s.v.*; *C.R.*, *s.v.*

79. For Proffett, see Surman, ed., 'Records of the Provincial Assembly of London', I, p. 269.

80. CLRO J.Co.Co., Vol. 40, fols. 42, 128; P.R.O., State Papers, 19/78, 60 d; Edward Finch, *An Answer to the Articles Preferd against Edward Finch* (London, 1641), p. 13.

81. CLRO J.Co.Co., Vol. 40, ff. 148, 176; Letter Books, QQ, ff. 180, 213b; Shaw, *loc. cit.*, II, pp. 401–402 (Russell was appointed Trier in 1645 for the Seventh Classis).

82. GLMS 1453/1, no fol. but see vestry minutes for the 1640s; GLMS 1455/1, front folio.

83. J.R. Woodhead, *The Rulers of London 1660–1689* (London, 1965), p. 77.

84. GLMS 1453/1, ff. 41, 44; GLMS 4458/1, ff. 125, 129, 147.

85. For Calamy, see *D.N.B.*, *s.v.*; *C.R.*, *s.v.*; GLMS 3570/2, ff. 43–58.

86. For Jackson, see *D.N.B.*, *s.v.*; *C.R.*, *s.v.*

87. For Bastwick, see *D.N.B.*, *s.v.*; Surman, ed., 'Records of the Provincial Assembly of London', I, p. 192, *s.v.*

88. GLMS 3570/2, ff. 50–57; CLRO J.Co.Co., Vol. 40, ff. 143, 176, 190, 199, 215; Letter Books, QQ, ff. 180, 213b, 216b, 234, 269–270.

89. See Firth and Rait, eds., *Acts and Ordinances*, III, p. 383, under Webb.

90. GLMS 2596/2, ff. 96, 100; GLMS 2597/1, ff. 80, 85; CLRO J.Co.Co., Vol. 40, ff. 153b, 174b; Letter Books, QQ, ff. 187b, 215.

91. For Cranford, see GLMS 4425/1, ff. 35b–54a; *D.N.B.*, *s.v.*; Hist. MSS. Comm., *Sixth Report*, pp. 67–68; Valerie Pearl, 'London Puritans and Scotch Fifth Columnists: A Mid-Seventeenth-century Phenomenon', in A.E.J. Hollaender and William Kellaway, eds, *Studies in London History* (London, 1969), pp. 313–331.

92. For Clarke, see *D.N.B.*, *s.v.*; *C.R.*, *s.v.*

93. P.R.O., State Papers, 19/78, f. 60b; Shaw, *loc. cit.*, II, p. 402; Charles M. Clode, *The Early History of the Guild of Merchant Taylors*, 2 vols. (London, 1888), II, p. 348.

94. GLMS 4526/1, ff. 54b, 58, 59b, 66; GLMS 4224/2, ff. 58a, 77; CLRO J.Co.Co., Vol. 40, f. 55.

95. GLMS 1303/1, no fol., see churchwardens' accounts for 1641–42 and auditors' signatories throughout the 1640s; Dale, *loc. cit.*, p. 38; CLRO J.Co.Co., Vol. 40, ff. 52b, 109b.

96. GLMS 4425/1, ff. 36b–42b; CLRO J.Co.Co., Vol. 40, ff. 213b, 302; Surman, ed., 'Records of the Provincial Assembly of London', I, p. 290; John Ruthworth, *Historical Collections*, 8 vols. (London, 1721), VII, p. 788.

97. For Spurstowe, see *D.N.B.*, *s.v.*; *C.R.*, *s.v.*

98. For Manton, see *D.N.B.*, *s.v.*; *C.R.*, *s.v.* Manton's moderation in religious polity was to be widely recognized. When he died in 1677, Ralph Thoresby wrote in his diary that Manton, 'deservedly styled the King of Preachers', had a funeral 'attended with the vastest number of ministers of all persuasions, etc., that ever I saw in my life. And the Ministers walked in pairs, a Conformist and a Nonconformist'. Thoresby, *Diary* (London, 1830), I, p. 7.

99. Pearl, *loc. cit.*, pp. 253–54, 260; Surman, ed., 'Records of the Provincial Assembly of London', I, p. 296; II, p. 6.

100. *D.N.B.*, *s.v.*

101. Woodhead, *loc. cit.*, p. 29; cf. GLMSS 9234/8, 9235/2.

102. *C.S.P.D.*, 1648–49, p. 247; 1649–50, p. 360. Later in the 1650s Legay became a leading

parishioner in the parish of St. Antholin's and was elected Common Councilman from 1651 to 1659. GLMS 1045/1, ff. 14–56.

103. For Whitaker, see *D.N.B.*, *s.v.; C.R.*, *s.v.*

104. For Rawlinson, see *C.R.*, *s.v.*; Hist. MSS. Comm., *Sixth Report*, pp. 127, 154.

105. Surman, ed., 'Records of the Provincial Assembly of London', I, p. 212, *s.v.*; II, pp. 7, 31.

106. Hist. MSS. Comm., *Fourth Report*, pp. 73, 74; Shaw, *loc. cit.*, II, p. 403.

107. Ruthworth, *loc. cit.*, VII, p. 788; Surman, ed., 'Records of the Provincial Assembly of London', I, pp. 190, 281, *s.vv.*

108. This subject cannot be explained fully here, but one of the fundamental reasons is probably that in few of the City parishes was there a real unity of religious sentiments among the parishioners – not even in parishes such as St. Mary Aldermanbury or St. Michael Cornhill, where both ministerial and civic Presbyterian leadership was very strong. See GLMS 3570/2, f. 58; GLMS 4072/1, ff. 179, 196, 198b.

109. These parishes are St. Bride, St. Dunstan in the West, St. Katherine Coleman, St. Margaret Lothbury, St. Mary Magdalen, Milk Street, St. Michael Cornhill, St. Peter Cornhill, St. Peter Westcheap, and St. Olave Jewry. See GLMS 6554/2, ff. 35b–37; GLMS 3016/1, f. 280; GLMS 1124/1, no fol., see vestry minutes for July 26, 1646; GLMS 4352/1, f. 178; GLMS 2597/1, f. 85; GLMS 4072/1, f. 178; GLMS 4156/1, f. 287; GLMS 642/1, no fol., see vestry minutes for July 19, 1646; GLMS 4415/1, f. 132b.

110. See Norman G. Brett-James, *The Growth of Stuart London* (London, 1935), pp. 187–212; Pearl, *loc. cit.*, pp. 11–12, 40.

111. See Brett-James, *loc. cit.*, pp. 127–149, 151–182; London County Council, *Survey of London*, Vol. X: *The Parish of St. Margaret, Westminster*, Part I (London, 1926).

112. See Brett-James, *loc. cit.*, pp. 214–222. We may remember that such men as Sir John Wollaston, Thomas Arnold, Roger Drake, all in this Ward, were for a strong Presbyterian church government and discipline. See CLRO J.Co.Co., Vol. 40, ff. 151–153b; Letter Books, QQ, ff. 195–196b.

113. For the unique role played by St. Antholin's in the history of Puritanism in London, see Pearl, *loc. cit.*, pp. 163, 167; Seaver, *loc. cit.*, *passim*; W.K. Jordan, *The Charities of London, 1430–1660* (London, 1960), pp. 286, 288, 289, 291.

114. For Offspring, see GLMS 1045/1, ff. 1–61; Seaver, *loc. cit.*, pp. 236–37; Pearl, *loc. cit.*, pp. 163, 165, 231; Calder, ed., *loc. cit.*, *passim*.

115. These nine parishes are St. Benet Sherehog, St. John the Baptist, St. Mary Magdalen, Old Fish Street, St. Mary Mounthaw, St. Mary Somerset, St. Nicholas Cole Abbey, St. Nicholas Olave, St. Pancras, Soper Lane and St. Thomas the Apostle. See CLRO J.Co.Co., Vol. 40, f. 297; Shaw, *loc. cit.*, II, pp. 103–4, n.; Jordan, *loc. cit.*, p. 41 n.

116. CLRO J.Co.Co., Vol. 40, f. 190b; Letter Books, QQ, f. 234.

117. CLRO J.Co.Co., Vol. 40, f. 193; Letter Books, QQ, ff. 237–237b.

118. *Ibid.*, f. 245.

119. *Ibid.*, f. 255.

120. [This was provided by Tai Liu, *Puritan London. A Study of Religion and Society in the City Parishes* (Newark, Delaware, 1986) ED.]

4

THE SIEGE OF PORTSMOUTH
IN THE CIVIL WAR

John Webb

During the early months of 1642 the long drawn-out war of words between King Charles I and Parliament was slowly transformed into a war of weapons.[1] In March, when Sir John Oglander, a steadfast loyalist and former Lieutenant-Governor of Portsmouth, recorded in his commonplace book at Nunwell the birth and baptism of his grandson and eventual heir, he added sadly, 'He was born in a miserable distracted time.'[2] All over the country men of local influence and power like Oglander were having to decide for themselves which of the many statements and orders issuing regularly from both sides their consciences allowed them to accept. 'Now', wrote Sir Thomas Knyvett, a practical East Anglian squire who surveyed the rapidly-changing political scene, 'there is so much declared as makes all officers in the kingdom traitors of one side or the other.'[3] During late spring and early summer, while the king and his retinue moved uncertainly about the North seeking moral support in town and country, John Pym and his fellow M.P.s increasingly took control of events. Resolving at last that the time had come to gather a military force, they appointed as Captain-General the dependable, if lethargic, Earl of Essex, whose more vigorous cousin, Robert Rich, Earl of Warwick, had already secured for Parliament the services of the navy. By mid-July a state of civil war virtually existed, although it was not until 22 August, when Portsmouth was already under siege, that the king formally raised his standard at Nottingham.

The great importance of holding what Clarendon described as 'the strongest and best fortified town then in the kingdom'[4] was manifestly apparent to both Charles and Parliament during the last months of peace. Situated in the south-west corner of the flat, pear-shaped isle of Portsea, which was linked to the mainland by Portsbridge (to the east of the modern crossing of that name), Portsmouth dominated the narrow entrance to the spacious harbour, on the other side of which lay the small fishing village of Gosport. To the north of the town and separated from it by the muddy tidal creek known as the Mill Pond was the royal dockyard, which had grown up around Henry VII's revolutionary dry dock. To the south-east, on the southernmost tip of the island, stood Southsea Castle, from which guns commanded the shore-hugging shipping channel into the harbour. Although always important as a naval centre, Portsmouth had been particularly favoured by the early Tudor kings. A period of comparative neglect had followed, but Charles I's reign had seen signs of a slow revival. In 1642, in its triple role of fortress, dockyard and key to the magnificent harbour, the town was obviously an important prize which both sides would try to secure.[5] The king, rebuffed at Hull, unable to rely on the loyalty of the principal ports, and deprived of Thamesside with its commercial and naval facilities, undoubtedly hoped that its possession would give him a military headquarters in the South and a gateway through which could come the men and supplies which he expected daily from his friends abroad.

Charles's loss of the navy, however, if permanent, would seriously reduce the importance of a Royalist Portsmouth, and this likely development must have dominated the thoughts of the local victuallers and merchants. Portsmouth without ships would be like a bank without money, and its adherence over a prolonged period to a party which did not control the fleet would lead to unemployment and economic decline. One may be certain that whatever political views they happened to hold, the leading burgesses were eager to continue to enjoy the sight of captains and crews passing regularly along Point and supply boats plying back and forth across the Camber.

The man upon whom rested the responsibility for deciding Portsmouth's allegiance during the impending war was the Governor, Colonel George Goring, the thirty-four-year-old son of Baron Goring, afterwards Earl of Norwich. The complex personality and military achievements of this officer, who later became one of the king's principal generals, still await detailed investigation by historians. Married at twenty-one to the third daughter of the Earl of Cork, from whom he had received a dowry of £10,000, he had, within a short time, amassed such large debts that he had been forced to seek his wealthy father-in-law's assistance. Like many of his contemporaries, he had attempted to find an outlet for his energies in the wars in the Low Countries, and there, in 1637, at the Siege of Breda, he had been wounded near the ankle and permanently lamed. A little later, during the two brief and ignominious campaigns against the Scots, he had added to his store of military experience.[6]

If to his duties as Governor of Portsmouth from 1639–42 Goring brought more than a casual knowledge of soldiering, he also brought serious imperfections of character. The king's adviser and publicist, Edward Hyde, later Earl of Clarendon, considered his extravagance, irresponsibility and repeated treachery deserving of the severest censure, and he declared his reluctance ever to participate with him 'in any action or counsel of trust and importance'. Money despatched to Goring at Portsmouth for official use, he asserted, had been spent 'in good fellowship, or lost . . . at play, the temptation of either of which vices he never could resist'.[7]

The weight of Clarendon's monumental prose has borne heavily upon Goring's reputation during the last three centuries. That he had many of the vices attributed to him there is no doubt. A quarrelsome, erratic, and in many ways immature man, lacking self-control and unable to subordinate himself completely to the common good, his drinking habits were notorious. Sir John Oglander tells in his commonplace book of the memorable visit to the Isle of Wight in 1639 of Goring's friends, Lord Portland, Captain of the island, and his brother Nicholas. One August day they crossed to Portsmouth, and with the colonel 'drank and shot, shot and drank, till they were scarce *compos mentis*. Then they all came into the island, where they did the like. I may truly say that in the space of six days there was never so much powder fired except against an enemy.' On several further occasions during this visit these excitable young men amiably quaffed together. Oglander describes them at Sandham Castle early in September, 'at every health tearing at one another's bands and shirts, insomuch as linen was very hard to be found amongst them'. Later that day, coming home by Newport, 'they got a ladder and drank healths at the top of the cage [i.e. lock-up], and there Goring made a recantation speech for his former disorders and wished the people, of which they had store about them, to take example by him how they came to that place'. Oglander concludes his account of these escapades with the note: 'The powder that was shot here and at Porsmouth in the space of 8 days was better worth than £300.'[8] High spirits and boisterous behaviour by young men are common enough in any age, but Goring's excessive fondness for the bottle seems to have increased over the years, and the habit which no doubt helped sometimes to provide a refuge from the recurring pain of his leg wound gradually undermined his health, so that in the later stages of the war he was a seriously sick man.

In spite of his many shortcomings, Goring was undoubtedly an attractive figure who had inherited many of the courtly qualities of his father. Even the highly-critical Clarendon was forced to admit grudgingly that he was 'a person very winning and graceful in all his motions', and there is a touch of envy in his catalogue of the colonel's charms. 'He had a civility which shed itself over all his countenance, and gathered all the eyes and applications in view; his courage was notorious and confessed; his wit equal to the best and in the most universal conceptions; and his language and expression natural, sharp, and flowing, adorned with a wonderful seeming modesty, and with such a constant and perpetual sprightfulness and pleasantness of humour, that no person had reason to be ashamed of being disposed to love him, or indeed of being deceived by him.'[9] Such qualities endeared him to the poets. His rumoured death on one occasion moved Davenant to write a dialogue in which, 'in manners and in fate', he was compared to Sir Philip Sidney, and he and some of the most celebrated of his riotous circle were the subject of two poems on 'The Gallants of the Times'. A lively drinking song, 'To General Goring after the Pacification at Berwick', by his friend Richard Lovelace, not only praises his glories, which 'shine so brave and high', but also extols the beauty of his 'lovely bride' Lettice, 'Whose eyes wound deep in peace, as doth his sword in wars'.[10]

There is no doubt, also, that on the field of battle he could be a clever opponent, capable of brilliant flashes. Of him Sir Richard Bulstrode said, 'He was, without dispute, as good an officer as any [who] served the king, and the most dexterous in any sudden emergency that I have ever seen.'[11] Clarendon spoke of 'the presentness of his mind and vivacity in a sudden attempt, though never so full of danger', but went on to add that in an enterprise 'that required more deliberation and must be attended with patience and a steady circumspection . . . his mind could not be long bent'.[12] It was this inability to plan coolly and methodically, and to subordinate his own whims to greater strategical considerations, that proved to be the fatal flaw in Goring's generalship. Yet, even so, two of the leading military historians of our time have pointed out that 'we cannot lightly dismiss a man who put to flight half the immense allied army at Marston Moor', and conclude that despite all his faults 'He had . . . the makings of a great leader of men, and as a supreme commander with a free hand, he would probably have made a great name for himself'.[13]

In his personal conduct and management of garrison affairs during the year before the outbreak of hostilities Goring showed the worse side of his character. A familiar figure at Court and like his father a special favourite of Queen Henrietta Maria, the young officer was to all appearances a stalwart supporter of the Royalist cause. More than once during 1641 he seems to have made it clear to the queen that in an emergency he would put Portsmouth at her disposal as a place of refuge in easy contact with the continent. Not surprisingly, when a group of discontented army officers plotted to give the king military support if his position should weaken further, they were successful in recruiting Goring to their number. However, upon learning that there was disagreement over a proposal to make him Lieutenant-General, he not only carried out his threat that 'If he had not a condition worthy of him, he would have nothing to do with the matter', but went even further, secretly revealing the details of the plot to some of the leading figures in the Lords while still keeping in communication with the dissidents. From those in the North he received at Portsmouth on 10 April a letter of support which had been carried down by Captain James Chudleigh, with whom he walked round the walls, at one point remarking that 'if there should be any mutiny in London, the queen meant to come down thither for her safety, and that she had sent him down money to fortify it'. Early in May, amid rumours that Portsmouth was soon to be taken over by a force of French, John Pym, who had been informed of the Governor's revelations, thought it wise to give details of the Army Plot to his fellow Parliamentarians. Still believing in Goring's loyalty, Queen Henrietta Maria decided to put herself under his protection, but, at the last moment, while her carriage stood waiting at the door, she was dissuaded from attempting such a rash act. Within a very short time she learned the harsh news of the colonel's betrayal, and, after his own part in the design had been investigated to the satisfaction of the Commons and his governorship confidently confirmed, it seemed that Portsmouth had been irrevocably lost to the Royalist cause.[14]

During these months Goring appears to have been making an effort to put the previously-neglected town defences into some state of readiness, although events were to show that he was either too late or too half-hearted to achieve much success. In September 1641 he wrote to Sir John Oglander seeking help. 'For the speedier finishing of the works begun here', he informed him, 'we have present want of a dozen of tumbrels. If you shall please to assist the bearer hereof in the procuring of them with all speed, you will, besides the service you do His Majesty herein, put a particular obligation upon your most affectionate servant, George Goring.' Timber, also, is known to have been brought from the island some time earlier for constructional purposes.[15] Parliament, trusting the Governor implicitly, readily promised to supply him with £3,000 'to relieve the great necessities and defects of the garrison of Portsmouth'.[16] In November, however, there was fresh cause for alarm. Letters from Hampshire warned the two Houses that all was not well in the town. Among other things, it was alleged that a post went between the queen and the Governor several times weekly, and 'the Papists and jovial clergymen thereabouts were merrier than ever'. Goring, who was Member for Portsmouth, was immediately summoned by his fellow M.P.s to answer the charges made against him. The aggrieved officer hastened to London 'with that undauntedness', comments Clarendon, 'that all clouds of distrust immediately vanished, insomuch as no man presumed to whisper the least jealousy of him'.

In his speech of defence Goring answered the charges one by one. A French Roman Catholic chirurgeon, it had been alleged, had been brought in to serve the garrison. This he did not deny. The man had attended the Earl of Holland during the war against the Scots in 1639 and had been able to give beneficial advice to Goring 'in respect of his own lameness'. As a reward for his professional skill he had been offered a post at Portsmouth. On another count, that he had tried, against the orders of the custom officers, to transport three geldings to France, he readily acknowledged an attempt to 'do a courtesy' for a French gentleman. He admitted, too, that he had received from the Low Countries arms for twenty horsemen, but thought these a very small provision for the personal use of the Governor of such an important place.

These particular acts, it was readily acknowledged after Goring had spoken, were nothing more than the indiscretions of a highly independent young officer. Of much greater concern were the fears aroused by his building operations at Portsmouth. His accusers had said that the sea defences had been seriously neglected and allowed to fall into decay, while on the landward side, commanding the town, new fortifications were being built upon which he was placing brass ordnance taken out of naval vessels. Goring, drawing on his military experiences in the Low Countries, patiently explained to the House the technical reasons why so much work was being done on the Mount. It was not a new construction, he explained, having been begun some years earlier, when it had been known as Fort Mountjoy. He had acted upon the most expert advice available and was convinced that it was in the best position for the defence of the town. There was nothing secret or sinister in his actions. He had, in fact, some months earlier, at the house of the Earl of Essex, fully explained his plans to Sir Walter Earle, now one of his accusers, who was also aware that the removal of the guns from the fleet to the fort had been done on the orders of the Master of the Ordnance. As for the sea defences, Goring denied that they were weak and reported that for greater strength he had added a 'dally' at the mouth of the haven.

The Members were convinced. For the second time within a few months Goring, consummate actor and superb public speaker, had been cleared by the House. He received 'so generous an applause', says Clarendon, 'that, not without some little apology for troubling him, they desired him again to repair to his government, and to finish those works which were necessary for the safety of the place'. They 'gratified him with consenting to all the propositions he made on behalf of his garrison, and paid him a good sum of money for their arrears'. Moreover, he was given a private assurance, later put into effect, 'that he should be Lieutenant-General of the horse in their new army when it should be formed'.

At the same time the two authors of the letters which had started the scare now came in for sharp criticism. One was an unnamed inhabitant of Portsmouth who had written to a London merchant. The other, also anonymous, had corresponded with Sir Walter Earle and was generally believed to be his son-in-law, Colonel Norton of Southwick Park, who later took a leading part in the siege. There was some talk of requiring them to compensate Goring for the libels they had spread, 'but the House conceived they were persons so mean and unworthy that they could not make reparation fit for a person of his worth to have, and therefore gave directions the letters should be burnt'.

At this distance of time it is impossible to disentangle all the twisted threads of Goring's skilful double-dealing, but it is clear that despite his full-throated allegiance to the Parliamentary cause during the last months of 1641, he was also in secret contact with the sovereign, whom he continued to assure of his loyalty. Once again, it seems, Charles believed him. Money for military expenses at Portsmouth now flowed in from both sides. Facts and figures are confused, but there is good evidence that on one occasion the queen sent him at least £3,000, probably much more, which she had raised from the sale of her plate and some of her jewels. During the spring and early summer of 1642 there are no overt signs of Parliamentary mistrust of Goring, and as late as 12 July Sir Philip Stapleton was ordered by the Commons to write 'to satisfy him with the clear opinion this House has of him and of his worth'.[17]

But the king's confidence in the Governor remained unshaken. In mid-June, in a document drafted at York, Goring received express orders to safeguard the town and the magazine, which 'is of very great consideration to the peace and quiet of this our kingdom', and was informed that 'we are well satisfied of your fidelity and care in that important service'. He was required to take control of all the gunpowder in Portsmouth and see that none of it was used except in the defence of the town. Furthermore, he was to take over the *Henrietta Maria*, a pinnace of sixty-eight tons which normally carried a crew of twenty-five, and use it in any manner he thought necessary to meet attack, 'with further authority to land the guns thereof and employ them for any land service you shall have occasion'. He was also empowered to build fortifications in any place on Portsea Island where he thought they were required and, since more foot and horse soldiers might be needed for the defence of the town, 'we likewise authorise and give power to you to make and appoint the several officers to the several companies so to be raised. And we likewise hereby authorise you . . . that upon any extraordinary occasion you command such number of our train-bands . . . in the places adjacent to march into our said town as may be answerable to the said danger you shall conceive our said town to be in'. In the light of subsequent events it is interesting to note the warning to Goring 'to be most careful for preventing of mutiny within the said town' by seeing that 'no person reside within the said town or be of the said garrison as you shall find disaffected to our service by refusing to obey our just and legal commands'. The Governor was also required to reside in Portsmouth 'and not to stir from thence without our particular directions signified unto you . . . ' Further royal dispatches were sent from Leicester on 25 July. These repeated some of the previous instructions and went on to urge Goring to show the 'utmost care and vigilancy in discharge of a trust so important to the safety both of us and our whole kingdom'.[18]

During the next few days events moved rapidly. With the king's commission in his possession and the arrival in the town of forty loyal horsemen armed with carbines and pistols, Goring decided to make public at once his undivided allegiance to the Crown. According to Clarendon, this premature declaration forced the king's hand, making it necessary for him to embark on war 'before he was in any degree ripe for action'. Whatever may have been the consequences for Charles, Goring's action was undoubtedly a sudden and unwelcome blow to Parliament, which as recently as 12 July had issued warrants for the payment of £5,030 for garrison purposes. Yet, despite this display of faith, it seems that new seeds of mistrust had already been sown at Westminster and were producing a rich crop of rumours in the weeks before Goring's declaration. Once more there had been talk of the Governor's close contact with men known to be loyal to the king, and some of his intimates had indiscretely revealed alarming information about his alleged designs. It had been noted, too, that in recent months he had failed to travel to London despite many letters from his Parliamentary colleagues urging him to do so. Excuses, even from such a glib tongue, were no permanent solution, as Goring must have realised when Lord Mandeville, 'his most bosom friend', wrote counselling him to pursue at once the offer of high command in the Parliamentary army, adding 'that if he did not come to London by such a short day as he named, he found his integrity would be doubted, and that many things were laid to his charge, of which he doubted not his innocence . . . '. So, feeling unable or unwilling to defer a decision any longer, Goring penned 'a jolly letter' of reply in which he stated that since he had been advised that Parliament was acting illegally, 'he might incur much danger by obeying all their orders'. He had received the command of the garrison from King Charles and dared not leave the town without his permission. At last the mask of deception was off.[19]

Events at Portsmouth at the time of Goring's public declaration of his loyalty are described by a contemporary pamphleteer. He tells how, on Tuesday, 2 August, the Governor summoned all those within the town who were capable of bearing arms to assemble during the afternoon, 'at whose appearance he made this speech unto them'. The highly polished oration which follows no doubt owes as much in literary style to the anonymous reporter as to the colonel, although it probably preserves the spirit of his call to arms. After reminding the men of their duty to the monarch, he appealed to them through their purses:

> And for you that are behind of your pay, although the Parliament hath made some promise to see you satisfied, yet such is the case and goodness of His Majesty towards you, that he hath provided you money, which I have in my custody to distribute amongst you so soon as you have subscribed to some few words and conditions in writing which I shall tender unto you, testifying your religious, honest, faithful, and ready intention to serve His Majesty in this business. Neither will I constrain or force any to stay in the town against their wills or free pleasure, but every man of what condition soever shall have free liberty to go and come with his wife and children, servants, and goods in safety and peace. And let every man assure himself that for his faithful service herein His Majesty will not see him unrewarded.

When he had ended, says the writer, 'some of the soldiers gave a great shout, the rest were discontented, and a great distraction was suddenly in the town'. Several other observers confirm that he was willing to discharge those who did not agree with his course of action and refused to take the required oath. The number of defaulters was said by some to be quite substantial, although the officers present later put it at only three or four. After his address to the military, Goring assembled the Mayor and townsmen and made a similar declaration.[20] That this series of events brought confusion there is no doubt, although the town records are unfortunately silent on the official response. In a news-letter published a few days later at the command of Parliament, it was stated that 'the inhabitants of the town are resolved to stand firm in their obedience to the Parliament, and withall to oppose as far as in them lies any forces that shall be brought in . . . that shall take part with the malignant party . . . '[21]

Most of the burgesses were undoubtedly more sympathetic to Parliament than to King Charles, but information on this important matter is limited. The Mayor and his brethren were men who normally could not be easily browbeaten. As recently as the previous April the Hampshire High Sheriff's two bailiffs, who had been sent to Portsmouth to proclaim the treason of the king's adviser, Lord Digby, had been committed into custody by the Deputy-Mayor and threatened with a whipping. Even the Sheriff himself, on coming to the town, had received similar insults, and had afterwards complained bitterly of the 'obstructions and great affronts' he had encountered. But the circumstances of such a quarrel, apparently over town privileges, were very different from those which prevailed during the critical days after Goring's declaration.[22] The townspeople, on the horns of a dilemma, knew that if they expressed their disapproval by leaving Portsmouth, their houses and property would almost certainly be looted by the garrison riff-raff, and this was undoubtedly a strong reason for compliance, if only until the reactions of Parliament were known. Some of the women and children were evacuated at an early stage, and others, but not all, were required by Goring to depart when the close siege of the town became an imminent reality.

Both Houses heard the news of Goring's treachery on 4 August. It is not difficult to imagine the anger and dismay that they must have experienced. One of the most important citadels in the kingdom had been lost. Believed to be immensely strong, its recovery would inevitably be a difficult and costly operation, particularly as the garrison commander was an energetic officer whose military experience they obviously respected. Joint consultations produced three immediate decisions. The first was to send a messenger to Portsmouth to summon Goring to deliver up the town and journey to London to answer for his conduct, which they thought merited a charge of high treason. The second was more practical. Recognising the close connection between Portsmouth and the Isle of Wight, they removed from office Goring's 'familiar friend', the Earl of Portland, 'suspected to be a Papist', and appointed in his place as Governor the more reliable Earl of Pembroke who, acting mainly through a deputy, ruled the island during the next few years. Finally, they resolved that the Earl of Essex, their military commander, 'shall forthwith appoint officers to levy horse and foot . . . and march to Portsmouth', and, should Goring prove to be obstinate, 'to lay siege against the town, and to suppress all that shall come to oppose them'.[23]

If Goring thought that there would be some delay before the island was cut off from the outside world he was quickly disillusioned. During the early days of August a sizeable military force seems to have been building up in the nearby mainland villages and on the slopes of Portsdown Hill, so that it became daily more difficult for the king's supporters to send in supplies. 'The gentry and commonalty of Hampshire . . . ', we are told, 'thought it most convenient to make a timely prevention . . . to which end they drew up such forces as the country could afford . . . so that no forces can either march in or out.' There is no doubt that this local initiative had important practical results. Goring and his officers afterwards admitted that many avowed Royalists had failed to reach the fortress 'by reason of the gathering together of the country forces, and the approaching of others from London'.[24] Throughout the region a careful watch was kept for men and equipment travelling towards the coast. On or about 10 August, for example, a certain Mr Knowles and a Dorset man named White were stopped, and on another occasion two fine horses belonging to Mr Waldegrave, a known Roman Catholic, were seized. At Salisbury, William Wroughton, apparently a junior officer from Portsmouth, was thrown into the gaol, and one of the aldermen went to Downton to turn back thirty Wiltshire recruits believed to be awaiting him there. Some had in fact already gone home, but others with more spirit had slipped away to Portsmouth where, a day or two later, they were intercepted by the vigilant Parliamentary watch.[25]

The growing assault force of trained-bands from Hampshire, Sussex and Surrey was joined on 10 August by two troops of horse. One was commanded by Colonel Hurry, and the other, consisting of forty-three men, by Sir William Waller, who now apparently took command of the besieging army. Not all was well, however, in the Parliamentary camp. A letter sent to Speaker Lenthall by the Hampshire Committee reveals that ammunition, twice promised, had not been received, and there was a shortage of horses and a slackening off in the supply of foot soldiers because of the opposition of some of the local gentry. A strong plea was made for money to pay those who had already arrived, because £1,000 which had been sent down earlier was soon likely to be exhausted. A postscript added a request for 400 muskets, bandoleers, rests and swords out of the Parliamentary stores. Since strong reinforcements for Goring were expected daily from the Marquis of Hertford and the Earl of Southampton, the Committee urged that the remainder of Waller's men and a regiment of foot under experienced officers should be sent down to Hampshire as soon as possible. According to one source, Sir John Merrick's regiment arrived in the area about this time, perhaps in response to the Committee's demand.[26]

Among the troopers under Waller's command was a Scottish contingent which soon gained a reputation for courage and an appetite for action. Some of these men were billeted at Havant at the house of the Rector, Francis Ringstead, a staunch Royalist. This 'most pestilent man' had, at the first sign of trouble, sent a light-horse to fight for the king, and the Scots, it was said, 'are with him therefore'. As a reprisal, too, for his action and opinions, he was required to pay for ten light-horse to serve Parliament. This unfortunate man seems to have had a most unpleasant time trying to cope with the wild northerners, one of whom, 'being aggrieved with him', is said to have 'basted him well favouredly'. When his attempts to escape were frustrated he seems to have come to terms with the situation. He 'waits upon them daily', it was reported, 'gives them good words, and tells them that he will gladly lie out of his own bed to make them room.'[27]

Although in mid-August a news-letter reported that 'about 240 horses, troopers, and 500 foot' had mustered for the final assault on the town, there is surprisingly little information about the exact composition of the Parliamentary force. Not much more is known about the Portsmouth garrison. If a statement made by the Royalist officers after the siege is to be believed, at the time of Goring's declaration there were 'of the ordinary garrison about 300 persons, and of the townsmen about one hundred that were able to bear arms, and of the island which was also under the command of the Governor about 100 fighting men more. Of officers with their servants there were then about 50. With their and the Governor's horses there was above 50 horse.' Another report says simply that at the time of Goring's speech those capable of bearing arms 'were about the number of three hundred'. Clarendon, in typical vein, stresses the paucity of the Governor's support among the gentry and men of his own rank. Except for Lord Wentworth and Thomas Weston, the Earl of Portland's brother, 'who came to enjoy the delight of his company, which was very attractive, and for whom he had promised to raise troops of horse', only three or four country gentlemen, 'with so small a number of men as was fitter for their equipage and retinue than for the defence of the place', were said to have joined him, together with an extra twenty or thirty men of humble birth recruited by sympathisers and added to the regular garrison.[28]

Some military support seems to have come from Chichester, which politically was a divided city. At an early stage, Christopher Lewknor, the Recorder and Member of Parliament, wrote to Goring to sound out his views, and after receiving a satisfactory answer he and others joined the garrison. The men that they brought with them soon gained a reputation for ruthlessness. 'Since Chichester men came to Portsmouth', a news-letter tells us in mid-August, 'there hath been harder usage of people by the colonel and his company than before, and some think by their or some of their advices'.[29]

No official lists of the fighting men now remain from the time of the siege, but some of the garrison accounts for the financial year ending 29 September 1640 are still available, and from these can be obtained a complete picture of Goring's peacetime force. During the last quarter of this period, for example, there were 135 men on the strength, a much lower figure than that given in the officers' description of the situation in early August 1642, by which time presumably the garrison had been built up in anticipation of the outbreak of hostilities. In 1640, receiving a daily wage of 8d. each, were a hundred soldiers, some of whom had specialist duties allotted to them. John Bigges was storekeeper and Thomas Beard the porter. The post of clerk of the garrison was held by John Lee, and that of clerk of the reports by John Webb. Receiving the same rate of pay as the soldiers but classed as officers were John Hunt (ensign), Henry Jenman (drum), Thomas Young (fife), Thomas Whitehorne (armourer) and Anthony Stevens (chirurgeon). John Lobb, the master-gunner, earned a daily fee of 10d., and was assisted by a force of twenty-nine gunners, fifteen of whom were each paid 8d. and the rest 6d. The total wage-bill of the garrison during the quarter was nearly £426.[30]

It was an age, however, when the pay of members of the armed forces was frequently in arrears, and in August 1641 it was stated that those serving in the Portsmouth garrison had not been paid for two-and-a-half years. In the following January the situation had apparently not improved, because a petition from the men was discussed in the Commons. Attempts were made to find the reasons for the delay and to earmark a source from which money might be forthcoming. In March it was resolved that £5,030 should be distributed to the garrison to cover a year's pay and some of the arrears, but warrants were not issued until July. Although early in August it was reported that the Governor 'had gotten a great sum of money from the county to pay his men', it is very likely that these financial arrangements were overtaken by events, and that Goring did not receive all that was due to him before the siege began, even though the cancellation of the order did not occur until 24 August.[31]

Nevertheless there is ample evidence that large sums of money had been sent to Goring by both sides during the last months of the peace, and it is difficult to believe that the financial needs of the men could not have been met earlier. In his speech of 2 August he admitted to the soldiers that 'Parliament hath made some promise to see you satisfied', but put pressure on them by making it clear that only those who stayed would benefit from the substantial sum of money which he said that he had received from the king. For the majority of the men who listened to him there could have been no real choice. Another large sum of money is said to have arrived in Portsmouth about 9 August. According to information given to Parliament by a London hackney-coachman, some gentleman had contacted him 'and hired his coach and six horses, agreeing with him by the day, not telling of him whither he should go'. Three other coaches, each with six horses, had been hired at the same time. Two had been sent off along one route and the third along another. Each vehicle had carried two gentlemen. The informant went on to say that one of the two passengers in his own coach had been Mr Weston, the Earl of Portland's brother. At Portsmouth, which had been their destination, the coachman 'understood that these gentlemen carried down along with them nine thousand pounds in silver, but before he came thither he knew nothing thereof. But he said that one Welch, another of these coachmen, told him after he came to Portsmouth that he knew of it, and did help to tell the money in London.' It is difficult to believe that as late as about 9 August large coaches pulled by teams of horses could rumble down the Portsmouth road and, without arousing the suspicion of the hawk-eyed Parliamentary watch, cross Portsbridge, the only point of entry by land to the island.[32]

Although he had been the master of events, Goring's preparations for a siege proved to be totally inadequate. 'Of victual there was not by estimation sufficient . . . above two days', we are told, and with the arrival of a naval squadron off the coast about 8 August there was little hope of securing further supplies by sea. The poor condition of the defences, even after Goring's repair work, was the subject of comment by observers. Much still remained to be done in the early days of August. He 'had relied too much upon probable and casual assistance', wrote Clarendon, 'and neglected to do that himself [which] a vigilant officer would have done'.[33]

During the early days of August the *Henrietta Maria* pinnace rode in the harbour under the walls of Portsmouth. It was the only naval vessel Goring had and was greatly outclassed by the growing force of ships which his adversaries were able to bring up to seal off the island by sea. Nevertheless in an emergency her six guns were capable of inflicting serious damage on the enemy. On the night of 9 (or 10) August the Parliamentary sea-captains allowed Brown Bushell, an officer on Captain Martin's ship, to attempt a bold stroke. Under cover of darkness he took one or more longboats through the heavily-defended harbour waters and captured the vessel. During the whole operation not a gun was fired or a blow struck. According to one account, the *Henrietta Maria* had forty soldiers on board, 'all which they took, put . . . under decks, and brought away . . . '. A Royalist version of the incident attributed the loss to the treachery of the master, and mentioned a crew of only twelve seamen and two officers. The prize was speedily taken across the harbour to a place near Fareham, where her rigging and guns were removed. It was a dazzling feat and a serious blow to Goring's pride and prestige.[34] The gratitude of the Commons was immediately conveyed to the captains and, more particularly, to the daring Brown Bushell, an able and indefatigable officer who, during the next few years, changed sides on several occasions and finally ended his career on the scaffold.[35]

Meanwhile the land forces of Parliament were willing to bide their time. Writing from Southwick on 12 August, the Hampshire Committee informed the Speaker that it was considered 'scarce proper' to summon Goring officially to give up the town 'till we have forces fit for the assault thereof should he refuse us', and pointed out that 'he could not but hang that trumpeter that should come to require his soldiers not to yield him any further obedience, with those other commands that you have directed for the Mayor and townsmen, which hath made us respite to proceed thereon'.[36]

Goring's supporters, however, thirsted for action, and several incidents which apparently occurred on the slopes of Portsdown Hill during this phase of the operations are vividly described in a letter which a Hampshire gentleman wrote to a friend in London in mid-August. On one occasion, he reported, a force of six Parliamentary horsemen put to flight a much stronger party of Cavaliers, one of whom was killed, another wounded, and a third taken prisoner. About this time, too, a serious clash was triggered off by a minor incident which occurred at Havant when a Royalist and his servant rode into the little market town and tried to incite the inhabitants to loot the Southwick home of Colonel Norton, one of

the leading Parliamentarians in the area. He, upon being informed, had the
trouble-makers arrested and sent to London. In retaliation, a Cavalier force
made a sortie towards Southwick, where they 'challenged Mr Norton forth,
saying "Where is this same Norton? Where is he? I warrant him he is a very
coward, let him come forth if he dare."' The colonel, buff-coated and suitably
armed, immediately rode out with his men and was fortunate enough to be
joined by a hundred mounted soldiers who had just arrived in the area. Against
such a formidable body the spirits of the Cavaliers flagged, and 'they posted
down the hill towards their fort with great speed'. The writer added that 'the
Scots that were among Mr Norton's auxiliaries would presently have flown on
upon the fort, but Mr Norton would not suffer them for fear of danger, there
being ordnance planted there'.[37]

This defence-work had been built at Portsbridge a little earlier. Across the road
stretched a strong wooden barricade and on the south side of the creek was 'a
little fort or bulwark of earth' which, until about 10 August, carried four guns
and was supported by a small force of a dozen or more horsemen. As the
Parliamentary troops began to arrive, however, Goring had second thoughts
about the military importance of this advanced position. Perhaps expecting his
foes to land men on one of the island's harbour shores, he ordered the speedy
removal of the Portsbridge ordnance to within the walls of Portsmouth. The
defence of the bridge was left to a few men armed with pistols and carbines
whose task was clearly to keep Waller's soldiers occupied while the Royalists, in
anticipation of a total withdrawal to the safety of the town, scoured the island for
additional supplies.

The contemporary writers who describe the events of the next two days were
supporters of Parliament and probably prone to exaggeration, but there is little
doubt that the large-scale requisitioning of foodstuffs caused the inhabitants
serious distress. From the 'fruitful isle of Portsea' hundreds of cattle, sheep and
pigs were driven into Portsmouth, 'whether they were fat or lean, to be all killed
and salted up', Goring forcing their luckless owners to act as drovers. One writer
tells how some of the unslaughtered animals were left to graze 'upon some
ground below the mounts that round the town, but the most of them they put out
without the town gate into a marsh near the town in the island, and there kept
them with some musketeers'. The soldiers were also reported to have stripped
bare the farms and cottages of 'corn, meal, flour, beef, bacon, bread, butter,
cheese, eggs, and all their poultry and ducks, not leaving half loaves of bread, nor
pieces of bread, nor pieces of cheese . . . to the great terror of all the people,
especially women and children, forcing poor and rich to come away and beg
about for bread to keep them alive . . . '.

The 'most mean' country folk, too weak to protect themselves, were rescued
from worse misfortunes by the seamen of the blockading squadron. Put ashore on
the eastern side of the island and protected against Goring's soldiers by the two

guns which they had brought with them, they ferried many of the women and children to safety on Hayling Island. According to one estimate, about one hundred cattle and two hundred sheep were taken with them across Langstone Harbour, some joined by ropes to the boats, after which they were forced to swim.

Meanwhile, at their headquarters at Southwick, the Parliamentary officers were making preparations for an attack on Portsbridge. During the afternoon of Friday, 12 August, their plans were thwarted by a heavy downpour of rain and the assault force remained under cover. That evening, however (one observer put it at about six o'clock), conditions had so improved that twenty troopers under the command of Sir William Waller and Colonel Hurry were able to break down the stout timber barricade – although only after some difficulty – and so take the bridge. Goring's tiny force, said to number only eight men, hastily withdrew with their enemies in pursuit. One of the Royalists was taken prisoner and another lost his mount but 'saved himself by his leaping from his horse and going over hedges into the cornfields, who had his hat cut and his head a little rased with a sword, but not much hurt'. So, swiftly and with little opposition, only a day or two after the *Henrietta Maria* incident, the first round of the military contest was won by the forces of Parliament. 'I must tell you the taking of this bridge is of greater moment than most think . . . ' wrote one observer, 'for it possesses them of the island Portsea, which hath 2000 acres of corn now standing upon it'. The success greatly encouraged Waller's troops. 'This hath put much mettle into the soldiers', it was reported, 'and it would make a faint-hearted man a soldier to see their spirits and resolution.'

Before tackling the new and much more formidable challenge presented by the walls of Portsmouth, within which Goring and his garrison were now penned, Waller set about strengthening the Portsbridge defences. Hundreds of men were soon at work constructing two mounts upon which were set up the guns which had been removed from the *Henrietta Maria* pinnace. One writer speaks of six pieces, 'three of them towards the town and three of them towards Portsdown'. If Waller's men had been more adventurous they might have added to their store of ordnance one of the guns which Goring had withdrawn from Portsbridge a few days earlier. Three had been successfully brought back to the town, but the fourth, which had suffered a damaged carriage, had been left in the highway about half a mile from the gate, guarded by two gunners, one of whom had subsequently been killed by a Parliamentary trooper who had managed to come up behind them. Despite the obvious value of the weapon to the Parliamentarians, Lord Wentworth seems to have met no opposition when he recovered it with sixty men on 13 August.[38]

It was probably soon after this incident that a series of skirmishes took place near the town walls. On several occasions the besieging force attempted to seize the cattle grazing outside the Landport Gate, and on another an attack was made on the watermill which stood close by on an arm of the sea, but the plan to fire the building and so prevent the grinding of the garrison corn was apparently foiled. In all these attacks, despite 'much playing of the ordnance', casualties were very small, and a hat and a sword the only trophies secured by the defenders. An eye-witness tells how, when one Royalist sally was beaten back, the pursuers included a brave member of Waller's Scottish contingent who 'followed the chase unto the very town', where six of the garrison attacked him. He defended himself bravely, 'but they gave him three gashes in the head, and for all that he was retreating and like to get away from them all had not one very suddenly shut the gate against him'. So, despite his valiant efforts, he was taken, but the Royalists admired his courage 'and procured the best chirurgeon they could to cure him, and let him want nothing for his conveniency'. In addition, Goring gave him some money as a reward when, two days later, he was exchanged for a Royalist prisoner at the first of several parleys which were arranged during the next few weeks. At the arrival of Waller's trumpeter, the Royalist sentries, 'being so ignorant that they knew not the sound of a parley from an alarum, let fly a piece of ordnance at him, but it hurt him not'. Despite this hostile reception he managed to convey his message, 'so the trumpeter brought in the prisoner behind him, and he took away with him behind him the said Scotchman, who being blindfolded was carried out to him to a place called Newgate, and there set up behind the said trumpeter'.

The last Royalist sortie of which we have record was the most ambitious and, with declining morale within the garrison, probably the most desperate. Two companies, commanded by Goring and Lord Wentworth and guided by a burgess named Winter, 'whom they call Lieutenant of Southsea Castle', went out by night to the enemy camp some distance inland. In the ensuing fight Goring and his friend Weston each lost a man, and Winter, who was riding a valuable horse belonging to Lord Wentworth, was taken prisoner. It was not an effective action, but it shows that Clarendon was unfair to Goring when he wrote that he 'suffered the enemy to approach as he pleased without disturbing him by any brisk sally or soldierly action'. Five musketeers who had been Parliamentary sentinels were captured and set to work carrying baskets of earth to strengthen the Portsmouth defences, but a trooper with an arm wound who was also brought in stubbornly refused to comply with the Governor's orders. Winter's son was later allowed to take clean linen to his father at Waller's farmhouse headquarters, and brought back word that the king was generally believed to be near Romsey and would soon be on the island to reward those who had supported him.

It was a wild rumour, like the story of a French supporting force which had circulated earlier, but although it was allowed to spread through the town in an attempt to whip up enthusiasm for the Royalist cause, its effect was negligible. Even when, some days later, one of Lord Wentworth's men arrived disguised in old clothes, 'as if he had been some country shepherd', and told how he had 'had entertainment on the Parliament side', few believed his news that King Charles was on his way from Oxford with a relief force. 'We continually led on and encouraged the soldiers with the expectation of the king's coming, or forces from His Majesty,' reported the Royalist leaders afterwards, 'but at length they finding themselves delayed grew impatient and so bold that they declared they would not fight against, but rather take part with, those without the town.' As a result, 'we were forced not only to keep watch over those that were without but those that were within the town'.[39]

If by mid-August morale was low and the number of defenders steadily decreasing it was not surprising. Many of the men had been pressed into service unwillingly and had no stomach for fighting over matters which they did not properly understand. The London hackney-coachman who had told of the transport of silver to Portsmouth early in the siege had added that he and his fellow drivers 'did very hardly get away from the Cavaliers, being very desirous to detain both them and their horses, and that they proffered to make them officers . . . '. Others had been less fortunate. A country farmer had been recruited against his will after coming into the town to sell his butter. Such men were not 'hot in the service', and if one report is true by 12 August half the soldiers and townsmen had already departed. Another described how 'the greatest part of the garrison soldiers were gone away by night, sometimes four, sometimes six, and more or less for a great many nights together. And the most of the best gunners were gone from them, and all gone to the Parliament side'. A member of the Commons told how 'every night some of the Portsmouth soldiers and gunners get away down the walls and come to the troopers, utterly disliking the colonel's cause and usage of the inhabitants of Portsea Island'. Even some of the more influential members of the Chichester contingent were said to wish they were in their own city again, and one of them, hoping to make his escape, was 'at charges 5 shillings a day only for a boat which lieth at hand . . . but cannot yet get away'. No doubt some of these reports and the frequently-repeated stories of the licentiousness of the soldiery were propaganda exercises which tended to exaggerate the true state of affairs, but it is clear that in spite of his natural charm and previous experience as a military commander Goring completely failed to keep the allegiance of more than a fraction of his men once the reality of the siege became apparent.[40]

Not surprisingly the siege produced a crop of stories about attempts to smuggle messages in and out of the town. At Havant a traveller's boots were found to contain letters despatched to the garrison from the North, and Colonel Norton sent both the packet and the bearer to Westminster for further investigation. At Havant, too, on 13 August, a horseman was intercepted carrying to a Portsmouth Royalist a suit of clothes in the lining of which ten letters had been sewn. On another occasion a messenger who had taken to the by-ways to avoid suspicion 'met him a man (conceive the simplest . . . that ever you saw and you have his image), who demanded of him whither he was going'. Not sensing any danger he told him, 'but that simple unlikely man laid hold of his bundle, bade him to stay, told him that he was an officer', and had him taken to Norton's house at Southwick. But probably the best-known story was about a woman who crossed Portsbridge nursing a bundle which she told one of the soldiers on guard was her baby. Closer inspection revealed that it was in fact a puppet of rags in the head of which was a black box full of correspondence.[41]

Although some messengers did manage to pass through the Parliamentary lines,[42] it is very unlikely that Royalist supporters were able to smuggle supplies into the town. During the early days of the siege a consignment of 135 quarters of wheat *en route* from Fareham was seized by Master Allyn and the Gosport watch, much to the annoyance of Goring who, until he was dissuaded 'for the women and children's sake', threatened to bombard the little town as a retaliatory measure. Another eighty quarters were on two ships which came into the possession of the blockading fleet a few hours after the capture of the *Henrietta Maria*. Some of the corn was left in the hands of the mariners as a reward, some was kept for the use of the besieging forces, and a small amount was distributed to poor folks in the coastal villages to encourage them to report news of any similar attempts to supply the garrison. Off the Isle of Wight the *Lion* of Leith, the colourful owner-commander of which was Captain Lovis (or Louis) Dick, who was rumoured to be a Scottish nobleman, successfully intercepted two Portsmouth-bound barks carrying salt, in one of which the seamen found a chest of money. On another occasion the *Lion* seized a small ship with a cargo of military saddles and harness intended, so it was said, for the use of Isle of Wight Royalists. When Captain Dick learned that the boatman had been promised nine shillings freight money, he paid the sum out of his own pocket and jocularly 'bade him withall to bring the horses' too.[43]

In addition to the free-lance *Lion*, Warwick's fleet by mid-August consisted of the *Paragon*, the *Charles*, the *Caesar*, the *Black James*, and two other vessels. Writing to his cousin at this time, someone on the *Paragon*, then in Stokes Bay, reported, 'Our greatest harmony is the thundering of cannon both day and night.' He was probably referring to the sound of the land batteries, not naval gunfire, because it was later stated that during the whole operation the fleet 'did not spend a shot upon the town'. But the ships were not merely sea-sentinels nor their companies passive observers of events after the *Henrietta Maria* incident and the Langstone Harbour ferrying operations. During the second half of August, Captain Richard Swanley of the *Charles*, who seems in the absence of Warwick to have been the senior officer in the fleet, initiated successful operations against the Isle of Wight and managed to wrest Carisbrooke Castle and the principal forts from the hands of supporters of Goring and put them under the command of trusted Parliamentary officers. In this work Captain Dick was particularly active. The good news of continued progress on both land and sea was heard at Westminster with great relief. 'The Parliament at the Lord Admiral's request hath given all seamen a month's pay extraordinary', it was reported on 18 August, and a *Commons Journal* entry for the same day tells us that the Committee for the Navy was ordered to send to each of the ships at Portsmouth a tun of wine in recognition of their good service. At the end of the month Captain Swanley, his fellow captains, and their men were again complimented and promised further reward.[44]

While the key points in the Isle of Wight were being secured, preparations were going on quietly for the next stage in the reduction of Portsmouth. By now Waller probably had the benefit of advice from Sir John Meldrum, a veteran warrior who had been knighted in 1620 for his services in the Netherlands. About 18 August 'much digging with pickaxes and driving of carts' could be seen across the harbour at Gosport by the Portsmouth defenders, 'whereby they sensibly perceived that they were framing some works to make a fort, whereat they were much troubled'. At once Goring ordered his gunners to eliminate this potential threat by bombarding the site with shot from the formidable battery mounted on the sea walls; but in spite of this distraction the Gosport men continued to carry out their orders, and by the end of a fortnight they had built two gun-platforms, one for ten pieces of ordnance behind a barn, and the other for two behind a pile of faggots. Apparently the only casualty was a ship's carpenter named Peter Baker, whose death was recorded in the church register of St. Mary's at Alverstoke on 24 August. He is said to have foolishly 'stood upon the work with a candle and lantern in his hand, whereby they took a true aim and shot him'. But it was also rumoured that he had been killed accidentally by one of the sentries on his own side.

During this period a last effort was made by Parliament to come to terms with Goring. On 27 August a trumpeter was sent to the town to sound a parley, and on the following day, at ten o'clock, Sir William Waller and Sir William Lewis came into Portsmouth and dined with Goring while Lord Wentworth and Christopher Lewknor were entertained at the Parliamentary headquarters by Sir Thomas Jervoise and others. But it was to no avail. Goring would not accept the terms offered to him and the bombardment of the Gosport emplacements was resumed. So low was the standard of his men's gunnery, however, that only the roofs of some houses were damaged. The new platforms and the Parliamentary camp on Portsea Island, which also came under fire at this time, both remained intact.

Until early September Portsmouth itself had apparently been subjected to little heavy enemy fire, but with the construction of the Gosport platforms and the mounting of ordnance, some of which the fleet provided, there was an important change in the military situation. On Friday, 2 September, the day began agreeably with the arrival of one of Waller's trumpeters who, having been

allowed into the town, presented Goring with a brace of bucks, 'which venison
had been by the Committee of the Parliament promised unto the Governor'. But
a few hours later, about four o'clock in the afternoon, social niceties were
forgotten when two of the Gosport guns began to lob shot across the harbour
mouth. It reached as far as the Town Mount, near the Landport Gate, where a
soldier carrying earth was killed and a Frenchman lost a leg. The accurate
shooting of the Parliamentary gunners terrified the defenders, and that night,
during a lull in the bombardment, all the men who could be spared from other
duties were set to work digging a trench on the Mount, into which, 'upon the
sight of the firing of the ordnance they might leap down . . . and save themselves'.
On Saturday the Gosport gunners opened up again, and on this occasion the
target was apparently the church tower, which was being used by the defenders as
a lookout, 'whereby they do espy all the approaches by sea and by land, and at
the tolling of a bell give notice both what ships come by sea and what number of
horses come by land'. The skilful Gosport gunners 'shot through the tower of the
church and brake one of the bells, and shot against the tower again, and that
rebounded and fell into the church and shot down another top of a house that is
near the church, and the end of the church, and shot through a great many
houses in the town, but killed not anybody'. The tower and nave of the old
medieval parish church lay in ruins and remained unbuilt until after the
Restoration. Also under fire that same Saturday was the town mill. A direct hit
was scored on the recently-vacated bed of the miller, who ever afterwards
'commended it for a good thing to rise betimes in the morning'.[45]

For more than twenty-four hours Portsmouth had been subjected to the
accurate shooting of the Gosport gunners, and it soon became clear that this
bombardment was designed not only to inflict the maximum amount of damage
on key buildings in the town but also to distract the defenders while final
preparations were being made for an assault on Southsea Castle, which was an
essential part of the harbour defences. Situated on the southernmost point of the
island about a mile from the town in a semi-wilderness of salt marsh, and
commanding the shipping channel into the harbour, it had been erected about
1544 as one of the links in a formidable chain of anti-invasion defences. Its
'device and fashion', so Henry VIII had been told, was 'strange and marvellously
praised of all men that have seen it'. In 1626 and 1640 the castle had been
seriously damaged by fire, but in spite of the financial difficulties of the
administration some rebuilding had apparently taken place in the years
immediately preceding the outbreak of hostilities. In a letter written in early
September 1642 by 'a clerk in the leaguer', there is an interesting description of
this compact but impressive building, 'which kept the ships from coming to aid
us, the strength of which is admirable, and I believe all men that have been in it
will say it is the strongest castle in England for the bigness'. Such language
probably exaggerated the state of the fort, which the writer had just seen taken by

his stout-hearted comrades, but there is no doubt that if it had been properly equipped and manned, and intelligently defended, it could have presented Waller with a serious obstacle. The square stone keep dominated an *enceinte* of sharp-angled walls which on the east and west sides embraced rectangular earth-filled gun-emplacements. 'It is walled about with a wall of three or four yards thick, about thirty foot high, a graft [i.e. moat] round about of some three or four yards deep and five yards in breadth', wrote the same clerk. 'It hath 14 pieces of ordnance planted round, all but two pieces shot 12 pound bullets, besides other small pieces; it hath dainty chambers in it, fit to entertain a prince; it was new repaired lately.'

The castle garrison normally consisted of two porters, one of whom was paid 8d. a day and the other 6d., a master gunner (8d.), fourteen gunners and eleven soldiers (6d. each). At the time of the siege the commanding officer was Captain Challoner (or Challender), who was one of the wealthiest residents of the island. He was entitled to 2s. a day for his official duties, and was assisted by a Lieutenant – no longer the unfortunate Alderman Winter, who had been captured – who received 1s. 1d. By early September only a dozen men remained for the castle's defence, Goring being unable or unwilling to provide reinforcements from his own shrinking resources, although an attack was known to be imminent. However, many of the town guns were trained on the castle entrance and the exposed track which led to it across the common, and most of Challoner's own weapons were mounted to resist an attack from the landward side. No doubt the serious military situation was discussed at length on Saturday, 3 September, when the Captain went into Portsmouth to confer with his friend, the Governor. Afterwards, despite the bombardment of the town by the Gosport gunners and his own state of inebriation, he was able to return to the castle, taking with him fresh supplies of biscuit, meal, and other necessities.

Later that same night, after protracted discussions at Waller's headquarters, a Parliamentary force, '2 troops and a matter of four hundred foot', set out with scaling ladders for the assault. With them went 'a very good engineer' whom observers did not name. To strengthen their resolve as they marched, the soldiers sang psalms, the booming Gosport guns providing a consoling accompaniment. Although a feint attack was made on the far side of the town to keep Goring's men occupied, the Southsea Castle assault force was not allowed to cross the open common between the two morasses without some harassment. But the Portsmouth gunners could not stop the progress of the Parliamentary troops and in the early hours of Sunday morning they 'came within two bowshot' of the building 'and there lay an hour'. Later they 'took away on the left hand, and the enemy expected them on the right, so we were not descried all this while'. Eventually they were seen, 'but we were got on the seashore before they could make shot upon us . . . and came between the sea and the castle, and leaped into the graft, where some of our men hurt themselves'. On these walls, we are told, 'were no ordnance, for they had removed them on the other side toward the heath'. Meanwhile some Parliamentary soldiers led by the intrepid Brown Bushell, who seems to have taken a prominent part in the affair, were on the bridge across the dry moat at the main entrance to the castle, and a trumpeter was ordered to sound a parley. Challoner, who had been brought from his bed, had some talk with the attackers. 'We propounded fair quarter in case he would fairly surrender the castle', wrote an eye-witness later. 'If not we would use our discretion in our proceedings against him. He being something in drink and withall newly wakened out of his deep sleep desired first of all that we should stay till the next morning and he would consider of it.' Nevertheless he asked Bushell who had sent him, and the latter replied 'that he had received his message from Colonel Waller, Colonel Norton, and Colonel Hurry, who were then not far off and waited for the resignation of that fort'. The exact sequence of events during the operation is not clear, but it was probably during this parley that Goring, having become acutely aware of the dangerous situation, began to fire off his guns furiously at the bridge. Captain Bushell narrowly missed injury and ten men who saw shot flying in their direction escaped only by flinging themselves to the ground, although the large log behind which they sheltered was hit. Lest Challoner should try to gain an advantage by procrastination, the foot soldiers were ordered to scale the walls. They met no opposition. An eye-witness reported later, 'Challoner seeing himself nigh lost demanded presently fair quarter, which he obtained with all his soldiers, though few in number, beside his lieutenant and ensign'. Sergeant-Major Harbert and Captain Bushell ordered the disarming of the prisoners, who were confined to their quarters, and a substantial garrison was placed in the castle to prevent its recapture. As for Challoner, 'he fell to drinking of the King and Parliament's health in sack with our officers, desiring that 3 pieces of ordnance might be discharged against the town of Portsmouth to let them know that now this castle was at another man's disposing; those being discharged, the town let so fly at us that I thought we should have been all cut off'.[46]

It had been a good night's work for Waller's men, and with this seemingly effortless success the morale of Goring's rapidly-diminishing force declined almost to vanishing point. The Mayor, a lieutenant, an ensign, and other officers, escaped over the wall, leaving behind a garrison so small and weak that Goring, scanning the Gosport gun-platforms through his 'prospective glass', realised that although supplies of gunpowder, ammunition, and most foodstuffs except provender for the horses were still fairly plentiful, militarily little more could be done. His entreaties to his men to hold out a day or two longer fell on deaf ears. All but a few 'desperate hellhounds' were openly rebellious and threw down their arms, 'being possessed with fear of having the town battered down on all sides, and being frighted more by their wives'. According to Goring's remaining officers, the number of men still willing to fight was 'not above . . . three score at most, and those [were] gentlemen and their servants which were not used either to traversing of great guns or use of muskets'.

Early on Sunday morning Goring held a Council of War at which it was unanimously decided to send a drummer to arrange another parley. In due course Lord Wentworth, Christopher Lewknor, and Mr Weston went out to Kingston as hostages while the Parliamentary representatives, Sir William Waller, Sir Thomas Jervoise, and Sir William Lewis, came into the town to discuss terms.[47] It is not clear from existing records whether the Governor of Portsmouth at this period used as his official residence the rambling building which served that purpose after the Restoration and which, except for the medieval section now known as the Garrison Church, was demolished early in the nineteenth century. If he did, it was almost certainly in one of the rooms of this building, which had once been the Domus Dei of Portsmouth, and where, twenty years later, Charles II married Catherine of Braganza, that the articles of surrender (see Appendix) were discussed.[48]

The terms were generous. The Civil War was as yet little more than an extension of the regular sporting activities of the country gentry, and the military operations had been conducted with caution, so that the total number of casualties was very small. During the negotiations the Royalist officers apparently used as a strong bargaining counter the large supplies of gunpowder which were still in their possession. In one magazine were stored two hundred barrels, while in the main repository, the Square Tower, were another twelve hundred, as well as a good stock of ammunition. 'If they had set them on fire', wrote a Parliamentarian, 'the whole town had been utterly spoiled, and not one person in the town could have been secured from destruction.'

On Wednesday, 7 September, the siege was officially at an end. The articles of surrender were sealed and the Parliamentary officers took possession. During that day the Royalist gentlemen and their followers left the town in accordance with the promise that all who had fought for the king, with the exception of those who had deserted to join the garrison, would have their safety guaranteed. As they rode out through the gates with their swords and pistols and personal possessions, they hid their humiliation in spirited cries that they meant to be back as victors before Christmas. 'And in the evening at six of the clock', one observer tells us, 'Colonel Goring took boat and rowed unto ship for Holland, but it is said he would go through France, and that his goods were carried to shipboard on Wednesday and Thursday.'[49]

There is a story that as he left the harbour Goring defiantly threw the key of the Square Tower magazine – or, according to another version, of the town – into the water, where it remained until its accidental discovery some time during the nineteenth century. Whether the key, now in Southsea Castle Museum, is authentic, or even whether the Governor's theatrical gesture has any real historical basis, cannot now be established. Such an act, however, would not have been out of character. During the siege the unreliable and self-willed young courtier had done little more than play at soldiers, as if for his own amusement, seeming rarely to take seriously his great responsibilities. He had misjudged the true extent of the king's local support, failed to put the town in an adequate state of readiness, and underestimated the cool determination of his adversaries. Perhaps because he lacked patience and perseverance, two of the essential qualities needed by a good garrison commander at a time of crisis, and found at Portsmouth little scope for the kind of swift, heroic action he craved, the siege proved to be an uncongenial military exercise with which he was soon bored. And since circumstances had deprived him of the chance to play host to Queen Henrietta Maria and her ladies, he thought the town 'too low a sphere for him to move in . . . And so', wrote the perceptive Clarendon, 'he cared not to lose what he did not care to keep.'[50]

Thus, only a few weeks after his impetuous call to arms, the swaggering colonel had been driven out of his stronghold and his place as Governor taken by Sir William Lewis, a Parliamentarian.[51] The news of these inglorious and unprofitable events 'almost struck the king to the heart',[52] yet so strong was Goring's influence that a few months later, when he returned from Holland, he was once again given high command. During the next three years, except for a period when he was a prisoner of Parliament, he was one of the king's principal military leaders, but he was an intractable subordinate and an unreliable colleague, and his erratic behaviour did considerable damage to the Royalist cause.[53] Early in 1645 he returned with a large force to Hampshire, where Portsmouth had remained loyal to Parliament; but if he saw the town again it was from the crest of Portsdown Hill or from across the harbour at Gosport, where his men set fire to the houses of the terrified inhabitants.[54]

It was one of his last campaigns in England. Towards the end of the year, on grounds of ill-health, he left abruptly for the continent, and in time became colonel-general of the English regiments in Spanish service in the Netherlands. In 1650 he went to Spain to collect his arrears of pay and seek assistance for King Charles II.[55] There, seven years later, this talented but undisciplined man died in comparative obscurity and poverty, dressed in his last days, so it was said, in the plain black habit of a Dominican friar.[56]

APPENDIX[57]

Articles agreed upon between the Committee for the Parliament in the County of Southampton, and Colonel Goring, for and on his own behalf and other the officers and soldiers within the garrison of Portsmouth, for the rendering up of the said town.

First, that the Committee for the Parliament shall this day, being the seventh day of September Anno Domini 1642, at or about six of the clock in the morning, put in two companies of foot in the town of Portsmouth for preventing of disorders and preservation of the magazine.

Secondly, that all such persons as are not of the old garrison, excepting Colonel Goring, the Lord Wentworth, Master Weston, Master Covist, with their ordinary servants, shall forthwith issue out of town, and have free liberty to pass and go wheresoever they please in this kingdom except unto any part of that army raised against the Parliament, with their horses, swords, and pistols, but no other arms, and all other their goods whatsoever, and that they may be allowed twenty days for their journey, they carrying themselves according to the laws, in a peaceable manner.

Thirdly, that Sir Thomas Jervoise, Sir William Waller, who with one servant a piece, and Sergeant-Major Lobbe, shall go into the town to take possession of the stores and several provisions in the town, and that for their security, Master Weston, Master Covist, Lieutenant-Colonel Donnet be delivered as hostages.

Fourthly, that if any of the said persons in the town desire to go beyond the sea, they may have liberty to pass with their proper goods in that town (arms only excepted) without the molestation of any one, and a ship to convey them.

Fifthly, that all officers and soldiers under the Governor that were formerly of this garrison, and now residing in town, shall continue their places, or have three months liberty to sell or otherwise dispose thereof to some other persons, except such as have been put in since the last of July.

Sixthly, that no person whatsoever now residing in town, and who within any time since the first of August hath resided in town, that hath done any act for the keeping, defence, or maintenance thereof, or used any other words in justification of the maintenance thereof, on the behalf of the King's Majesty, shall be questioned or molested.

Seventhly, that such soldiers as are run from their colours to the town shall be excluded out of this treaty.

Eighthly, that there shall be no train left to any mine or to the magazine whereby to blow up the town or endamage the garrison that shall be put into it. And that the Governor, gentlemen of quality, and all the officers of the said town shall discover upon their oaths what they know concerning any such things, and that sufficient hostages be given for performance thereof, who are to be retained two days in the custody of such person as shall be put in the town as Governor.

Ninthly, that carriages shall be provided for the use of such persons as shall issue out of the town, they paying the usual rates for them.

Tenthly, that all prisoners on both sides be released, excepting such as are sent up to London.

Eleventhly, that the Governor shall presently after delivery up of the town, which shall be on Thursday next, by nine of the clock in the morning, have permission from the Committee to despatch such a gentleman to the king as he shall name.

Notes

1. For the national background see C.V. Wedgwood, *The King's War 1641–1647* (London, 1958), pp. 15–136.

2. *A Royalist's Notebook*, ed. Francis Bamford (London, 1936) [hereafter Bamford], p. 105.

3. *The Knyvett Letters 1620–1644*, ed. Bertram Schofield (Norfolk Record Society, xx, 1949), p. 105.

4. Clarendon, Edward, Earl of, *The History of the Rebellion and Civil Wars in England* (6 vols, Oxford, 1888 edn) [hereafter Clarendon], II, p. 314.

5. H.J. Sparks, *The Story of Portsmouth* (Portsmouth, 1921), pp. 113–19, 144–72.

6. *The Dictionary of National Biography* [hereafter *DNB*]; C.V. Wedgwood, 'George Goring, Soldier and Rake', *Sussex County Magazine*, March 1935, pp. 164–9.

7. Clarendon, II, pp. 314–15, IV, p. 25.

8. Bamford, pp. 97–9.

9. Clarendon, II, p. 269.

10. Sir William Davenant, *The Shorter Poems and Songs*, ed. A.M. Gibbs (Oxford, 1972), pp. 69–73, 387–9; *Minor Poets of the Seventeenth Century*, ed., R.G. Howarth, (London, 1959), pp. 286–7; *The Muses Recreation: Wit Restor'd . . . 1658* (London, 1817), I, pp. 134–7.

11. Sir Richard Bulstrode, *Memoirs and Reflections* (London, 1721), p. 134.

12. Clarendon, IV, pp. 102–3.

13. A.H. Burne and Peter Young, *The Great Civil War* (London, 1959), p. 232.

14. S.R. Gardiner, *History of England . . . 1603–1642* (London, 1884, 10 vols.), IX, pp. 313–64 *passim*, 384–6; Wedgwood, 'George Goring', *op. cit.*, pp. 165–6.

15. Isle of Wight Record Office [hereafter IWRO], Oglander MSS, 16/159, 21/3. I am indebted to the late Major Denys Oglander for permission to quote from these records.

16. *Commons Journals* [hereafter *CJ*], 14, 17 August 1641.

17. *The Journal of Sir Simonds D'Ewes*, ed. W.H. Coates (Yale, 1942), pp. 146, 169–70; *CJ*, 19 November 1641, 24 March 1642, 12 July 1642; Clarendon, II, pp. 268–72. Col. Richard Norton (1615–91) had married Anne, daughter of Sir Walter Earle, M.P., in 1636.

18. IWRO, Oglander MSS, 21/2.

19. Clarendon, II, pp. 268, 272–3. The principal source for the description of events at Portsmouth at the time of the siege is the collection of Thomason Tracts [hereafter TT] in the British Library, the most important being: *A New Discovery of a Designe of the French who are lately arrived at Portsmouth*, E 109 (21); *Ioyfull News from Portsmouth and the Isle of Wight*, E 109 (25); *A Joyfull Message sent from both Houses of Parliament to Portsmouth*, E 109 (28); *His Maiesties Message to Colonell Goring of Portsmouth*, E 109 (32); *True Newes from Portsmouth being Colonell Goring his Speech*, E 112 (1); *The King's Resolution concerning Portsmouth and Colonell Goring*, E 112 (2); *A True Report of the occurrences at Portsmouth*, E 112 (8); *An Uprore at Portsmouth*, E 112 (28); *An Exact Relation of Fourteen dayes passages from Portsmouth*, E 112 (34); *A Relation from Portsmouth wherein is declared the manner how the Castle was taken*, E 116 (15); *The taking of the Castle of Portsmouth with the Circumstances thereof*, E 116 (21); *A true and briefe Relation how and by what meanes the Isle of Wight was secured in August 1642*, E 116 (40); *A Declaration of all the Passages at the taking of Portsmouth*, E 117 (10); *A True Relation of the Passages and Occurrences that happened at the towne of Portsmouth at the late siege*, E 118 (22). Of the above, other copies of TT, E 112 (28) and E 117 (10) are to be found in the Portsmouth Central Library (hereafter PCL), as well as an original *The Copy of a Letter presented by a*

member of the Commons . . . concerning divers passages at Portsmouth and photocopies of TT, E 118 (22) and *His Maiesties Two Proclamations to the Counties of Southampton and Dorset.* The account of the siege in J. Vicars, *Jehovah-Jirah, God in the Mount,* 1641–3, is printed in W.G. Gates, *Illustrated History of Portsmouth* (Portsmouth, 1900), pp. 249–55.

20. Clarendon, II, p. 273; TT, E 112 (1), E 117 (10).

21. TT, E 109 (25).

22. *CJ*, 29 April 1642.

23. TT, E 109 (28, 32).

24. IWRO, Oglander MSS, 16/156, 21/3; TT, E 112 (2).

25. Historical Manuscripts Commission [hereafter HMC], *Portland Papers*, I, pp. 49–51.

26. *Ibid.*, pp. 50–1; J. Rushworth, *Historical Collections* (London, 1708), IV, p. 412. Colonel Hurry's name was sometimes given as Urry. For Waller see J. Adair, *Roundhead General* (London, 1969).

27. TT, E 112 (34).

28. Clarendon, II, p. 315; TT, E 112 (1), E 117 (10); PCL, *The Copy of a Letter . . . concerning divers passages at Portsmouth.*

29. TT, E 112 (34), E 117 (10).

30. British Library [hereafter BL], Add. MSS, 33,278, ff. 14–19.

31. *CJ*, 5 August 1641, 13 January 1642, 24 March 1642, 12 July 1642, 27 July 1642, 24 August 1642; TT, E 109 (28).

32. TT, E 112 (1).

33. Clarendon, II, pp. 294, 315; TT, E 117 (10), E 118 (22).

34. HMC, *Portland Papers*, vol. 1, pp. 50–1; TT, E 117 (10). The master of the vessel was John Goodwin of Portsmouth, who was described as 'one of the four masters of attendance'.

35. *CJ*, 15 August 1642. For Bushell see *DNB*.

36. HMC, *Portland Papers*, 1, pp. 50–1.

37. TT, E 112 (34).

38. TT, E 112 (8), E 117 (10), E 118 (22); PCL, *The Copy of a Letter . . .*

39. TT, E 117 (10), E 118 (22); Clarendon, II, p. 315. William Winter, a rich brewer, was mayor of Portsmouth 1635–6 and 1646–7. He had renounced his military connection on becoming mayor in 1635. (R. East, ed., *Extracts from Records . . . of the Borough of Portsmouth* (Portsmouth, 1891), pp. 159–60, 314, 348.)

40. TT, E 112 (1, 8, 34), E 118 (22); PCL, *The Copy of a Letter . . .*

41. TT, E 112 (34); PCL, *The Copy of a Letter . . .*

42. TT, E 117 (10).

43. TT, E 112 (8, 34); HMC, *Portland Papers*, 1, pp. 50–1.

44. *Documents Relating to the Civil War 1642–1648*, eds J.R. Powell and E.K. Timings, (Navy Records Society, 105, 1963), pp. 36–7; *CJ*, 18 and 30 August 1642; TT, E 116 (40), E 118 (22).

45. TT, E 118 (22); Portsmouth City Records Office, CHU 42/1A/1.

46. A. Corney, *Southsea Castle* (Portsmouth 1967), *passim*; TT, E 116 (15, 21), E 118 (22); BL, Add. MSS, 33,278.

47. TT, E 116 (21), E 117 (10), E 118 (22).

48. H.P. Wright, *The Story of the Domus Dei of Portsmouth* (London, 1873), pp. 1–34 *passim*.

49. TT, E 116 (21), E 118 (22); HMC, *Portland Papers*, 1, p. 61; E. Warburton, *Memoirs of Prince Rupert and the Cavaliers* (London, 1849), pp. 379–80. John Evelyn, the diarist, then only twenty-one years of age, visited the town at the time of the surrender. He wrote: 'October 3rd [*sic*] to Chichester, and thence the next day to see the siege of Portsmouth . . . It was on the day of its being rendered to Sir William Waller, which [gave] me opportunity of taking my leave of Col. Goring the Governor now embarking for France.' *The Diary of John Evelyn*, ed. E.S. Beer (London, 1959), p. 45.

50. Clarendon, II, p. 315.

51. For his disbursements from 1 August 1642 see Public Record Office, SP 28/129.

52. Clarendon, II, p. 315.

53. *DNB*.

54. G.N. Godwin, *The Civil War in Hampshire (1642–45)* (London, 1882), p. 203.

55. *DNB*.

56. For a possible explanation of this unlikely story see M. Bence-Jones, *The Cavaliers* (London, 1976), pp. 98–9.

57. TT, E 117 (10).

5

BRISTOL AND THE CIVIL WAR

Patrick McGrath

In the late summer of 1642 England drifted slowly, unwillingly and
incredulously into civil war, a horror which she had not experienced for over
one hundred and fifty years. Bulstrode Whitelocke commented at the time:
'It is strange to note how we have insensibly slid into this beginning of a civil war,
by one unexpected accident after another . . . and we scarce know how, but from
paper combats by declarations, remonstrances, protestations, votes, messages,
answers and replies, we are now come to the question of raising forces, and
naming a general and officers of the army.'[1]

On 23 October 1642 two armies faced each other at Edgehill in the first major
engagement of war. There was a feeling that it could not really be happening in
'this warr without an Enemie', as Sir William Waller was to call it later when he
confronted in arms his old friend and neighbour Sir Ralph Hopton.[2] It is, of
course, wrong to imagine that every one in England was either a royalist or a
parliamentarian, and historians in recent years have laid great stress on the
importance of neutralism.[3] Thomas Barrow, a linendraper in Cheapside,
represented the views of many of his contemporaries when he wrote: 'Iff I might
butt stand an newtrall I should then be well; for I should . . . butt follow my
owne, and not looke after another's busines.'[4] Nevertheless, between 1642 and
1646 there were four years of fighting in which Englishmen killed and wounded
each other and destroyed property on a large scale. People do not behave in this
way unless they have strong motives, and so we must ask briefly what made
Englishmen take up arms and how far these motives affected Bristolians.

For a number of politically-conscious people, the question was whether the
king could be trusted to accept permanently the constitutional restraints placed
upon him in 1641. Some thought that he could not be trusted and that further
restraints must be imposed. Others thought that enough had been done and that
parliament was now trying to seize power which rightfully belonged to the king.
Another issue was religion. Should the Church of England be radically reformed,
or even abolished and replaced by something else? Those who thought it should
be were opposed by religious conservatives, who feared both Presbyterians and
Papists and who had no desire to tolerate the sects. Some fought, or thought they
fought, for principles, but others fought for personal reasons, out of loyalty to
king or parliament or to some nobleman or gentleman to whom they had
obligations. In some counties, the civil war was primarily a conflict between rival
factions. Many soldiers fought for pay and plunder. Large numbers were

conscripted and had no choice. Motives were many and varied, and they changed from time to time in particular individuals. The majority of Englishmen managed to avoid fighting.

Before examining the attitude of Bristolians to the war, it is necessary to say a little about the city itself. It was a flourishing port trading primarily to the Iberian peninsula, France and Ireland. Regional and overseas trades, with all their subsidiary industries and services, were the most important characteristics of the place, but there was a great variety of other occupations. It had a population of about 15,000 on the eve of the civil war.[5] This was tiny compared with London, which had between a quarter and a half a million people, but nevertheless Bristol impressed visitors, even Londoners, who compared it very favourably with the capital. During the war, Prynne wrote of it: 'The Parliament, his Excellency, London, and the whole kingdom, looked upon Bristol as a place of the greatest consequence of any in England, next to London, as the metropolis, key, magazine of the West.'[6]

Bristol was governed by a closed oligarchy of some forty-three members, consisting of a mayor, twelve aldermen and a number of common councillors. The merchants were the wealthiest and most influential group in the city and dominated the governing body. They also had their own organisation in the Society of Merchant Venturers, but in many ways the Common Council was simply the Society wearing another hat.[7] However, the Common Council also included a small number of people from other occupations such as mercers, vintners, haberdashers, brewers and innkeepers. There were few gentlemen living in Bristol, and they played no part in the city's affairs. Some merchants, of course, had land in the neighbouring counties, but they lived and worked in the city. They were not country gentlemen, and they were not involved in county affairs. Moreover, the gentry of Somerset and Gloucestershire had not been allowed to take over the Bristol parliamentary seats, as they had in many other boroughs. The two Bristol M.P.s were normally merchants, although occasionally the City Recorder was allowed to hold one of the seats. Thus, as the country moved towards war, decisions about the role of Bristol were in the hands of some 40 people out of a population of 15,000, and these 40 were not closely involved with the gentry of Somerset and Gloucestershire and would not necessarily follow their lead.

When we try to assess the role of Bristolians, we must bear in mind the unsatisfactory nature of the evidence. As far as the records of the Society of Merchant Venturers are concerned, there might not have been a civil war, for it is not mentioned in them.[8] The decisions, but not the debates, of the city's Common Council are recorded in the Books of Proceedings,[9] but these minutes are often uninformative, and it is possible that there was no desire to write down evidence which might be dangerous. When we try to find out from the minutes what happened on 9 December 1642, when a parliamenary force first got into

Bristol, we find that there are two relevant minute books. One goes up to 19 October 1642, then jumps to 7 December, and then has fifteen double pages which have been left blank. The second book begins on 23 October, runs on to 7 December, for which it has a different entry from the first book, and then jumps to 23 January 1643, when it records the dismissal of a schoolmaster. Thus, as far as the official minutes are concerned, the dramatic events of 9 December did not happen, and during the critical period from 8 December 1642 until 23 January 1643 the Common Council not only took no action but did not even meet.

Much that was written at the time was straightforward propaganda. The often-quoted comment of the Puritan minister, John Corbet of Gloucester, that in Bristol ' . . . the king's cause and party were favoured by the two extreames in that city; the one the wealthy and powerfull men, the other of the basest and lowest sort, but disgusted by the middle rank, the true and best citizens'[10] has frequently been treated by historians as though it were a well-informed, balanced judgement rather than a piece of wishful-thinking meant to give comfort to the supporters of parliament.

A few contemporaries, and some later historians, have made generalisations about the attitude of Bristolians to the civil war which fail to take into account the fact that the number who can be shown to have given positive support to one side or the other is very small indeed. Even for these, we often do not know what their motives really were. John Latimer, who had a great influence on those who have written about Bristol, was very ready to attach the labels 'royalist' and 'parliamentarian' to people, merely because they made loans or gifts to the king or to parliament, even though their motives may have been no more than a desire to avoid trouble or to curry favour with the occupying forces.[11] Moreover, people were not consistent, and their attitude often changed with circumstances. As the evidence to the Committee for Compounding amply demonstrated, men were very anxious to play down the help they had given to the side which eventually lost.[12]

Did Bristolians, or some of them, have any positive attitude to the conflict which broke out in 1642? Why did they go to war? As far as the Common Council, the governing body of the city, is concerned, it can be argued that it did not go to war. It was dragged very reluctantly into a conflict which it did not want and which it had done its best to avoid. It would have preferred to remain non-aligned. At no time in 1642 did the Common Council declare for king or parliament. It merely strengthened its defences and tried to keep both sides out. Although the war had begun some time before the king raised his standard on 24 August 1642, Bristol remained neutral until a parliamentary force somehow got into the city on 9 December without the consent of the Common Council.[13]

That Bristolians showed so little initial commitment is hardly surprising. In 1642 there were no deep political, religious or economic motives to make them anxious to support one side or the other, and there were certainly very strong reasons for keeping out of war. It is true that the city had had a number of grievances in the 1630s and that it was very vocal about them, but complaints from aggrieved merchants should not always be taken at their face value, and this city, which was supposed to have so many grievances, sent back to the Long Parliament two M.P.s who were certainly not ardent reformers and who were expelled in 1642 as favourers of monopolies.[14] It then replaced them by two more members who were in due course to support the king and one of whom died defending the city against parliament in 1645.[15] The grievances which had troubled the city had mostly been economic, and they had been dealt with before the war began. The great constitutional issues which stirred men like John Pym and William Prynne did not seem to have aroused much enthusiasm in Bristol, and the Bristol M.P.s were more concerned with local issues than great issues of principle.

Religious problems, too, seem to have aroused little interest. There was hardly any trace of Puritanism in Bristol before 1640, and it was of no importance in the city on the eve of the war.[16] No one in the governing body wanted radical religious change, and the city seemed well content with the established church. A visitor in 1634 remarked that the eighteen city churches were all 'fayrely beautify'd, richly adorn'd, and sweetly kept, and in the maior part of them are neat, rich, and melodious Organs, that are constantly play'd on.' He added: 'Their Pulpitts are most curious all which the citizens have spared no cost, nor forwardness to beautify, and adorne . . . for they dayly strive in euery Parish, who shall exceed other in their generous, and religious bounty, most to decke and inrich those sanctify'd Places, and Heauenly Mansions, heere on Earth, to Gods glory, and good example to others'.[17] The visitor may have been too enthusiastic, but it seems clear that Bristolians were taking a good deal of trouble to beautify their churches and were not going in for puritan simplicity. There may have been some dissatisfaction with the Laudian church, for, after the city had fallen to parliament, four aldermen took a petition to the king in January 1643 which refers, among other things, to prelates forcing new doctrines on the Church of England, but this is evidence of religious conservatism and not of religious radicalism.[18] In 1645, a Puritan commented bitterly that the people 'sitt in darkness and the collegiate men still chaunt out the Common Prayer booke to the wonted height and in private pariches they thinke of noe other discipline, here being hardly three sermons in the whole citty, on the Lords-day, and but one upon the last fast, the late holly-dayes being more solemnly observed than the Sabbath.'[19]

It seems that neither politics nor religion moved many Bristolians to the point when they were willing to suffer and die for a cause. In so far as there still were economic grievances in 1642, they concerned the monopolies of the great London trading companies, which parliament had not abolished, but there were few who were prepared to risk their lives to destroy the privileges of the Merchant Adventurers, the Levant Company or the East India Company.

It is also necessary to remember that the people who governed Bristol were not men who would normally think in terms of carrying swords and fighting. They were merchants and business men, and war, particularly civil war, would be bad for business, as well as meaning higher taxation. Some of the merchants, it is true, played at being soldiers in the 1630s, and we have an interesting account of the Trained Bands from the same visitor who remarked on the churches. He said that in the Marsh the City Captains constantly drilled and exercised and mustered the city forces. The river on three sides 'causeth a sweet and pleasant Eccho of their martiall Musicke, Drums, Fifes, and volleys of Shot.' He noted that the city had three foot companies 'besides a voluntary Company, of gentile, proper, martiall, disciplin'd men, who haue their Armes lodg'd in a handsome Artillery House, newly built vp in the Castle Yard, where one in a yeere, they inuite, and entertaine, both Earles, and Lords, and a great many Knights and Gentlemen, of ranke, and quality, at their Military Feast; And this yard affoords them, a spacious, and a large place to drill, and exercise in.'[20] The visitor may have taken the Bristol Trained Bands more seriously than they deserved, but there was a chance that they would be useful if the governing body decided to defend the city against outsiders. Bristol was protected by its rivers and its walls, it could keep out bands of soldiers in the way that country villages could not, and it would be difficult to take. No one dreamed that the war would last four years, and as long as there was some kind of balance between the military forces in the areas around Bristol, there was at least a chance of staying neutral.

It is not possible to examine in detail here all the actions of the Common Council in the critical months of 1642 after the king had left London and the slow drift towards armed conflict had begun.[21] The city was busy looking to its stock of arms and taking various measures for its own security, but from May onwards it was also busy with a petition to king and parliament asking them to be reconciled.[22] Latimer said that both 'parties' in the Common Council were equally represented on the committee for drawing up the petition,[23] but it is quite wrong to talk of 'parties' in Bristol at this time. Latimer was continually surprised to find that people often failed to behave in a way consistent with the labels he had put on them. Thus, when the two Bristol M.P.s were expelled from the House in May 1642, they were replaced in June by the Recorder, Sir John Glanville and Alderman John Taylor, both of whom subsequently adhered to the king. Latimer thought their election contradicted the policy of the Common Council which, he said, had by this time definitely abandoned the royal cause.[24] In fact, the Common Council was not committed, it wanted to remain non-aligned, and it was anxious to avoid giving offence to any one.

In June 1642, Parliament asked for a loan for the defence of the king and kingdom and for the support of the army in Ireland. The Council contributed

£1,000, and various individuals lent a total of £2,625. Latimer expressed surprise that Robert Yeamans and Thomas Colston who, he says, were 'afterwards famous as royalists', each contributed £50,[25] but the loan was not some kind of political test. Most Englishmen wanted to put down the Irish rebellion, and this was not an issue on which would-be neutral Bristol was likely to refuse cooperation with the House of Commons. Equally consistent with this desire to avoid making a stand was the willingness of the city to entertain the Marquis of Hertford when the king sent him to the west to execute the commission of array. On 11 July the Common Council decided to offer him suitable hospitality if he came to stay in Bristol.[26] The city could hardly refuse to entertain the king's representative, and as the country was not at war, this was not an obviously hostile act as far as parliament was concerned, although it might not be too pleased about it.

Fortunately from the point of view of Bristol's neutrality, the Marquis decided not to come to the city and eventually set up his headquarters in Wells. Clarendon tells us that those who urged the Marquis to come to Bristol pointed out that it was 'a great, rich, and populous city' and that from it he would be 'easily able to give the law to Somerset and Gloucestershire'. Those who advised him not to come said that it was not clear that he would be well received and that there were 'visibly many disaffected people in it, and some of them of eminent quality . . . '.[27] We do not know who gave this advice or whether they were really in touch with Bristol opinion. What was called disaffection may have been merely reluctance to admit troops of any kind. A little later the mayor refused permission to Hertford to send a troop of horse to Bristol, but he argued that this was simply because the king had ordered him not to admit troops.[28]

The Marquis of Hertford at Wells had great difficulty in getting support, and in early August Alexander Popham and other Somerset gentlemen, who were putting into execution the Militia Ordinance, assembled at Chewton Mendip a force of about 10,000 men to oppose him.[29] This force was alleged to include not only men from Somerset, Gloucestershire, Wiltshire and elsewhere, but also 'above 300 lusty stout men, of very good ranke and quality of the City of *Bristoll*, all of them on Horseback, with Swords, Pistolls, or Carbines', as well as two wains loaded with powder, bullet and match, and two more with small field pieces, sent from Bristol contrary to the order of the mayor and sheriffs. The evidence for this alleged contribution from Bristol is a letter of 7 August sent to the House of Lords by the wealthy clothier and committed parliamentarian, John Ashe.[30] Ashe was writing to urge the Lords to send the Duke of Bedford to support the parliamentarians in the west, and he was endeavouring to show 'the condition and stout resolution of our good Countrymen, however heretofore ill thought of . . . '. The Lords instructed one of the Bristol M.P.s, John Taylor, to thank the city for its help, but the story seems highly improbable, although it does credit to Ashe as a propagandist. It is difficult to believe that Bristolians, with or without official support, could have mustered 300 horsemen and sent them with ammunition and arms to Chewton. There is no evidence relating to this in the city's records, and such commitment is highly unlikely in view of the city's cautious neutralism.[31]

In the face of the strong parliamentary forces on Mendip, the Marquis of Hertford had to withdraw, and Somerset passed into the control of men favourable to parliament. It was going to be very difficult for Bristol to maintain its neutrality, but during the next four months it made determined efforts to do so.

In August 1642 the city obeyed an order from parliament that Denzil Holles should be admitted to review the Trained Bands.[32] Latimer claimed that this was 'a fact which excludes all doubt as to the principal animating the majority both of the Council and of the civic militia,'[33] but he is wrong. The city had not declared for parliament and had no desire to do so.

In September, Richard Aldworth was chosen mayor. He was later to show sympathy for parliament, but his election does not mean that the Council supported parliament, any more than the choice of Alexander James as Master of the Society of Merchant Venturers in November 1642 showed that the Society was committed to the royal cause which James later supported.

On 19 October 1642 Bristol was asked to admit 2,000 troops who were on their way to Ireland. The cool attitude of the city to parliament is shown in its reply that it would admit as many troops at a time as might be consistent with its safety, but all must be disarmed except the officers.[34] A request for a loan conveyed through the two M.P.s was at first rejected, and although under pressure the Corporation and certain individuals eventually lent £2,600, it seems clear that Bristolians were not eagerly seeking to place their fortunes, let alone their lives, at the disposal of parliament.[35]

A policy of non-alignment was, however, becoming increasingly difficult to maintain. On 23 October the Council considered a letter from the Association of Somerset, Gloucestershire and Wiltshire desiring a mutual association with Bristol for the defence of the king and kingdom against all forces sent without the consent of parliament. The Council decided to agree to the association and set up a committee of four to confer about it. Nothing was done. Bristol was in no hurry to declare for parliament.[36]

The real feelings of the city governors were probably better expressed in a motion passed in the Common Council on 5 November which stated that 'This day, the Mayor, Alderman, Sheriffs and Common Council have declared themselves to be in love and amity one with another and do desire a friendly association together in all mutual accommodation.' They proceeded to draw up for signature a petition appealing to the king and parliament to be reconciled.[37]

On 24 November the Council ordered earthworks to be made at all needful places round the city for its necessary defence.[38] It might well be asked against whom they intended to defend it. The only troops in the area were the parliamentary troops of Somerset and Gloucestershire.

Alexander Popham now began to increase the pressure on Bristol to commit itself. He wrote to Captain Harrington, one of the captains in the Bristol Trained Bands, telling him to be ready to join forces with him when he came to Bristol. Harrington evidently ignored Popham's request that this should be kept secret, for the Mayor and Aldermen wrote thanking Popham but saying they did not need his friendly assistance at present. Popham, who had come as far as Pensford, denied that he intended to march on Bristol, but gave a warning that the city's lack of enthusiasm was a danger to the surrounding areas.[39]

At the end of November, when the royalists were alleged to be threatening, the House of Commons ordered Bristol to admit into the city a force of foot and horse.[40] Before this was known, Bristol representatives met Popham and other gentlemen at Bath on 28 November, but would not commit themselves.[41] They were still playing for time on 2 December when they wrote to Popham saying they were distracted by the movement of troops into Bedminster and Westbury with intent to advance on Bristol. They wanted to know what all this meant.[42]

According to one account, the city government, understanding that Colonel Essex was about to march on Bristol, sent three aldermen to him to ask him not to do so, but he 'finding the malignity of their Message, detained their persons, and set forward his march thither.'[43] Colonel Essex was evidently not sympathetic, but the mayor and aldermen hoped for more considerate treatment from Popham and the Somerset militia. On 7 December they wrote again to Popham saying they had sent messengers to say what force of Trained Bands they were prepared to entertain, but the messengers had been detained by Colonel Essex who was at Thornbury with the intention of entering Bristol next day. They asked Popham to come to the city early next morning before Colonel Essex arrived 'to avoid effusion of Bloud, which otherwise will undoubtedly happen'.[44] It looks at this stage as if the city government, with troops advancing from Gloucestershire and Somerset, had decided to come to terms and was trying to arrange a planned admission of troops to avoid bloodshed. The Council evidently feared there might be some resistance unless it allowed troops to enter. The government of Bristol did not declare for parliament, it merely recognised the reality of the situation. It had no heart for a fight. Yet even at this date it was giving orders to the committee for the defence of the city to treat with the people who owned houses against the castle with a view to demolishing them.[45] It seems as though it was trying to keep its options open to the last.

We have no really satisfactory account of how parliamentary troops got into Bristol. If the city government made some sort of agreement with Essex or Popham, we have no record of it. According to the eighteenth-century historian of Bristol, William Barrett, Colonel Essex's troops approached the city on 5 December. The citizens were preparing to defend it, and the Common Council was discussing how it might be best held for the king, when the mayor's wife and many more women came to the Tolzey and persuaded the Council to agree to open the gates, to the great grief of the commons who were prepared to fight.[46] According to Samuel Seyer, Colonel Essex appeared before the city on 2 December, but was resisted for two days by the loyal citizens. The Common Council made a show of supporting the king, but in fact wished to surrender, and when a party of 100 women led by the mayor's wife came to the Tolzey 'in a tumultuous manner', the magistrates ordered the gates to be opened. There was, however, fighting at the Frome Gate, and while this was going on, Newgate was 'opened by the contrivance of a woman (as was said) . . . ', and Colonel Essex entered with two regiments of foot. Seyer thought the smallness of Essex's force showed that 'they depended more on the favour of some within, than on themselves.'[47]

There are accounts of the surrender in various pamphlets, but it is difficult to know how reliable they are, and they contain a good deal of propaganda. The most detailed account we have is in the form of a communication sent by Mr John Ball in Bristol to James Nicolls in London. It is dated 23 December 1642, and it was printed and sold in London.[48] The writer was not a member of the Common Council and was presumably relying on hearsay for much of what he said. Ball deals at great length with the circumstances leading up to the entry of the troops, and his account is worth summarising.

Ball alleged that there were 'many malignants of the great ones amongst us as Colston, Yoemans, and their brethren' and also among some of the clergy, but he thought 'the major part of this city and best part stands firm for the Parliament'. He gave an account of a Council meeting of which we have no record at which the Council discussed a letter from the king telling it not to admit parliamentary troops, a letter from parliament requiring it to do so, and a letter from the Marquis of Hertford in Wales offering to send 1,500 men. Then Colonel Popham and Sir John Seymour came to Bristol, and 'there was much agitation of the question, some being for admitting forces, some against it'. Sheriff Jackson, Alderman Locke and Mr James went to tell the Gloucestershire men that if they came with their forces, then 'upon their perill be it'. The Gloucestershire men were so incensed 'that they clapt them up, and would not set them at liberty, untill they had ingaged their lives for the admission of a Garrison in Bristoll'. Popham and Seymour came a second time to Bristol to ask for an answer to parliament's request, and then 'A very great combustion there arose.' Some said it would be 'an invitation of the Kings Army suddenly,' others argued that it would be best to join with the neighbouring counties against the Cavaliers. The writer then goes on: 'there is news brought that unlesse a strength were admitted into the City, the Country would starve the City.' Then 'the well affected women (some of the chiefest) as M. Maioresse, M. Holworth and others, to the number of 200' came with a petition saying that if the parliamentary forces were opposed, 'the effusion of bloud would be great', and food supplies from Gloucestershire and Somerset would be cut off. To prevent this and 'the mischiefs that might arise by a violent entring the town', they asked that 'parliaments forces might in a faire and peaceable manner be admitted.'

According to Ball's account, the Council agreed to act on the women's petition, but when the parliamentary forces reached Bristol the next day, the malignants tried to raise a mutiny and insurrection in the town. They hired some seamen and placed ordnance at the Frome Gate. When the mayor himself came to the gate and turned the ordnance away from it, they resisted him and turned it back again. They were, however, 'prevented of their purpose', because the horse and foot entered at Newgate and 'Pitty-gate'. When they heard this, they ceased to resist.

Another pamphlet has an interesting variation on the theme of the three aldermen who went to meet Colonel Essex and the Gloucestershire men. Essex was so angry that he detained them and 'set forward his march thither, where he found strong resistance; but setting the aldermen in the front of the battell, by that means abated their rage, and with the assistance of the good party in the City, they got entrance.'[49]

These accounts were pieces of propaganda written for a London audience, and we cannot be sure what went on when the Gloucestershire men reached the city gates, but an interesting piece of evidence has recently come to light. This is a sworn statement made by Mary Stephens, wife of William Stephens, soapmaker.[50] She said that on Friday 9 December, the day the troops came in, Francis Belcher, soapmaker, came to the door of her house and 'demanded the bolt of the Chaine that goeth athwart the streete nere Froome Gate'. She asked him whether he would not obey the mayor and sheriffs who had been taken there a little earlier. He replied: 'litel care wee fore the Maior and Sheriffes. There are wiser than they.' He went on: ' . . . if a daie should come as we hope will, we will remember you'. She continued: 'the said Belcher being verie earnest and much busying himselfe to kepe fast the said gate, the said examinants husband wishing him to give over and let open the gate, and Mr Butcher then coming by, the said Belcher spoke to the said Mr Butcher and said la saith he that Iacanapes (meaning the said William Stephens) would have us open the gate'. This evidence is difficult to interpret, but it seems that on 9 December there was talk of opening the Frome Gate and that the mayor and sheriffs were in some way concerned. Francis Belcher was trying to stop them. Belcher was later involved in the plot to let Rupert into the city.[51] Mr Butcher may possibly be the George Butcher or Bowcher who was hanged for his part in the plot. He had a house in Christmas Street near the Frome Gate, and after the plot had failed, he confessed that he had provided chains and locks to bar the passage at St. John's Gate while the royalists were being admitted.[52]

There is another deposition referring to events about this time.[53] On

10 December, the day after the troops had come in, Richard Tyler, baker, stated that on 9 December in the afternoon he was in Wine Street where the parliamentary force of horse was standing when William Knight, a tailor, with 'either a small piece or carbine' on his shoulder asked one of the horsemen if all the foot soldiers had come in. The horseman said he did not know, and Knight said: 'Well now, if ye doe not plunder soundly, I would you were hanged, and we will show you the places.' The horseman replied that he should forbear of that then and that they would talk of it soon.[54]

On 9 December, then, Bristol was occupied by troops supporting Parliament. Ten days later the Earl of Stamford informed the House of Lords by letter from Bristol that he had heard while he was on his way to the city that 'some commotion' had occurred after the entry of the troops, but that all was now in order. He said: 'I find the city infinitely well affected towards the good cause.'[55] In view of what was to happen in March 1643 he was clearly too optimistic, but it is interesting that no one was removed from the Common Council by the occupying forces.[56]

Occupation by a garrison inevitably meant billeting of troops on civilians and large contributions in taxes and loans for maintaining the occupying forces and strengthening the defences of the city. Moreover, Bristolians cannot have found it pleasant to have to endure the presence of soldiers over whom they had no control.[57] Within a month of the occupation, four aldermen took to the King a petition asking him to be reconciled with parliament.[58] The petition stressed the economic consequences of the war: 'Our ships lie now rotting in the Harbor without any Mariners freight or trade unto forraigne partes by reason of our home-bred distraction.' The king returned a gracious answer, but the war went on.

In the early stages of the occupation, the troops were under the command of the drunken and unreliable Colonel Essex who was alleged to be much distrusted by 'the best affected of the City' and intimate with those suspected to be malignants.[59] In February, Colonel Nathaniel Fiennes was sent to Bristol to investigate. He arrested Colonel Essex and took over as military governor, but there was no decrease in the demands for money.

By March 1643 there was enough discontent in Bristol to lead to a formidable plot in which a hundred or more Bristolians were prepared to risk their lives to help Prince Rupert take the city.[60] It is impossible to say how far this was a reaction against the occupying forces and how far it was genuine royalist commitment. There must also have been considerable poverty and unemployment, and some may have come in for payment or in the hope of plunder. The chief leaders were Robert Yeamans and George Bowcher or Butcher, who were both Merchant Venturers. They had the support of some other merchants, including John Taylor, Thomas Colston, Edmund Arundel, Edward Caple, John Butcher, John Heyman, Rowland Searchfield and William Yeamans. Others involved included two ropemakers, two hauliers, two Oxford scholars, a soapboiler, a vintner, a goldsmith, a doctor, a plumber, a tiler, a carpenter, a cooper, a hatter and a grasier.[61] It was alleged that the leaders had associates to the number of 2,000 in and around Bristol, and that they hired the services of sailors, butchers, halliers and the like. There may have been exaggeration in all this by those who wanted to show how dangerous the plotters were and how much they deserved death, but it is clear that a considerable number of Bristolians were involved. This is one of the rare occasions in the war when they showed commitment in any numbers.

Yeamans had received some kind of commission from the king to raise troops in Bristol before it had fallen to parliament. He now belatedly acted on this and enlisted support in the occupied city.[62] There seemed a good chance of success since some of the officers of the garrison were not completely loyal to parliament. Fiennes explicitly stated that it was 'a wicked conspiracy, plotted between divers inhabitants . . . and some of the officers of Col. Essex his regiment . . .'.[63] Contact was made with the king, and the plan was for Prince Rupert to come towards Bristol on the night of 7 March and to have his advance party as far forward as the gallows on St. Michael's Hill. One group of conspirators was to assemble at Yeaman's house in Wine Street, another at Bowcher's house in Christmas Street, and there were two other assembly points. The Frome Gate was to be seized with the help of Captain Hilsdon and disloyal troops from the Guardhouse, and the Guardhouse itself was to be surrendered to Yeamans' party by another traitor, Lieutenant Moore. When the Frome Gate had been seized, the church bells would give the signal to the conspirators outside and to Rupert's troops, and they would move in and take the city. All royalists were to wear white tape, and the watchword was 'Charles'.

On the night of 7 March 1643, the conspirators assembled at their rendez-vous points, and Rupert's troops came near the city, but the conspiracy was betrayed, possibly by 'some tattling women', possibly by the parliamentary officers who were alleged to be involved, possibly by indiscretion on the part of some of the conspirators.[64] Fiennes moved quickly, and before morning some hundred people had been arrested. There was no serious resistance. The conspirators had been caught unawares and had no contingency plans.

Four of the conspirators, Robert Yeamans, George Bowcher, Edward Dacres and William Yeamans, were put on trial before a Council of War. They were found guilty and were condemned to death. The royalists threatened reprisals if they were executed, and the king wrote to the mayor and aldermen ordering them to raise the city in order to rescue the condemned men, but Yeamans and Bowcher were hanged in Wine Street. They died bravely.[65] They left between them sixteen children, and another was born posthumously to Yeamans' widow. Mrs Dorothy Hazzard, whom we shall meet later, was alleged to have said: 'it is a pity but that their childrens' brains should be dashed out against the stones, that no more of their race might remain on the face of the earth . . .'.[66]

There are some puzzling features about the plot and its aftermath. If four officers of the garrison were involved, it is surprising that none of them was court-martialled. It is possible that they deceived Yeamans and never intended to help him, but on the other hand Fiennes explicitly said that some officers were involved. There is no explanation of why Dacres and William Yeamans were selected for trial, or of why they were spared. Since so many people were involved, one would have expected more to be put on trial. It is possible that Fiennes preferred to take money from the plotters, although he later complained that most of them were poor and that he did not get much from them.[67] It may be that the royalist threats made some impact and Fiennes may have thought that a large number of executions would be counter-productive. According to Clarendon, many fled from the city, and the affair 'exceedingly enraged a great part of the city, which longed to be freed from the yoke of servitude they were under.'[68]

The attempt at self-determination thus failed, and the future of Bristol now depended on what happened elsewhere. On 13 July 1643 Sir William Waller was caught between two royalist forces at Roundway Down, and his army was destroyed as a fighting force. There was no longer an effective parliamentary army in the west, and Bristol and Gloucester were obvious targets for the royalists. On 18 July Prince Rupert rode out from Oxford, and on 23 July he took up his quarters in the College of Westbury-on-Trym. Meanwhile, the Western or Cornish Army, nominally under the Marquis of Hertford but in fact led by Sir Ralph Hopton and Prince Maurice, moved up from the south, and Bristol was surrounded.

A good deal had been done to put the city in a state of defence. Apart from the rivers Avon and Frome, the city walls and the castle, there was a new line of defences which the city had begun to construct at the end of November 1642 and which had been continued under Colonel Essex and Colonel Fiennes. This consisted of earthworks and ditches and a number of forts and strong points extending for some four miles. On the north and west, the defences followed the line of the Brandon Hill to Kingsdown escarpment, but the rest of the line was on low ground in the valleys of the Frome and the Avon (see sketch, pp. 109). The Dutch engineer, Sir Bernard de Gomme, who came to England with Prince Rupert and who was present at the storming of Bristol, wrote a long description of the line and works,[69] and some of the points in his account may be briefly noted. On the southern skirt of Brandon Hill was the Water Fort (more or less at the junction of the present Hotwells Road and Jacobs Well Road). Then the line ran up to Brandon Hill Fort, which was 18 feet square and 18 feet high. Here the moat was shallow and narrow because of the rockiness of the ground. The line then ran downhill to a barn and spur where the royalists eventually broke through, known later as Washington's Breach (near Bristol City Museum). From here the line and ditch went up the hill to the Windmill Fort (which was later enlarged under the royalists and called the Royal Fort). It ran on to a battery on St. Michael's Hill, near Alderman Jones's house, then to a redoubt on Kingsdown, and then on to Prior's Hill Fort. From here it ran down hill to a work at Stoke's Croft, and round to Lawford's Gate and the Avon. According to de Gomme, the curtain wall and ditch were on average about 4½ feet high and 6 feet at the highest, and about 3 feet thick at the top. The ditch was on average 6 feet broad and 5 feet deep, but was as much as 9 feet deep around the forts.

The long line of outer defences was on the face of it not easy to defend with a comparatively small force, and Fiennes was thought to have only 300 horse and 1,500 foot, while estimates put Rupert's total forces at between 14,000 and 20,000. In fact, the royalists were to find the defences far more formidable than they expected.

What was the attitude of those inside Bristol? There was certainly some sympathy for the royalists, and those in Rupert's army who argued for a siege rather than a storm thought that, given time, this sympathy would show itself openly.[70] As we shall see, two merchants did in fact arrange for eight ships to be handed over to Rupert.[71] The civilian population cannot, however, have felt much enthusiasm about either a siege or a storm, and the status quo must have appeared less unsatisfactory than the prospect of the violent capture of the city by Rupert's men. Some of those who later gave evidence against Colonel Fiennes maintained that he was getting a lot of help from the citizens, and it seems that he had armed some of them with weapons he had taken from the Trained Bands.[72] Sergeant Major Wood said that there were a considerable number of volunteers, 'for I had, as I believe, at that part of the Line that was in my charge, no lesse than one hundred Citizens that defended the work voluntarily'.[73] Mary Smith deposed that 'divers of the City . . . went out to the Works and fought Valiantly to her knowledge, she being oft among them to carry provisions'.[74] Moreover, there was the famous incident of the Frome Gate.[75] We must remember, however, that the horrors of a storm may have encouraged a number of people to try to keep the royalists out, and that such action did not necessarily mean commitment to parliament. Moreover, most of the evidence on this point comes from people who were trying to show that Fiennes should not have surrendered and that he was getting plenty of help from the inhabitants. Many soldiers died in the storming of Bristol in 1643, but there is no record of any civilian being killed or wounded.

On Sunday 23 July, the two besieging armies moved into position.[76] Between 2 and 3 in the afternoon Prince Rupert with a large escort, including Colonel Washington's dragoons, came to Clifton Church 'to take a view of their forts and line . . . ' and to see where to put his batteries. De Gomme related how while he was in the churchyard, 'the enemies forts made two or three canon shot at us, but hurt nobody'. Colonel Washington was left in Clifton with a strong force. He repulsed an enemy skirmishing party and blazed away at Brandon Hill Fort and the Water Fort, which fired back throughout the night.[77]

On Monday 24 July, the whole of the Oxford army 'with a very Large front', as De Gomme puts it, 'marched to the edge of the downe that the forts might see them', and the Western army likewise demonstrated its strength on the southern side of the city. Then, at 11 o'clock, Prince Rupert sent a trumpeter to summon Bristol to surrender. Colonel Fiennes, as was proper in a man of honour, replied that he could not relinquish his trust 'till he were brought to more extremitye'. The royalists then set up their batteries, and both sides blazed away at each other. De Gomme said that the guns firing at Brandon Hill Fort were meant 'onely to awe and keep them in, so that they did ours the lesse mischiefe. Onelye (as we heard) one of theyr Canoniers vaporing in his shirt on topp of the fort was kill'd there for his foole hardynesse.' We do not know the name of this unknown soldier who seems to have been the first casualty.

This Monday, also, two Bristol merchants, Mr Fitzherbert[78] and Mr William Bevan[79] arranged for the handing over to the royalists of eight ships anchored in Kingroad. Clarendon says that the ships were 'not only laden with things of great value, as plate, money, and the best of all sorts of commodities, which those who suspected the worst had sent abroad, but also with persons of quality, who, being unwilling to run the hazard of a siege, thought that way to have secured themselves, and to have escaped to London; who were all taken prisoner.'[80]

When darkness fell on Monday, the guns stopped firing, but at midnight two cannon were fired by the royalists, and the defenders blazed off with shot and musket, expecting an attack. De Gomme remarked: 'Twas a bewtyfull peece of danger, to see so many fires incessentyle in the darck . . . for a whole hower together . . . And in these military Maskerado's was this Munday night passed.'

On Tuesday 25 July, Prince Rupert went over the river to the Western Army and held a Council of War about whether to proceed by way of storm or by way of approach (that is to say, by gradually pushing the lines and works nearer to the defences and in the end mining or making a breach). Rupert's officers were for storming, but the officers of the Western Army favoured the approach method, since they thought the place would be difficult to storm, and if they proceeded slowly, the royalist fifth column in Bristol might be better able to influence the defending garrison.[81] In the end, Rupert's officers prevailed. It could be argued, in view of the heavy casualties and the fact that the storm very nearly failed, that this was the wrong decision.

The attack was to begin at dawn on Wednesday 26 July. De Gomme tells us that 'The word for the Soldyers was to be Oxford: & the signe for the two Armyes to know one another, to be green Colours, eyther boughs, or suchlike: & that euery officer & Soldjer, to be without a band or handkerchief about his neck.' When the infantry had broken through the lines, they were to level the defences and fill up the ditches to let in the cavalry. The commanders-in-chief were to agree among themselves in what manner Redcliffe Church should be possessed, and if possessed, how maintained, and they were to appoint officers for that purpose. The signal for the attack was to be the firing of two demi-cannon from Lord Grandison's post near Prior's Hill Fort. Firing was to be kept up all night before the attack 'to interteyne the Enemy with Alarms'.

On 26 July, the Western Army, contrary to orders, began the attack before dawn, at about 3 in the morning, 'out of a military ambition (I suppose) to winne the worckes first . . . ', according to de Gomme.[82] When Rupert realised from the noise that the Western Army had begun the attack, he ordered the signal shots to be fired, and the attack began from his side too. This premature attack was unfortunate, since all the preparations in the way of ladders and other materials had not been completed.

There were three separate divisions or tertia attacking from the north-west. Lord Grandison's division was directed against the defences in Stoke's Croft and Prior's Hill Fort. Colonel Bellasis attacked first to one side and then to the other of the Windmill Hill Fort. Colonel Wentworth's troops attacked the line between Brandon Hill Fort and Windmill Hill Fort. The attacks went on more or less simultaneously.

Grandison's men first attacked the Stoke's Croft fortifications, threw grenades into the works and exploded a petard on the entrance. It did not make a big enough hole, and the line held. After an hour and a half's fighting, Grandison shifted the attack to Prior's Hill Fort. His men got into the ditch around it, but the scaling ladders had not come up, because, says de Gomme, the attack had begun too soon. Colonel Lunsford found a ladder lying about and climbed up to the pallisadoes at the top, but he could not get over and had to come down again. The men retreated, but Grandison led them on again and was shot in the leg. The wound was eventually to prove fatal. Colonel Owen, to whom he handed over, was shot in the face, and the soldiers then retreated. When news came of the breakthrough at Washington's Breach, this force moved over to join the troops who had broken through.

Colonel Bellasis's men attacking on the right and left of the Windmill Hill Fort ran into great trouble. De Gomme states that 'fynding there an impossibilitye of entring, for that they wanted fagots to fill up the ditche, & Ladders to skale the Worcke', they retreated to a stone wall to the right of the fort. One group apparently fled even further back and was rallied by Prince Rupert, who had his horse shot under him.

Thus, at two points the attack failed, but Colonel Wentworth's men were successful. It has sometimes been suggested that this was a lucky breakthrough by Colonel Wentworth, but the attack had in fact been planned at a midnight meeting of the officers of the army group.[83] They decided to attack the line between Brandon Hill Fort and Windmill Hill Fort. Sir Jacob Astley's and Sir Edward Fitton's regiments were to lead, Colonel Bowles and Colonel Herbert were to follow, and Colonel Washington was to bring up the rear. It did not work out as planned, because of the uneven ground and the furze bushes, and because as they advanced from the area near the present Victoria Rooms, they came under heavy fire from the forts. The men ran as fast as they could to the line and found shelter in the dead ground between the forts. There was also a barn near what is now George's Bookshop which gave cover against the fire from Brandon Hill. De Gomme relates what happened next: 'being gotten to the Line, Leift. Wright, Leift. Baxter, with others, throwing hand-granados over among the Enemyes, made them stagger & recoyle a Little: so that ours more courageously coming on to storme over the Line, the Enemys quitt it, & rann towards the Towne. Ours thereupon helping over one another, fell presentlye to fling down the work with theyr hands, halberts & partizans to Lett in theyr fellowes . . . In the meane tyme, Leift. Colonel Littleton ryding along the inside of the Line with a fire-pike, quite cleered the place of the defendants: some of them crying out Wyld fire. Thus was the Line cleared, for a great waye together.'[84]

There was later an argument about the strength of the line at Washington's Breach. Those who wished to show that Fiennes was inefficient as well as cowardly claimed that he had been warned about the weakness of the defences at this point. Thus, Captain Henry Loyde gave evidence that 'A Souldier of my company pointing with his finger to that Part of the Line between Windmill-Hill Fort and Brandon Hill Fort (where the said Line was not yet perfected, and where the Enemy afterwards entred) advised the Governor to have a care of that place as the only likely place for the Enemy to enter at and further did admonish the Governor that the line in that place was very weakely manned, for which the said Governor called him sawcey knave.'[85] Fiennes maintained at one time that 'the place where the enemy entered, was not a likely place for the enemy to enter by, was weakliest assaulted, could not have been better guarded without drawing forces from other places, which were in more apparent danger . . . '.[86] Elsewhere, however, he admitted that here 'the works were not quite perfected . . . '.[87] De Gomme said that 'the conquest was not to be attributed so much to the weaknesse of the place, as to Gods blessing on our Soldjers courage'.[88] Colonel Birch, however, remarked acidly: ' . . . the line was unhappily *entred*, for I cannot call it *stormed*, because at that entrance there was not a man slain on either part'.[89]

Thus, between 3 and 4 o'clock a small force of infantry had got over the line. At Fiennes' court martial, a number of witnesses alleged that it was only a very small force of between 150 and 200 men, that they were not reinforced for a long time, and that they could easily have been destroyed. One witness maintained that the men 'were so afraid of being cut off, that they gave themselves all for dead men . . . none of their own party knowing of their entry till two hours after they entered, nor sending any relief'.[90] Witnesses also stated that the men who got over the line had not been counter-attacked, as they should have been. Fiennes maintained at his trial that Sergeant Major Langrish had been ordered to charge with the horse if the line was broken and he failed to do so,[91] but de

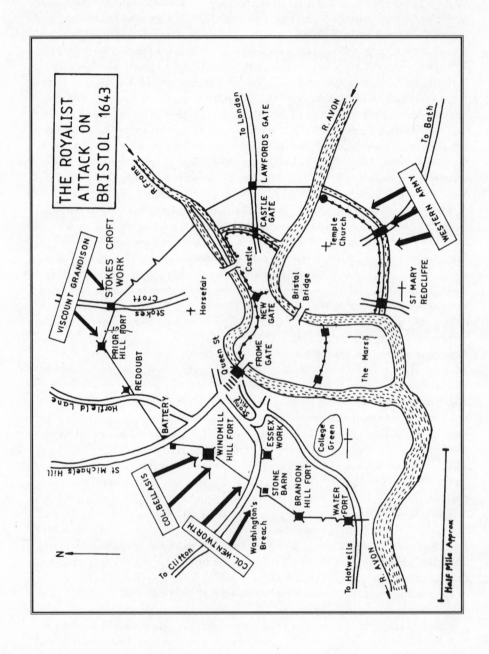

THE ROYALIST ATTACK ON BRISTOL 1643

Gomme says that the cavalry did attack the infantry more than once, and that there was fierce fighting. In the end, Captain Clerk, Ancient Hodgekinson and some others met the attackers with their fire pikes, and 'neither the men nor the horses were able to endure it'.

This breakthrough of the outer defences, which was at only one point in the line, did not mean that the city itself had been taken. One body of troops now moved towards the town, presumably along Park Row, not realising that in front of them lay a strong point known as the Essex Work, which was garrisoned by the enemy. It seems that some of the royalist foot were moving rapidly to get out of the way of the enemy horse, and, according to de Gomme, the defenders of the Essex Work, 'suspecting our mens running hast, to be the courage of such as pursued the victorye, & were resolved to carrye all before them', ran out of the Work.[92] Colonel Wentworth and Colonel Washington found a ditch across the street near the Essex Work and filled it up to make way for the horse. They came under fire from the town and the houses, but they held on to the Work and the lane until relieved by Colonel Bellasis's men. Other troops had come up by now. Colonel Wentworth and Colonel Washington's men marched to College Green and occupied the Cathedral and the two churches near it.[93] From here they fired on 'a Little Worck & a hows where the Enemy had a peece of Canon and beat them from it'. The royalist troops came under fire from the quay and from the houses as well as from the redoubt below Brandon Hill (the Water Fort). They now advanced to near the quay and could have set fire to the ships, but when the Prince was informed, he forbade this, as he wished to preserve the town.

A number of witnesses at the Court Martial maintained that once the outer line had been pierced, Colonel Fiennes quite unnecessarily ordered all his men to come off the line into the town, even though they were extremely reluctant to leave it, and that he refused to authorise an effective counter-attack.[94]

The way into the city was across the Frome river over the Frome Bridge and through the Frome Gate. This gate had two separate gatehouses, one at each end of the bridge. The inner gatehouse was eight yards long and had a stone room over it. Beneath this were two gates secured with chains. The outer gatehouse was six yards long and also had a room over it.[95] From this gate during the next two hours the defending garrison made a number of fierce sallies, and in one of them the royalist Colonel Lunsford was shot through the heart on what were later called Lunsford Stairs (Christmas Steps). There were heavy royalist casualties,[96] but the defenders also suffered, and, according to de Gomme, 'this made them thinck of nothing but Parlee: for now (they knew) could wee without interruption have brought our Canon or Petards up to the verye ports, or might have fired the Shipps and howses, or have mined'.

Nothing has been said so far about the attack by the Western Army on the other side of the city, except that it began prematurely. Three columns attacked with great courage, but the ditch before the walls was deep and full of water, and efforts to fill it up with faggots and carts were unsuccessful. The men tried to scale the walls, but were driven back with heavy casualties. As one observer put it: 'as gallant men as ever drew sword . . . lay upon the ground like rotten sheep . . . '.[97] The Western Army had to fall back on its defensive positions, and after Rupert's men had broken through, the Prince ordered Maurice to bring 1,000 men round as reinforcements for the attack on the northern side.

Before the surrender, there occurred the curious incident of the women at the Frome Gate. The legend, as given by John Latimer, runs as follows: 'When the news of Washington's entrance reached the city, Mrs Dorothy Hazzard, a Puritan lady . . . rushed with about two hundred women and girls to this Gate . . . and with the help to some men the portal was solidly blocked up with woolsacks and earth'. Mrs Hazzard then went to the Governor and urged him to stand firm, assuring him 'that her Amazons would face the besiegers with their children in their arms "to keep off the shot from the soldiers if they were afraid"'. Latimer added that her entreaties were of no avail, but some of the women stood firmly with the gunners in the Gate, and it was not until after repeated assaults that the royalists were able to enter.[98]

The story rests primarily on the evidence of three people who made statements at Fiennes' trial. William Deane, a baker and member of the Trained Bands, said that he had heard some women urging the soldiers to go courageously against the enemy. He went on: ' . . . and if they feared the Canon, we (they said) and our children will put ourselves between the Canons mouth and you, to dead and keepe off the Bullets . . . '.[99] Another witness, Joan Batten, said she was one of two hundred women who went to Colonel John Fiennes 'offering themselves to worke in the Fortifications in the very face of the Enemy and to go themselves and their children, into the mouth of the Canon to dead and keepe off the shot from the Souldiers . . . '. She said that shortly afterwards a message came from Colonel Nathaniel Fiennes, the Governor, telling them to go to the Frome Gate and make a bulwark of earth, 'which by the direction of the Engineer they did'. However, when they had almost finished the bulwark, which was fifteen or sixteen feet thick, Colonel Fiennes surrendered the city.[100] The third witness, who in the course of time stole all the limelight, was Mrs Dorothy Hazzard. She deposed that with diverse other women and maids and with the help of some men, they stopped up the Frome Gate with woolsacks and earth. The women then went to the gunners and told them that if they would stand and fight, the women would stand by them, and they would not want for provisions.[101] At the Court Martial, Fiennes denied that he had heard about the women offering to dead the bullets with themselves and their children, and remarked that he did not think this was a fit means to dead cannon bullets.[102]

In her evidence Mrs Hazzard did not claim that she took the lead, and, indeed, it is possible that Joan Batten was the more important person in the affair. It also seems that the order to build the barricade came from Colonel

Fiennes himself and was not a spontaneous reaction of the women, as has often been suggested. Mrs Hazzard may in the long run have got all the credit because she was very prominent in organising a fanatical group of separatists in Bristol.[103] She was furious that she had lost all the property which she had put in the castle on the undertaking from Fiennes that the castle would be defended. She was hardly a typical Bristolian, and there were many in Bristol who feared 'the sad consequences of an enraged Enemy entring such a City by force, having been exasperated by the losse of above a thousand of their men . . . '.[104] If we can believe Clarendon, the Bristolians, fearing they would be made a prey to the soldiers, urged the Governor to treat for terms.[105] It would have been possible for the garrison to defend the city street by street and to make a last stand in the castle, and Fiennes was accused of cowardice because he did not do this. In his defence, he maintained that his men were disheartened and were withdrawing from the colours to go off drinking or sleeping, and that when he ordered fourteen companies to muster in the Marsh, not more than one hundred men turned up. He said: 'they could not get six men a-piece of their companies together, they ran so fast over the key to the enemy'. He maintained that there was no hope of holding the castle for more than two or three days, that not more than fifty barrels of gunpowder remained and there was no match.[106] All this was denied by William Prynne who more or less compelled the House of Commons to put Fiennes on trial and who produced many witnesses, most of them refugees from Bristol, to give evidence against him. Fiennes was found guilty and condemned to death, but the Commander in Chief, the Earl of Essex, pardoned the son of his old friend Lord Saye and Sele.

Before he surrendered the city, Fiennes had obtained good terms from Rupert, who was glad to end the storm in which he had suffered very heavy casualties, and the parliamentary garrison with a number of civilians marched out from Bristol. The terms were not properly kept and there was some violence and looting as the column left the city. Rupert and his officers did their best to prevent it, as Fiennes himself acknowledged, but some of the royalist troops got out of hand.[107]

The fall of Bristol was a great encouragement to the royalist cause. As Captain Richard Atkyns put it: 'When we were posessed of Bristoll, and the lesser garrisons came tumbling in to the obedience of the king, I took the King's crown to be settled upon his head again . . . '.[108]

A royalist garrison now occupied Bristol, and the city remained in royalist hands for over two years. Inevitably, the moving in of a conquering army meant disturbances and a certain amount of looting until things settled down.[109] Equally inevitable was the heavy taxation in the form of 'voluntary' gifts and assessments for the upkeep of the garrison and for strengthening the defences.[110] Latimer gave various details of what Bristolians had to pay, and he seemed to think the burden was 'intolerable', but it must be remembered that the whole country during the war years was subject to systematic taxation on a scale never before known in English history. In the present state of knowledge it is not possible to say whether Bristol was particularly heavily burdened compared with other towns.

After the royalists had taken Bristol, they did not engage in a large-scale purge of the governing body or take reprisals against those who had favoured parliament. The mayor remained in office, and only two members of the Common Council were removed.[111] There was some delay before the king granted a General Pardon, but when it was issued on 24 February 1644, the only people excepted were those who had been on the Council of War which condemned Yeamans and Bowcher to death.[112] This lenient treatment suggests that there were few Bristolians who had shown themselves deeply committed to parliament.

There were some compensations for Bristolians during the years of royalist occupation. In December 1643 the king granted a new Charter to the Society of Merchant Venturers of Bristol, throwing open to them the trades of the Eastland Company, the Russia Company, the Levant Company and the Merchant Adventurers of England, trades which had hitherto been restricted to London-dominated monopolies. The Charter was granted 'in consideration that the merchants of Bristol have expressed their loyalty and fidelity to us in these late times of differences, even when the merchants of London, who have enjoyed many more privileges and immunities, have many of them traitorously rebelled against us . . . '.[113] The king was trying to build up Bristol as a counter-weight to London, and had the fortunes of war gone differently, this Charter might have been of great value.

Other indications of the increased importance of Bristol were the establishment of a mint[114] and the setting up of a printing press.[115] Moreover, in spite of heavy taxation, Bristolians enjoyed relative peace and did not have to worry about marauding troops and threats from without. This relative security may have compensated in some measure for interference with trade at home and abroad.

During these two years, a number of prominent Bristolians became involved, willingly or unwillingly, with the royalist cause and were in trouble later as malignants.[116] No doubt there were others who disliked the royalists, but there is little indication of active opposition. Clarendon, however, tells us that in March 1645 Sir William Waller advanced with his horse and dragoons towards Bristol 'in hope . . . to have surprised that city by some treachery within, and being disappointed there, retired towards Dorsetshire . . . '.[117] Nothing seems to be known about this alleged conspiracy.

In 1645 the fate of Bristol was once again determined by the military situation outside. On 14 June the king was defeated at Naseby, and on 10 July General Goring was defeated at Langport. The king's forces were not totally destroyed, but the balance swung overwhelmingly in favour of parliament. The parliamentary armies now proceeded to reduce the royalist strongholds. Bridgwater was stormed on 21 and 22 July, Bath surrendered on 29 July, and Sherborne Castle fell on 14 August. Fairfax then had to decide whether to campaign against Goring in the south-west or to take Bristol. He and Cromwell feared that if they left Bristol alone it would be reinforced from Wales and might also get help from the disaffected Clubmen of Somerset, Wiltshire and Dorset, once the parliamentary forces had turned their backs.[118] Fairfax was aware that there was plague in and around Bristol, but he is reported to have said 'as for the sickness, let us trust God with the army, who will be as ready to protect us in the siege from infection, as in the field from the bullet.'[119]

As the enemy approached, Rupert asked the advice of his Council of War. The general view was that 'notwithstanding the Workes and Line were very defective, the circuit long, our number few; yet if we could repell one generall storm, the enemy would be discouraged from attempting the second time; and the season of the year might advantage us, and incommode them.' As there was some uncertainty, Rupert asked whether he should break out with the horse and leave what could be spared in the fort and castle, but it was felt that this was neither safe nor honourable. A suggestion that he should defend the castle and fort was also rejected 'in regard of the Nobility, and Gentry and such of the Town as appeared well affected'. It was not honourable to leave those who could not be accommodated in the castle and fort to the sword of the enemy. And so the decision was taken for a general defence.[120]

Prince Rupert was confident that he could hold Bristol for a considerable time. His garrison was a good deal larger than that with which Fiennes had defended the place in 1643,[121] and the defences had been greatly strengthened since then.[122] The inhabitants had been ordered to lay in provisions for six months, and Rupert had bought a store of corn for those who could not afford to do so. Cattle were driven in from the neighbouring countryside as the enemy approached.[123]

We have little information about the attitude of the citizens as the parliamentary armies closed in. At the end of May, the Committee of Both Kingdoms had written to Colonel Massey saying: 'We conceive that the townsmen may be very well affected to us if you can but find means of correspondence with them',[124] and a little later, when the attackers were considering whether or not to storm the place, Cromwell noted that one of the arguments against storming was 'the report of the good affections of some of the townsmen to us.'[125] On 25 August, Fairfax and Cromwell issued a statement promising pardon for past disloyalty to those who endeavoured to deliver the city into parliamentary hands. This was intercepted, and Rupert caused 'several suspected, and active persons to be restrained, which prevented the designe, and withall by his personal presence secured the great fort from surprizall.'[126] There may have been a small fifth column in Bristol, particularly as it was now clear to many people that the royalists were not likely to win the war, but if there was, it has left very little trace in the records.

The Trained Bands were expected to play their part in the defence of the city.[127] In May 1644 the Common Council had decided to increase their numbers to 1,000, but by the time of the attack they had been reduced to about 800 'by interruption of Trade and Commerce, by the Pestilence then raging there, by their poverty and pressures laid upon them.'[128] Indeed, on 3 September, the Common Council decided to give relief to the necessitous members of the Trained Bands and other auxiliaries, and Colonel Taylor and Colonel Colston were told to bring in lists of those in need.[129]

It is likely that by this time morale was low among the civilian population. In Rupert's *Declaration* it was alleged that 'The Commissioners for the Contribution and support of the Garrison, upon the enemy's approach, abandoned the Towne, and many considerable persons had libertie given them, and quitted the Town which much weakened and dis-heartened the rest.'[130]

The advance of the parliamentary army took the defenders by surprise. Ireton was sent ahead with 2,000 men to preserve the places adjacent to Bristol,[131] and in addition, a regiment of foot reached Hanham, three miles from the city, before the garrison was aware of the imminent attack.[132] The royalists set fire to Bedminster, Clifton and some other villages, and they would have carried this scorched earth policy still further but for the unexpected arrival of the parliamentary forces.[133]

On 21 August the main army reached Chew, and Fairfax and Cromwell came towards Bedminster to view the town. They moved their headquarters to Hanham on 22 August, and to Stapleton on 23 August. On that day, the defenders made the first of a number of sallies which were to tax the besiegers to the full by imposing on them 'exceeding great duty' considering 'the paucity of our men to make good their posts, and the strength of the enemy within . . . '.[134] There were further sallies on 24, 26 and 27 August.[135] There was the additional worry that General Goring seemed to be getting ready to move towards Bristol, but it was thought that Colonel Massey's brigade near Taunton would be able to hold him up till the horse could be brought from Bristol.[136]

On 28 August the fort on Portishead point was taken by the parliamentarians, and the way was open for co-operation with the navy, which could now bring ships up the Avon to Kingroad.[137]

A Fast was held among the parliamentary forces on Friday 28 August to ask God's blessing on the design, and there was a debate in the Council of War about whether to storm Bristol or besiege it. There had been bad news from Scotland where Montrose was moving on Edinburgh; the king had advanced to Bedford without being followed; and Goring was thought to be moving nearer Chard. An intercepted letter of Goring's, dated 25 August, said that he hoped to be ready to interrupt the siege of Bristol in about three weeks time.[138] Sprigg thought that the parliamentary army was 'in a great strait', since it was adequate to deal with Bristol, but no more. In view of all this, the Council of War decided to make preparations for a storm but to postpone the final decision.[139]

On Monday 1 September Prince Rupert made a sally with 1,000 horse and 600 foot, but he was beaten back.[140] It is surprising that he was not able to inflict more damage in these sallies, since he could concentrate his striking force, and he was operating against an enemy spread out thinly over several miles.

There was a long debate on Tuesday, 2 September, about whether to storm the city. We know from Cromwell that 'there appeared great unwillingness to the work, through the unseasonableness of the weather, and other apparent difficulties'. Nevertheless, once the decision had been made to storm Bristol, it was accepted with great enthusiasm by both officers and men.[141] A committee was instructed to prepare detailed plans and to report to the Council the next day.

The plan of attack presented on 3 September was as follows: Colonel Weldon with four regiments was to storm the city on the Somerset side; Colonel Montague with four regiments was to attack on both sides of Lawford's Gate; Colonel Rainsborough's division of five regiments was to attack the line between Prior's Hill Fort and the Frome and was to take the fort itself. There were plans for some 200 soldiers to help the sailors take the Water Fort if the occasion arose. A regiment of horse and a regiment of foot were to move up and down before the Royal Fort to 'alarm' it, and a regiment of dragoons and two regiments of horse were to carry ladders with them and attempt the line by Clifton at Washington's Breach.[142]

The plan obviously had some similarities with the royalist plan of 1643, but the main weight of the attack was now to be on the line from Prior's Hill Fort down to Lawford's Gate instead of from Prior's Hill Fort to Washington's Breach. Moreover, the whole defensive line was threatened or at least 'alarmed' in some way, which had not been the case in 1643.

At the Council of War it was also decided that the attack should be launched about 1 o'clock in the morning on Wednesday 10 September. It was hoped to achieve surprise. When the line and forts were taken, the troops were to halt until daybreak so as not to fall foul of each other.[143]

On 4 September the weather 'that had been so extreme wet before, that many soldiers and horses died thereby (and with extreme hard duty) in that wet season' altered for the better, and the drooping spirits of the soldiers revived.[144] Furthermore, about 2,000 'well-affected countrymen' joined the besiegers. They were given quarters and assigned guards 'as an effectual caution against their revolt' and because their presence would discourage the defenders, rather than because they were likely to be of great use.[145] That day, Fairfax summoned Rupert to surrender.

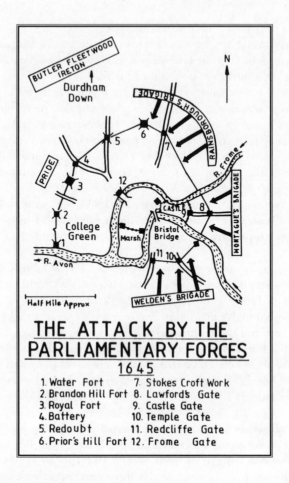

THE ATTACK BY THE
PARLIAMENTARY FORCES
<u>1645</u>

1. Water Fort	7. Stokes Croft Work
2. Brandon Hill Fort	8. Lawford's Gate
3. Royal Fort	9. Castle Gate
4. Battery	10. Temple Gate
5. Redoubt	11. Redcliffe Gate
6. Prior's Hill Fort	12. Frome Gate

There followed protracted negotiations, for Rupert was playing for time. He does not seem to have been in communication with either the king or Goring or to have had any assurance that help would come, and he wanted to postpone the crisis as long as possible.[146] At length, on 9 September Fairfax sent a trumpeter to say that if the terms were not immediately accepted, negotiations were at an end. Rupert kept the trumpeter until 10 o'clock at night and then sent back an unsatisfactory answer. At midnight Fairfax went into the field to give the order for the storm.[147]

Cromwell states that the attack began about 1 o'clock in the morning. He notes that the burning straw and discharge of cannon, which were the signal for the attack, were 'very well perceived by all' and 'truly the men went on with great resolution, and very presently recovered the line, making way for the horse to enter.'[148] According to Sprigg, the attack began about 2 o'clock with 'setting on fire a great heap of straw and fagots on the top of an hill' and the firing of the great guns against Prior's Fort. He adds: ' . . . immediately the storm began round the city, and was terrible to the beholders.'[149]

Four regiments were launched against the line on either side of Lawford's Gate. Cromwell tells us that Colonel Montague and Colonel Pickering stormed the double work at Lawford's Gate, beat the enemy from their works and took the cannon. They laid down bridges for the horse to enter, and Major Desborowe with the horse came in and seconded the foot. The foot then advanced to the city walls, took the gate opening into Castle Street and put a hundred men in it. Sir Hardress Waller and Lieutenant Colonel Jackson also broke through the line in this section and joined the rest of the brigade, so that four regiments and the horse were through the outer defences.[150]

At the same time, an attack was launched against the line from Prior's Hill Fort down to the Frome. Colonels Rainsborough and Hammond attacked round the Fort itself and also had support from part of Colonel Pride's regiment, while Birch and Skippon attacked further down towards the Frome. Colonel Hammond got over the line very quickly and made way for the horse to enter, the line being broken down by the pioneers. Colonel Rainsborough had the hardest task of all and almost despaired of taking Prior's Fort. While he was still attacking it, the horse which had come in under Captain Ireton encountered a party of enemy horse and drove them off, mortally wounding Colonel Taylor who had been one of the Bristol M.P.s. The royalist horse were so disheartened that they did not attack again but retreated to the protection of the Great Fort and Colston's Fort.[151]

It was very difficult to take Prior's Fort. It was very high and a ladder of thirty rungs hardly reached the top. Many of the ladders were too short. The royalists had four cannon there and fired round and case shot, and there was fighting with pikes for two hours. Colonel Hammond's men, attacking from inside the line, eventually got in the portholes and on to the roof. The royalists retreated to the inner rooms below, hoping for quarter, but after three hours of fierce fighting, the attackers were in no mood to grant it and they put almost all the defenders to the sword, including Major Price, the Welsh officer who commanded there.[152]

Dawn was beginning to break when the fort was taken. Sprigg comments how fortunate it was that the attack began so early, for in daylight they could not have taken Prior's Fort. They would have been shot down by the guns from the Great Fort and Colston's Fort and from the castle. In the dark the royalists dared not fire in case they killed their own men drawn up between the Great Fort and Colston's Fort.[153]

The attack from the Somerset side was as unsuccessful in 1645 as it had been in 1643. Cromwell noted that the works were higher than had been reported, that the ladders were too short and the approach very difficult. The attackers were repulsed and lost about 100 men.[154]

Nothing very serious was attempted from the north-west, but three regiments of horse were on Durdham Down to prevent any attempt by Rupert to cut his way out, and some of these men 'alarmed' the Great Fort and the line there, while others 'alarmed' Brandon Hill Fort and the line towards Clifton, presumably to keep men tied down there so that they could not reinforce other places.[155] The attempt of the seamen against the Water Fort came to nothing because of the tide, but the seamen were used elsewhere on the line.

All this did not mean that Bristol had fallen. Cromwell relates what happened next: 'Being possessed of thus much as hath been related, the town was fired in three places by the enemy, which we could not put out; and this began a great trouble to the General and us all, fearing to see so famous a city burnt to ashes before our faces.' While they were discussing what to do next, Prince Rupert sent a trumpeter to request negotiations, and Fairfax agreed, provided that the fires were put out. It is not quite clear whether they had been started by accident or whether the garrison had deliberately started them, as Cromwell and Sprigg suggest.[156] If they were started deliberately, presumably the purpose was to make the attackers' task more difficult or to put pressure on Fairfax to come to terms.

Fairfax gave Prince Rupert very reasonable terms, and the next day at 2 o'clock in the afternoon the Prince marched out from the Royal Fort. A contemporary account states that he 'was clad in scarlet, very richly laid in silver lace, mounted upon a very gallant black Barbary horse . . . '. He was accompanied by many ladies and persons of quality. Fairfax accompanied him for two miles over Durdham Down and treated him with great courtesy.[157]

In his letter to the Speaker of the House of Commons, Cromwell concluded: 'Thus I have given you a true, but not a full account of this great business; wherein he that runs may read, that all this is no other than the work of God. He must be a very atheist that does not acknowledge it.'[158]

The king's reaction to the disaster was to send Rupert a savage letter pointing out that the prince had assured him, that if no mutiny occurred, he would hold Bristol for four months. Charles asked bitterly: 'Did you keep it four days?' He required Rupert henceforth to seek his subsistence 'somewhere beyond the seas', and he sent him a pass to enable him to leave the country.[159] Rupert demanded to be heard, and he had printed a defence of his proceedings in *A Declaration of His Highness Prince Rupert with a Narrative of the State and Condition of the City and Garrison of Bristol.*[160] He put his case with great ability, and he had the support of his officers. Eventually, at his insistence, the matter was brought before the equivalent of a Court Martial on 18 October and 21 October. As a result of its findings, the king accepted that Rupert was not guilty of treachery or cowardice, but still expressed the view that the Prince ought to have held the castle and citadel longer, since he intended to relieve the place.[161] It is not clear that he was planning to do so, or that he had the necessary resources.

There has been much debate since then as to whether Rupert should have held out longer. On the whole, opinion has inclined to the view that he had little option but to surrender on terms, once the outer defences had been pierced. It is argued that the city itself was indefensible and that further resistance would have led to pointless slaughter of soldiers and civilians.[162] Nevertheless, it is surprising that Rupert did not put up a more determined defence or even try to cut his way out with the horse, as the parliamentarians had done at Lostwithiel. He could have left some one else to negotiate the surrender of what remained. Common sense and accepted military conventions justified his action, but in desperate situations great commanders can sometimes successfully ignore these things. There does seem to have been a lack of determination and fighting spirit such as inspired, for example, Colonel Massey at Gloucester, Colonel James Wardlaw at Plymouth, the Marquis of Winchester at Basing House, the Countess of Derby at Lathom House, and a number of others who held out when the sensible course was to surrender.[163]

The departure of Rupert meant that the fighting was over as far as Bristol was concerned, even though the conflict continued elsewhere and the king did not surrender until May 1646. And now those Bristolians who had unwisely committed themselves too far to the royalist cause had to pay the price. It was not in fact as high as they feared it would be.

The victors purged the Common Council much more drastically than the royalists had done in 1643. By an Ordinance of 28 October, Parliament removed from the governing body of Bristol those who had shown themselves so disaffected and so active in promoting the royalist cause that they could no longer continue. These consisted of the Mayor, Francis Creswicke, who had actually been chosen mayor after the city had fallen, five aldermen and seven common councillors. John Gonning junior was appointed mayor, a fact which Latimer found puzzling, since he thought his previous record pointed to royalist sympathies. The sheriffs were instructed to assemble the Council as soon as possible to elect replacements for those who had removed. The new councillors were to be 'well-affected persons' and were not to include those who had been in prison or whose estates were liable for sequestration.[164] On 1 November another Ordinance put back on the Council Richard Aldworth, Richard Vickris and Luke Hodges who had been removed without lawful causes.[165] On 26 January 1646 Richard Aldworth and Luke Hodges were chosen M.P.s to replace John Glanville, who had been expelled for supporting the king, and John Taylor, who had been killed when the city was stormed in 1645.

There must have been considerable trepidation among those whose conduct left them open to the charge of being 'malignant', but it is clear from the papers of the Committee for Compounding[166] that in Bristol, as elsewhere, there was a good deal of obstruction and collusion when efforts were made to make the guilty men pay. No doubt there were a number of people in the governing body whose hands were not entirely clean and who did not want to proceed with excessive vigour against their fellow Bristolians. Some of them clearly wanted the unpleasant business to be conducted in as gentlemanly a way as possible. Thus, on 8 November 1647 the parliamentary committee in Somerset wrote to the mayor of Bristol, William Cann, and other committee men in Bristol, pointing out that they had said at a meeting in Bristol at Michaelmas 1646 that there were several gentlemen in Bristol liable for sequestration but that the Bristol committee had thought it better that these men should be asked to give an engagement to prosecute their sequestrations and that in the meanwhile their estates should not actually be sequestered. The guilty men had not in fact taken any action, and the central committee at Goldsmiths' Hall in London was getting impatient. The Somerset Committee said the Bristol delinquents must compound quickly, otherwise every one would be in trouble for negligence.[167]

In November 1650 a Captain Mason wrote to the Committee in London complaining that 'by the dark actings of men who are unwilling to come into light, because their deeds are so evil . . . malignants, both of this county and Bristol, are very well pleased, and in Bristol particularly, have time to convey away their personal estates'.[168] There were other complaints about the unsatisfactory behaviour of the Bristol committee, and allegations that Captain John Burgess associated with cavaliers, favoured malignants and was a drunkard, a swearer and a cheat.[169] It was also claimed that Edward Caple, merchant of Bristol, bribed an agent of the Committee of Sequestration not to prosecute him for delinquency.[170] As late as November 1651 the mayor and aldermen were accused of obstructing the Somerset committee, denying that it had jurisdiction in Bristol and refusing it access to the old records. The Committee for Compounding in London wrote to Bristol in February 1652 informing it that the city did come under the jurisdiction of the Somerset committee. It said that it was aware that Bristol wanted to manage its own affairs, but, it added sharply, 'We know not how far any not yet detected are concerned herein, but we believe there is a desire rather to conceal than punish offenders.'[171]

The number of Bristolians who eventually compounded was very small. It included about a dozen fairly prominent men, mostly merchants, and five or six smaller fry, one of whom alleged he had been falsely accused. Some of the accused minimised the role they had played and emphasised their subsequent loyalty. Thus William Bevan, who had been a captain in the Trained Bands, asserted that he had laid down his arms ten months before Fairfax took the city and that he had submitted, taken the National Covenant and lent money to parliament,[172] and Humphrey Hooke alleged that he had never been active against parliament.[173]

A study of the part played by Bristol in the first Civil War from 1642 to 1646 makes it clear that it was never a committed 'parliamentary' or 'royalist' city, still less a 'puritan' city. Of the two hundred or so merchants in Bristol, not more than thirty showed even minimal commitment to one side or the other, and of these about twenty were involved with the royalists.[174] The generalisation that the wealthy and the basest elements supported the king and that the 'middle rank, the true and best citizens' supported parliament cannot be substantiated. The governing body would have preferred to adopt a policy of non-involvement. When this proved impossible, it co-operated without too much fuss with whatever garrison occupied the city. Bristol was twice taken by storm, but it was not a Plymouth or a Gloucester, and the role of the citizens in the fighting was of little significance. Bristol in these years failed to play the important part that might have been expected from a large and rich port, and it had no relish for a civil war in which men were fighting for reasons which did not fill most Bristolians with any great enthusiasm. War meant the presence of the brutal and licentious soldiery, threats to life and property, taxation on an unprecedented scale, and a decline in the foreign and domestic trade on which the city depended for its wealth. In the two sieges, many men died, but few were Bristolians. Yeamans and Bowcher gave their lives for the king, and Joan Batten and Dorothy Hazzard claimed that they were prepared to 'dead the bullets' with their bodies and those of their children, but these people were not typical Bristolians, and few of their fellow citizens had the political or religous commitment which made men ready to lay down their lives for the king or for the Good Old Cause.

Notes

1. Bulstrode Whitelocke, *Memorials of the English Affairs* (4 vols. Oxford, 1853), i. p. 176.

2. Waller's letter is transcribed in F.T. Edgar, *Sir Ralph Hopton* (Oxford, 1968), p. 99.

3. For a very influential pioneer work, see B.S. Manning, 'Neutrals and Neutralism in the English Civil War 1642–1646', Oxford D.Phil., 1957. David Underdown wrote of Somerset: 'The war had been fought between two minorities, struggling in a sea of neutralism and apathy'. *Somerset in the Civil War and Interregnum* (Newton Abbot, 1973), p. 117.

4. *The Oxinden and Peyton Letters, 1642–1670*, ed. D. Gardiner (1937), p. 41.

5. See D.H. Sacks, *The Widening Gate. Bristol and the Atlantic Economy, 1450–1700* (Berkeley and Los Angeles, 1991). ED.

6. *A Complete Collection of State Trials*, ed. T.B. Howell (1817), iv. p. 229.

7. *Records Relating to the Society of Merchant Venturers of the City of Bristol in the Seventeenth Century*, ed. Patrick McGrath, Bristol Record Society, xvii, pp. xxviii–xxx.

8. The Society did, it is true, get a new Charter from the king. See p. 112.

9. Bristol Record Office: Common Council Proceedings 1627–1642 and Common Council Proceedings 1642–1649.

10. John Corbet, 'An Historicall Relation of the Military Government of Gloucester', printed in *Bibliotheca Gloucestrensis*, ed. J. Washbourn (Gloucester, 1823), Part 1, p. 14. The judgement seems to be accepted as valid by Brian Manning, *The English People and the English Revolution 1640–1649* (1976), p. 241.

11. John Latimer, *The Annals of Bristol in the Seventeenth Century* (Bristol, 1900), hereafter referred to as Latimer, *Seventeenth Century Annals*. Latimer had a very detailed knowledge of Bristol history based on a

study of original sources, but he also had a strong bias in favour of parliament and against the Stuarts.

12. *Supra*, pp. 119–20.

13. *Supra*, p. 98 ff.

14. Humphrey Hooke and Richard Long. For the wine project in which Bristol merchants were involved, see McGrath, *Records Relating to the Society of Merchant Venturers*, Bristol Record Society, xvii, pp. 221–5.

15. *Supra*, p. 117.

16. Latimer, *Seventeenth Century Annals*, pp. 150–1, gives a misleading picture of the strength of separatism.

17. *A Relation of a Short Survey of 26 Counties by a Captain, a Lieutenant and an Ancient*, ed. L.G. Wickham Legg (1904), p. 92.

18. For the Bristol petition and the king's answer, see British Library: *Thomason Tracts*, E 84131.

19. Historical MSS. Commission: *Manuscripts of the Duke of Portland*, i. p. 310.

20. *A Relation of a Short Survey of 26 Counties etc.*, pp. 91, 93–4.

21. There is a great deal of material relating to the purchase of arms and to other military preparations in the Proceedings of Common Council and in the Mayors' Audit Books in the Bristol Record Office. The payments show that the Council was aware it lived in dangerous times, but not that it was preparing to fight for king or parliament.

22. Bristol Record Office: *Common Council Proceedings 1627–1642*, f. 119. In July they decided not to send the petitions 'in regard they have bin soe long retarded'. *ibid.* 11 July 1642.

23. Latimer, *Seventeenth Century Annals*, p. 156.

24. *Ibid.*, pp. 156–7.

25. *Ibid.*, p. 156.

26. Bristol Record Office: *Common Council Proceedings 1627–1642*, 11 July 1642.

27. *Clarendon's History of the Rebellion and Civil Wars in England*, ed. W.D. Macray (6 vols., Oxford, 1888), ii. pp. 294–5. Hereafter referred to as *Clarendon's History.*

28. British Library: *Thomason Tracts*, E 83/3, pp. 1–2; Latimer, *Seventeenth Century Annals*, p. 157.

29. For developments in Somerset at this time, see David Underdown, *Somerset in the Civil War and Interregnum* (Newton Abbot, 1973), pp. 28–38; *Bellum Civile*, ed. Charles E.H. Chadwyck Healey, Somerset Record Society (1902), pp. 2–10; *Clarendon's History*, ii. pp. 290–1; F.T. Edgar, *Sir Ralph Hopton* (Oxford, 1968), pp. 34–40.

30. *Journal of the House of Lords*, v. 278–9; *A perfect relation of all the passages and proceedings of the Marquesse Hartford, the Lord Paulet, and the rest of the Cavelleers that were with them in Wels . . . as also, what helpe was sent from Bristoll to theyr ayd*, etc. 12 August 1642, p. 5. (Avon County Reference Library, Bristol).

31. It is true that both Clarendon and Hopton say that Horner and Popham had help from Bristol, but they may simply have accepted what was being spread by the other side. Neither mentions three hundred lusty horsemen.

32. Bristol Record Office: *Mayors' Audits 1640–1644*, f. 175.

33. Latimer, *Seventeenth Century Annals*, p. 159.

34. Bristol Record Office: *Common Council Proceedings 1627–1642*, 19 October 1642. It is curious

that Latimer does not mention that the city insisted that the soldiers should come in without their arms.

35. *Ibid.*, 19 October 1642. A committee was set up to consult about the reasons to be given to parliament for not lending: Latimer, *Seventeenth Century Annals*, pp. 159–60.

36. Bristol Record Office: *Common Council Proceedings 1642–1649*, 23 October 1642.

37. *Ibid.*, 5 November 1642.

38. *Ibid.*, 24 November 1642; *Mayors Audits 1640–1644*, f. 237.

39. Latimer, *Seventeenth Century Annals*, pp. 162–3.

40. *Journals of the House of Commons*, ii. p. 869, 29 November 1642.

41. Latimer, *Seventeenth Century Annals*, p. 163.

42. *Ibid.*, p. 163.

43. Avon County Reference Library, Bristol: *A Letter from Exceter . . . Also, the true Copy of a Letter sent from Bristoll, declaring the manner and means how that city was secured from the Cavaliers*, B 10568, p. 7.

44. Bristol Record Office: *Common Council Proceedings 1642–1649*, 7 December 1642.

45. Bristol Record Office: *Common Council Proceedings 1627–1642*, 7 December 1642.

46. William Barrett, *The History and Antiquities of the City of Bristol* (Bristol, 1789), p. 226.

47. Samuel Seyer, *Memoirs Historical and Topographical of Bristol* (Bristol, 1823), ii. p. 311.

48. British Library: Thomason Tracts, E 83/3, *A Declaration from the Citty of Bristoll: By the Maior, Aldermen, Sheriffes, and others of the City: Declaring their Resolution and fidelity to the Parliament and their designes: Also a Petition from M. Maioresse, M. Holworthy and 200 of the best Citizens wives in Bristoll, to the Maior and Common Councell of the City, for admitting the Parliaments Forces into their City, and many other things worthy of observation. Sent from M. John Ball in Bristoll, to M. James Nicolls, a Merchant in Fanchurch-street, London. Printed for Joseph Matthews and John Nicolls, and are to be sold in the old-baily, Decemb. 23 1642.*

49. *A letter from Exceter* etc. See n. 43.

50. Bristol Record Office: *Sessions 1634–1647*, 04446, 17 December 1642.

51. See List of conspirators printed in *The Copy of a Letter sent from Bristoll*, British Library: *Thomason Tracts*, E 93/3, p. 6.

52. *The Severall Examinations and Confessions of the Treacherous Conspirators against the Cittie of Bristoll*, British Library: *Thomason Tracts*, E 104(4).

53. Bristol Record Office: *Sessions 1634–1647*, 04446, 10 December 1642.

54. See *Clarendon's History*, iii. p. 112 for an account of how some of Fiennes' men went over to the royalists after the fall of Bristol in 1643 and led their new friends to plunder the houses of alleged supporters of parliament.

55. *Journal of the House of Lords*, v. 511, 22 December 1642. He gives Colonel Essex the credit for restoring order.

56. See pp. 110–11, 117–18.

57. A small illustration of the trouble from the soldiers is given in the *Mayors' Audits* 04026(ii)f.231: 'payde 2s 6d for a new Chamber pott for the Tolze, the other being stolen by the Souldiers'.

58. British Library: *Thomason Tracts*, E 84/31. *The Humble petition of the Citie of Bristoll for an Accommodation of Peace between His Majestie and the Honourable the High Court of Parliament etc.* Oxford, 1642.

59. *A Full Declaration of All Particulars Concerning The March of the Forces under Collonel Fiennes to Bristol*, April 1643, British Library: *Thomason Tracts*, E 97/6, p. 2.

60. There is a considerable pamphlet literature on the subject to be found in the *Thomason Tracts* in the British Library and in the excellent collection in Avon County Reference Library, Bristol. Seyer printed a number of the documents, including statements of the plotters in his *Memoirs Historical and Topographical of Bristol*, (Bristol, 1823) ii. pp. 341–400.

61. From various sources, Seyer compiled a list of over 100 conspirators. He was able to give their occupations in thirty-two cases. Seyer, *op. cit.* ii. pp. 359–62.

62. See his confession, printed in Seyer, *op. cit.* ii. p. 389.

63. *A Complete Collection of State Trials*, ed. T.B. Howell (1817), iv. p. 195: ' . . . a wicked conspiracy, plotted between divers inhabitants . . . and some of the officers of Col. Essex his regiment . . . '. See also British Library: *Thomason Tracts*, E 93/10, *An Extraordinary Deliverance* etc. which says that Colonel Essex's regiment was 'something distempered' by his dismissal.

64. Seyer, *op. cit.* ii. p. 389; *Military Memoirs of Colonel Birch*, ed. T.W. Webb, Camden Society (1873), p. 2.

65. The documents relating to the attempt to save them are in Seyer, *op. cit.* ii. pp. 377–80. The best known of the royalist pamphlets is *Two state martyrs; or, the murther of R.Y. and G.B., citizens of Bristoll, committed on them by Nathaniel Fiennes*. Typical of the pamphlets on the other side is an *An Extraordinary deliverance from a Cruell Plot and bloudy Massacre, contrived by the Malignants in Bristoll . . . related in a letter from Colonel Fines . . . and three letters more, Thomason Tracts*, E 93/10.

66. *Records of a Church of Christ in Bristol 1640–1687*, ed. Roger Hayden, Bristol Record Society, xxvii, p. 293.

67. Avon County Reference Library, Bristol: *A Relation Made in the House of Commons, by N.F.* etc., 5 August 1643 (ref: 10576, p. 25). He said that since the stop of trade and the withdrawal of their estates from Bristol by many malignants, Bristol was not nearly as rich as some conceived, and he had not made £3,000 out of the plotters, 'there being never a rich man among them'.

68. *Clarendon's History*, iii. p. 103.

69. Printed as 'The Siege and Capture of Bristol by the Royalist Forces in 1643,' ed. C.H. Firth and J.H. Leslie, *Journal of the Society of Army Historical Research*, iv. no. 15, 1925. This is referred to hereafter as De Gomme. His account is also printed with modern spelling in Eliot Warburton, *Memoirs of Prince Rupert and the Cavaliers* (3 vols., 1849), ii. pp. 236–264.

70. *Clarendon's History*, iii. pp. 108–9; *'Colonel Slingsby's Relation'* printed in Somerset Record Society, xviii (1902), p. 92.

71. *Supra*, p. 105.

72. British Library: *Thomason Tracts*, E 64/12, p. 6: *A Relation Made in the House of Commons by Col. Nathaniel Fiennes, Concerning the Surrender of the City and Castle of Bristoll*, 5 August 1643. See also *Thomason Tracts*, 97/6, p. 3, for a statement that Col. Essex refused to let the Bridge-men, that is the Roundheads, have their arms back for the defence of the city. Some of the wealthiest citizens had houses on the Bridge.

73. Avon County Reference Library, Bristol: *A True and full Relation of the prosecution . . . of N.F. late colonel and governor of the city and castle of Bristoll* by William Prynne and Clement Walker, part ii, Catalogue of Witnesses, p. 10.

74. *Ibid.*, p. 33. William Powell deposed optimistically that there could have been raised in Bristol at least six or eight thousand men fit for service.

75. *Supra*, p. 110.

76. The account that follows is based on De Gomme unless otherwise stated.

77. De Gomme, p. 183.

78. William Fitzherbert was a member of the Common Council 1632–45 and he was removed by parliament. He was sheriff 1632–3 and Treasurer of the Merchant Venturers 1638–9.

79. One of the captains in the Trained Bands. Sheriff 1644–5 and Warden of the Merchant Venturers 1644–5. Removed from the Council in 1645 and had to compound as a delinquent.

80. *Clarendon's History*, iii. p. 108.

81. For accounts of the discussion, see *Clarendon's History*, iii. pp. 108–9; *De Gomme*, p. 188; *Bellum Civile*, Somerset Record Society, xviii. p. 92.

82. This suggests that they were enthusiastic, but Clarendon indicates that the Cornishmen were dissatisfied with the particularly difficult task assigned to them.

83. De Gomme, p. 191.

84. *Ibid.*, pp. 191–2.

85. *A True and full Relation of the prosecution of N.F.* etc. by William Prynne and Clement Waker, part ii, Catalogue of Witnesses, p. 20. See also pp. 27–8.

86. *A Complete Collection of State Trials*, ed. T.B. Howell, iv. p. 200.

87. British Library: *Thomason Tracts*, E 64/12, *A Relation made in the House of Commons by Colonel Nathaniel Fiennes*, August 1643.

88. De Gomme, pp. 192–3.

89. *Military Memoirs of Colonel John Birch*, ed. T.W. Webb, Camden Society (1873), p. 3.

90. *A Complete Collection of State Trials*, ed. T.B. Howell, iv. p. 222. James Coles deposed that the attackers 'thought they should have been shut in and the breach made good against them' (*A True and full Relation of the prosecution . . . of N.F.* etc., p. 30).

91. *A Complete Collection of State Trials*, ed. T.B. Howell, iv. p. 222; *Thomason Tracts,* E 64/12. p. 7.

92. De Gomme, p. 193. At the Court Martial, two witnesses said that the Essex Fort commanded the place where the enemy entered and 'if manned with twenty or thirty Musketeers, would easily have kept out all the enemy partee . . . ' (*A True and Full Relation of the prosecution . . . of N.F.* etc., p. 9).

93. St. Augustine the Less (now demolished) and the present Lord Mayor's Chapel.

94. *A True and full Relation of the prosecution . . . of N.F.* etc., pp. 15, 17, 24–7, 31, 33–4.

95. J.F. Nicholls and John Taylor, *Bristol Past and Present* (Bristol, 1881), i. p. 64.

96. The total casualties in the attack were put between 1,000 and 1,400.

97. *Military Memoirs of the Civil War: Richard Atkyns*, ed. Peter Young (1967), p. 28. See also *Bellum Civile*, Somerset Record Society, xviii, pp. 92–4, and *Clarendon's History*, iii. p. 103.

98. Latimer, *Seventeenth Century Annals*, p. 179. He seems to suggest that the Frome Gate was stormed, but there is no evidence of this.

99. *A True and full Relation of the prosecution . . of N.F.*, part ii. pp. 25–7.

100. *Ibid.*, pp. 31–2.

101. *Ibid.*, pp. 32–3.

102. *A Complete Collection of State Trials*, ed. T.B. Howell, iv. p. 200.

103. For Dorothy Hazzard, see *Records of a Church of Christ in Bristol 1640–1687*, ed. Roger Hayden, Bristol Record Society, 1974, pp. 12, 13, 18, 19, 154, 293.

104. Avon County Reference Library, Bristol: *A Check to the Checker of Britannicus*, p. 10.

105. *Clarendon's History*, iii. p. 105.

106. For his defence, see *A Complete Collection of State Trials*, ed. T.B. Howell, iv. p. 194; and *Thomason Tracts*, E 64/12.

107. De Gomme, p. 198; *Clarendon's History*, iil. p. 111.

108. *Military Memoirs of the Civil War: Richard Atkyns*, ed. Peter Young, p. 29.

109. For a propaganda piece on the horrors, see Avon County Reference Library, Bristol, B 10561, *The Tragedy of the Kings Armies Fidelity since their entry into Bristol, Together with the too late repentance of the Inhabitants Wherin is set forth the Extreme Plunderings, Rapes, Murthers and other Villanies*, London 1643.

110. According to *A True Relation of the taking of Bristoll (Thomason Tracts*, E6669, f.8(19)) Bristol paid £14,000 to save itself from plunder. Two documents relating to taxation and the royalist military establishment in Bristol were printed by Edmund Turnor in *Archaeologia*, xiv, 1803, pp. 121–8.

111. Luke Hodges and Richard Vickris. See A.B. Beaven, *Bristol Lists*, Bristol, 1899, pp. 198, 295, 311.

112. For the Pardon, see *Bristol Charters 1509–1899*, ed. R.C. Latham, Bristol Record Society, xii, pp. 63–5, 166–75. Latham thinks that only three of those excepted from the pardon were Bristolians – Thomas and Robert Hippisley and Robert Baugh.

113. J. Latimer, *The History of the Society of Merchant Venturers of the City of Bristol* (1903), pp. 106–7; Patrick McGrath, *Records relating to the Society of Merchant Venturers*, Bristol Record Society, xvii, 1952, p. xx.

114. L.V. Grinsell, *The Bristoll Mint* (Bristol, 1972), pp. 17–18.

115. Latimer, *Seventeenth Century Annals*, pp. 188–9.

116. *Supra*, p. 120.

117. *The History of the Rebellion and Civil Wars in England* (Oxford, 1843), p. 544. Seyer, *Memoirs Historical and Topographical of Bristol*, ii. p. 428, says two or three of the conspirators fled; Latimer, *Seventeenth Century Annals*, p. 195.

118. *The Writings and Speeches of Oliver Cromwell* by W.C. Abbott (Cambridge, Mass., 1937), 4 vols., i. p. 374, Cromwell to Fairfax, 14 September 1645. Hereafter referred to as Abbott, *Cromwell*. Joshua Sprigg, *Anglia Rediviva*. Oxford, 1854, pp. 97–8. Hereafter referred to as Sprigg.

119. Sprigg, pp. 98, 122. He says that when they came to Bristol people were dying in the city at the rate of a hundred a week and that the sickness was also in the towns and villages where they quartered their men, but only one man died of the plague. See also *Calendar of State Papers Domestic, 1643–1645*, pp. 493, 495.

120. *A Declaration of his Highnesse Prince Rupert with A Narrative of the state and condition of the City and Garrison of Bristol, when his Highness Prince Rupert came thither*, London, 1645, pp. 7, 8. This is also printed in Eliot Warburton, *Memoirs of Prince Rupert and the Cavaliers*, iii. pp. 168–9.

121. Sprigg, p. 97, says he could have put 3,000 men in the field and still have enough left to garrison Bristol. Latimer says his effective strength was nearly 4,000, exclusive of auxiliaries, but Rupert claimed that he had no more than 2,300.

122. Latimer, *Seventeenth Century Annals*, p. 197. Rupert and his officers maintained that the defences were still very defective. Eliot Warburton, *Memoirs of Prince Rupert and the Cavaliers*, iii. pp. 168–70.

123. Warburton, *op. cit.* iii. p. 168. In Rupert's *Declaration* it was claimed that 'upon a strict survey'

there were found to be 2,500 families in the city, of whom 1,500 could not maintain themselves.

124. *Calendar of State Papers Domestic 1644–1645*, p. 519, 24 May 1645.

125. Abbott, *Cromwell*, i. p. 375. Cromwell added 'but that did not answer expectation . . . '.

126. Eliot Warburton, *op. cit.*, iii. pp. 171–2.

127. There are a number of payments to Colonel Lathom for training the men recorded in the Mayors' Audits.

128. Rupert's *Declaration*, p. 6.

129. *Common Council Proceedings 1642–1649*, 3 September 1645.

130. Rupert's *Declaration*, p. 6.

131. Abbott, *Cromwell*, i. p. 374.

132. *Ibid.*, i. p. 374; Sprigg, p. 99.

133. Abbott, *Cromwell*, i. p. 374.

134. *Ibid.*, i. p. 375.

135. Sprigg, pp. 101–2.

136. *Ibid.*, p. 136.

137. *Ibid.*, p. 101.

138. *Ibid.*, pp. 103–4.

139. *Ibid.*, p. 104.

140. *Ibid.*, p. 104; Abbott, *Cromwell*, i. p. 375.

141. Sprigg, p. 104; Abbott, *Cromwell*, i. p. 375. Enthusiasm may have been increased by the fact that the men were paid 6s. per head which the General had promised them for their service at Bridgwater.

142. The plan is given in detail in Sprigg, pp. 104–6. It was subject to amendment. No attempt was apparently made at Washington's Breach.

143. Abbott, *Cromwell*, i. p. 375.

144. Sprigg, p. 108.

145. *Ibid.*, p. 110.

146. For the negotiations and the terms which Rupert would accept, see Sprigg, pp. 105–15.

147. Sprigg, p. 115.

148. Abbott, *Cromwell*, i. p. 375.

149. Sprigg, pp. 116–17.

150. Abbott, *Cromwell*, i. p. 375. Cromwell says Hardress Waller and Jackson entered 'on the other side of Lawford's Gate, towards Avon River'. Sprigg says they entered between Lawford's Gate and the River Frome. Either Cromwell or Sprigg confused the Avon with the Frome.

151. Abbott, *Cromwell*, i. p. 376; Sprigg, pp. 116–17.

152. Abbott, *Cromwell*, i. p. 376; Sprigg, p. 117.

153. Sprigg, pp. 117–18.

154. Abbott, *Cromwell*, i. p. 376; Sprigg, p. 118.

155. Sprigg, p. 118.

156. Abbott, *Cromwell*, i. pp. 376–7; Sprigg, pp. 118–19.

157. Sprigg, pp. 119–22 gives the terms of surrender and describes Rupert's march out of Bristol. See also Morrah, *Prince Rupert of the Rhine*, pp. 195–6.

158. Abbott, *Cromwell*, i. p. 377. Fairfax's letter to his father about the taking of Bristol, dated 12 September 1645, is in Bristol Record Office 8029(9).

159. Warburton, *Memoirs of Prince Rupert and the Cavaliers*, iii. p. 185. The original pass granted by the king is in Bristol Record Office, 8029(8).

160. See note 120.

161. Morrah, *Prince Rupert of the Rhine*, pp. 203–4.

162. *Ibid.*, p. 197. There is a good discussion in Ashley, *Rupert of the Rhine* (1976), pp. 100–7. See also Eliot Warburton, *op. cit.* iii. p. 184.

163. There are a number of short studies of sieges in P. Young and W. Emberton, *Sieges of the Great Civil War 1642–1646* (1979). For Gloucester, see J.R.S. Whiting, *Gloucester Besieges* (Gloucester, 1975). Obviously, many more studies could be added to the list.

164. Firth and Rait, *Acts and Ordinances of the Interregnum*, i. pp. 797–8, 28 October 1645. The men removed were: Francis Creswicke (mayor), Aldermen Humphrey Hooke, Richard Long, Ezekiel Wallis, Alexander James, Thomas Colston, councillors William Fitzherbert, Henry Creswicke, William Colston, Nathaniel Cale, William Bevan, Richard Gregson, Giles Elbridge (A.B. Bevan, *Bristol Lists*, p. 199).

165. *Acts and Ordinances of the Interregnum*, i. p. 801.

166. *The Calendar of the Proceedings of the Committee for Compounding 1643–1660*, ed. H.M. Everett Green (1892), 5 vols. Henceforth referred to as *Cal. Committee for Compounding*.

167. *Cal. Committee for Compounding*, Part i. p. 453, 24 June 1651.

168. *Ibid.*, Part i, p. 351, 6 November 1650.

169. *Ibid.*, Part i. p. 453, 24 June 1651.

170. *Ibid.*, Part i. p. 227, 17 May 1650.

171. *Ibid.*, Part i. pp. 511, 545.

172. *Ibid.*, Part ii. p. 1556, 3 November 1646.

173. *Ibid.*, Part ii. p. 1629. Latimer, *Seventeenth Century Annals*, pp. 202–3, states that Hooke did 'something considerable' in support of the Puritans, and Sir Thomas Fairfax undertook that he would not suffer. When Hooke was in trouble for delinquency in 1650, Cromwell stayed proceedings against him and said what he had done was 'for many reasons desired to be concealed'. I have not been able to trace the reference in the Cromwell papers.

174. This is based on a study of the merchants in the Civil War which I have not yet published.

6

'WHOLE STREETS CONVERTED TO ASHES': PROPERTY DESTRUCTION IN EXETER DURING THE ENGLISH CIVIL WAR

M.J. Stoyle

Few historians would now regard the English Civil War as a conflict which was 'eminently humane'.[1] Ever since the publication of Ian Roy's seminal article, 'England Turn'd Germany', in 1978, awareness of the extent to which the Civil War impinged on the day-to-day life of the civilian population has been steadily growing.[2] Scholarly interest in this subject has grown particularly fast over the last few years, and as a result the devastating effects of wartime taxation, requisitioning, plundering, destruction and disease are at last receiving the attention which they deserve.[3] 'Impact studies' are still very much in their infancy, however, and a great deal remains to be discovered, not least about the war's long-term effects.

One field in which particularly interesting advances have recently been made is that of property destruction. The work of Stephen Porter has demonstrated that urban communities right across England suffered extensive physical damage during 1642–46.[4] Archaeological excavation has confirmed and amplified this overall picture. Digs at Chester, Exeter and Gloucester have revealed considerable evidence of wartime destruction, and these discoveries have in turn spurred further writing and research.[5] At Exeter, documentary research into wartime demolition has been going on for some years now, under the auspices of Exeter Museum's Archaeological Field Unit.[6] As a result, an unusually detailed picture of the Civil War's physical impact upon a single English city has emerged. The purpose of this paper is to communicate the Exeter findings to a wider historical audience; to explain where, when and why the worst devastation occurred and to show what happened to the luckless residents of the city suburbs in the immediate aftermath of the Civil War.

Before examining the war's events in detail, something should be said about the civic community upon which the disasters of the 1640s fell. Early modern Exeter was the regional capital of south-west England, the very 'centre, heart and head of the West' according to one proud contemporary.[7] And as the city was to the region, so the ancient medieval core of Exeter was to the city itself. Encircled by the old town walls, the fourteen wholly intra-mural parishes of this district housed the majority of the better-off inhabitants, including almost all the civic elite. Outside the city walls lay the sprawling suburbs, inhabited almost exclusively by the poor and the 'middling sort'.[8] By 1640 these suburban areas had become extremely large and extensive.

To the north of the city lay the parish of St Davids (see map, p. 131). Most of the people who lived here worked in the cloth trade, or in industry. To the east lay St Sidwells, the largest and most unruly of the suburban parishes. There were over 1,500 people living here in 1642.[9] Many of them were very poor, and the parish was notorious for riots and popular disturbances. The parishioners had a strong sense of parochial identity and were collectively known as the 'Grecians'.[10] The southernmost of the city suburbs was that of Holy Trinity. Unlike St Davids and St Sidwells, Trinity contained an intra-mural as well as an extra-mural area. Needless to say, it was in the former district that the most prosperous parishioners tended to dwell. Trinity parish without the walls was as poverty-stricken as St Sidwells.[11] The fourth suburban area lay on the western side of Exeter, between the city and the River Exe. Two crowded and populous little parishes stood here, St Edmonds and St Mary Steps. The west quarter was one of Exeter's most heavily industrialised areas; the chief trade being that of cloth-making. During the 1660s, as in later centuries, the west quarter was considered to be a rough, tough and dangerous area. In the mid 1650s the inhabitants of St Edmonds and St Mary Steps were described as 'the most ignorant and profane' people in Exeter.[12] Like the people of St Sidwells the residents of the west quarter possessed their own nickname, being popularly referred to as 'the Algerines'.[13]

Across the River Exe lay St Thomas. Although outside the city boundaries and therefore not an Exeter parish in the strictest sense, St Thomas was integral to the local economy. Many of its houses were owned by rich Exeter citizens and the links between the city and the parish were extremely strong. For all practical purposes, then, St Thomas can be classed as a suburb of Exeter. This parish too was a large one. During the 1650s, it was claimed that some 2,000 people dwelt here.[14] This was almost certainly an exaggeration, but we need not doubt that the population of St Thomas was very considerable. All in all, there were probably around half as many people living in the suburbs of Exeter in 1642 as dwelt within the city proper, that is to say as dwelt within the city walls.[15]

So much for the physical setting. What of the political background? On the eve of the Civil War, Exeter was a deeply divided city. That this was so was chiefly because of religious differences. From around 1610 onwards, the city's governing body, the Chamber or 'Council of Twenty Four', had been dominated by a powerful puritan faction. This group was led by Ignatius Jurdain, the 'arch puritan of the west'.[16] Jurdain's religious beliefs can only be described as extreme. Whilst representing Exeter in Parliament, he introduced a bill demanding that adultery should be made punishable by death – and was angered when other MPs declined to support the motion.[17] On this particular occasion Jurdain's

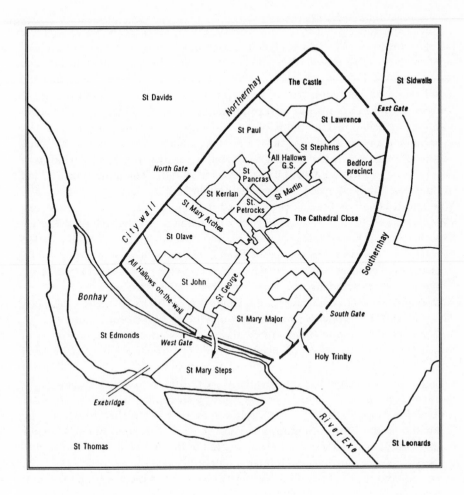

desire to regulate the moral behaviour of his fellow men and women was thwarted. But in his attempts to push through a far-reaching moral reformation at the local level, Jurdain achieved much more success. During the 1620s and '30s he and his followers strove to turn Exeter into a 'godly city upon a hill', a new Jerusalem, free from drunkards, swearers, revellers, fornicators, and profaners of the sabbath.[18] Those who were found guilty of such offences were strictly punished, and there can be little doubt that, under Jurdain, Exeter became a quieter, less turbulent and more strictly regulated place than ever before. Whether it became a more pleasant place to live in is another matter.

There were undoubtedly many local people who sympathised with Jurdain. Had this not been so, his campaign for moral reformation could hardly have achieved the success which it did. Yet there were also many who hated the puritans and resented the loss of their accustomed sports and pastimes. There were many to echo the words of the Exeter man who spat out that 'all such puritan rogues that come to sermons be as bad as the divell . . . and that the devill might as well come out of hell and be saved . . . as some of them'.[19] Resistance to the puritans was strongest amongst the city's religious conservatives – and the cathedral was the centre of opposition to the puritan regime.

Important though the conservative and anti-puritan elements were in Exeter, it was the puritans who held the upper hand, and it was they who decided which way the city would go when England began to divide in 1642. The terms 'Puritan' and 'Roundhead' were regarded as virtually interchangeable during the Great Civil War, and it comes as little surprise to find that the puritan faction on the city Chamber was determined to secure Exeter for Parliament.[20] By August 1642 they had effectively achieved this goal.[21] At the time the councillors undoubtedly felt themselves to have won a great victory. Exeter, they thought, was on the verge of a glorious era of godly rule. Could they have foreseen what the city would look like in four years time, their feelings might well have been rather different.

During August–December 1642, the Chamber took stock of Exeter's defences. The city walls were repaired, companies of soldiers raised and cannon bought and mounted.[22] Despite such activity, there is no sign that any demolition of property occurred in 1642. All this was to change at the beginning of the next year. On New Year's Day 1643 Exeter was menaced by a large force of Royalist soldiers, who made a violent attack upon Cowley Bridge, to the north of the city. Fortunately for Exeter's defenders the Royalists were repulsed, and four days later a powerful force of Parliamentary soldiers marched into the city under the command of the Earl of Stamford.[23] The events of 1–5 January led to major changes taking place at Exeter. To begin with, the Royalist attack had shown that the city's defences were woefully inadequate and would have to be improved. More importantly, the arrival of Stamford's soldiers and the Earl's appointment as governor of Exeter meant that the citizens were no longer in control of their own destinies. Henceforth, the civic dignitaries were to have less and less say in local affairs, as a succession of military commanders took ever more ruthless decisions concerning the upkeep and extension of the city defences.

The first signs of this new order were not long in coming. On 23 January a detailed set of instructions was issued, setting forth how the city defences were to be improved. Included amongst these directives was the order that 'the dikes about the city be made deeper and more falling . . . and the walls and houses removed'.[24] The 'dikes' referred to were the ancient medieval ditches which had once served to protect the city. Over the years, these had become silted up and house and gardens had been built upon them. Now the dwellings would have to be swept away. As 1643 went on, more destruction occurred. The public gardens which had been laid out in Northernhay just a few years before the war were dug up and destroyed, and fortifications built in their place.[25] In addition a systematic assault was launched upon Exeter's trees. Not only was wood needed for the fortifications but it was also feared that the trees might provide cover for future attackers. Accordingly, all the trees in Southernhay and many of those in the Bonhay were felled and brought into the city. The ancient elms in Northernhay suffered a similar fate. A wood belonging to the Dean and Chapter in St Sidwells was completely destroyed, as was a stand of 500 trees in St Leonard's parish. Orchards, both within and without the city walls, were savagely cut back.[26]

By early 1643 Exeter was already beginning to assume an aspect very different from that of its pre-war self – and worse was to come following the defeat of the Parliamentary army at Stratton in Cornwall. As the victorious Royalist forces advanced across Devon during May, the Exeter Roundheads launched themselves into a new and ambitious defensive project. Simply put, this involved the construction of a deep trench around the entire southern and eastern side of the city, the area which was most vulnerable to attack. This trench would act as the defenders' front line, as a forward position in advance of the already deepened city ditch. Needless to say, the construction of the trench caused a great deal of destruction in the city suburbs. St Sidwells suffered particularly badly. Here, Mr Hurst's Almshouses, the White Swan Inn and many houses outside Eastgate were laid waste. Properties belonging to the Dean and Chapter, said to be worth over £110 per annum in rents alone, were also pulled down, as was St Sidwells Guildhall.[27] In Holy Trinity parish the damage was much less great. Most of the houses here were included within the defensive line and thus preserved from destruction.

The very different treatment accorded the two suburbs partly reflected the fact that it was the eastern side of the city which was most vulnerable to attack. Yet the pre-war rivalry between the city and the cathedral may also have been significant. Much of St Sidwells belonged to the Dean and Chapter and therefore lay outside the city's jurisdiction. As a result the puritan group which had dominated Exeter before the war had been unable to impose godly discipline upon the inhabitants. In 1624 a city constable exclaimed that 'everyone about Eastgate are rogues, knaves and whores', whilst a few years earlier it was claimed that there was 'not one honest woman in all Paris Street'.[28] It is easy to appreciate why the puritan/Parliamentarians who ruled Exeter in 1643 should have seen the poor, unregenerate and Chapter-dominated parish of St Sidwells as much more expendable than the relatively well-governed suburb of Trinity.

The new defences were constructed only just in time. By early June Royalist forces had begun to move in close to the city, and a few days later they launched a major assault, capturing St Anne's Chapel at the far end of Sidwell Street and part of the 'south subburbs'.[29] After this promising start, the Royalists found they could make no further headway, so, around the beginning of July, they abandoned their initial positions and occupied St Thomas instead. From here the King's men directed a galling fire upon the city, damaging many houses in the western suburbs. Mr John Reed's house near West Gate was later noted to have suffered greatly 'by reason of the battering thereof by shooting etc'.[30] Some buildings had to be completely destroyed as a result of the bombardment. On 15 July a resident of St Mary Steps parish was paid for his services in 'drawing downe of thetcht houses that endangered ye cittie'. More thatched houses were demolished in the following week.[31] Presumably the defenders feared that the Royalists might try to set the roofs of these buildings alight with red-hot shot or fire arrows, in the hope of starting a general conflagration within the city.[32] Eventually the Royalist bombardment became too much for the defenders to bear and on 31 July an 'extraordinary sally' was launched over Exe Bridge by the Parliamentarians. The aim of this operation was to destroy the buildings which the Royalists were occupying in St Thomas and from which they were directing such a punishing fire upon the city. All the evidence suggests that the Parliamentarian sortie was successful. The West Indies Inn, many houses in Cowick Street and the mansion house at Hays Barton all seem to have been burnt down and destroyed on this occasion.[33]

As time went on, the besiegers were reinforced and pressure on Exeter built up. Still further destruction of property occurred as a result. In July the Parliamentarians were forced to abandon the Magdalen Hospital which they had been holding as a forward position. During the course of this evacuation, the buildings themselves were burnt down. By mid-August increasing Royalist pressure from St Thomas had compelled the defenders to demolish the central spans of Exe Bridge in order to prevent the structure from being captured.[34] In St David's, meanwhile, hedge banks were levelled for fear that they would provide the advancing Royalists with cover.[35]

Towards the end of August a second Royalist army arrived to join the besiegers, under the command of Prince Maurice, Prince Rupert's younger brother. A few days later the final attack was launched upon the city. Maurice had quickly perceived that the weakest point of the defences lay to the south of Exeter, where the line of the fortifications had been extended to include the suburb of Trinity, and it was here that he decided to strike. Early on 4 September, 1,000 Royalist soldiers launched themselves upon the 'line of communication' which connected the Parliamentary outworks to the south of the city with Exeter's inner defences. The assault was successful and the line taken. As a result, 400 Parliamentarian soldiers were cut off and captured. The Royalists soon improved their position still further, by turning the captured cannon in the outworks upon the city itself.[36] During this attack the Royalists also showered Exeter with 'granadoes' or mortar shells, setting light to 'a good part of the suburbs' and shaking the town walls in several places.[37]

The Parliamentarians' position was now quite hopeless. They had no hope of relief, their supplies were running out, and many of their best men had been captured. Not only this, the Royalists had now lodged themselves so close to the city walls that any further assault was bound to succeed. Accordingly negotiations for a surrender were entered into, and on 6 September the Parliamentarians marched out, leaving the inhabitants to face two and a half years of Royalist occupation under Sir John Berkeley, the new Governor.[38] By the end of this first siege a great deal of damage had already been inflicted upon Exeter. The worst destruction had occurred in St Sidwells and St Thomas, where the buildings nearest to the city had been completely razed to the ground. In Trinity and St David's, however, the damage had been much less great. The western suburbs, too, had so far escaped relatively unscathed, apart from those houses which had been damaged by Royalist bombardment from St Thomas.

Following their capture of the city the Royalists carried out some vital repairs. In September 1643 Exebridge was ordered to be 'forthwith repaired in the defects thereof, especiallye in that parte which was of late pulled downe for the supposed safetye of this cittie in the tyme of the late siege'.[39] In addition, the 'waterpipes without Eastgate', which had once carried the city's water supply, but had been 'of late broken up and wasted by his Majesties forces lying thereabouts' were ordered to be repaired.[40] The most important project undertaken during the Royalist occupation was the repair of the shattered town defences. During 1643/44 almost £400 – an enormous sum – was spent on repairing the city walls in Southernhay, whilst during 1644/45, over £200 was laid out on the walls to the west of the city, which had presumably been damaged by Royalist artillery fire from St Thomas during the previous siege.[41]

With Exeter safely in Royalist hands, the pace of destruction slowed down. No houses were destroyed between September 1643 and June 1645, the period during which the Royalists were generally dominant in the west of England.[42] Yet by mid-1645, the King's armies had been forced onto the defensive. Following his defeat at Naseby, Charles I had fled to Wales, leaving Parliament's New Model Army free to advance into the West Country. It was clear that the King's local strongholds were about to come under fierce attack, and Exeter's Royalist garrison made feverish efforts to strengthen their defences. Large earthen mounds or 'mounts' were built at various points along the city wall. These structures were intended to act as artillery platforms and were therefore constructed on a large scale. It is possible that some houses adjoining the walls were knocked down as a result of this work. The city's 'places of easement', or public latrines, hitherto situated at Snayle Tower, were certainly demolished during the construction of a defensive work there known as 'Mount Truck'.[43] Yet once again it was in the extra-mural parishes, rather than within the walls, that the greatest devastation occurred.

This new destruction was occasioned partly by the Royalists' construction of bigger and better defensive outworks. Not only was the system of ditches and trenches which surrounded the city extended at this time, but four completely new forts were also built. Unfortunately, little is known about these structures. The most important was built to the south of the city at Mount Radford. The second was constructed on St David's Down, near the church. The third fort stood in Cowick Street, St Thomas, and was built around the prison or 'Sheriff's Ward' there.[44] (This work was referred to as 'Hunks Fort' and was probably named after Sir Fulk Hunks, an officer in the Royalist garrison).[45] The fourth major fort was situated on the eastern side of the city; perhaps at St Anne's chapel, more likely near St Sidwell's church. Other minor outworks are also known to have been built around the city at this time. One was erected in the Bonhay, for example.[46]

The damage caused by the construction of these works was not nearly as limited as one might think. Not only was everything standing on the actual site of the forts demolished, but extensive fields of fire had to be cleared as well. It should be remembered that the works were built of earth, which had to be bonded together with quantities of turf. Wherever a fort or defensive line was built, therefore, the ground for some distance round about had to be stripped of its turf and topsoil. This process could be extremely damaging. After the war, one man complained that some 20 acres of his land had been 'spended up upon the very gravill' by these means. As a result, the land had fallen in value 'in judgement of most men, att least £100'.[47]

Throughout the summer of 1645 the Royalists continued to labour away at Exeter's defences. During this period they concentrated on the construction of works, rather than the demolition of houses, presumably because they were keen to hold off the evil day of destruction for as long as possible. Yet by September 1645 news-pamphlets were reporting that 'they burn down houses neer Exeter', and once the Parliamentary army had marched into Devon, full-scale demolition began to occur.[48] On 21 October the Royalist General Goring oversaw the destruction of a large part of St Sidwells and St Thomas, 'pulling downe and burning both the townes'.[49] Soon afterwards, the Royalists reportedly 'burnt downe the greatest part of four parishes', by which St Sidwells, St Thomas, St Davids and St Edmunds were probably meant.[50]

Trinity's turn came soon afterwards. On 26 October the New Model Army marched to Topsham, just south of Exeter. According to the Parliamentarian chaplain Joshua Sprigg this move prompted the Royalists to fire 'the houses in the suburbs of Excester, to the number of about 80, which sent many out of the city, complaining of the cruelty of the enemy'.[51] Sprigg's claim is backed by the London pamphleteers. One diurnalist commented that 'the Governor [of Exeter] continues his cruelty. He hath anew caused 80 houses to be burnt down in the suburbs, which were left, and would not suffer the inhabitants to come into the city, but forced them to seek harbour abroad'.[52] Another lamented that 'Jack Berkley . . . makes fuell of the inhabitant's houses, converting whole streets into ashes . . . [and] turning out the people to the mercy of the besiegers'.[53] Recent archaeological excavations have confirmed the truth of these reports, revealing Civil War destruction-layers in St Sidwells, St Thomas, St Davids and Holy Trinity parishes.[54]

By November 1645 the demolition seems to have stopped. But this was only because there was nothing left to destroy. The destruction had been immense and the four extra-mural areas were now quite simply devastated. St Sidwells and St Davids had been flattened. There is no evidence that any houses close to the city in these two parishes had survived. Every dwelling house in St Sidwells, from Eastgate to St Anne's Chapel (a distance of over one third of a mile) had been razed to the ground.[55] In St Thomas, too, all the houses between Exebridge and the hospital had been 'utterly ruined by fire to the undoing of many of the parishioners'.[56] Trinity parish 'without the South Gate' was 'totally demollished by fyreing & pulling down the howses'.[57] Things may have been a little better in St Edmunds and St Mary Steps. These parishes were sheltered by the river, and did not need to be secured quite so brutally. Yet even here, a great deal of damage occurred. George Leach, a brewer of St Edmonds, later deposed that his brewhouse was demolished 'and my outhouses were also puld downe, and the trees of my orchard cut up, and all the walls and mounds puld downe, being worth at least £100'.[58]

By November 1645 'Fortress Exeter' squatted, bleak and forbidding, amidst a vast circle of ashes. Berkeley's measures could hardly have been more ruthless – and they succeeded in halting the Parliamentary advance. During the winter of 1645 the New Model Army – too weak either to storm the city defences or to advance further into the west (where a large Royalist army was quartered) – settled down for a long siege of Exeter. Nearby houses were occupied and a system of counterworks erected to offset those of the Royalists. Local people were forced to provide the Parliamentarians with all sorts of supplies at this time – and were sometimes punished by marauding Royalist bands for doing so. Robert Babb, an Exminster farmer, later recalled that he had been awoken at dawn and arrested by a party of Royalist soldiers merely for 'selling of cider to the enemy'.[59] Local people also had to help the Parliamentarians to build their siege-works. Little information survives about the precise nature of these fortifications, but it is clear that they were very extensive, and that the damage which they caused to the surrounding countryside was correspondingly great. This is well illustrated by the petition of John Cupper, an Exeter merchant who owned a mansion in St Thomas. In early 1646, Cupper later recalled, 'his Excellencie Sir Thomas Fairfax . . . haveing made the dwelling house a garrison, the barnes, stables and other outhouses there were burnt by his forces, and much of the land turft for the making of fortificacons, and the orchards, gardens, hedges and inclosures in manie severall places pulled and cut downe to make avenues and fierwood, and the dwelling house much spoyled and ruined'. Cupper later estimated that the value of his property had been halved as a result of the Parliamentary visitation.[60]

The occupation of Cupper's house marked the beginning of bitter fighting in St Thomas. On 29 January Fairfax summoned Berkeley to surrender, urging him to consider the condition of Exeter's inhabitants, made 'poor and miserable . . . by [the] fireing of so many of their habitations'.[61] Berkeley, who had high hopes of relief from the Royalist forces to the west, refused to listen, prompting Fairfax to step up the pressure on the western side of the city defences. As the Roundhead troops moved closer, Berkeley decided to destroy the few building left in St Thomas that might provide them with cover. Accordingly a party of Royalist soldiers 'sallied out and fired St Thomas Church and the Lady Carewes house'.[62] (This affair can be precisely dated, for it is noted in a contemporary hand on the fly-leaf of St Thomas parish register that 'the 30 of Januari 1646 was the parish church of St Thomas burned'.)[63] The destruction of the church did not prevent Fairfax's advance. Soon afterwards Roundhead troops occupied the burnt-out shell of the building and the remains of the hospital nearby, promptly fortifying these positions with trenches and redoubts.[64] For some time after this, fighting raged back and forth between the Parliamentarians dug in around the church and the Royalists entrenched at Hunk's Fort.

Preparations for a full-scale storm of Exeter now began, but before matters could proceed to a conclusion, news arrived that the King's Western Army was advancing from Cornwall to the city's relief. Anxious to counter this threat, Fairfax marched away from Exeter with the bulk of his men. The ensuing campaign sealed the city's fate. Towards the end of March 1646, the Western Army – the King's last major field force in England – surrendered to the Parliamentarians at Truro. Exeter's defenders were now without hope of relief and during the last days of March, Parliamentarian forces advanced very close to the city defences. On 31 March Berkeley was again summoned to surrender.[65] Even now, some of the most ardent Royalists felt that the city should hold out to the last. A certain Mary Cholwill asserted 'that she had rather the Turks should come into the cittie than . . . the Parliament's forces, and that rather then they should have the said cittie, the castle and cittie should be sett on fyre'.[66] The majority of the citizens were desperate for the fighting to end, however, and the garrison had little choice but to come to terms. On 3 April Berkeley entered into negotiations and ten days later Exeter was finally surrendered to Parliament; Oliver Cromwell himself leading the first Roundhead troops to enter the city.[67] The war in the west was over.

Exeter was at peace at last. But the war's events had crippled the city, rendering between a third and a half of the inhabitants homeless. What happened to these unfortunate people? How did they survive in the immediate aftermath of the war? Where did they go to find shelter? The city itself tried to house a few. In December 1645 'an almeswoman of Palmer's Almeshowses without the South Gate was elected into one of the houses in Billiter Lane . . . her owne house being of late burnt or demolished'.[68] Few were as fortunate as this woman. Many of the civic almshouses had been destroyed, so other places had to be found to house the majority of the homeless.[69] Eventually, the main places utilised for this purpose seem to have been the old ecclesiastical properties in the Cathedral Close, and Bedford House, the town house of the Earls of Bedford.[70] Some of the homeless found other places of refuge. Soon after the war's end it was deposed that the guard-house at East Gate 'is now inhabited by such poore people as were burnte out of theire houses in the suburbs . . . by the king's army'.[71] The poor of St Thomas, meanwhile, had congregated in the remains of the Sheriff's Ward, which had survived destruction by virtue of its having been incorporated within a Royalist fort.[72]

For those unfortunates who could find no shelter within the city, there was no recourse but to make their way to the surrounding villages.[73] Some refugees from Exeter are known to have arrived in Heavitree, two miles to the east of the city, whilst others went to Upton Pyne, three miles to the north.[74] Some travelled even further afield. John Chubb, a fuller, later recalled that 'he did dwell in a house' in St Sidwells 'till that house and many others were burnt to the ground by the king's partye during the late warres', forcing Chubb and his family to seek lodgings five miles away, in Broadclyst.[75] This sudden influx of displaced persons put a great strain on the inhabitants of the villages around Exeter. The refugees had to be supported in some way, and local finances must have been stretched to the limit. The county bench was anxious to ensure that Devon would not have to continue footing the bill for the Exeter refugees, and in the immediate aftermath of the war it was ordered that those refugees 'that belong to Exeter' should be sent back to the city 'according to the law, or if they be settled for the present in any adjacent parishes . . . that it may be so done as that the . . . city shall at all times receave them agayne when they shall be sent unto them'. The point was reiterated at the Michaelmas sessions of 1646, when the bench declared that 'the poore people lately inhabiting in the citty . . . of Exeter and now residing in any parish of this county are to be returned home to the said citty and by them [i.e. the city authorities] provided for, and Devon to be spared of all charges'.[76]

The process of resettlement was slow, however. In 1647 the parishioners of Heavitree were forced to present a petition at the sessions 'for the removal of the poore of the cittie out of the parish'.[77] As late as July 1649, a considerable number of refugees were still camped out at Alphington, two miles south-west of Exeter. The parishioners informed the county bench of this sad fact, commenting that 'since the beginning of these late warrs in these western parts, many tradesmen, labourers, and other poore people to the number of sixty nine poor persons have by reason of fire and other mischiefe attending the war been inforced to forsake their own habitacions and take up their dwellings in Alphington'.[78] The sufferings inflicted on the Exeter poor as a result of the demolition were still causing concern in 1652, when the Chamber agreed that a petition should be sent to Parliament, asking 'for some relief to and for the poore of this cittye . . . [impoverished] by fyreing and other sad accidents in the time of the late warrs'.[79]

Some idea of the human suffering caused by the demolition is provided by a clutch of petitions to the city Chamber, in which those who had lost their houses begged for relief. Perhaps the most poignant of these documents is the petition of Richard Lowman of St Sidwells, husbandman, who, 'haveing formerly lost an

estate in 4 severall houses in the same parish, burnt with fyre [in] the late
unhappy warr', complained that he 'hath [now] beene necessitated to sell his
goods to maintaine him and his sick wife who, haveing nothing left to subsist, are
like to perish in want'. Other sufferers were Richard Pasmore, whose house and
garden in Southernhay 'were pulled downe and spoyled', Edith Blake, whose
house outside East Gate was 'consumed by fire in those unnatural warrs' and
Valentine Bishopp of Trinity, 'hee having two howses burn[t] in the first siege,
neere the Mawdlyne, which was his utter undoing'.[80] For all these poor, distressed
people the Civil War had proved an unmitigated disaster.

How long did it take for the damage to be repaired? The answer, it seems, is a
great many years. Fortunately, a good deal of information survives about the efforts
which the Chamber made to repair its property during the post-war period. The
Chamber had three main priorities in its campaign of reconstruction. The first of
these was to repair the public utilities; the bridges, waterpipes, almshouses and
other communal buildings. Work on such tasks began relatively quickly. In April
1647, for example, the windows and woodwork of the Guildhall 'broken upp and
spoyled by ill-affected souldiers' were replaced.[81] Later that year, the major task of
repairing the Magdalen Hospital began, with an order that the chapel there should
be re-edified.[82] By the end of the 1640s the warehouses on the Quay, previously in
sad decay, had also been patched up.[83]

During the next decade a concerted effort was made to restore the city's
almshouses to their former condition. In December 1651 Palmer's Almshouses were
ordered to be rebuilt, whilst in 1653 the Chamber began badgering a certain Mr
Speke to repair the Wynard's Hospital.[84] This work was well advanced by 1655,
during which year the Chamber also directed that the task of building houses to
replace those which had formerly stood at the Magdalen should begin.[85] The lead
pipes which had once brought water into the city, but 'had byn in the late troubles
cutt and stolne awaye' were ordered to be replaced in 1656.[86] By 1660 a great deal
of damage had been repaired, but much still remained to be done. Neither Wynards
nor the Magdalen were completed as late as 1665, whilst one or two public utilities
had to wait even longer to be restored to their pre-war condition. The 'houses of
office' at Snayle Tower were not rebuilt until 1693.[87]

The Chamber's most pressing concern during 1646–50 was undoubtedly to
ensure that the many demolished houses belonging to the city were rebuilt. These
dwellings were vital because of the revenue which they brought in in the shape of
rent. In 1647 the Council ordered that five civic dignitaries should carry out a
survey of 'the severall lands and tenements' belonging to the Chamber 'lying in
the suburbs, which have been of late burnt, wasted, or otherwise demolished'.[88]
The bounds of these ruined tenements were to be carefully set out, so that they
might be leased again in the future. Around the same time, leases of the wasted
city lands began to be made to various persons, with the proviso that the new
tenants should build new dwelling houses upon the site of the old, demolished,

buildings. At first there was a mere trickle of applicants for such leases. Yet during the early 1650s the number of applications swelled. Between 1650 and 1660 the Chamber issued no fewer than sixty-three separate leases specifying that property should be rebuilt.[89] Presumably the rebuilding of privately-owned houses followed a broadly similar pattern. Preliminary research has revealed only one privately owned house which was rebuilt during the 1640s, so it seems fair to assume that it was not until after 1650 that reconstruction of such properties got properly underway.[90]

Rebuilding of private houses, like civic properties, may well have peaked during the 1650s. Even so, scattered references make it clear that many dwellings continued to lie in ruins long after 1660. A glebe terrier for St Thomas noted in 1680 that 'here hath been no house . . . that can be rightfully claimed by the incumbent . . . ever since the last unhappy warrs, by the callamity of which the minister's house was utterly destroyed'.[91] During the 1680s and '90s many properties were erected on Exebridge, presumably to replace those which had been demolished when the bridge was pulled down in 1643.[92] And rebuilding continued until well into the eighteenth century. As late as 1713 a tenement was being built in Cowick Street, St Thomas, to replace premises 'burnt and demolished by the late civill war'.[93] It may well be, therefore, that Exeter did not return to its pre-war extent for some sixty years after the disastrous firings of the 1640s. The scars left by the Civil War were enduring ones indeed.

Notes

1. The quotation is taken from G.M. Trevelyan, *England Under the Stuarts* (1904), p. 230.

2. I. Roy, 'England Turned Germany? The Aftermath of the English Civil War in its European Context', *TRHS*, 5th Series, 28 (1978), pp. 127–44. For subsequent important studies, see D. Pennington, 'The War and the People', in J. Morrill (ed), *Reactions to the English Civil War, 1642–49* (1982), pp. 115–35; and A. Hughes, *Politics, Society and Civil War: Warwickshire 1620–60* (Cambridge, 1987).

3. In, for example, C. Carlton, *Going to the Wars: The Experience of the British Civil Wars, 1638–51*, (1992); J.A. Dils, 'Epidemics, Mortality and the Civil War in Berkshire, 1642–46', *Southern History*, 11 (1989); J. Morrill (ed), *The Impact of the English Civil War* (1991); P. Tennant, *Edgehill and Beyond: The People's War in the South Midlands, 1642–45* (Stroud, 1992); J. Wroughton, *A Community at War: The Civil War in Bath and North Somerset, 1642–50* (Bath, 1992).

4. S. Porter, 'The destruction of Urban Property in the English Civil Wars, 1642–51' (unpub. Ph.D thesis, London, 1983). See also, S. Porter, 'Property Destruction in the English Civil War', *History Today*, 36 (August 1986). I am most grateful to Stephen Porter, George Bernard and Ian Roy for their comments on a preliminary version of this paper, which was given at the Institute of Historical Research in 1991.

5. See S. Ward, *Excavations at Chester: The Civil War Siege Works, 1642–46* (Chester Museum, 1987), p. 37; M.J. Stoyle, 'St Thomas, near Exeter, during the Civil War', (Exeter Museum, Green Report 87.08, 1987), p. 2; and M. Atkin, *Gloucester and the Civil War: A City Under Siege* (Stroud, 1992), *passim*.

For a summary of recent developments in Civil War Archaeology, see P. Harrington, *Archaeology of the English Civil War* (Princes Risborough, 1992).

6. I am most grateful to Mr C.G. Henderson, the Director of Exeter Archaeological Field Unit, for his assistance and advice.

7. J. Bond, *A Doore of Hope* (1641), p. 49.

8. For a discussion of Exeter's social geography in the post-Civil War period, see W.G. Hoskins, *Industry, Trade and People in Exeter, 1688–1800* (Manchester, 1935), pp. 120–3.

9. S. Lawrence, 'A Population Study of St Sidwells Parish, Exeter, During and After the Civil War of 1642–46' (Certificate course dissertation, Exeter University, 1993) p. 3.

10. D(evon) R(ecord) O(ffice), Exeter, Book 73/15 (James White's Chronicle), p. 134. The name still lives on in the popular nickname for Exeter City Football Club, whose home ground lies in St Sidwells.

11. See Hoskins, *Industry, Trade and People*, p. 21, for evidence that this continued to be so after the Restoration.

12. S. Palmer (ed), *The Non-Conformists' Memorial*, by E. Calamy (3 vols, 1802), II, p. 37.

13. D.R.O., Book 73/15, p. 134.

14. Bod(leian Library), Oxford, J. Walker MSS, 5, f. 352.

15. In 1646 a Parliamentarian observer commented, admittedly with some exaggeration, that the pre-war suburbs had been 'as populous as the citie, and for buildings not much inferior'. See E.332 (23) (*Sir Thomas Fairfax's Further Proceedings in the West*, 22 Apr. 1646).

16. P(ublic) R(ecord) O(ffice), London, STAC 8, 161/10. I am currently preparing a paper on Jurdain's life and career.

17. The incident is described in C. Russell, *Parliaments and English Politics, 1621–29* (Oxford, 1979), p. 29.

18. See D.R.O., Exeter Quarter Sessions Order Books, 61 (1618–21); 62, (1621–30) and 63 (1630–42), *passim.*

19. Exeter Quarter Sessions Order Book, 62, f. 152r.

20. See M.J. Stoyle, 'Divisions within the Devonshire "County Community", *circa* 1600–1646', (unpub. Oxford D.Phil thesis, 1992), p. 276.

21. I hope to explore the outbreak of the Civil War in Exeter in a future paper.

22. For a full account of work on the city defences during 1642–46, see M.J. Stoyle, *Documentary Evidence of the Civil War Defences of Exeter, 1642–43* (Exeter Museum, 1992) and M.J. Stoyle, *The Civil War Defences of Exeter and the Great Parliamentary Siege of 1645–46* (Exeter Museum, 1990).

23. Stoyle, *Documentary Evidence*, pp. v–vii.

24. D.R.O., DD.36995.

25. S. Woolmer, *A Concise Account of the City of Exeter* (Exeter, 1811), p. 11.

26. D.R.O., DD.36995; Woolmer, *Concise Account*, p. 11; Bod., Hope Adds, 1133 (*Mercurius Rusticus*, 16 Mar. 1643); P.R.O., S(tate) P(apers) Domestic, 23/185/603; D.R.O., Exeter Chamber Act Book, 1/8 (1634–47), f. 143.

27. Bod., Hope Adds, 1133, (*Mercurius Rusticus*, 16 Mar. 1643). The value of the destroyed Chapter properties may well have been exaggerated, see Lawrence, dissertation, p. 3.

28. Exeter Quarter Sessions Order Book, 62, f. 218r; and Exeter Quarter Sessions Order Book, 61, f. 197.

29. J. Bamfield, *Colonel Joseph Bamfield's Apologie* (The Hague, 1685).

30. Exeter Chamber Act Book, 1/8, f. 165.

31. D.R.O., Letter Book 60F ('Exeter Siege Accounts'), f. 41r.

32. Fire arrows are known to have been employed for this purpose at Lyme in 1644, see G. Chapman, *The Siege of Lyme Regis* (Lyme Regis, 1982), pp. 37–8.

33. See Stoyle, *Documentary Evidence*, pp. xi–xii.

34. *Ibid.*, pp. xii–xiii.

35. D.R.O., Letter Book 60F, f. 43.

36. Bamfield, *Apologie*.

37. Bod., 4.M.68.Art (*Mercurius Aulicus*, 3–10 Sept. 1643).

38. *Ibid.*

39. Exeter Chamber Act Book, 1/8 f. 149r.

40. *Ibid.* See also Porter, thesis, p. 165.

41. See D.R.O., Exeter Receivers' Books, 1643/44 and 1644/45.

42. The temporary alarm caused by Essex's expedition to the West in the summer of 1644 did not result in the demolition of any houses at Exeter.

43. For the destruction of the 'houses of office', see D.R.O., D1/24/120A.

44. For the surrender of 'the ward in St Thomas parish', see W(est) C(ountry) S(tudies) L(ibrary), Exeter, SB/Exe/1646/Art.

45. For Hunks, see E.327 (25) (*The Moderate Intelligencer*, 5–12 Mar. 1646). His career is summarised in P. Newman, *Royalist Officers in England and Wales: A Biographical Dictionary* (1981), p. 205.

46. See, for example, Exeter Chamber Act Book, 1/8, f. 166.

47. P.R.O., S.P. 23/184/905.

48. E.262 (42) (*Perfect Occurrences of Parliament*, 8–15 Aug. 1645); and B(ritish) L(ibrary), Burney Collection, *The Moderate Intelligencer*, 4–11 Sept. 1645.

49. E.266 (10) (*Perfect Occurrences of Parliament*, 24–31 Oct. 1645).

50. B.L., Burney, *A Perfect Diurnal*, 27 Oct. to 3 Nov. 1645.

51. J. Sprigg, *Anglia Rediviva: England's Recovery* (1647, reprinted Oxford, 1854), p. 161.

52. B.L., Burney, *The Moderate Intelligencer*, 30 Oct. to 6 Nov. 1645. See also E.308 (25), (*The True Informer*, 1–8 Nov. 1645); and E.309 (2) (*The City Scout*, 4–11 Nov. 1645).

53. B.L., Burney, *Mercurius Brittanicus*, 3–10 Nov 1645.

54. For example, during the excavations at Exe Street (1985/86) and South Gate (1988).

55. E.266 (10) (*Perfect Occurrences of Parliament*, 24–31 Oct. 1645).

56. *Ibid.*; and J. Walker MSS, 5, f. 352.

57. J. Walker MSS, 4, f. 300.

58. P.R.O., S.P. 23/183/285.

59. P.R.O., S.P. 19/157/89.

60. P.R.O., S.P. 23/184/409.

61. E.320 (22) (*Mercurius Veridicus*, 25 Jan. to 1 Feb. 1646).

62. E.322 (8) (*The Kingdom's Weekly Intelligencer*, 3–12 Feb. 1646); see also E.322 (7), (*The Moderate Messenger*, 3–10 Feb. 1646); and Porter, thesis, p. 105.

63. W.C.S.L.; T.L. Ormiston (ed), 'St Thomas Parish Registers, 1, 1541–1691' (Devon and Cornwall Record Society, 1933), p. 185.

64. See Sprigg, *Anglia Rediviva*, pp. 313–14; B.L., Burney, *Speciall and Remarkable Passages*, 6–13 Feb. 1645; E.322 (8) (*The Kingdom's Weekly Intelligencer*, 3–12 Feb. 1645).

65. Sprigg, *Anglia Rediviva*, p. 241.

66. D.R.O., Exeter Quarter Sessions Order Book, 64 (1642–60), f. 102.

67. E.332 (23) (*Sir Thomas Fairfax's . . . Proceedings*, 22 Apr. 1645).

68. Exeter Chamber Act Book, 1/8, f. 170r.

69. For the destruction of the civic almshouses, see Porter, thesis, p. 106.

70. For the homeless in the ecclesiastical properties, see Porter, thesis, p. 201.

71. P.R.O., S.P. 23/85/173.

72. D.R.O., Devon Sessions Order Book, 8 (1640–51) (unpaginated), entry of Bapt 1646.

73. A similar flight to the country occurred during the Exeter Blitz of 1942. I owe this point to Mr D. Langdon.

74. D.R.O., St Loyes Wardens' Account Book, 1589–1651, f. 217; and Devon Sessions Order Book, 8, entry of Bapt 1647.

75. Devon Sessions Order Book, 8, entry of July 1649.

76. *Ibid.*, entries of Bapt and Mich. 1646. For comparable cases near Bridgewater, see Porter, thesis, p. 197.

77. St Loyes Wardens' Account Book, 1589–1651, f. 217.

78. Devon Sessions Order Book, 8, entry of July 1649.

79. D.R.O., Exeter Chamber Act Book, 1/9 (1647–52), f. 87.

80. D.R.O., Y5, 'Miscellaneous petitions to the Chamber for Relief', (uncalendared and unnumbered).

81. D.R.O., Exeter Receivers' Vouchers, Box 2.

82. Exeter Chamber Act Book, 1/9, f. 3.

83. Exeter Receivers' Vouchers, Box 2; and D.R.O., Exeter Receivers' Accounts, 1646–50, *passim*.

84. Exeter Chamber Act Book, 1/9, f. 85r; and D.R.O., Exeter Chamber Act Book, 1/10 (1652–63), f. 16.

85. Exeter Chamber Act Book, 1/10, f. 61r.

86. *Ibid.*, f. 73r.

87. D.R.O., D1/24/120A.

88. Exeter Chamber Act Book, 1/8, entry of 23 September 1647.

89. A total of sixty-four leases specifying rebuilding work are referred to in the Chamber Act Books for 1646–60, see Porter, thesis, p. 207. Three more stray leases are contained amongst the city deeds: D1/5/136 [1648], D1/5/4 [1655] and D1/26/11 [1655].

90. The one privately-owned house known to have been rebuilt during the 1640s belonged to Mrs Elizabeth Flay, and lay in St Sidwells. 'Burnt and utterly wasted' during the Civil War, the house had been 'built of new' by June 1649. See D.R.O., ED/FC/83.

91. D.R.O., Exeter Glebe Terriers, 1601–1745, no. 123.

92. See, for example, D.R.O., D1/25/8; D1/25/21 and D1/7/47.

93. D.R.O., D7/946,36B.

7

Epidemics, Mortality and the Civil War in Berkshire, 1642–6

Joan A. Dils

T he pattern of demographic change in England, including the incidence of abnormally high mortality, is well established, as is the realisation that the national situation might not have been reflected in every local community since it could have been the result of a 'countrywide peppering of local epidemics' or of one which was 'widely present but only within a limited region'.[1] Factors peculiar to a locality would determine whether it experienced a national mortality crisis severely or moderately, escaped it totally but saw neighbouring communities affected, or was almost unaware of its existence.

Table 1

COMPARATIVE MORTALITY IN ENGLAND AND BERKSHIRE IN CRISIS YEARS 1559–1750[2]

Year Jan–July	England Deaths per cent above average	Berks. Burials per cent above average	Jan–Dec
1558/9	124.23	66	1559
1597/8	25.61	62	1597
1625/6	42.99	38	1625
1643/4	29.27	119	1643
1657/8	42.93	30	1657
1728/9	41.23	28	1728

Between 1642 and 1646 such factors produced the highest death rates recorded in Berkshire in the early modern period whereas other southern counties report nothing out of the ordinary.[3] Along with the rest of the Thames Valley, its strategic importance to both sides in the Civil War made it the scene of extensive military activity and severe depredation, with consequent increases in civilian mortality, the extent of which is indicated by Table 1. Compared to a national death rate of nearly 30% above the norm, Berkshire's burials were more than doubled.

The survival for the period 1630–50 of 74 registers from the county's 147 parishes has made possible a detailed examination of the effect of hostilities on the civilian population though defective registration becomes a problem after mid-1644, reflecting the troubled times. An east Berkshire register records no entries between 1641 and 1653 'by reason of ye tumults and confutions of this Civil War which then raged in England'.[4] More serious is the absence of some urban registers, Faringdon, Wallingford, Wokingham, and 1 of the 3 Reading parishes. Of the extant registers only 55 were used, the rest being from extremely small parishes. Annual and monthly burial totals for the years 1631–50 were recorded from which 20-year mean averages were calculated.[5]

The severity and widespread nature of the crisis is apparent from Table 2. In the worst year, 1643, nearly 1 parish in 5 experienced very high burial rates. In Reading 2 parishes had a total of 529 deaths compared with an average of 152; the adjacent rural parish of Sonning recorded 88 (average 42) and its neighbour, Hurst, 113 (average 32). The crisis lessened in 1644 but not until the latter part of 1645 did the situation approach normality.

Table 2

EXTENT OF MORTALITY CRISIS 1642–6

CALENDAR YEAR BURIAL TOTALS

Date	Total of parishes	Total with 3 or more x average burials	Total with 2 x average burials	Total with 1½ x average burials	Total with crisis
1642	55	2	5	4	11
1643	55	10	9	12	31
1644	53*	1	9	8	18
1645	51**	0	2	7	9
1646	48***	2	1	1	4

*   no data for Abingdon St. Helens, Reading St. Giles.
**   no data for Abingdon St. Helens, Reading St. Giles and St. Lawrence or Windsor.
*** no data for Abingdon St. Helens and St. Nicholas, Reading St. Giles and St. Lawrence, and Pangbourne.

The proximity to the scene of military engagements of some of the parishes experiencing the worst mortality figures suggests the possibility of a causal link, the troops spreading to the local communities the diseases which were rampant in both armies, resulting in the high civilian mortality figures which the registers record.

The opportunities for such contact were many: soldiers in small bands or large formations frequently crossed the country which lay between the King's headquarters at Oxford and the City of London, the goal of both contestants; the Thames, which formed the county boundary to the north, was a major supply route, especially for corn, to the capital. As a result the inland ports of Reading and to a lesser extent Henley, attracted the attention of both sides. Several important roads provided direct communication between strategic areas: the east-west road from London via Maidenhead, Reading and Newbury to Bristol; the Oxford-Gloucester road through the Vale of White Horse; the north-south route from Southampton to Oxford via Newbury. In addition the corn, livestock and especially the horses of this rich agricultural area were coveted and fought over by raiding parties which attacked villages within striking distance of strategic towns and major roads.

By the beginning of 1643 the Royalists were established at Oxford, Faringdon and Reading and Parliamentary troops at Windsor, and Henley in Oxfordshire. Skirmishes and pillage occurred over a wide area, especially near Reading prior to the successful siege in April by the Earl of Essex who advanced on the town from the east while the King failed to relieve this vital strategic centre by an attack from the north. However, widespread sickness among the troops prevented Essex from exploiting his victory, forcing him to transport 100s of men to London by cart and barge, and to move others to the higher and supposedly healthier land north of the Thames. A contemporary, Dr Thomas Willis, noted that 'this disease grew so grievous that in a short time after, either side left off, and from that time for many months fought not with the enemy but with the disease'.[6]

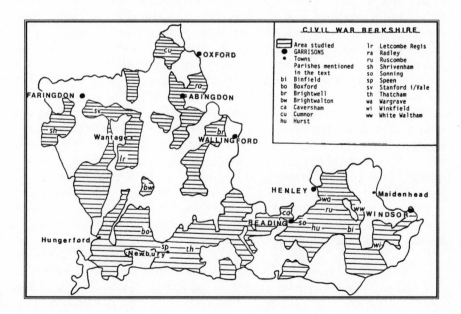

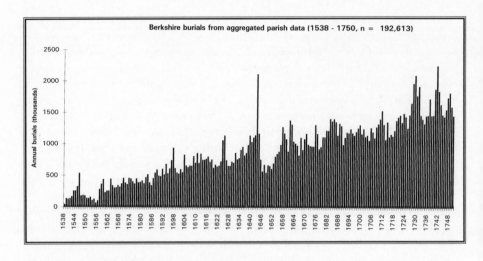

Berkshire burials from aggregated parish data (1538 - 1750, n = 192,613)

However, before the siege, epidemic disease was already present in Reading, its population swollen by the Royalist garrison, and in some of the surrounding parishes. In the first 4 months of 1643, 52 villagers were buried in Hurst and 25 in Ruscombe, compared with 32 and 7 respectively in a normal year. There the similarity ends, for in Ruscombe the worst was over by May whereas in Hurst the situation worsened in early summer with 48 deaths between May and July. In the neighbouring parishes of Sonning and Wargrave high death rates also occurred in midsummer, but continued into late autumn. There is no obvious explanation for the apparently random spread of disease in the early part of the year, since troops from Reading and elsewhere seem to have been operating over the whole area. Yet the worsening crisis following the outbreak of disease in both armies during and after the siege is very apparent. In the countryside around Reading the number of parishes 'in crisis' rose from 2 in April, to 4 in May, 6 in June and 7 in July, declining to 3 between August and September. With 70% of the parishes affected, the situation here was undoubtedly worse than elsewhere in the county. It is hard to resist the conclusion that these villages suffered from their proximity to disease-ridden armies in and around Reading. They were also at risk from the Royalists and Parliamentarians quartered successively in and around Henley. The damage inflicted on people and property here was graphically described by Bulstrode Whitelocke. Henley parish registers recorded 228 burials in 1643, more than 3 times the average, with exceptionally high figures in April, June and July, there being every likelihood that the disease was transmitted beyond the town on one of the many marauding and skirmishing expeditions.[7]

In June there were reports of 'a contagious disease' among the royalist troops who had recently taken Abingdon and Wallingford;[8] high burial rates were recorded in Abingdon's parish registers as early as January, reaching a peak in

July. It is possible that disease was spread from the town by troops travelling to and from Oxford, itself very unhealthy and a possible source of rural infection, or by marauding expeditions stealing horses. In June there was an epidemic in the largely extramural parish of St. Nicholas, Abingdon, and by July it devastated the adjacent village of Radley. To the north, Cumnor had its worst month in August.

The early autumn of 1643 saw the scene of military activity move to the south and west of the county, affecting villages there and over the border in Hampshire near Basing House. Burial rates rose in the parishes along the main road from Reading as early as July, but not until October in Newbury and later still further west. The timing of the outbreak of epidemics in this area may well have been connected with the massing of troops for the First Battle of Newbury in September, and the major exodus by both sides which followed, but nowhere was the disease so lethal or so longlived as in the Reading area.

During the last 3 months of 1643, among other military operations, the Royalists retook Reading. Further privations were caused to the local populace by the cutting down of Thames bridges, the destruction of mills, and the requisitioning of wood and wheat, especially to the east of the town. On October 20th Sir Samuel Luke reported 'At Reading there was a house yesterday shut upp in the market place of the sicknes' and on November 18th 'The plague is very much in Oxford, and also in Reading.'[9]

The evidence from the areas around Newbury, Abingdon and Reading, especially where the parish register survival is good, would seem to indicate a close causal connection between the presence of troops and high civilian mortality. A county-wide analysis of all surviving registers month by month illustrates the effects of the 1643 campaigns on Berkshire as a whole. Table 3 shows for each parish the extent to which burials for a given month exceeded the mean average for the period 1631–50.

Table 3
Monthly Burial Pattern Jan–Dec 1643

Extent of burials above average	Number of parishes 'in crisis' each month											
	J	F	M	A	M	J	J	A	S	O	N	D
7 times average	–	1	–	1	–	4	7	3	–	3	3	2
5–6 times average	2	–	1	1	4	4	4	3	3	–	2	1
3–4 times average	1	1	6	7	7	10	8	9	8	8	5	5
twice average	4	2	1	2	1	1	1	2	4	5	4	2
Total parishes 'in crisis'	7	4	8	11	12	19	20	17	15	16	14	10

Total parishes analysed: 55

There was a continuing, severe mortality crisis in the county in 1643, beginning, at the latest, in April, when 20% of the parishes surveyed had very high burial rates. At its height in July it was affecting nearly ²⁄₅ of the parishes, the majority concentrated near the strategic towns. In Reading and the surrounding area only 1 of the 12 parishes had a normal burial pattern. Within the borough the death rate was at least 3 times the average between April and July, but nearly 6 times greater in June and July in the poorer suburban parish of St. Giles where 147 deaths were recorded in just 4 months, compared with 106 in the larger and more prosperous parish of St. Lawrence. The register in Caversham, the base for the unsuccessful Royalist attempt to raise the siege, and the destination of some of Essex's sick troops, listed as many deaths in June, 15, as in a normal year, and another 11 in July.

Elsewhere small parishes near the centre of military operations, on the main roads, or in areas subject to looting, suffered for long periods, including Stanford in the Vale near the garrison at Faringdon, and Brightwell just outside that of Wallingford. Villages on the roads connecting Wallingford and Newbury with Faringdon form a consolidated area of high morality. In the east of the county where few registers have survived, Windsor suffered a lengthy and severe mortality crisis between February and July, and the total of 149 burials for the year was nearly 3 times the average; the only neighbouring parish with a register. Winkfield, experienced only a short-lived epidemic. The whole of this eastern area was less prosperous and fertile and it is possible it was more remote from military operations, holding less attractions for the armies in terms of supplies.

The following year, 1644, was marked by similar military activities. In March, in an attempt to build up his reserves, the Royalist commander of Reading requisitioned all food above 7 days' supply, while elsewhere there was pillage, especially near the major garrisons. May saw Reading and Abingdon fall to Parliament whose armies now held most of the county. A Royalist counter-attack on Abingdon in August resulted in many casualties, 16 cart loads of sick men being sent back to Oxford. During the summer and early autumn large numbers of troops crossed the county to the remaining Royalist strongholds, especially Donnington Castle, and Basing House in Hampshire, though the largest contingents were those involved in the Second Battle of Newbury in October. After this the Royalist position in Berkshire rapidly worsened as the Parliamentary armies took over one stronghold after another, the last garrison loyal to the King, Wallingford, holding out until July 1646.

Despite the widespread military activities of the spring and summer of 1644, the pattern of epidemics of the previous year was not repeated. A few parishes near Reading and Abingdon recorded short bursts of increased burials, but with a few exceptions, such as Caversham, there was little out of the ordinary. Only on the Downs near Wantage were there many significant rises in the death rate. An epidemic began in the town early in the summer and continued into the following year. It is possible that the disease came into the county from the west: deaths rose in Shrivenham in February, Letcombe Regis in April and reached Wantage in May. From here it may have spread south to Brightwalton where burials rose in June, and to Chaddleworth and Boxford in July. However, some caution is necessary in reaching any conclusions since, with the exception of Wantage, these are all small parishes where a few extra deaths could have had an inordinate impact on the overall total.

It was not until the winter of 1644–5 that a situation similar to that of 1643 occurred, though the major crisis lasted only 4 months, from November to February.

Table 4
MONTHLY BURIAL PATTERN JAN 1644–JUNE 1645

Extent of burials above average	J	F	M	A	M	J	J	A	S	O	N	D	J	F	M	A	M	J
7 times average	–	1	–	–	1	–	–	–	–	1	–	4	–	1	–	–	–	–
5–6 times average	3	–	–	1	–	–	1	1	–	1	5	2	3	1	–	1	–	–
3–4 times average	2	3	2	–	3	4	–	–	4	1	6	9	8	5	2	3	2	–
twice average	2	1	3	4	4	3	2	2	2	1	3	2	4	3	3	2	3	–
Total parishes 'in crisis'	7	5	5	5	8	7	3	3	6	4	14	17	15	10	5	6	5	–

Total parishes analysed: 51

Some of the parishes near Reading, such as Sonning and Wargrave, affected in the previous year, again appear among the casualties, but others, such as Hurst, do not, and yet others, Binfield and White Waltham, occur instead. In general the high burial rates lasted for short periods under 1 month, so that many parishes may record an occasional high monthly total yet fail to appear among those with abnormal annual figures. The south west of the county reflected the impact of the military operations of the autumn on its population. Parishes on the east-west routes such as Thatcham, Speen and Newbury had above average figures for 2 or 3 months, while those between Newbury and Hungerford to the west, and Wantage to the north, were also badly affected. The intrusiveness of the war in a rural parish is indicated by a note in the parish register of Chaddleworth regarding a burial in November 1644: 'This is that Thomas Nelson that fought two dragoons in Hangman Stone Lane in the time of the Civil

War and was never well afterwards.'[10] Occasional burials of soldiers are noted in the register, though without a hint of whether they died of wounds or disease. In 1 or 2 instances, as at Lambourn in November, the rise in the civilian death rate follows closely enough on the death of a soldier in the village for there to be a possible connection between them. A further description of the situation in 1644–5 is prevented by defective registration over a wide area, particularly in the boroughs. This almost certainly reflects the confusion caused by the war, and possibly the difficulties of recording increasing numbers of burials, ending in the failure to record any at all.

After March 1645 the pattern of short crisis periods in scattered parishes, usually lasting less than a month and less severe than before, becomes more general. A new threat appeared in the summer when plague made a short-lived appearance in Wantage, and Reading in July 1646.[11] Apart from this, there is little evidence of widespread high burial rates in Berkshire during the closing months of the war.

The connection between heavy troop concentrations and high civilian mortality is very positive. The one did not always follow the other, but did so often enough for the correlation to be beyond coincidence.

It needs to be stressed that the overwhelming majority of recorded deaths are those of the local population and not of the military. In general, relatively few soldiers' burials are found in the Berkshire registers. Reading St. Lawrence records 47 in all, 37 of these in 1643, the year of the siege; Newbury has at least 52 for whose burials payment was made to the churchwardens in 1644–5;[12] the rest of the county can muster less than 50, of whom 13 died in 1 village, Ruscombe in 1643 and 1644. With the exception of Reading, there is no indication of whether these men died of wounds or of disease, or a combination of these. Those killed on the field of battle appear to have been buried in mass graves. After the Second Battle of Newbury, the greater number of the slain found a grave near where they fell, while many of those who died of their wounds in the town of Newbury were buried in St. Nicholas' churchyard. A letter from Essex to the Rector and Churchwardens of Enborne ordered them to bury all who lay dead in and about Enborne and Newbury West, while the King ordered the Mayor of Newbury to bring in to the town all sick and wounded Parliamentary soldiers from the surrounding villages and 'carefully provide for their recovery'.[13] Doubtless some did not recover and it is these who are found in the registers.

However, it is clear that military casualties are not responsible for the large numbers of deaths between 1643 and 1645. A very detailed analysis was made of the registers of 18 parishes from all areas of the county which were in crisis in either 1643 or 1644 or both. There were 4 registers that gave no information other than names, making it impossible to identify children with certainty, though there was usually sufficient information to indicate that all soldiers were identified. Apart from those in St. Lawrence in Reading, only 13 soldiers were named in the other 17 registers. In each year the proportion of burials of men to women was almost identical at about 53:47, although a significantly large number of parishes had more men than women buried in 1643. The proportion of children ranged from 18% to 39% of the totals, the most frequent being about 20%. It is reasonable to conclude, first that the deaths being recorded are predominantly those of the civilian population, and secondly that whatever diseases were responsible for the epidemics, they were not those that attacked children rather than adults.

There is no shortage of diagnoses for the diseases prevalent during this period. Contemporaries made frequent references to sickness both among the troops and the civilian population. Sir Samuel Luke mentions contagious disease and plague in various centres including Oxford and Reading, and in the autumn of 1643, 'the "new disease" as they call it'.[14] One major epidemic in Oxford in 1643 was described as 'morbus campestris' – camp fever, which could well have been typhus. Thomas Willis, a doctor serving the Royalists in Oxford, also suggested the disease resembled that which had affected armies in the past, 'morbus castrensis', 'it being seldom or never known that an Army, where there is so much filth and nastiness of diet, worse lodgings, unshifted apparell etc. should continue long without contagious diseases'. The same disease he found in Reading during the siege of 1643 which 'at length assailed everywhere the weak multitude, to wit the persons of the houses where the soldiers lodged. . . . About the Summer Solstice the Fever began to spread . . . and to sieze a great many husbandmen and others living in the Country'.[15] It is significant that the death rate shown in the parish registers reaches a peak in midsummer 1643, though the gradual spread from town to country is not so evident. With the constant movement of troops, especially to the major centres of Reading and Oxford, it is highly likely that the contagion spread wherever armies were to be found, and that the infection was a form of typhus. In addition modern authorities cite as a characteristic of the disease that it affects adults more than children, a feature of the Berkshire mortality already noted from the registers. In the hot summer of 1643 victims displayed plague-like symptoms of buboes and spots, which it is suggested is also typical of the 'war typhus' which affected Berkshire, Oxfordshire and elsewhere in 1643. Whether or not this was the only infection responsible for the extremely high mortality of these years is questionable since contemporaries also identified 'squinancy, dysentry or deadly sweat' in the area.[16]

Of the cause of the winter epidemic of 1644–5 there is almost nothing written. It too may have been caused by a combination of diseases, including typhus which frequently occurred during the colder months, and which could be the 'spotted fever' which Creighton suggests was widely prevalent in the autumn of 1644. There is a single reference to a death from smallpox in the Vale of White Horse, but it may have been more widely active. Any epidemic would have had a serious impact on a population short of food and fuel as a result of constant requisition and pillage, and suffering from the loss of employment consequent on the disruption of trade. Thomas Dulbie of Botley in the parish of Cumnor voiced the concerns of many local people when in his will made on 24th November 1643 he ordered the sale of a house in Abingdon 'being free land which I bought latelie and seeing the pillage of it and fearing more may happen in these tymes'.[17]

These early years of the first Civil War were undoubtedly the worst for Berkshire in terms of the scale of deaths, not only during these hostilities but for the whole of the seventeenth century. The overall effect on the county's death rate can be judged by the total burials recorded in the 2 years 1643 and 1644 in the parishes so far discussed. Against a 20-year average of 859 must be set a figure of 1,759 for 1643 and 1,192 for 1644. Just how widespread was the mortality crisis in the adjoining counties can only be gauged by a similar study of the parish register data, but it is likely that the whole region had cause to regret the choice of Oxford as the King's headquarters, and its own proximity to the capital, which for the rest of the century was instrumental in promoting its prosperity.

Addendum

Since this article was published, a cemetery in Abingdon dating from 1644–8 has been excavated by the Oxford Archaeological Unit. Bone analysis of 250 or so skeletons indicates that it contained a larger proportion of young males than would be expected in a conventional graveyard of the period. Some appear to have died of wounds received in military activities. In 1644–5 the churchwardens of Abingdon St. Helens were paid for the burial of 69 soldiers and some are also recorded in the parish register in 1643 and 1644. However, the register is defective and so was not used after 1643 in the calculations on which this article is based.

Acknowledgements

The research on which this paper is based was carried out as a consequence of an extramural class at Reading University, and is part of a general study of mortality patterns in Berkshire before 1750. Several students contributed to the work, but the major portion has been undertaken by Anne Crabbe, Gillian Clark and Deirdre Schwartz.

Notes

1. E.A. Wrigley and R.S. Schofield, *The Population History of England 1541–1871* (1981), p. 645.

2. Figures for England taken from Wrigley and Schofield, op. cit., p. 333, and for Berks from a sample of parish registers. 'Average' here means 25-year moving average.

3. M.J. Dobson, *A Chronology of Epidemic Disease and Mortality in South-East England 1601–1800* (1987). For a county similarly affected see D. Palliser 'Dearth and Disease in Staffordshire 1540–1670' in M. Havinden and C. Chalkin eds., *Rural Change and Urban Growth* (1974), p. 65.

4. Sunninghill parish register (Berks. Rec. Off. D/P126/1). The map indicates which registers were used for this study.

5. The parish registers of Berkshire are mainly deposited in the Berks. Record Office, Shire Hall, Shinfield, under the general reference D/P. Caversham, once in Oxfordshire but now mostly part of Reading Borough, has been included in the data base. The statistical methods used by Wrigley and Schofield seemed inappropriate to this study. In particular the 20-year mean average has been chosen in preference to a 25-year moving average which would have restricted the number of registers used by demanding good registration for a much longer period. Whenever the term 'average' is used hereafter in this paper it refers to the mean unless otherwise stated.

6. D.S. Disbury, *The Civil War in Berkshire* (1978), Chap. 3; quoted in C. Creighton *A History of Epidemics in Britain* (1891), Vol. I, p. 549.

7. Quoted in E.J. Climenson, *A Guide to Henley on Thames* (1896), pp. 18–19; Henley Parish register (Oxon. Rec. Off. transcript). Details of many raids are given in civil war tracts, e.g. *The Late Famous Victory obtained by Captain Lamley, Sunday, Jan. 29th 1643* (1643).

8. I.G. Philip ed., *The Journals of Sir Samuel Luke*, 3 vols (Oxfordshire Record Soc. 1947–1953). Vol. II, p. 102.

9. Ibid. p. 172.

10. Chaddleworth parish register (Berks. Rec. Off. D/P32/1.

11. J.M. Guilding ed., *Reading Records. Diary of the Corporation*, Vol. IV (1892), p. 201.

12. H. Money, *A History of Newbury* (1887), p. 533–4. The burial of a soldier wounded in the battle is recorded in the parish register of All Hallows the Less, London: September 28th 1643, 'Maddocks, Robert, clothworker, one of whose legs was shot off at the Battaile of Newbury' (transcript at Society of Genealogists' Library).

13. E.W. Gray, *History and Antiquities of Newbury and its Environs* (1839), p. 14.

14. *Journals of Sir Samuel Luke* Vol. III, p. 217.

15. Quoted in F.J. Varley, *The Siege of Oxford* (1932), pp. 97–8.

16. Creighton, op. cit., p. 5.

17. E. Lockinge parish register (Berks. Rec. Off. D/P82/1); Will of Thomas Dulbie (Berks. Rec. Off. D/A1/M16).

8

PARISH AND PEOPLE: SOUTH WARWICKSHIRE IN THE CIVIL WAR

Philip Tennant

In recent years academic interest in the English Civil War has increasingly focused on its regional context, and the result has been to transform popular notions of a conflict confined essentially to politicians and military commanders, with a few set-piece battles taking place in suitably remote areas, leaving the bulk of the population unscathed or even, perhaps, actually unaware of events. The deafening silence of most of the earlier *Victoria County History* articles on the impact of the war at parish level[1] and the persistence of folk legends illustrating the ignorance of the native inhabitants of momentous events unfolding on their very doorstep have both helped to perpetuate such a myth. The Marston Moor ploughboy astonished at being interrupted at his work by the arrival of two armies may perhaps appear inherently implausible,[2] but nearer home Dugdale's story of Richard Shuckburgh blithely intent on hunting near Edgehill, oblivious to his king's preparations for a supposedly decisive battle, or the anecdote of the Tysoe youth surprised by the arrival of a troop of cavaliers and quite unable to identify them – these surely have the ring of authenticity.[3] Yet if the extent to which the Civil War fundamentally and permanently changed English society is still cause for legitimate debate among historians, the more one examines a specific area the more it becomes clear that, for a few short years at least, the lives of ordinary people, with their age-old preoccupations of field and market, weather and harvest, labour and rest, were profoundly disrupted. The purpose of this essay is to substantiate this claim by exploring the impact of the war on a limited area of the south Warwickshire Feldon for the period 1642–46 and to attempt to determine to what extent it is true that 'the Civil War from below remains hidden'.[4] The emphasis will be on military campaigns (already well documented in standard histories) only insofar as these directly involved ordinary men and women, named individuals whose very obscurity testifies to the all-embracing nature of the conflict in which they were unavoidably caught up.

Warwickshire as a whole was, as is now known, heavily implicated in the events of the Civil War,[5] and nowhere was this more so than in the extreme south of the county where a combination of strategic factors, deep and long-standing religious dissension, apparently random events and the presence of influential local personalities made the district a military thoroughfare from the outset and ensured that it staged 'the dress rehearsal for the entire English Civil War'.[6] The

major determining factor in this was the initial establishment of the Court at
Oxford, with Banbury as '(its) most important outpost . . . and an integral part of
the Royalist scheme of operations in the southern midlands'.[7] The early Royalist
re-occupation of Worcestershire and Herefordshire provided a corridor between
the King's base at Oxford and the loyal strongholds of Wales and the south-west,
a corridor soon broadened by Prince Rupert's conquest of Bristol. Oxford itself
was progressively surrounded by a circle of protective bases extending north into
Warwickshire and south into Berkshire and Buckinghamshire. Equally important
was the King's dependence on the West Midlands and Marches as a major
recruiting base, as well as a vital manufactory containing iron-working regions,
arms depots and workshops.[8] A string of staging posts was established throughout
this corridor, which were periodically fought over before changing hands with the
ebb and flow of the war, thus ensuring a constant stream of convoys escorted by
local commanders on the east-west transit. From the Parliamentary viewpoint the
Cotswolds and Severn Valley were equally vital, to keep open communications
between the ports of Bristol and Gloucester with London on the one hand, and
to safeguard the north-south route via Warwick, Coventry and Northampton on
the other. The result was that not only major market towns like Evesham,
Warwick, Stratford, Cirencester, Stow and Banbury assumed strategic
importance but that what now seem rural backwaters on modern tourist circuits
witnessed some of the most recurrent military operations as bases like Sudeley,
Bourton-on-the-Water, Chipping Campden, Woodstock and Burford were
activated. Even in lulls of activity, temporary 'courts of guard' were kept in
countless hitherto peaceful villages throughout the Feldon and beyond, like
Kineton, Ratley, Balscote, Burton Dassett, Adderbury, Shuckburgh and
Combrook, all necessitating burdensome local provisioning in addition to the
ever-present gathering of taxes by both sides. Moreover, historians' stress on
'localism' and the notorious reluctance of soldiers to serve outside their home
region should not obscure the interdependence of localities or the regularity with
which 'foreign' troops crossed regions far distant from their point of origin. The
relief of Gloucester, besieged by the king in the summer of 1643, was largely
achieved by Londoners trekking across the south Midlands, but many other
similar expeditions, less well known, affected the region. The Warwickshire
parish archives refer with almost monotonous regularity to forces from Newport
Pagnell, Northampton, Tewkesbury and Aylesbury criss-crossing their territory
on some mission, besides the unwelcome incursions of the standing armies,
including eventually Fairfax's New Model and the dreaded Scots.[9] Such regional
interdependence is acknowledged by contemporaries: a Royalist commander
writes to Prince Rupert that 'the loss of Evesham . . . cut off all the intercourse
between Worcester and Oxford'; John Corbet, Massey's chaplain at Gloucester,
bewails the loss of Sudeley Castle as 'a great stop to our entercourse with
Warwick, which was the only way of commerce with London'; and the

Parliamentary commander, Colonel Whetham, stressing the importance of Banbury Castle, 'of more concernement to Oxford then any other', notes that 'the taking of this Den of Theeves would much conduce to the straitning of Oxon, and give liberty of Trade to London from many parts'.[10] Often the Warwickshire constables are conscientiously explicit in their reports on troop movements: 'Nuport men when they came from Worcester', 'the carryage of Coll. Whalleys amunition to Evisham & other places', 'when the seege was at Banbury', 'Northampton men going to Worcester', 'Coll. Crumwells when they went to Stow fight', 'when Sir Thomas Fayrfaxe marcht by Stratford', and 'the Scots Army when they came throughe Warrwicke'. Sometimes the contemporary reference remains obscure: what were 'dragooneers when they came from Yorke fight' doing loitering at Sherbourne, outside Warwick? Why were Parliamentary troops from Gaunt House, near Standlake, Oxon, stationed in Brailes, or soldiers from 'a castle in Wales' in Tysoe?[11] Often the manoeuvrings seem almost motiveless, a mystery even to the weary victims like Richard Randall in Little Wolford: 'For 8 weekes Last I have had foote Souldiers under [*blank*] and for this last Fortnight, 3 Horsmen & how long they will Continew I know not'. Each one of these military expeditions – which considerations of space must exclude from further discussion here – brought to the villagers of south Warwickshire the realities of war, in the shape of quarter and plunder if no worse.

If south Warwickshire was, therefore, undoubtedly a major thoroughfare, it was the dominating presence of the two powerful rivals, Lord Brooke and the Earl of Northampton, which ensured that sooner or later, actual armed conflict would break out in the district. Once Parliament had pointedly replaced Northampton as Lord Lieutenant by Brooke, on 5 March 1642, neither peer lost time in acting. The Earl of Northampton, evidently converted overnight from courtier to military commander, was prominent among the group of peers publicly declaring loyalty to the King at York on 5 June, while Lord Brooke's adherence to the Puritan cause was well established long before that. Both magnates, with influential regional allies, were active in the summer of 1642 recruiting local forces, holding musters, offering handsome financial inducements to attract volunteers and generally ensuring that issues were becoming dangerously polarized. There was already much warlike activity in the towns. Even in January, following the doubling of the watch throughout the county, tensions were apparent, as at Stratford, where the Corporation thought it advisable to replenish the town's armoury.[12] Soon the town's 'armer howse' was being renovated, barrels of gunpowder bought, old armour refurbished, while armed and unarmed volunteers were swelling the numbers of the regular militia and many others trooping in to Warwick Castle, whose small garrison trebled within a month and where large-scale tree-felling was taking place to improve fortifications. By early June the King, through the Earl of Northampton and others, was ready to call the county to arms via Commissions of Array,

Warwickshire's being the first such to be issued.[13] This already antiquated procedure involved delegating local loyalists to call open-air rallies, usually in a meadow outside an important town, as at Worcester, Stratford, Warwick and Coleshill. Two took place, however, in the only recorded instances in the south Warwickshire countryside, in Winderton and Tysoe meadows, at the centre of the Northampton estates, organized by William Baldwin, whose family had provided bailiffs for the ancient royal manor of Brailes as far back as the Middle Ages, and who subsequently saw his estate sequestered for his pains.[14] No description of the proceedings at this gathering survives, but it cannot have been very different from those picturesquely evoked by Richard Gough in Shropshire or, nearer home, by William King at Pitchcroft Meadow outside Worcester, which was attended by 'a great number of men – of mean and base quality as they seemed to me – and having hedgebills, old calivers, shep pikes and clubs'.[15] Lord Brooke, for his part, declared the Parliamentary Militia Ordinance at Stratford in June and July, for which he was thanked in an official petition from Warwickshire notables, by which time his panic – or foresight – was such as to attract comment when he unsuccessfully attempted to seize the county armour from the shop of the Warwick armourer, Tibbot, to whom it had been sent for repair. Tibbot was probably the Thomas of Rowington who was an ally of the Earl of Northampton and himself a Commissioner of Array, and who had recruited some twenty Solihull men for the King's service 'with colours in their hats and acted as their captain'. The Warwick shopkeeper stoutly refused to surrender his charge, and the incident led one commentator to condemn Lord Brooke for 'fuelling jealousies and fears in these days [when] there is none or very little reasons for them'.[16] Northampton had already been designated a 'delinquent' by the House of Commons, an act countered a short time later by the King's warrant to Sir William Dugdale naming Brooke as traitor.[17]

July and August saw the first violence in south Warwickshire in a series of incidents marking a significant escalation towards outright war: the armed confrontation between the two peers over the county magazine, at Warmington and Banbury, the abortive siege of Warwick Castle by a small force of the Earl of Northampton's (the Earl somewhat unprofessionally lodging at the Swan Inn for the purpose), and the sacking of 'malignant' Southam, with the pillaging of its parson, the elderly scholar Francis Holyoake, by a contingent of Parliamentary troops boasting of their Puritan zeal.[18] In August came the King's commission from York to the Earl of Northampton 'to imprest, raise, enroll and reteyne one Regiment of one thousand Foote furnished and armed', and the proclamation from Stoneleigh of the royal threat to Coventry.[19] Troops of both sides were now manoeuvring and quartering in south Warwickshire villages, Northampton's at Aston Cantlow on one occasion, Colonel John Fiennes's Roundheads at Kineton on another.[20] By the time the King raised his windswept standard at Nottingham on 22 August, divisions within the county were hardening, unease and suspicion were rife, forces were being mobilized. Opinion was sufficiently polarized to inspire at least one petition, from 'the Knights, gentlemen and others' of the shire 'to adventure the utmost hazard of our lives and fortunes' for the King.[21] 'Here is nothing but providing of arms', Midland commentators noted apprehensively, 'the country is like a cockpit, one spurring against another'.[22] The more politicized clergy were beginning to take the initiative in some parishes: Richard Wootton, rector of Warmington, collected arms, ammunition and horses for Parliament in August, finally deserting his parish to captain a troop at Warwick, Robert Kenrick abandoned Burton Dassett to join the King; while others, like the obstreperous Royalist, Walwyn Clarke, rector of Oxhill, contented themselves with publicly abusing the enemy.[23] Edgehill, on 23 October 1642, was to be the logical climax in the district of this spiral of violence, but even before then so many cartloads of royal booty were trundling in to the courtyard of Warwick Castle from plunder and ambush that a cellar in the castle was set aside to house it and popularly dubbed 'the pillage house'.[24] It is inconceivable, in view of such activity and the intense pressure on the leading families to declare themselves, that the villages could remain ignorant of the drift of events; in Richard Baxter's oft-quoted observation from neighbouring Worcestershire, where he had to flee for his life, 'the war was begun in our streets before the King or Parliament had any armies'.[25] Those able rustics who had not willingly escaped the economic depression of 1642 by volunteering to join local garrisons were labouring on fortifications at Banbury, Warwick or Compton Wynyates or being recruited as scouts or spies, like Thomas Earle of Alveston who joined Lord Brooke's company and, learning of the plan to fetch the magazine from Banbury to Warwick, deserted at Stratford and promptly warned the Earl of Northampton.[26] In September, in what seems retrospectively a symbolic event, the county Quarter Sessions were suspended when armed Roundheads broke into the courtroom: they would not be resumed until Michaelmas 1645. Warwickshire was 'alive with national politics' long before 'like two great blind moles the rival armies quested across Warwickshire for six days' to collide at Edgehill.[27] In Warwickshire at least the point of no return had been reached.

THE IMPACT OF EDGEHILL AND CROPREDY

If 'Kineton fight' gave the Feldon its first experience of warfare, the effects were far from temporary or confined to the actual soldiers who faced each other on the 'great broad Field' below Edgehill.[28] The army in 1642, consisting, it must be remembered, mainly of amateur volunteers, was a cumbersome, ill-disciplined, many-headed monster whose ramshackle progress in any given direction bore little relation to the purely symbolic, neat arrows beloved of military historians. Strategy was rudimentary and professionalism patchy. Moreover, abysmal roads after the recent appallingly wet weather meant that foot marchers as well as cavalry would often prefer to cut across this unenclosed, virtually hedgeless landscape peopled with the labouring poor toiling at their strips, deviating to loot whenever a promising hamlet or mansion appeared on the horizon. Urgency was seemingly a low priority, quartering was often for several days at a time and troops were scattered over a wide area. This was the reality at Edgehill and after. The King's approach, from Birmingham and Solihull via Kenilworth, Southam and Edgcote, was too tangential to affect much of the area under discussion, though Royalist troops quartered in a triangle of villages from Ratley to Wormleighton, Mollington, Cropredy and Wardington. Although there is no conclusive evidence, and although things were soon to deteriorate, the Royalists seem to have been relatively well-disciplined on this approach through what Clarendon describes as hostile territory.[29] The main Parliamentary force under the Earl of Essex, however, intending to relieve Banbury and intercept the king's march towards London, approached Edgehill in an easterly direction from Worcester, quartering unhurriedly as they entered Warwickshire on a very broad front extending from at least Alcester and Studley in the north, for a leisurely two to three days, to Ilmington, some 15 miles to the south, with Stratford and surrounding villages heavily quartered in between. Although unattributed in the archives, it was clearly Essex's men who, disregarding their commander's express proclamation at Worcester only weeks previously,[30] had time to plunder the wealthy Catholic landowner, Richard Canning, at Foxcote manor, Ilmington. Canning, along with his Royalist neighbour, the rector of Ilmington, Dr Thomas King, was subsequently to be victim of repeated acts of Parliamentarian plunder in addition to suffering the sequestration of his estate when he took up arms for the King and being forced to pay £100 in ransom. Essex's army, still unaware of the proximity of the Royalists, then converged ponderously on a whole cluster of unsuspecting south Feldon villages; Halford, Pillerton Priors, the Tysoes, Radway and Kineton were all heavily invaded 'upon ye Saturday before Kineton fight', with provisions demanded from surrounding villages. At Halford, for example, John Baron received fifty men and horses and the conspicuous Royalists William and Thomas Halford suffered nearer 200, 'a great part of the Earle of Essex his army, before and after Kinton fight'. Similarly at Tysoe, a whole troop of soldiers quartered on the wealthy Francis Clarke alone, and 'a Captaine and his Troope of horse whose name I know not' at William Bickerton's at Pillerton Priors. Essex himself – who insisted that his coffin accompany him at all times, though its presence is not recorded here – quartered at Kineton, the village constable later reporting: 'The Earle of Essex with his whole Army at the Battell lay here from Saturday untill Tuesday night'. Unavoidably, the district experienced its first plunder and destruction during this long week-end, Kineton alone losing stolen coal, wood, and farmyard equipment such as ploughs, harrows, sheepracks, hurdles, pails, ladders and gates, with the odd hovel or cowhouse for good measure, to fuel the camp fires in the frosty autumn nights. The effect of the soldiers' presence in the household was evidently devastating; in a typical example from Tysoe, for instance, Thomas Calloway:

> . . . had taken forth of his house by souldiers under the comand of the Earle of Essex bookes worth xxs ten Cheeses worth xs five yards of flannell worth ten shillings two Coates worth xxs provision spent in his house worth xxs and seaven sheepe taken forth of his ground worth iiili. . .

while women, usually widows where recorded, were no more exempt than anyone else. Hester Wootton of Tysoe lost:

> . . . twelve Cheeses worth viiis halfe a pigg worth six shillings foure yards of new Cloath worth xiiiis a flaggon and foure sawcers worth iiis. . .

By now quarter and theft were usually inseparable; Ralph Ellis of Butlers Marston was not only obliged to provide quarter for twenty men and their horses for two days, losing thirty loads of hay in the process, but also 'Lost att Kineton Fight by the parliament Soldiers 73 sheepe att 10d. p.Sheep'. In view of such experiences nothing appears more credible than traditional folk memories, like that of Essex's soldiers hammering on Oxhill church door during divine service, or those from Upper Tysoe of the theft of the housewife's newly-baked bread from the oven or her husband's hiding valuables by lowering them down the well in a pot until the soldiers had passed.[31]

Meanwhile several other Parliamentary units had converged on Edgehill from opposite directions, though precise movements are difficult to establish: Lord Brooke's from Droitwich, Lord Saye's from his ancestral Broughton in the south-east, where a tradition persists that troops slept on the eve of the battle, and Lord Willoughby of Parham's which, fresh from an encounter with Prince Rupert near Kings Norton, marched its 800 horse and foot southwards, liberally pillaging Stratford on the way. Willoughby himself, apparently separated from his men for some unknown reason, billeted himself at Thomas Wilks's in Brailes, costing the yeoman over £2 on that occasion as a prelude to much more substantial losses suffered later in the war. Also in the district was Sir William Waller who, whether at the battle or not, quartered at Tysoe with thirty of his men at this time, at the house of the wealthy William Browne. The sounds of the battle itself carried far and wide on the still autumn air, clearly audible to the fidgety parishioners at Alcester listening to their Sunday afternoon sermon.[32]

The impact of Edgehill on the locality extended well beyond the day of battle, for the district was anything but quickly vacated. The fit dispersed in orderly fashion in all directions, the Parliamentarians, cold and hungry, loitering for days seeking out their old quarters in and around Kineton, Halford, Pillerton, Warwick, Stratford and beyond, (with the harrying of Rupert's cavalry not preventing more looting as they went), abusing the hospitality of Giles Eliot, the Tysoe alehousekeeper or, according to tradition, quenching their thirst at the tavern at Whatcote. The sick and maimed lingered week after week, left to their own devices in alien billets, dependent on the compassion of the cottager's wife when not being attacked by the hostile villagers as they sought relief,[33] unless the rudimentary surgery at Warwick Castle were their lot. So many Parliamentary wounded resulted from this first major encounter that carts from the King's former train were used for 'the releife of maimed souldiers which were to ye number of 3 or 4 hundred sent to Warwicke from Edgehill fight to be cared for and cured of their wounds'. A year later, hundreds of wounded Parliamentarians were still being cared for in the castle.[34] Plundering expeditions were now becoming routine, more ambitious and highly organized: in one typical of many, the mansion of the influential Catholic landowner, William Sheldon, at Weston, near Long Compton, was pillaged shortly after Edgehill by a Parliamentary troop of horse from Warwick, while a Kenilworth contingent even had the leisure to drive a quantity of Sheldon's cattle over 20 miles back to their garrison.[35] The Royalists dispersed equally slowly, towards Oxford, capturing Broughton and the crucial garrison at Banbury *en route*, and entrusting local activists, like William Loggins of Butlers Marston, to continue their work of collecting much-needed arms. From now on, the Royalist garrison at Banbury Castle, according to its adversaries a 'most pestilent, pernicious, and vexatious den of Theeves and Royall Robbers',[36] was constantly reinforced and provided a continual focus of military activity in the region, while its marauding raids far and wide in Oxfordshire and Warwickshire were to become notorious. The Parliamentary garrison at Warwick was an equally oppressive presence throughout the war and arbitrary imprisonment of innocent wayfarers on the orders of its governor, Colonel John Bridges, became a frequent and lucrative pastime. Anne Malms of Tysoe reported that 'her husband going to Warr. to seeke for his [stolen] horses was there imprisoned & payd to Collonell Bridges for his libertie 4ʜ'. Henry Middleton of Tysoe testified to a similar experience when:

> . . . his sonne going towards Stratford Market with two horses and a quarter of barley was taken by Collonell Bridges his souldiers to Warwick Castle and Imprisoned, where he payed to Coll. Bridges for his liberty Six Pounds and for his horses and barley eight pounds.

The Parliamentary authorities made repeated, conscientious attempts to curb such malpractice, writing to Bridges on one occasion:

> We are informed that Major Castle at Warwick takes money for the prisoners in his custody, and so turns them off. Inform yourself further herein . . . that he may be proceeded against for such misdemeanour as it deserves.[37]

Edgehill constituted, therefore, a unique experience for peaceful south Warwickshire and a foretaste of what was to come, presenting substantial material losses to many villagers and unquantifiable fear and insecurity to as many others. Above all, free quarter and plunder, inseparable companions, were endemic from now on. Altogether, such an experience could not but etch itself indelibly on the community, for not only were there poignant reminders like the quantity of battlefield relics, many surviving today, but also the Edgehill grave-pits containing, according to a local antiquarian vicar, 1,200 corpses, together with others buried in local churchyards and, soon, the odd monument, like that to Daniel Blackford, the Oxhill churchwarden. The almost instant appearance in the folk memory of battlefield ghosts is itself eloquent testimony to the hold these events exerted on the popular imagination.[38] Less than two years later Cropredy Bridge underscored these lessons and ensured that those villages which had largely escaped the effects of Edgehill learnt them.

Strategically, the prelude to Cropredy (1644) presented superficial parallels to Edgehill. While once again the immediate approach of the Royalists, under the King westwards from Buckingham to Banbury, lay well outside the area under consideration, the Parliamentary army under Sir William Waller struck directly across south Warwickshire north-eastwards from Gloucester, in accordance with Waller's pledge 'to follow the King wherever an army can march', and hoping 'that there may be an universall conjunction of forces agt the ennemy which, with Gods blessing, will make the worke short'. Taking a route roughly parallel to the ancient Fosse Way, after quartering a night near Stow and – such was the rudimentary fieldwork – literally going round in a circle,[39] Waller's forces entered Warwickshire near the Four Shires Stone and spent the next two days and nights scattered in a wide circle of villages centred on Shipston, extending from the Wolfords, Whichford, Burmington, Cherington, Willington, Barcheston and Brailes in the south to Oxhill, Halford, Pillerton, Kineton and Radway in the north. There was thus a distance of some 12 miles at least separating the rearguard at Wolford from the forward contingents, with groups of officers being 'lodged in town' and the common soldiers 'lodged in field', as a contemporary report states. Waller himself, with an increasingly demoralized army awaiting a convoy of supplies and pay, quartered at Oxhill, where he had time to write to Parliament a letter yielding interesting incidental detail:

I onely desire that it may not be expected, that I should take long marches and not sometimes rest, this extreame hott weather, especially with the foote, who are very much diminished, and would quickly be ruined if I should not spare them as much as I can. I am come to Oxhill, neare Keynton feild, and the foote are at Shepstone, and purpose to march in ye coole of ye Evening. I have receed some spplies of Horse & foote from Gloucester & Warwick & Coventry. I humbly desire yt Maior Genall Browne, & such forces of ye Association as can

be drawne into ye feild may march to Bedford, & I shall by ye meanes of Sr
Sam. Luke, direct a way how wee may ioyne. I humbly beg that a months pay
(wch was pmised), may be sent downe wth Maior Genll Browne, and it will be
a meanes to prserve this Army from dissolving. I desire all expediency may bee
used in this.[40]

Once again, all the surrounding villages must have been humming with
activity as they were harassed and impoverished by the occupying forces – all the
more so as Waller, in view of the exceptionally warm weather, had decreed a
day's rest to his forces, giving them time to indulge themselves at the expense of
the more affluent local yeoman. Once again William Sheldon was victimized, his
servant Thomas Savage later reporting to a Parliamentary committee that an
official warrant from Waller had ordered the seizure of 200 of the landowner's
best sheep.[41] As before, not just twos and threes but huge contingents of men and
horses were foisted upon the unfortunate villagers, especially those known to be
Royalist sympathizers like Lot Keyte, of Great Wolford, who reported providing
quarter to 'ye rere of ye Army that Night' (24 June 1644). A 300-strong Tower
Hamlets detachment battened on the vicar of tiny Barcheston, Nathaniel Horton,
for 2 days and nights, enlivening the Warwickshire lanes with their outlandish
London accents. Neighbouring Willington and Burmington suffered particularly;
160 men and 30 horses invaded Thomas Walker's at Willington, with another
140 at Thomas Fletcher's and further units of 100 each with William Ashby and
William Humphreys. Other large detachments were billeted in nearby
Burmington, 60 foot soldiers spending 2 days and nights with Nicholas Hunt,
another 60 each with Francis Court and Richard Hall, 50 more with Richard
Sammon, 40 more each with Giles Thomas and Robert Beale. In all, well over
1,000 of Waller's men were quartered, with all the attendant imaginable chaos, in
Willington and Burmington alone in those 2 long summer days before moving on
to disaster across the hills at Cropredy. As at Edgehill, quartering and plunder
resumed unabated in the villages once the battle was over as the various
Parliamentary units scattered haphazardly in all directions, falling back in some
cases, one suspects, on the same villages vacated only days previously. A
dispirited Waller, pressed by a former lady friend to change sides, reported to
Parliament that his army was plagued with desertions;[42] yet the indefatigable
general was soon back in Tysoe, intent on following the King westwards,
quartering with 'about 120 of his Commanders & souldiers, some of them
quartered five Dayes', with the same unfortunate Francis Clarke already imposed
on by Essex's troops at Edgehill. The hapless Clarke would be forced to entertain
further Parliamentary units on at least three more occasions, in August,
September and October of this same year, 1644. Each parish for which the Civil
War records have survived (and almost certainly several, heavily quartered,
whose records have not, like Tredington, Shipston and Long Compton)

conscientiously itemises its by now familiar litany of losses, complaints and costly provisioning, all recollected years later as the constable went his rounds gathering information on the time when 'the army marched through our town'. Incidental personal comment occasionally adds a further human dimension, like that of John Wilton, vicar of Great Wolford, who touchingly notes:

> for as much as the most part of the sayd Inhabitants are husbandmen and unlearned men and have kept no Accompt of theyr great charges and losses for these fower or five yeares last past, nor can possibly so call to mynd the sayd charges . . . therfore they desyre to be excused for making any further Account.

For their part, the morale of the Cavaliers after the battle was high enough to transform the King's march westwards into a splendid royal progress as it skirted Warwickshire within sight and sound of Long Compton and Barton-on-the-Heath: 'his Majestie with all his army, drums beating, colors flying and trumpets sounding, marched over the Cotswold Hills'.[43]

THE YEAR WITHOUT A BATTLE: 1643

If Edgehill and Cropredy, as intensely local dramas, both profoundly marked the consciousness of the village community of south Warwickshire, these two campaigns were far from being the only ones to affect the region. Military offensives well outside any given region often had an unpredictable local impact, and the spring and summer of 1643, for example, were particularly eventful for the Feldon even though the main theatres of war were distant. For one thing, 'foreign' troops of either side passing through a district were often even more unprincipled than when nearer home, irrespective of local allegiance: mindless plunder of one's own supporters was not uncommon. In one blatant example, Sir Thomas Aston's Royalist cavalry, which had already plundered largely loyalist Worcestershire on its way north in January 1643, again ran amok as they careered southward in June, smarting from defeat in Cheshire, provoking angry complaints from the inhabitants of the Bromsgrove-Droitwich area and an official petition to the King's Commissioners from the people of Armscote and Blackwell in the parish of Tredington. The text is worth quoting in detail for its sheer human interest:

> . . . according to or late Information, uppon Satturday the Third of June instant [1643] we were plundered and bereft of 40 of or best horses . . . Uppon our diligent and chargeable search and Inquiry we have found out or horses in the Regimt of Colonell Sr Thomas Aston att their quarters about a place called Black Burton neere Burford in the county of Oxon. But soe incomisserate and unreasonable are theis Plunderers That (not content with

thewrongfull takeing or said horses, beating and abusing us for onely
requesting to buy them agayne, and att their departure wilfully trooping away
neere a quarter of a Mile over a furlong of or Beanes & Pease in a body of 7 or
8 score horse, when a fayre high way of 30 yards broad lay all along by the said
furlong) But when or Messengers and servants whom wee ymployed in
seekinge after or horses wth 4 or 5 dayes expence of tyme found them in the
said Regimtt att Black burton aforesaid The soldiers there . . . (in contynuance
of theire mischeivous practizes) did imprison & threaten our said Messengers
and servants & rob them & pick their pocketts and take away & deprive them
of all their moneyes wch they tooke wth them for their necessary expences. Soe
that we dare pceed noe further in pursuance of our said horses Except you
wilbe pleased honorably to afford us yor assistance and aide herein . . .
And we shall allwayes pray for yor happinesse both here & hereafter.[44]

That horse theft was one of the commonest crimes in the Civil War and that
some cavalry units were admitted by their own side to be little better than
unscrupulous horse-dealers (Colonel John Fiennes's regiment was a particularly
notorious local one)[45] was scant consolation to the inhabitants of these two small
hamlets for such a catastrophic loss at midsummer, and the sense of outrage is
palpable.

Although 1643 saw no battles in the region comparable to Edgehill or
Cropredy it was a period no less disturbing for the village communities. Some of
the military activity was relatively painless. Neither the passage of Prince Rupert
south in January to storm Cirencester, when he quartered successively at Butlers
Marston and Shipston-on-Stour, his return northwards in March when he again
quartered at Shipston and then Stratford on his way to assault Birmingham and
Lichfield, nor his return to escort the Queen south from her sojourn with
Shakespeare's grand-daughter at New Place, Stratford, to her emotional reunion
with Charles near Kineton in July, seems to have adversely affected the district.[46]
However, consolidation of the Royalist bases at Oxford and Banbury, the brief
occupation of Stratford by the Royalists in January and February before Lord
Brooke 'beate [them] out of the towne' and the Parliamentary relief of
Gloucester, besieged by the King in the summer, were events among many others
that ensured that the threat of armed violence was never lifted from south
Warwickshire this year. The King's cause was now at its height: in March a
Royalist source alleged that even the Parliamentary garrison at Warwick was
much enfeebled by desertions '. . . and the Townsmen & Souldiers at greate
varians'. The Parliamentary commander, Sir Samuel Luke, later warned of the
heavy Cavalier presence throughout the region: 'all the townes betweene
Banbury and Stratford are full of the King's soldiers . . . and a troope of horse
keepe a constant centry upon Edgehill to prevent any forces that may come from
Warwick and Coventry'.[47] Many of these Royalists units had been quartered in

the villages since the winter, busy collecting contributions, the Earl of
Northampton appealing from Banbury to all his tenants on his south
Warwickshire estates to assist to the maximum. Both he and Colonel Gerard
Croker, one of the first local loyalists, from Hook Norton, to be equipped with a
regiment of horse, were authorized by the king to cover the entire district for this
purpose:

> Whereas our deare Nephew Prince Rupert Generall of the Horse of our Army
> hath by severall orders under his hand and Seale given and assigned for the
> Quarters of the Regimt of Horse under your Comand the Townes of Long
> Compton, Barton on the Heath, Storton, Cherington, Brayles, Wichford and
> Ascott, in our County of Warwick; Little Compton, Sutton under Brayles and
> Shinington in our County of Glocester – and Hooke norton in our County of
> Oxon; and Authorized you to receive contribution out of the same after the
> rate of Tenn shillings six pence weekly for each Trooper . . . requiring the
> Inhabitants thereof to make good unto you all the Arreares . . . Hereunto wee
> expect full obedience to be given by all whome it may concerne, as they will
> avoid our high displeasure . . .

There is evidence, however, of local resistance in Warwickshire, as elsewhere,
to the increasing burdens of quarter and taxation. Already, by January 1643,
within days of the King's warrants authorizing collection of contributions,
neighbouring Oxfordshire parishes were reported to 'deny the mayntenance of
the sd Troopes' and by May several Warwickshire villages were seriously in
arrears. Croker's harshness in his task of collecting taxes so alienated the local
population, however, that bitter complaints arose from several parishes, involving
the rector of Sutton-under-Brailes, Dr Henry Watkins, and Long Compton,
Cherington and Brailes particularly, and finally provoking more than one appeal
from the Earl of Northampton to Prince Rupert himself:

> Sr I made bold to trouble your highness before concerning Collonel Crokers
> threatening to plunder Brailes and some other townes thereabouts. I likewise
> Signified unto your highness ye unreasonable sums hee required of ye
> constablerie of Brailes, whiche is to great a sume for them to beare, they being
> as before I wrote very willing to do any thing yt lay in their powers, for ye
> Kings service. Sr I have raised some troopes whiche have been in service, and
> now there quarters lying conveniently, either for them to quarter in or to fetche
> provision from, and mightily complayning of Crokers hard usage I thought
> good to acquaint yr highness with it, besides Sr if thy pay yt sum whiche hee
> exacts a great share will fall to my part to pay, besides ye hindrance of my
> tenants rents, whiche I beleeve is contrary to your highness intents, being yt I
> have devoted my selfe and all my fortune to his Matie Service, Sr I know yt

Croker hath given you misinformation, I shall desire to know your highness pleasure, as soon as conveniently you can, for none shall bee more readie to obey your commands then
Your highness Most humble and faithfull servant

Northampton

The seriousness of the situation is emphasized by a marginal note:

Sr to prevent to farther inconveniencies I desire your highness would bee pleased to send a protection under your hand for my tenants in ye constablerie of brailes, and for ye towne of Long Compton, which is mine, being both townes well affected.

Rupert either never received or ignored this appeal, for a few days later the King issued a threatening warrant:

Whereas by my Orders of the 14th of Janray Last past Colonell Croaker was quartered in your Townes of Long Compton & Brales, and to receive Contribution from your said Towns for such horse as hee did quarter therein: the payment of which Contributions you have till this tyme utterly neglected . . . Therefore by Vertue of my Authority and Power streightly Charge and command you . . . immediately after sight hereof (all delays and excuses set aside) to pay in to the said Colonell or his Assigns, all such Arrears as are from you to him due . . . wherein you may in no wise faile, as you will answer it at your utmost perills . . .

In June Croker was still engaged in the task, but the fact that the collecting process was then shared between him and the doubtless more respected Colonel Charles Compton, one of the young Northampton sons, who was assigned specifically to Long Compton, the Wolfords, Burmington, Brailes, Whatcote, Tysoe and Compton Wynyates, may hint at an attempt to defuse local hostility.[48] Not that this virtual occupation of south Warwickshire by the Royalists in 1643 made the district much more secure from harassment. Besides the highway kidnapping exploits of Major Bridges, indiscriminate plundering is still reported by marauding troops from the garrisons at Kenilworth and Warwick – in Tysoe in February, Warmington in March, Winderton during the summer – as well as more substantial disruptions to the lives of individuals as when, for example, a massive Parliamentary contingent of Waller's cavalry descended on Widow Meakins of Tysoe Lodge:

. . . in June the 4th 1643 the Souldiers in Sr William Wallers Army spent her in mansmeate and horsemeate haveing the number of 500 horses in her groundes besides teames of Oxen with the pvision and goodes they tooke from her was worth . . . 12li 10s 0d.

As though exorbitant tax enforcement and continued plundering were not enough, the entire district was being forcibly ransacked for men and materials to assist in the Royalist convoys on their east-west journeys already referred to. One order dated 15 June 1643 authorized two officers:

. . . to impresse and take vpp in the citty of Worcester or in any towne parish or village within ye Severall Counties of Gloucestr Worcester Warwicke and Oxford As many Horses Carts and Carters as shalbee requisite and vsefull for the draweinge and carriinge of all such Ordnance as are now to be brought from ye saide citty of Worcester to this citty of Oxford.

Little wonder indeed that local trade was by now becoming severely disrupted, with the fair at Stow – and, no doubt, many other markets – mere shadows of their former selves and that at Evesham actually cancelled.[49]

A good example of the local reverberations of distant events is provided by the Parliamentary relief of Gloucester in the autumn of 1643. In a concerted operation Parliament assembled a substantial army under the Earl of Essex, which marched north-west from London via Bicester and Brackley, while a lesser force under Lord Grey of Groby was ordered south from Leicester. Essex and Grey joined forces near Aynho and skirmished with Royalist forces at Deddington before resuming their march on Gloucester via Stow. Their route should therefore in theory have avoided Warwickshire altogether, yet as we have seen, Civil War troop movements rarely meant a disciplined and unified advance. In the event, detachments of Essex's army, including the London Trained Bands who quartered at Hook Norton, strayed deep into Warwickshire. Quartering and plundering were reported from several villages in the locality, including Brailes, Cherington, Willington and the Wolfords, the two latter being particularly affected. Lord Grey meanwhile, having approached via Stratford on his way to meet Essex and establish his headquarters at Adderbury, quartered virtually his entire force, in groups of tens and twenties for a seemingly interminable three days and nights, in Ascott and Whichford. Grey himself, with his officers and men amounting to 200 men and horses, quartered on the unfortunate Royalist vicar of Whichford, Dr Richard Langston, 'in harvest time', as the village constable pointedly adds in a hint at the price exacted by war on the rural community. In what looks like a calculated insult the parson had his Bible stolen by the soldiers.[50] About the same time, Parliamentary troops of Colonel William Purefoy were also scavenging in the locality, Tysoe being once again particularly victimized: five horses, bedding, pewter, brassware and clothing taken from

Ralph Wilcox; shirts, linen and another Bible from John Middleton. Even the barber's shop was broken into:

> [Edward King] had taken from him by the souldiers in Collonell Purefoys Regement the 14th day of September 1643 a new broad cloath coate a paire of bootes a paire of layd spurs and a box of Barbers Instruments worth . . . 2li 10s 2d.

The conduct of the troops on these occasions is well captured in a report by John Eades of Tysoe that:

> in September 1643 he had taken from him foure mares by Collonell Purefoys souldiers on by Capt Halfords sergeant cost him to have her againe xxxs. on by Capt Lovehils Lieuetenant cost him to have her againe of Capt Lovehill foure nobles on mare cost him to have her againe xxxs vid and on mare Capt Atwood had would not let him have her under ten pound, but she was well worth five pound.

The irresistible target for foraging soldiers in the area was the wealthy Catholic landowner, William Sheldon of Weston House, Long Compton. Already plundered at Edgehill, and later at Cropredy too, Sheldon was now targeted by Grey's troops, losing five more horses and mares and £300 worth of goods from his mansion. Sheldon's loyal servant, Thomas Savage, himself an active Royalist, attempted to avenge this outrage by publicizing news of the Parliamentary march on Gloucester to alert the besieging Cavaliers.[51]

Before condemning the indiscriminate pillaging by both sides which was such a notable feature of the war, it must be remembered that pay, when it materialized at all, was almost invariably in arrears and that troops were appallingly treated. If a London sergeant's testimony is to be believed, Essex's troops, as they skirted Warwickshire from Hook Norton to Rollright, were literally starving: having eaten little at Aynho, where 'we were very much scanted of Victualls', near Chipping Norton:

> Our Regiment stood in the open field all night, having neither bread nor water to refresh ourselves, having also marched the day before without any sustenance, neither durst we kindle any fire though it was a very cold night.

The following day too, 'we lay all in the open field, upon the plowd-land, without straw, having neither bread nor water . . . '. Little wonder that a few months later the conscientious Essex should bitterly complain to his superiors of 'not being able to stay [with his army] to hear the crying necessity of the hungry soldiers'.[52]

Not surprisingly, given the heavy presence of troops of both sides in the district at this time, armed skirmishes occasionally involved the villagers themselves. In one incident, at Little Wolford in August, a Cavalier attack on the manor house of the conspicuous local Parliamentarian, Hastings Ingram, forced the occupants to flee for their lives, a neighbour reporting:

> about August 1643 one Hastings Ingram Esquire taking up armes then for ye Parliamt I did furnish him with 4 souldiers whereof one was my eldest sonne wch soldiers did stand out in his house wth him in their defense against part of ye Kings army till he was forced to yeald & they to fly the house being fired over their heads.

In a largely Royalist area where substantial numbers of inhabitants were tenants of either William Sheldon or the Earl of Northampton, Ingram, who was captured and imprisoned at Oxford only to escape and join the Parliamentary garrison at Kenilworth with 130 fresh recruits, evidently enjoyed local notoriety. In an ingratiating letter to the regional commander, the Earl of Denbigh, Ingram later claimed that his known Parliamentary sympathies had forced him to adopt a lower profile: 'For my p'te thr malignitie & power agt me was ye occasion of ye layinge downe my armes'. This did not, however, prevent a local Parliamentary victory at Stow, where Prince Rupert made an abortive attempt to arrest Essex's advance on Gloucester, after which he 'retreated and that night lay in the field by Compton'.[53]

Such, then, were a few – by no means all – of the events which enlivened the existence of south Warwickshire villagers in 1643. Within the space of a few months they had suffered an almost constant military presence, with free quarter, plunder and harassment from both sides becoming commonplace. Moreover, it must be remembered that providing quarter, intolerable in itself, was also highly dangerous, since the 'beating up' of enemy quarters was deliberately and routinely practised by both sides. In many cases, the parson was being investigated as politically suspect, and would later be ejected. Above all a crippling financial burden was now a permanent feature of life, for the enforcement of 'contributions' by the Royalists already referred to is only a fraction of the tax-gathering story. Various levies had been imposed on the villages by Parliament from the outset, but the spring of 1643 saw the systematic adoption of compulsory assessment of each village proportionate to its estimated wealth. Colonel William Purefoy, appointed Parliamentary commander for Warwickshire in February, set about this task with his customary zeal. Henceforth no village was to escape heavy taxation, the county as a whole protesting officially at its unfairly high assessment.[54]

THE COMPTON GARRISON

Of all the crosses borne by the long-suffering villagers none was worse than that of having to endure a local garrison. Quarter and plunder associated with

periodic troop movements, though intolerable to the individual when they
occurred, were random and intermittent, dependent on the vagaries of orders
and strategies decided elsewhere, but a neighbouring garrison was a permanent
burden. Not only did it invite the constant threat of attack and perhaps
prolonged siege, with unforeseeable local repercussions, but even in lulls of
activity when the flames of war were flickering elsewhere a local garrison meant
an oppressive presence of ill-disciplined troops kicking their heels under an
arrogant commander accountable to virtually no-one. Some became notorious
even with their own side: to Clarendon's disgust the Royalist garrison at
Chipping Campden 'brought no other benefit to the public than the enriching
the licentious governor thereof, who exercised an illimited tyranny over the whole
country'.[55] Of the major garrisons affecting south Warwickshire, including the
'den of thieves' of Banbury, none fits this description better than the Earl of
Northampton's captured seat at Compton Wynyates. Warwick and Kenilworth
were recognized as virtually impregnable and after the initial months of the war
were largely left alone by the Royalists. Banbury's two sieges did indeed affect a
wide region and attracted heavy and prolonged quartering, constant pillaging,
requisitioning of men, materials and provisioning, as well as excessive financial
levies, from all the surrounding villages as far away as Brailes at least. But
Compton was even more centrally situated for the region and was not only
besieged twice, in June 1644 and January 1645, and threatened at other times,
but was manned for two interminable years by a strong Parliamentary force
under a particularly unscrupulous commander, Major George Purefoy, an
arrogant younger kinsman of the indomitable Warwickshire puritan, Colonel
William Purefoy. The impact on the local community of the Compton garrison,
curiously ignored by modern historians, is difficult to exaggerate. It was clearly
considered almost as important as Banbury by both sides – judging on the one
hand by the initial succession of royal warrants issued from the Court at Oxford
guaranteeing its protection and, on the other, once taken by Parliamentary
troops, by the substantial taxes levied on neighbouring parishes to support it, the
scale of the fortifications and repairs undertaken to maintain it as a viable base,
the Royalist attempt to recapture it and, above all perhaps, by the vastness of the
area deemed necessary by Parliament to support it. From Alcester in the west to
Bicester in the east and comprising literally half of Oxfordshire, dozens of
parishes in the two counties were compelled to support it financially, besides
those nearer home which were bled to provision it.[56] Compton Wynyates was in
effect stragetically important to both sides as the farthest frontier post between
their respective areas of influence, in what was effectively a buffer zone for much
of the war.

Intense activity had been building up in the south Midlands for some time
before the capture of Compton House in June 1644, which was only one of many
campaigns. Parliament considered Coventry to be 'in imminent danger' in

February, while anxious at the same time to transport a vital convoy of money, weapons and ammunition from London via Warwick to their garrison at Gloucester. Royalists were heavily concentrated throughout the Cotswolds to prevent this, Colonel Massey at Gloucester reporting to the Earl of Essex in March:

> Prince Rupert, with much of the horse from Oxford, is come to Stow. Lord Northampton and the rest at Campden, Sudeley, Evesham, Broadway, Upton, Bredon and Tewkesbury lie very strong, at least 2,000 horse besides dragoons, and 2,000 foot lie between us and Warwick on purpose only to keep back our relief.

On one occasion in March the Parliamentary convoy under Colonel Hans Behr was forced to turn back outside Stratford in face of a determined Royalist attack,[57] while further east the King had ordered greater reinforcement of Banbury. Tension was heightened by a systematic Royalist campaign of destroying the Feldon bridges, like the strategically important ancient one at Halford on the Fosse Way, 'being a great bridge and very useful to passengers from Warwick to Shipston and . . . divers other great towns', the Earl of Denbigh reporting to Parliament from Coventry:

> the great [Royalist] forces drawn towards these confines and about Gloucestershire purposely to intercept this convoy, a number too considerable and much superior to our forces . . . have likewise cut down the bridge of Halford, and intend to do the like to all the other bridges which lie in the way; and to make the passage more difficult they are cutting trenches in all the fordable places of the River Stour.[58]

One armed clash which probably took place at this time resulted in fatalities at Newbold-on-Stour; the Tredington burial register recorded 'Two men killed at a skirmish betwixt the Kings Maties soldiers and the Parliaments above Newbold church bridge'.[59] In addition to those Parliamentary forces assigned specifically to escort the convoy to Gloucester under Behr, which included substantial contingents from Warwick and even Newport Pagnell, several other Parliamentary regiments were scattered throughout the area: Brailes alone quartered units belonging to Waller, Denbigh and Fiennes, while Cromwell's were keeping guard further north, at Radway and beyond. As usual, therefore, plundering was rife, with known Royalist sympathizers the first victims; Simon Underhill, of the Idlicote Royalist branch of the family, was divested in June of 'a Beaver hatt a sword a payre of silke stockings 3 gold capps a new payre of bootes one fyne Holland table cloath conteyninge 6 els in length, valued at . . . 5li' and many other items. The indiscipline of Behr's troops was particularly notorious, the Earl of Denbigh condemning 'Commissary-General Behr's forces [who] by their plundering and intolerable insolences discontented the people'.[60] Finally in May came a concerted but abortive Parliamentary attempt to recapture Banbury, before the successful assault on Compton House, which finally fell to Parliament on 9 June 1644 after a two-day siege, as noted in the terse official communiqué:

> Major Bridges wth his forces from Warwickshire & Coventry, having laid before Compton howse Friday & Satturday last, on Sunday morning tooke it, and in it the Earle of Northtons brother, Captaine Clarke Capt Bradwell wth about 12 officers more and 120 common soldiers, 80 good horses with all their armes and Ammunition, and sent them to Warwicke . . .

A slightly different Parliamentary version, naming Colonel William Purefoy as the victorious commander, records, probably accurately, that 'besides 120 prisoners, he took £5,000 in money, 60 horses, 400 sheep, near 160 head of cattle and 18 loads of other plunder; besides 5 or 6 earthen pots of money which he afterwards discovered in the fishpond'. The Royalist Dugdale, adding yet another slant, alleges that the Parliamentarians 'drove the park and killed all the deer, and defaced the monuments in ye Church'.[61]

The great Tudor mansion was promptly stripped of its contents, Colonel William Purefoy taking charge of the plunder operations using carts requisitioned locally via hapless village constables like Richard Wilcox of Tysoe and Edward Walker of Brailes to convey the goods to Warwick. An inventory of the stolen goods was later compiled by the Earl of Northampton's trusty bailiff, William Goodman, himself a substantial yeoman farmer from neighbouring Winderton who had in happier times supplied the earl with meat and other goods. The inventory, interesting though it is, suggests that the house had been largely emptied of the most valued possessions by its owner, of late almost entirely absent on active service. Goodman's loyalty to his 'good Lord & Maister' cost him dear: he subsequently claimed on oath that on this occasion alone he lost almost 1,500 sheep, 24 cattle, 80 loads of hay, £140 in cash divided between money bags, a locked box 'in an inner Roome' and 'a Trunke in one of ye Chambers which was broken up by ye souldiers', besides his wife's purse containing more than £20, three or four gold rings taken from his maid and a further £10 worth of his own gold. He himself was physically searched and robbed in the presence of the officer-in-charge, Major Castle, already notorious with his own Parliamentary superiors for illegal extortion from his prisoners in Warwick Castle. Not content with this, the newly-appointed garrison commander, Major George Purefoy, ordered a large quantity of malt, wheat and peas from Goodman's Winderton farm. The unfortunate Goodman had already had his other estate at Prescote, near Cropredy, plundered the previous October, when over 400 sheep, 25 cattle and 3 horses had been seized and driven to Warwick, besides suffering also at the hands of the Earl of Denbigh's soldiers on another occasion.[62] Nor were such outrages confined to the wealthy, able, it could be argued, to recoup losses. Certainly the more affluent were particularly victimized, especially if Royalist connections were evident. William Calloway of Tysoe, one of those managing the sequestrated Northampton estates, was at one point imprisoned in Compton House and released only on producing 8 cwt of butter and 7 cwt of cheese for the garrison commander. Other notables like Francis Clarke of Tysoe, Richard Canning of Ilmington and Sir Hercules Underhill of Idlicote, together with the many supposedly 'papist' clergy of the district, were persecuted more than once. Some even, like the prominent Brailes Catholic, William Bishop, went abroad for a time, probably as a direct result of the conflict.[63] However, those of very modest means and even the downright poor suffered too, as the new governor, George Purefoy, set about systematically terrorizing the entire neighbourhood. Swingeing taxes were imposed on all the nearby communities, with additional fines as punishment for their past disaffection.

The inhabitants of the adjacent parish of Tysoe, in particular, were appallingly treated, being immediately subjected to a stream of imperious ultimata demanding men, materials and food supplies, the preamble to a typical 'warrant', dated 17 June 1644, reading 'To the most base, malignant Constable and Townes of Tysoe . . . upon paine of imprisonment and plunderinge'. Scores of labourers, carpenters and teams of oxen and horses were demanded for week after week of unpaid labour on improved fortifications, the scale of which is evident from one warrant alone among others demanding 'on(e) labourer forth of every houshold in all the three Townes and three Draftes of each towne to continue their all that weeke', together with the length of service exacted of husbandmen uprooted from their fields: 'Humphrey Tennant was labouring at Compton cutting Downe trees thaching hayrickes and about the workes Forty Dayes and upwards.' A glance at these Tysoe indemnity claims, among the most detailed and circumstantial of the parish books,[64] leaves the impression indeed that virtually the entire male population was for a time dragooned into Purefoy's service, seriously dislocating the life of the community in the height of summer. Little escape was possible in a close-knit community and arbitrary summonses were issued by the governor to appear at improvised courts, 'charging the constable and other of the Inhabitants to appeare at Cumpton to Answere to such thinges as should be laide to their charge'. The Compton barns were replenished free of charge with thirty loads of straw and new-mown hay from the Tysoe pastures pending the arrival of more substantial supplies from further afield:

Itm Comanded by my warrants for ye use of my garrison 120 loads of hay, from ye townes neare adjoynenige to the same as Tysoe, Brayles, Oxhill, Idlicott, Whatcott, Epwell, ye Pillertons & Eatenton ye said quantity beinge burned in the barne wn ye enemy stormed ye Garrison.

Considerable quantities of utensils and food – bread, cheese, butter, bacon, salted beef are repeatedly mentioned – made their way to Compton from the surrounding villages and suggest that the members of the garrison intended to make the most of their temporary quarters and live comfortably. Bedding was particularly prized, with sheets, linen blankets, bolsters, pillows and beds themselves all specified, as many a former ploughboy or shepherd slept more comfortably than ever before in the stately home on sheets supplied by rich and poor alike, from Sir Hercules Underhill in his mansion at Idlicote to the cottage of widow Saul at Brailes. That not all thefts were intended directly for the maintenance of a military garrison is clear, too: besides the usual food and utensils, for example, Thomas Wilkes's losses at Tysoe included a riding coat, waistcoats and petticoats, boys' hats and stockings, silver clasps for a Bible and a pair of 'sifters tipped with silver'. Lest such robbery be ascribed to indisciplined subordinates, the victim insisted on specifying 'the Maior being present himselfe'. Only a few months previously, a Thomas Wilks of Brailes (whether the same man settling in the nearby parish or a case of father and son is unclear) reported losing, at the taking of Compton House, 'in mony plate, household goods & all manner of waring clothes of my owne my wives & 4 children . . . to the value 214li 16s 0d.' Such episodes were repeated countless times throughout the district as Purefoy's marauders descended on village and hamlet in the Feldon and across the border into Oxfordshire. Alkerton, where the Royalist rector and scholar, Thomas Lydiate, was brutally treated, was raided several times, Shutford was threatened 'upon paine of plundering, imprisonment and other extremities . . . At your perils', and Over Norton similarly: 'I will plunder yor towne and hang yor Constable'.[65] The character of such expeditions may be judged from a petition submitted later by Thomas Tasker, a labourer of the neighbouring Oxfordshire parish of Epwell, to the Parliamentary authorities:

. . . yor Petitioner being a poore man and aged, in December 1644, in the middle of the night, a Partie of Maior Purefoys souldiers comanded by Corporal Dizon came into his house, and violently tooke away the most parte of his household goodes, to the valew of tenne Pounds or upwards, and also tooke away yor petitionr to Compton where he was uniustly imprisoned by the space of Five or Six Dayes, and nothing being alleadged against him, the Maior came to him and used many harsh speeches & so gave order to the Marshall for to release him, but never examined him of any thinge at all, neither would he give him leave to speake for himselfe to Desire any of his goodes againe . . . His humble request unto Yor Worps is . . . in regard he and his wife are aged, and the sudden fright hath made them both so sickly and weake that they are altogether unable for to get their liveing . . .[66]

The highways too were kept under surveillance by Purefoy's men for goods being transported which were liable to be seized and brought back to Compton: 'taken 3 horseloads of Poltry & cheese going to ye enemys garrison', 'taken 6 oxen going to Oxford', 'taken from Mr Osburston within 4 mls of Oxford to victual 40 sheep & 10 qr wheate', 'a Pryze of hatts going to ye enemys garrison of Worcester', a side baron of beef which the Brailes butcher (though unnamed, probably Francis Shirley, a local Catholic) was carrying to the royal garrison at Banbury, 'and the said Beafe was disposed of by the Govnor of Compton who had halfe of it and the soldiers the Rest', £3 taken from the constable of Whichford which was suspected of being taken to Banbury Royalists. In periods of inactivity the garrison's horses were grazed indiscriminately on neighbouring pastures, provoking frequent anger. At other times the tedium was relieved by morale-boosting reprisal raids on notorious, or simply defenceless, local Royalist sympathizers or anyone unfortunate enough to be associated with them, like the curate of Whichford, Lieutenant Henry Smith later confessing:

> I had commande from Major Puryfoy to seise upon the person of Doctor Langstones Curatt, and such cattle of the Doctors as I coulde finde upon his groundes, and to bring the said Curatt and Cattell to Compton Garrison wch I did according to the Govnors Commannde, to the best of my knowledge the Govnor of Compton had eleaven or twelve pounds for the inlargemt of him selfe and the Cowes of wch monies my selfe nor the soldiers had anie parte.

If by now the unscrupulous Cavalier, Colonel Gerard Croker, had withdrawn from the conflict, his north Oxfordshire family remained as a tempting target for Purefoy:

> Also I was Commanded by the Governor of Compton Garrison to fetch into the Garrison fiftie sheepe from Mr Henry Croker of Hooke Norton, wch sheepe were disposed of by the Governor to his owne particular use . . .

Vindictive reprisals were also carried out against former enemy soldiers now disbanded, like Robert Rose and William Bratford returning home to Tysoe hoping to resume their peaceful former existence. Rose was promptly imprisoned by Purefoy and even though 'he had his Dyett sent him from his Mother' was retained until £5 ransom was paid.[67] As the war dragged on the Royalists threatened more than once to recapture Compton, the most spectacular attempt coming at the end of January 1645 and graphically described by the defending governor, Purefoy himself. The Royalist newsletter, *Mercurius Aulicus*, whose objectivity is, however, clearly somewhat suspect, alleges that the Earl of Northampton's local strength cooped up the Parliamentarian at Compton to such an extent:

> that his cummings abroad are more like a theife than a souldier, creeping

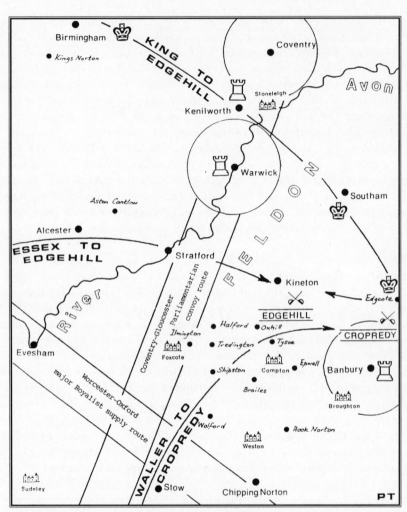

South Warwickshire was disputed territory for much of the war. Two major permanent garrisons were established at the outset, at Banbury (Royalist) and Warwick (Parliamentarian), together with the Parliamentarian administrative headquarters at Coventry. Among many other garrisons set up periodically by both sides throughout the district the most active were Evesham (Royalist) and Compton Wynyates (Parliamentarian). The main military supply lines, west-east for the Royalists and north-south for the Parliamentarians, provided additional hazards for the local community, while the two major battles at Edgehill and Cropredy attracted the major field armies to the district. The arrows show only the general direction of marching; in reality units strayed far and wide beyond these on the approach to the battles, and scattered very widely after.

sometimes in the darke, where he steals contributions to keepe himself in heart to pen blustering warrants.[68]

All in all, the colourful George Purefoy is worth rescuing from oblivion, such was the undoubted impact of his presence on south Warwickshire and beyond during these two years. Although very different in character from those of his formidable relative, William Purefoy, his swashbuckling exploits earned the distinction of attracting comment in Parliament. He suffered a preposterous riding accident in Hyde Park in which he knocked himself unconscious and lost a diamond-decorated hat worth £150 in the process and he rigged local elections in Warwickshire. Not content with managing for a time to enjoy the huge profits from the Earl of Northampton's sequestrated estates, he was not averse to appropriating the schoolmaster of Combrook's salary, forcing the unfortunate parson of Butlers Marston, Edward Langley, to teach the children at the new school without remuneration. If the words *plunder* and *highwayman* both made their entry into the language during the Civil War, they might almost have been coined specifically in memory of George Purefoy. He had a good war.[69]

As has already been suggested, the poor were hardly less exempt from the effects of the war than the wealthy, although burdens were differently distributed. Even villagers of very modest status were called upon to provide the quarter. Among the sixty inhabitants of Brailes submitting complaints of quarter and plunder few were wealthy; Nicholas Bishop was a labourer, Thomas Eddon a shoemaker, and many others, twenty years later, still had only one or two hearths to their name.[70] For many a modest husbandmen the war meant severe hardship, as proved by the few cases – the tip of a considerable iceberg – finding their way into the State Papers, like Christopher Mills of Warwick or Silvester Warner of Marston, the latter despairingly ending his petition with the hope 'that God will either take him out of this world or make him more able to undergo these burdens'.[71] As for the destitute living at or below subsistence level, the situation was even worse, compounded by the breakdown of the administration of justice and poor relief at parish level. At Leek Wootton, which had already been regularly plundered by the Royalists, one inhabitant pleaded to the Parliamentary tax authorities: 'I am A poore Tenant which have nothing but upon the rack rent, being tenant at will', while the constable recorded of another: 'Thomas Barnet is very poore and hath nothing but what he getts by his dayly labour'.[72] The situation in most parishes cannot have been very different. In the most populous of all, Brailes – which not so long ago had been receiving assistance from other parishes under the old Elizabethan Poor Law because its own resources were inadequate to relieve its many destitute, and with a substantial proportion of indigent cottagers, including recusants 'soe extreame poore that they have neither lands nor tenements, goods or Chattels' – lists of inhabitants in arrears of taxes and others assessed, significantly at 1s were regularly returned by the constable.[73] In other parishes the Quarter Sessions records alone cite cases of hardship arising directly from the war: masters refusing to take back apprentices after serving in the war on the wrong side; war widows requesting relief, like Margery Browne of Pillerton, whose husband was killed at the siege of Banbury; rates being interrupted; an alarming increase in the numbers of pedlars and beggars.[74] In such parishes, complaining, like Barton-on-the-Heath, that taxes had been unjustly raised 'in these late unhappy wars', driven, like Rowington and Cubbington, to protest officially at excessive quartering, or unable to continue payment of the poor levies, the simple cumulative effects of swingeing taxation, economic depression, harsh winters, disruption to markets, harvests and trade, 'much decayed . . . in the time of the late distractions', must clearly have affected the whole community.[75] An occasional random jotting in the archives conceals, one imagines, many a silent personal crisis aggravated by the hardships of these years, like the touchingly simple note scrawled on a page of the parish book of Ascott in Whichford: 'Jane Sturch, a poore widow, behind'.

At least one scholar, in a nevertheless invaluable study, has concluded that apart from Catholics, 'in civil war Warwickshire the bulk of the population appeared to be relatively unaffected by the traumatic experience of warfare'.[76] Examination of the surviving indemnity claims submitted by parishes to the Parliamentary authorities – and it must be stressed that those for several populous parishes like Long Compton and Shipston and many smaller ones like Barton-on-the-Heath, Ettington, Honington, Sutton-under-Brailes, Whatcote and Tredington have not survived – suggests otherwise, however: that both the village community itself and substantial numbers of individuals, and not only the wealthy, were indeed severely affected. Moreover, space has excluded all but the most cursory reference to at least two major aspects of the conflict from the present discussion. The disruption to religious life, still central to a village community, along with the persecution of the clergy, and above all, the whole question of the crippling financial burden on rich and poor alike, have not been dealt with here. Were adequate examination of these added to the picture drawn above from a mere selection of events, the sheer human toll on the south Warwickshire rural community would undoubtedly appear even more evident.

Notes

1. E.g. Warwickshire's Kineton Hundred, Vol. V. The section on Stratford-upon-Avon by Philip Styles in Vol. III (1945) is one good exception to the rule. Regrettably, subsequent contributions, like those on Warwick and Coventry (Vol. VIII, 1968), did not follow this lead and are pitifully brief.

2. Told by M. Ashley, *England in the Seventeenth Century* (1952), p. 79; P. Young, *The English Civil War, a Military History* (1974), p. 53, etc., but rejected as apocryphal by I. Roy in Bond and Roy, *War and Society* (1975), p. 31, and R. Hutton in J. Morrill, ed., *Reactions to the English Civil War, 1642–1649* (1982), p. 51.

3. William Dugdale, *Antiquities of Warwickshire*, W. Thomas, ed., 1730, I, p. 309, and often repeated since. Dugdale was closely involved in events in Warwickshire and had unrivalled local contacts and knowledge. The Tysoe story is a long-standing tradition.

4. J.F.C. Harrison, *The Common People, a History from the Norman Conquest to the Present* (1984), p. 203.

5. *VCH* II contains a short (and occasionally inaccurate) summary of some main events, but no serious treatment of the Civil War in the county appeared between M.H. Bloxam's *Warwickshire during the Civil Wars* (Warwick, 1880), and the academic theses of D.F. Mosler, 'A Social and Religious History of the English Civil War in Warwickshire' (Stanford, 1975) (unpublished; copy at Warwick CRO) and A. Hughes, published as *Politics, Society and Civil War in Warwickshire* (Cambridge, 1987). My own *Edgehill and Beyond: the People's War in the South Midlands, 1642–1645* (Stroud, 1992), and *The Civil War in Stratford-upon-Avon* (Shakespeare Birthplace Trust/Stroud, 1996), provide a straightforward chronological account of the impact of the war on the local community.

6. R. Hutton, *The Royalist War Effort, 1642–1646* (1982), p. 19. Cf. Bloxam, *op. cit.*, p. 3, who claimed that the county was 'destined to be the trysting ground in which the first blow was to be struck'.

7. C.D. and W.C.D. Whetham, *A History of the Life of Col. Nathaniel Whetham*, (1907), p. 75.

8. This section is based on the excellent introduction by I. Roy to *The Royalist Ordnance Papers*, Oxford Rec. Soc., xliii, 1963–4.

9. Public Record Office, SP.28/182–6, from which all subsequent parish details are taken unless otherwise indicated. Other miscellaneous Wks items are found in SP.28/136, 201, 215, 247–9, etc. These classes are uncalendared, unindexed and without any internal arrangement.

10. Lord Digby to Rupert from Oxford, 2 Apr 1645, in British Library (BL) Add. Ms. 18982, ff. 44–5; cf. Clarendon's *History of the Rebellion and Civil Wars in England* (Oxford, 1888), iv, pp. 37–8; Corbet in J. Washbourn, *Bibliotheca Gloucestrensis* (1823), i, p. 63; 'A Full Relation of the Siege of Banbury Castle', Sept 1644, in BL, Thomason Tracts (TT), E 8(9).

11. Distances travelled by soldiers were often impressive, and must have been a major talking-point among the amazed villagers in small, close-knit communities. Like many others, tiny Ashow, near Kenilworth, saw not only local soldiers but others from Evesham, Norfolk, Lincolnshire, 'Darby men as they went to Bristow' [Bristol] and 'Darby men as they came back', as well as the Scots.

12. *CSPD 1642, passim*; 1641–3, p. 166; Wks *Quarter Sessions Order Books*, S.C. Ratcliff & H.C. Johnson, eds, Warwick, 1935–53, p. 116; Shakespeare Birthplace Trust, BRU 2/3, C.203, 209, and Chamberlain's Accounts, BRU 4/2 ff. 164–5.

13. Warwick: PRO SP.28/183, 253B. Commission of Array: Hutton, *Royalist War Effort*, pp. 5–6.

14. *Calendar of the Committee for the Advancement of Money, 1646–1656* (hereafter *CAM*), M.A. Green, ed., HMSO, 1888, for 13 Jul 1646. Baldwin: PRO SP.19/21 f. 253: Baldwin was 'the principall Man yt published & read ye Comission of Array in the psence of many hundred people called together for that purpose both in Winderton & Tisoe Meadowes'.

15. *The History of Myddle*, W.G. Hoskins, ed., (1968), p. 67; Historical Manuscripts Commission (HMC) *Portland MSS.*, i, p. 53 (12 August 1642), quoted in A. Fletcher, *The Outbreak of the English Civil War* (1985), p. 359.

16. BL Harl. 669 f.5; *CAM*, p. 1109; PRO SP.16/491 f. 89, A Letter from Stoneleigh, 25 Jul 1642. Brooke's activities were scathingly condemned by the (Royalist) author of *The Life of that learned antiquary Sir William Dugdale, Kt* (London, 1713), p. 13.

17. *Journal of the House of Commons*, 27 June 1642; Royal Warrant dated York, 4 August 1642 and printed in full in *Life . . . of Sir William Dugdale*.

18. *CSPD* and *Journal of the House of Commons*, 26 August 1642; W.B. Compton, *A History of the Comptons of Compton Wynyates*, Bodley Head (1930); SP.28/253B; *Letters of Nehemiah Wharton* (a subaltern in the Earl of Essex's army), in *Archaeologia*, xxxv, 1853, H. Ellis, ed., p. 310.

19. Compton papers, Castle Ashby, 1083/3.

20. *CSPD*, 26 September 1642, SP.28/182 (Kineton).

21. Compton Papers, Castle Ashby, 1083/1.

22. BL, TT: E 109 (3), 'Some Special Passages from Warwickshire'; E 108 (26), 'Terrible News from Leicestershire, Warwickshire and Staffordshire'; cf. Fletcher, *op. cit.*, containing many other references.

23. SP.28/182 (Warmington), A.G. Matthews, *Walker Revised* (Oxford, 1948) and BL Add. MSS. 15670–71; *CAM*, iii, p. 1412 (Oxhill).

24. *CSPD, 1645–47*, pp. 240, 522, etc; *VCH*, III, pp. 459–60; *House of Lords Journals*, vi. p. 196; SP. 16/511; SP.28/253B. The Warwick booty was later the subject of protracted enquiry, still continuing in 1651.

25. *A Holy Commonwealth*, (London, 1659), p. 457.

26. *CAM*, p. 1413.

27. S.C. Ratcliff and H.C. Johnson, eds, *Warwick County Records, Quarter Sessions*, ii, pp. xxiv–xxv, 125–6; Mosler, *op. cit.*, pp. 57–8; Hutton, *op. cit.*, p. 32.

28. 'The Account of the Battel at Edgehill, Oct. 23. 1642, as publisht by Order of the Parliament', quoted in P. Young, *Edgehill 1642* (1967), p. 306.

29. Clarendon, *op. cit.*, ii, pp. 358–9, 364.

30. Wharton, *op. cit.*, letter of 24 September 1642.

31. Parish details from SP.28/182–6. Oxhill and Tysoe traditions repeated in G. Miller, *Rambles Round the Edge Hills* (Banbury, 1896, repr. Kineton, 1967), pp. 66–7, 106–7, and often since.

32. SP.28/136/56; SP.28/183, 201. Willoughby presents a puzzle, since Brailes is the only parish to mention him (and not his men); Whitelock says he joined late evening 23 Oct: *Memorials of the English Affairs* (Oxford, 1843). Waller poses a problem too: one Parliamentarian source says he fought bravely, another (Peacock, *Army Lists*, p. 48) that he arrived too late. Young, *Edgehill 1642*, compounds the confusion, listing him as absent p. 99, then present pp. 100, 102. Alcester: R. Baxter, *Reliquiae Baxteriana* (1696), I, p. 43.

33. Clarendon, *op. cit.*, ii. pp. 364, 373.

34. 'The Answer and Defence of Col John Bridges, June 1651', in SP.28/253B; SP.28/184; SP.28/33 ff. 457–8; SP.28/36 ff. 254–6; *Journals of the House of Commons*, III, p. 187.

35. SP.16/511, f. 106; 'Examination of Thomas Savage, servant to W. Sheldon', 6 Feb 1645/6.

36. John Vicars (puritan chronicler), *England's Parliamentary Chronicle, Magnalia Dei Anglicana* (London, 1642–44), iv. p. 421.

37. *CSPD*, 3 June 1645, p. 562.

38. Young, *op. cit.*, pp. 330–1; G. Miller, *op. cit.*, p. 70. The Oxhill epitaph is quoted by many local historians, from Dugdale to the present church notes by Betty Smith, 1971. For the Edgehill ghosts, see Young, *op. cit.*, pp. 162–6.

39. R. Coe, 'An Exact Dyarie . . . of the Progresse of Sir William Waller's Army', 24 June 1644, in BL TT. E 2(20).

40. PRO, SP.21/16, f. 74 (Oxhill, 26 June 1644); cf. *CSPD*, June–July 1644 *passim*.

41. Cf. n. 35 above.

42. Quoted with source in J. Adair, *Roundhead General, a Military Biography of Sir William Waller* (1969) p. 162; *CSPD*, June–July 1644, *passim*.

43. R. Symonds, *Diary of the Marches kept by the Royal Army*, C.E. Long, ed., Camden Society, 1859, p. 25.

44. *The Diary of Henry Townshend, 1640–1663*, J.W.W. Bund, ed., Worcestershire Historical Society, 1920. BL Harl. Ms 6804, ff. 78–9, The King's Papers.

45. Sir Samuel Luke to his father, 12 Nov 1644, in H.G. Tibbut, ed., *The Letter Books of Sir Samuel Luke, 1644–45* (1963), p. 76.

46. 'The Journal of his Highnesse Prince Rupert's Marches . . . ', C.H. Firth, ed., *English Historical Review*, xiii, (1898); *VCH*, III, p. 235, quoting E. Warburton, *Memoirs of Prince Rupert and the Cavaliers*, ii (1849), p. 227.

47. *VCH*, III, p. 235. Tibbut. *op. cit.*, p. 20; Prince Rupert's Correspondence, BL Add. MS. 18980, f. 23, dated 2 Mar 1642/3; Tibbut, *op. cit.*, pp. 121, 136.

48. Compton Papers, Castle Ashby, 1083/20; BL Harl. MS. 6851, ff. 70, 105–6, 6852, f. 7; 6851, f. 120; Compton Papers 1083/21a; BL Add. MS. 18980, f. 58; BL Harl. MS. 6852, f. 7. Resistance is also reported from Buckinghamshire in BL Add. MS. 18980, ff. 66, 68 (Lord Wentworth to Rupert, May 1643, quoted by R. Hutton, 'The Royalist War Effort', in Morrill, *op. cit.*, p. 60, with comment.)

49. M. Toynbee, ed., *Papers of Capt. Henry Stevens*, Oxford Rec. Soc., xlii (1962), p. 16; R. Hutton, 'The Worcestershire Clubmen in the Eng. Civil War', *Midland History* V, (1979–80), p. 41, quoting the Townshend Diary. Stow and Evesham: Kent Arch. Off., Maidstone, U.269/1, E.126; Hutton, *Royalist War Effort*, p. 99.

50. BL TT. E 69 (15); 'A True and Exact Relation . . . of the Trained Bands of the City of London', 2 Oct 1643, reprinted in Washbourn, *op. cit.*, TT. E 70 (10), 'A True Relation of the late Expedition of his Excellency the Earle of Essex, for the Relief of Gloucester', 7 Oct 1643, also in Washbourn.

51. *CAM*, p. 1289.

52. Sergeant Henry Foster, in 'A True and Exact Relation of the Marchings of the Trained Bands of the City of London', in Washbourn, *op. cit.*, pp. 255–6; C.H. Firth, *Cromwell's Army* (1962), p. 23. Royalist finances were equally shaky; cf. R. Hutton, 'The Royalist War Effort', in J. Morrill, *op. cit.*, p. 60.

53. HMC IVth Rpt. (Denbigh), p. 270, dated 19 Aug 1644; W. Hamper, ed., *The Life, Diary and Corresp. of Sir Wm Dugdale* (1827), p. 47; 'The Journall of . . . Prince Rupert's Marches'. 'Compton' is likely to be Little Compton rather than Long Compton, where Rupert would have had William Sheldon's palatial Weston House at his disposal, or Compton Wynyates, much further away.

54. BL Harl. 158, f. 277 and cf. *CSPD, 1645–47*, p. 289. The financial burden on the community is a huge subject well beyond the scope of a short article. Sums quoted in the parish books and elsewhere suggest very heavy taxation indeed; cf. A. Hughes, *op. cit*. Warwickshire claimed more than once that the whole county was unfairly overtaxed and harshly treated: cf. BL Harl. MS. 158, f. 277; *CSPD, 1645–7*, p. 289, etc.

55. Clarendon, *op. cit.*, iv, pp. 37–8.

56. BL Harl. MS. 6804 (The King's Papers), ff. 101–2; SP.28/43 Pts. IV, V; SP.28/136, 184 (Maj. Purefoy's Account Books).

57. *HMC*, IVth Report (Denbigh), p. 264, dated 4 Feb 1644, *CSPD*, Feb-Mar 1644. *passim*; BL Eg. MS. 785/5, 7, dated 11 Mar 1643/4; *CSPD, 1644*, pp. 64, 67–8, 70, etc.; *HMC*, Vth Rpt., p. 271.

58. *Quarter Sessions*, iii, pp. 21, 33, 65; *HMC*, IVth Rpt., p. 264; *CSPD*, 29 Feb 1643/4. pp. 29–30. Many local bridges were destroyed, often deliberately, during the war; Kites Hardwick, Bretford, Barford, Bidford, Tachbrook and Clopton Bridge, Stratford; cf. *Quarter Sessions* index.

59. Warwick County Record Office, DR 79.

60. *CSPD*, 19–20 Mar 1643/4, 2 Apr 1644; *HMC*, Vth Rpt., p. 265.

61. Sir Samuel Luke's Letter Books, 1643–45, BL Eg MS. 785, i (12 June 1644); J. Vicars, *England's Parliamentary Chronicle, Jehovah Jireh*, 1643–46; Dugdale, *Diary*.

62. Warwick CRO, CR 556/285, 286, etc.; SP.16/539/2/207; PRO, Will (PROB 11/216) dated 8 May 1651; SP.28/253B.

63. SP.28/184, 215; BL Add. MS. 35098, 'The Book of Sequestrations 1646', f. 25r (Bishop).

64. SP.28/184 (Tysoe).

65. *VCH, Oxford*, IX, quoting A. Wood, *Athenae Oxoniensis* (London, 1813), iii, p. 187; Beesley, *op. cit.*, p. 397; SP.28/43/IV, f. 577.

66. SP.28/184 (an Oxfordshire stray).

67. Maj. Purefoy's Account Books, SP.28/136, SP.28/184.

68. BL TT. E 268 (12), 7 Feb 1644/5, reproduced in full in W.B. Compton, *op. cit.*; cf. *CSPD*, 24–25 Dec 1645, pp. 276, 278, and Beesley, *op. cit.*, pp. 390, 400 ff.; BL, TT. Mercurius Aulicus, p. 1513.

69. A. Hughes, *op. cit.*, pp. 235, 251, 248, etc.; BL Add. MS. 35098. 'The Book of Sequestrations 1646', f. 3; SP.28/201 (Combrook).

70. SP.28/184; PRO. E. 179/259/9, 10.

71. *CSPD, Addenda, 1625–49*, p. 692 (6 Feb 1646); *HMC*, IVth Rpt, p. 264 (and another case, p. 266).

72. Cf. *Quarter Sessions*, ii, pp. xxiv–xxv; SP.28/185.

73. Huntington Library, Cal., USA, Stowe Mss. St 1444, 110; PRO. E, 179/395/23 (22 Oct 1641); Compton Papers 1083/33. Cf. the large number of Hearth Tax exemptions, e.g. PRO. E 179/194/334; E 179/347 etc.

74. *Quarter Sessions*, iii, pp. 134, 161; ii, pp. 177, 179, 231, 256, (cf. *CSPD, Addenda 1625–49*, p. 693, the case of Hester Whyte); iii, pp. 107, 274; iv, pp. 185–6; cf. *Quarter Sessions*, index, 'Poverty'.

75. *Quarter Sessions*, iv, p. 178: *HMC*, IVth Rpt (Denbigh), p. 272; *Quarter Sessions*, ii, pp. 177, 248–9; iv, pp. 185–6.

76. Cf. Mosler, *op. cit.*, p. 177.

9

THE CITY OF WORCESTER DURING THE CIVIL WARS, 1640–60

Philip Styles

I

Local studies of the Civil War tell us more about its effects than about its causes. The meeting of the Long Parliament on 3 November 1640 released a flood of pent-up grievances from all over the country. The old personal monarchy of the Tudors had collapsed and there had to be some great change. But there seemed as yet no likelihood that it would culminate in armed conflict. It was the rapid movement of events during the next eighteen months that made war inevitable: and, as the revolution acquired its own momentum, it was from the centre that the impetus came. There were many, even in Court and Parliament, who faced the nearing prospect of war only with reluctance. In the provinces the prevailing attitude was often that of bewildered spectators. In every county in England there were, of course, convinced Royalists and Puritans, men, who, when a choice had at last to be made, made it without hesitation. But in tracing the history of these momentous twenty years in any locality, as here in Worcester, we have to think in terms less of embattled and coherent sides than of response to swiftly changing circumstances.

Worcestershire was under Royalist military control for more than half the first Civil War and the city was the last of all the King's strongholds to surrender. Its strategic importance is obvious – guarding the principal crossing of the Severn between Oxford and Wales and the Marches, a vital source of supply, not only of troops, but of iron and ordnance.[1] It was, besides, the largest city in the West Midlands: 'pleasantly seated, exceedingly populous, and doubtless very rich' it seemed to Nehemiah Wharton, who came here in Essex's Army in September 1642.[2] A census, not quite complete, taken before the final siege in 1646, gives 5,676 inhabitants, representing a total civil population of perhaps 6,500 to 7,000.[3] In the hearth tax assessments of 1662–4 it ranks eleventh among the provincial towns in number of hearths.[4] Its highly organized textile industry, though somewhat declined from its peak in the previous century when, according to Leland, 'no town of England . . . maketh so many cloths yearly', was still the predominant source of wealth.[5] By his charter of 1621 James I had conferred upon Worcester the status of a county of itself, with its own sheriff, making it independent of the neighbouring shire.[6] The attitude of the citizens in the conflict was to be not a little influenced by the need to safeguard this newly acquired and cherished privilege.

The development of the situation between 1640 and 1642 is illustrated in Worcestershire by the elections to the Long Parliament. Though most of the leading gentry were to fight for the King, both the Knights of the Shire, Humphrey Salway of Stanford-on-Teme and John Wilde, serjeant-at-law, of Droitwich, became active Parliamentarians. They replaced two Royalists who had served in the Short Parliament, Sir Thomas Littleton of Frankley and Sir John Pakington of Westwood. Wilde was recorder of Worcester and afterwards (1645–53) Chief Baron of the Exchequer and was regarded by the city fathers as a valuable friend at Court during the Interregnum. Worcester returned two aldermen, members of prominent city families, John Coucher and John Nash. Coucher, aged seventy-nine, had sat in five previous Parliaments since 1604, and though he lived until 1652 there is no evidence that he attended after 1641.[7] Nash (1590–1662) remained in London throughout the War and retained his seat until he was expelled by Pride's Purge.[8]

The contentious measures of the 'Eleven Years Tyranny' aroused resentment in Worcester, as elsewhere. By 1640 there were three grievances of which the corporation hoped for redress from Parliament. The first, a local issue, was the project of William Sandys of Fladbury to make the Avon navigable from Tewkesbury up to Stratford, which was complained of as prejudicial to the city's trade.[9] On 18 January 1636 the corporation decided to petition the Council against it.[10] Nevertheless the navigation was completed by 1639. On 7 January 1641 a committee was appointed to draw up a petition to Parliament[11] and a fortnight later Sandys, who sat for Evesham, was expelled from the House as a monopolist.[12] During the War the 'Waterworks' fell into disuse. But the dispute bore little relation to politics and the local opposition was led by Sir William Russell of Strensham, soon to become the first Royalist governor of Worcester.

The second grievance was the jurisdiction of the Council of the Marches, of which the city had attempted to free itself as long ago as 1574.[13] The Council was included in the Act abolishing Star Chamber, which became law on 5 July 1641, but its powers as a civil court remained unaffected. A bill exempting the border counties of Shropshire, Herefordshire, Gloucestershire and Worcestershire and the cities of Gloucester and Worcester from its jurisdiction passed the Commons on 19 July but foundered in the Lords.[14] Another bill, for its total abolition, was thereupon introduced, towards the expenses of which Worcester corporation voted £5 on 10 August. This, however, got no further than the second reading.[15] It was perhaps because of the failure of this bill that we find the mayor attempting to make use of the Council by persuading the Lord President to grant the city control of its own militia, independent of the county:[16] a privilege which, had it been obtained, might have made some difference to the course of events a few months later. The Court of the Marches, though it lapsed during the Interregnum, survived in an attenuated form until the Revolution.

The third grievance, more directly related to the central issues of the time, concerned relations with the Dean and Chapter. The cathedral and its precincts were in the parish of St. Michael in Bedwardine, within the walls but outside the city boundaries; a potential source of conflict going back to the Middle Ages, though until the 1630s it seems on the whole to have worked reasonably well. By then, however, the clericalizing policy of Laud was making the Church more and more unpopular. In 1636 there arose a sharp dispute, such as broke out in other cities, for instance in Salisbury and Chester,[17] over the provision of seats in the cathedral for the mayor and corporation: an issue, petty in itself, which seemed to involve the whole question of the relationship between the ecclesiastical and the civil power. At Worcester it was embittered by the active zeal of two successive Deans, Roger Mainwaring (1634–6) and Christopher Potter (1636–45), both prominent Arminians. The earliest reference to the Long Parliament in the city's Chamber Order Books is the appointment on 18 December 1640 of a committee to draw up a case against the Dean and Chapter.[18] The complaints ranged from the stone altar and altar rails set up by Dean Mainwaring to the right of burial in the cathedral churchyard, the management of the Grammar School, the Chapter's contribution to the poor and highways, and the licensing of alehouses in the Close.[19] The city's petition to Parliament was referred, on 16 February 1641, to the committee which was considering the articles of impeachment against Matthew Wren, Bishop of Ely,[20] and no more is heard of it. But in the city records there are recurrent references to the case down to 29 November.[21] As the proceedings in Parliament dragged on, efforts were made locally to settle the differences by negotiation, apparently with some success. Certainly the alleged 'popish practices' in the cathedral were abandoned.[22] The corporation enlisted the support of their recorder, the two burgesses for the city, the Bishop and even one or two of the prebendaries. The membership of their committee, including both future Royalists and future Parliamentarians, indicates the wide range of opposition before which the Laudian system collapsed in 1641 like a house of cards.

Religious discord was not confined to the cathedral. The advowson of All Saints was one of those purchased by the Feoffees for Impropriations. When, in 1633, their activities were declared illegal by the Court of Exchequer, it was forfeit to the King, who granted it to a more orthodox group of clergy and laymen.[23] The rector they presented, John Ricketts, gave vent to his anti-Puritan feelings in Latin in his parish register: 'A Diabolo et latrante populo Deus liberet Ecclesiam.' Bishop Thornborough, a man of advanced years and old-fashioned orthodoxy, was less inclined to look for trouble. His report to Laud on the state of the diocese in 1636 mentions that there are only two lecturers in the city, 'both very conformable, and that they shall not continue longer than they are so'. The Archbishop was evidently not satisfied by these assurances, for in his Injunctions of 26 May 1637 he ordered that 'Mr Hardwick shall not be suffered to preach neither in the cathedral nor in any church in the city of Worcester any more, and for Mr Halseter he shall attend the Dean and Chapter, and give satisfaction to them concerning his abilities and conformity, and obtain their good will, or else he is to be forbidden also, and not suffered to preach any more in the said cathedral church'.[24] Humphrey Hardwick was rector of St. Mary Witton, Droitwich, and John Halseter, whom even Dean Potter thought 'an honest harmless man',[25] was rector of St. Nicholas in the city. Both of them, together with Henry Hacket, rector of St. Helens, afterwards deserted their cures and joined Essex's army. Hacket, however, the son of Alderman Thomas Hacket, soon returned and was buried in St. Helen's on 28 October 1643, leaving his widow and family on the parish.[26]

That the tone of feeling in the corporation was, in a general sense, Puritan appears from the payment on 14 August 1640 of 5s. 8d. 'to a Companie of players . . . to prevent theire playeing in the Citie'[27] and in the appointment of a committee on 2 January 1644 charged, among other things, 'to admonish the severall inhabitantes for the well ordering of their children and servantes that they forbeare swearing and prophaneing the Lordes day'[28] – or, in other words, to protect them from being corrupted by the Royalist soldiery. But Worcester was not, like Gloucester, a centre of militant Puritanism, partly perhaps because all the city livings except All Saints were in the gift either of the Bishop or the Chapter. On the eve of the War St. Martin's was held by one of the prebendaries and St. Andrew's, St. Swithin's and St. Clement's by minor canons. Nehemiah Wharton, that ardent Puritan, found little comfort here. 'Like London', he says, 'it abounds in outward things of all kinds, but for Want of the Word the people perish'. He goes on to liken it to Sodom and Gomorrah and believes that, but for the visitation of a Godly army 'it would have been worse than either Algiers or Malta, a very den of thieves, and refuge for all the hel-hounds in the country'.[29] Richard Baxter describes how, in the summer of 1642, 'As I past but through a corner of the Suburbs of Worcester, they that knew me not, cried, "Down with the Roundheads", and I was glad to spur on and be gone. But when I came to Gloucester, among strangers also that had never known me, I found a civil, courteous, and religious People, as different from Worcester, as if they had lived under another Government'.[30]

The 'corner of the Suburbs' through which Baxter rode would include St. Michael in Bedwardine, where the unusually full churchwardens' accounts give a vivid picture of the religious life of the parish. Because of its close connection with the cathedral it may not have been wholly typical, but there was here clearly a genuine enthusiasm for Church and King. A strong sense of the 'beauty of holiness' appears in the meticulous inventories of plate and ornaments. They include a communion cup and cover 'of silver parcell guilte', worth £5 4s. 0d., and a case of leather for the handsome keepinge of the same'; two pewter flagons and plates to stand them on 'to preserve the cloth and carpett from spillinges of wine'; and two sets of 'carpet' and cushion for the communion table, one, worth 40s. given by Richard Warmerton, shoemaker, in 1624 and the other, given by Nicholas Archbold, gentleman, in 1627, worth £5. All these were removed by Cromwell's soldiers after the battle in 1651.[31] The church was decorated with rosemary and bays at Christmas and with boughs at Rogation-tide.[32] The custom of ringing bells on 27 March, the King's Accession day, was observed, in obvious defiance of the Parliamentary Committee, as late as 1647.[33] The living was poorer even than most of those in Worcester and was augmented by pensions of £3 from the Dean and Chapter, 10s. under the will of Nicholas Archbold and £2 from the parish stock. The rector, Nathaniel Marston, attended Sir John Byron, probably as his chaplain, when he entered Worcester in September 1642 and in consequence was 'very barbarously plundered' by Essex's troops soon afterwards. He appealed to the King for compensation and Charles recommended him to Bishop Prideaux for one of the cures deserted by Halseter and Hacket,[34] but apparently without effect. Marston inspired the devotion of his flock, even through the years of adversity. After the War he was summoned to London and then for a time was banished from Worcester and on each occasion the churchwardens gave him 20s. On 22 July 1647 he received £2, 'to buy him a suite of cloathes'.[35] Probably about then he was deprived and it seems likely that the church was closed for regular services, the congregation being provided for by the weekly lecture in the cathedral. Marston lived on in the parish, mainly supported by charity. By 1654 the overseers were making him a monthly allowance of 2s., later raised to 2s. 6d., and gifts of a few shillings 'in regard of his greate want' or 'his poverty' recur in the churchwardens' accounts. In 1651, 5s. was paid towards the burial of his wife and on 14 November 1657 'Mr Nathaniel Marston our late Minister was buryed in the churchyard'.[36] In 1660 the return to the old order was spontaneous. The church was restored and cleaned and the bells rehung in time to ring for the anniversary of the Gunpowder Plot. On 30 July 3s. was paid 'for two partes of the rayles which stood in the chancell and were plundered from the church' and on 20 December two new prayer books – the 1559 Version – were purchased for the minister and the clerk. The church was decorated at Christmas for the first time since 1645. From 12 May onwards, services were taken by a succession of ministers, many of them ejected Royalists of the neighbourhood who had returned to their livings:[37] St. Michael's is an interesting case of the survival of an Anglican tradition at parish level and there must have been many others.

II

Charles I's efforts to coerce the Scots had given the country a foretaste at least of the financial burdens of war. Worcester had to provide thirty-six men at a cost, in 1640 and 1641, of nearly £200, most of which was raised by four double-fifteenths;[38] a double-fifteenth, the regular unit of taxation at this time, being reckoned to yield £35.11.8. Whatever the wealth of its citizens, the corporation of Worcester was poor. A petition to the King in 1643 speaks of 'our whole revenue not amounting to £100 a year',[39] a figure which corresponds to the total of rents in the chamberlains' accounts. The rental even of so small a borough as Stratford was estimated in 1637 at £279 14s. 5½d.,[40] and at Gloucester, the corporation rents during the early 1640s averaged over £470 and the total annual revenue about £800.[41] But, whereas in both these towns the bulk of the rents came from land and tithe, Worcester held mainly urban properties let on long leases of forty-one years. Civic insolvency, therefore, was common enough, even in times of peace. Any extraordinary expense could only be met by loans or taxes, by voluntary subscription or by levies on the two companies of the Chamber, the Twenty-four and the Forty-eight. All these methods were frequently resorted to during the Civil War and bore especially hard on members of the governing body.[42] Refusals to serve office and resignations or removals for having left the city were sometimes due to financial rather than political reasons.

The vote by the Chamber in March, and again in June 1641, of a double-fifteenth for the repair of the walls and the bridge shows how the threat of war was beginning to move nearer home.[43] On 18 December the office of Muster-Master, appointed to train the troops for Scotland, was discontinued, but with the significant proviso, 'unlesse there bee order taken by Parliament for that purpose'.[44] Then came, on 4 January 1642, the attempted arrest of the five members, on 9 January Charles's final departure from London, and on 5 March the Militia Ordinance by which the two Houses claimed control of the militia, independently of the King. That spring and summer were occupied by both sides in raising troops, Parliament under the Ordinance and the King by issuing commissions of array for various counties, as he did for Worcestershire about the end of June. It was to be put in execution at the county Quarter Sessions on 13 July when all freeholders charged with arms were ordered to appear before the commissioners at the Town Hall in Worcester.[45] The plan was frustrated by the Knights of the Shire, Salway and Wilde, who were hurriedly sent down from Westminster and arrived in the city on the night of 11 July. By their influence a grand jury was impanelled which drew up a petition to the Justices to execute the Militia Ordinance and this was carried 'with a great acclamation of the company then present, and further intimations of ten thousand hands more to have been added to it, if time would have permitted'.[46] At the city Sessions on 11 July there is no record of any proceedings in the matter, no doubt because the Mayor and the aldermen did not control their own militia.

The Parliamentary triumph, however, was short-lived. At the Summer Assizes on 3 August the petition was repudiated and a 'Declaration and Protestation agreed upon by the Grand Jury' was carried and was afterwards printed at York. It bears 59 signatures: 26 knights, esquires and gentlemen, 11 of whom were commissioners of array; the Clerk of the Peace, two coroners and three high constables; and the grand jurors, 14 for the county and 13 for the city. As it is the only direct statement we have of Royalist opinion in Worcestershire it is worth quoting in full:

We do with all thankfulnesse, acknowledge ourselves very sensible of those
sundry good Lawes which through His Majesties great Grace and Goodnesse,
have been obtained for us this Parliament. And we do no lesse rejoyce in His
Majesties Pious and tender care repeated by His gracious Declarations in
print, and expressions by letter read unto us, and all the County at this Assizes,
in open Court, to defend and maintaine the true PROTESTANT RELIGION by
Law established, against Popish Recusants, Anabaptists, and all other
Separatists. And that the Laws of the Land shall be the Rule of His Majesties
Government; whereby the Subjects Liberty and Property is defended: And that
His Majesty will preserve the freedom and just privilege of Parliament, with all
which promises and expressions we are so abundantly satisfied, that we do not
in any way distrust His Majesties Constancy in these Resolutions. And we do,
declare, that we will be ready to attend His Majesty in all lawfull ways, for the
putting of the County in a posture of Arms, for the defence of His Majesty, and
the peace of His Kingdomes. Therefore we do resolve, according to our oathes
of Supremacy and Allegiance, and late Protestation, to adventure our lives and
fortunes in defence of His Majesties Royall Person and Honour, and the just
Rights and Priviledges of Parliament, and the knowne Lawes of the Land, and
Liberties of the Subjects, That thereby the Distractions and Disturbances of
His Majesties Kingdoms may be reduced to His Majesties Legall Government.
And whereas the Grand Jury at the last Sessions, delivered a Petition, thereby
desiring the exercising of the Militia, we utterly disavow it as not agreeable to
the intents or desires of us, or any considerable number of the said County.
And we do hereby declare, that by the information which we have received
from severall of the persons then of the Grand Jury that it was not of their own
framing, but contrived and prepared for them by some few persons, not well
affected to the peace and quiet of this County.[47]

This, with its emphasis on law, is the constitutional Royalism of Hyde and of
the Oxford Parliament of 1644. The profession of readiness 'to attend His
Majesty in all lawfull ways' avoids any explicit endorsement of the commission of
array: and the whole tone suggests that it was intended, not so much as a call to
arms as to throw the onus of beginning hostilities on to the other side.

Besides the thirteen grand jurors for the city, the Mayor, Edward Solley, the
Sheriff, Henry Foord, and two aldermen, John Hanbury and George Street, sign
among the esquires and gentlemen. We can thus identify seventeen Royalists in
Worcester at the outset of the struggle. A study of their subsequent careers throws
some light on the changing fortunes and attitudes of urban Royalists during the
Revolution. Except for Thomas Rea, they are all known to have been members
of the Chamber. One of them appears to have defected, William Gibbes, who
was removed from the Forty-eight on 21 December 1643 for having 'absented
himselfe from all chamber meetinges for the space of one yeare and more,

although he hath bin oftentymes summoned and required hereunto and that he is refractorie and obstinate in all other his paymentes and dueties concerning the common charge of this citty'.[48] The rest all continued in office while Worcester was held for the King and took some active part in administration. Three became officers in the city regiment under Sir Martin Sandys, though their service would consist mainly of garrison duty: Edward Solley as Lieutenant Colonel, Francis Sharman as Lieutenant and Francis Hughes as Ensign.[49] Sharman, Hughes, Robert Sollers (or Sellers) and Thomas Licens were compounding for their estates with the Committee between 1646 and 1648.[50] Apart from Solley, all the survivors accepted the new regime, though Sharman, Hughes, William Taylor and George Brooke resigned, doubtless under pressure, in the purges of 1648–9,[51] as in 1653 did Thomas Licens,[52] who as Mayor had welcomed Charles II and the Scots army. In 1660, Solley, Licens and Hughes were restored to their places and Alderman Henry Foord was removed in 1662.[53]

Worcestershire was thus, though narrowly, secured for the King and the commission of array was already established at the Talbot in Sidbury and busily engaged in raising troops.[54] But the city corporation was still at pains to avoid becoming involved. This appears from the wording of their resolution of 2 August, to purchase the private stock of arms of the late Lord Lieutenant, Lord Windsor, 'for the generall use and defence of the cittie and not to be imployed but by consent of the chamber' and in those of 25 August to take a view of the arms of the citizens and to buy powder, shot and match and ordnance.[55] Besides this defensive neutrality, however, there was a good deal of positive support for Parliament, both in the Chamber and among the townspeople, in which Serjeant Wilde, the Recorder and a leading figure at Westminster, was a prime mover. When the Declaration was carried at the Assizes a contrary petition was presented by 'divers of the best Freeholders of the County' but the Judge refused to read it.[56] In the summer of 1642, when the air was thick with rumours of Popish atrocities in Ireland and of the excesses of the wilder Cavaliers, it was easy to present the King's forces as the chief danger to peace. Even the claim that it was the Royalists who were 'disaffected persons', disingenuous as it sounds to us, could seem plausible with Parliament in control of London and the press, and the King, operating from York or Nottingham, still trying desperately to raise an army. On 30 August the King's commissioners wrote to the Mayor asking how many troops could be billeted in the city and how many volunteers raised.[57] This provoked a vigorous response in a petition of 'the trained soldiers and commons' complaining of the influx of 'divers strangers, gentlemen and others whereof some of them are voted by the Parliament to be delinquents and some other papists or popishly affected, whereby it is generally suspected and feared they have some design upon this city, or at leastwise may occasion the bringing an army upon this city to the Ruin thereof'; and asking that 'those Troopers and all Adherents to the unlawful Commission of Array, which daily appear here to the terror of the citizens, the hindrance of our trade and market, and tend to be dividing of the King and Parliament' should be put out, and that no billeting or recruitment of volunteers should be allowed and a strict watch be kept at the gates and the quay head: to which the Mayor, the same Edward Solley who was soon to become so active a Royalist, fully acceded.[58] As a result the commissioners agreed to move elsewhere and, not surprisingly, told the King's Council that 'the ill entertainment of the citizens of Worcester have so scattered our thoughts, that they cannot be so suddenly recollected'.[59] About the same time the corporation itself petitioned the House of Commons declaring its adherence to 'King and Parliament' and asking that the city militia and volunteers might be embodied under Captain Rea. This was approved in an order, drawn up by Salway and Wilde, which was passed on 13 September.[60]

III

The Chamber Order Book contains no record of any meeting between the annual elections on 29 August and 7 October. In the interim the situation had dramatically changed and Worcester had become the seat of war. With the King at Shrewbury and Essex marching westwards from Northampton to interrupt his advance on London, it lay in the path of both armies. Byron's dragoons, with money and plate from Oxford, entered on 16 September and were joined by Rupert and Maurice a few days later. On 23 September, the Royalists sallied out and cleared the way to Shrewsbury by defeating a Parliamentary force at Powick Bridge: and, after pausing for a few hours in the city, resumed their way to the King's headquarters. On the day after Rupert had crossed the Severn bridge, Essex's main army marched in at Sidbury Gate.

No resistance seems to have been offered to these successive occupations. Indeed, the citizens were in no position to resist. Wharton describes the fortifications as 'much decayed',[61] in spite of the money that had recently been spent on them, and, according to Clarendon, though he had no first-hand knowledge, the town 'was open enough to have been entered in many places, though in some it had an old decayed wall, and, at the most usual and frequented entrances into the city weak and rotten gates to be shut, but without either lock or bolt'.[62] After the deep divisions of the past few weeks, each side might have expected to be well received by some, at least, among the townspeople. Wharton writes of Rupert's entry, 'most of the City crying "Welcome, welcome," but principally the Mayor, who desired to entertain him' and that the 'treacherous citizens' went out 'in multitudes with muskets' to Powick Bridge to support his army.[63] The sexton of St. Michael's received 2s. 8d. for ringing 'at the Princes comeinge in', which, if the payment was proportioned to the length of the peal, indicates a specially hearty welcome.[64] In July 1646 when Worcester had endured two months of siege at the end of nearly four years of military occupation, Henry Townshend notes that 'though the middle and lowest sort of citizens be cordially bent for to stand it out courageously, yet many of the best rank draw very backward in their Actions'.[65] The 'best rank', of course, had most to lose. But while we cannot really discern any alignment in terms of class, least of all in that final, desperate plight, the King's cause must have had roots, even among the poorest.

Worcester was held for Parliament for about six weeks. Essex's first act, on the night of his arrival, 24 September 1642, was to arrest the Mayor in his house and he was sent up under guard to London. The occupation was at first intended to be permanent. Soldiers and citizens were set to work on the fortifications. £20,000 was sent down from London and a levy of £5,000 imposed upon the townspeople.[66] A Parliamentary Committee was set up which carried out the first of many purges of the corporation; three aldermen – Solley, John Hanbury and George Street – being removed and replaced on 17 October by Richard Heming, Humphrey Vernon and Roger Seaborne, afterwards a major in the Parliamentary army.[67] But on 19 October Essex withdrew with the bulk of his forces to follow the King, leaving as governor Colonel Thomas Essex, who, feeling his position isolated, abandoned Worcester and marched off to Gloucester sometime in early November.

The Parliamentary army numbered something like 15,000 men, but there are only a few hints in the city records of all the problems that their presence must have created: such as the order of 11 October doubling the number of constables annually elected for each ward,[68] a petition to the Lord General about the supply of coals for the guard, and the voting of two double fifteenths – a pitifully inadequate sum – towards the various charges of occupation.[69] Essex's prohibition of plunder on pain of death was, on his own admission, not obeyed,[70] and his troops were ill-disciplined, as Nehemiah Wharton's letters show. The zealots among them sacked and defiled the cathedral, destroying the organ and the stained glass windows, defacing the monuments, rifling the library, tearing up bibles and service books and 'putting the surplices and other vestments upon their Dragooners, who rode about the streets in them'.[71] Colonel Essex at his departure was paid £40 by the corporation to save the city from further plunder. The Town Clerk, Francis Street, with whom the Colonel himself had lodged, afterwards received £5 compensation for 'the spoylinge of his goods'.[72]

Perhaps because of these experiences, the next Parliamentary threat to Worcester in the summer of 1643, by Waller, whose troops had a worse reputation than those of Essex for 'barbarous and ungentlemanlike Qualities',[73] met with civilian as well as military resistance. It was resolved to demolish buildings and works outside the walls which might give cover to the enemy. To relieve the soldiers this was freely undertaken by 400 of 'the ordinary sort of women out of every ward within the City joined in companies and with colours and drums, striking up with spades, shovels and mattocks . . . in a warlike manner . . . (in imitation of the She Citizens of London)'. After sixteen hours exchange of fire on 30 June Waller drew off.[74]

IV

Apart from this attempt of Waller's, Royalist control of Worcester remained unchallenged between Colonel Essex's withdrawal in November 1642 and 1646. Sir William Russell entered the city, with the King's commission as governor, on 10 November 1642.[75] The ringing of the cathedral bells and the customary presents to him of sugar loaves and claret from the corporation are the only evidences of the take-over, nor is there much sign of its effect during the next two or three months in the municipal records. The commission of array, though it normally sat in Worcester, was responsible for the county as well as the city and consisted entirely of members of county families. The relation between the civil and military authorities was, therefore, different from that at Gloucester, which had its own commission of lieutenancy and where the corporation during Massey's governorship appointed a Council of War at which officers were present. The Worcester corporation had to execute the orders of a socially superior body, for whom the county town was simply a part of the area under their charge.[76] After 1646, though the constitutional position was unchanged, some of the city aldermen took a leading part in the county Parliamentary organization.

In December, January and February 1642–3 9 troops totalling about 700 horse and dragoons are stated to have been raised.[77] The list is certainly incomplete and probably between 1,500 and 2,000 men were being mustered or trained or quartered in the city during these early months of the War. Worcester was the headquarters of all the county forces, apart from the small garrisons at Evesham and Hartlebury Castle, though we cannot say how many were stationed here at any one time. In addition there were the trained bands and volunteers raised for the defence of the city under Captain Martin Sandys. These would mainly be local men 'who performe their duties in turne'. They numbered 300 in March 1643, 800 in June 1644 and 1,800 in March 1645.[78] This last figure, almost equal to the whole male population of military age, may perhaps have included gentlemen volunteers. Even so, the continuing increase, at a time of mounting hardship and diminishing hopes, is some measure of the strength of loyalty in the 'Faithful City'. In May 1646, at the beginning of the siege, the garrison consisted of 1,500 men, 'Besides the Gentlemen and all the City Bands'.[79] From time to time the movements of the field armies imposed a heavy additional burden, as when Charles I was at Worcester for a week in June 1644 and 3,000 of his army of 7,000 were quartered on the city.[80] The wartime population was further increased by strangers, country gentlemen and their families, many of them papists who had taken refuge within the walls.

Since neither King nor Parliament could legally impose taxes without consent of the other, the war effort of both sides was at first financed by loans and gifts. Only tentatively did either advance from these *ad hoc* methods to direct taxation.

In Worcestershire, Quarter Sessions at Epiphany 1643 granted the King £3,000 a month (for three months in the first instance, but made permanent at Easter) 'towards the payment of His Majesty's forces sent and raised for the defence of this County'.[81] This did not, however, include the city of Worcester and the corporation showed itself very reluctant when Russell approached them about the end of February with propositions which 'are not cleerlie by us understood'.[82] To his demand that they should lay a regular assessment on the citizens in proportion to that of the county they pleaded that they had already raised £700 by loans and contributions and that they might be allowed to decide for themselves how best to meet their share of the burden.[83] On 15 March the Council of War at Oxford sent a strongly-worded letter requiring them to settle 'a certeine Contribution for the constant payment' of war charges in agreement with the governor;[84] and the chamber meeting on the following day voted £180 a month 'toward the fortification and other publique uses of the cittie as the governor shall appoynt'. It was to be assessed after the usual manner of fifteenths and the soldiers enlisted under Captain Martin Sandys were to be exempt 'in respect of their service'.[85]

A comparison of these monthly assessments of £3,000 for the county and £180 for the city, with the figures in the last regular Parliamentary grant, in 1641, of £5,802 10s. 6d. and £356 4s. 9d. respectively, spread over twelve months,[86] shows the sudden and drastic increase in taxation which the War involved. When a county was assessed by both sides the Royalist demand seems always to have been the higher.[87] In the Parliamentary ordinance of 24 February 1643, which fixed weekly assessments for the whole country, whether or not they could be collected, the rate for Worcestershire was £550, or £2,200 a month, and for Worcester, £16 10s. 0d., or £66 a month. The £180 monthly assessment was certainly unrealistic and was always heavily in arrears. As early as June 1643 it was found necessary to withdraw the concession to the soldiers and to require those who served personally to pay half and those who served by substitute two-thirds of their assessment.[88] But the 'gentlemen strangers', not being permanent residents, seem to have escaped all payment until the final siege. Both the administration and the spending of the monthly pay caused confusion which, by the end, had almost dissolved into chaos. Responsibility for assessment lay with the Mayor and aldermen. The money was collected by the constables, who paid it to the chamberlains, who paid it to the Governor, so that it did not normally pass through their accounts. The accounting was at best irregular. In March 1645 the claim of Lady Anne Gerard, widow of Sir Gilbert Gerard, Russell's successor as governor, for £200 of arrears due to her and her late husband was questioned 'for it is alleadged that the governor had divers moneths contribucon in his owne collection, and it doth not appeare that he hath receaved'. In June the Chamber confessed themselves unable to pay her anything because of all their other debts and expenses, though by the end of August she was promised £10 out of the arrears.[89] By that time the situation had become desperate and since there was 'little or noe obedience given unto the mayor and his officers' it was decided to call on the troops to enforce payment. On 4 September Captain Cheyney and Captain Field were made collectors, together with such constables as the Mayor and aldermen should appoint. This was a drastic expedient and on 21 October a return was made to the old method, but with stipulations that reveal into what disorder the business had fallen: the constables were to account monthly to the chamberlains, who were to keep a book of assessments and receipts: the August and September contributions, of which, presumably, nothing had yet been paid, were to be collected together and arrears previous to August were to be accounted for by the old chamberlains, for 1644–5.[90] The results of this attempt at reform appear in receipts from the monthly pay totalling £62 7s. 4d. in the 1644–5 accounts and £27 14s. 6d. from the constables of five of the seven wards, in 1645–6.[91] More, no doubt, was collected. But it was too late, four months after Naseby, to make the system work efficiently.

Payments out of the contribution money could be made only on the governor's order. But it was quite inadequate to finance current war expenditure, which had often to be met by the Mayor or the chamberlains or individual citizens who were reimbursed from it, sometimes by grants of arrears, if and when they could be recovered. However disappointing its yield, it was a grievous burden on the inhabitants. The excise, a still more unpopular tax, granted to Charles by the Oxford Parliament, was imposed on Worcester in early May 1644.[92] On 27 November 1645 the corporation petitioned the governor that in compensation for it the monthly pay should be reduced or abolished, especially in view of 'the great decay of families within this citty'.[93] The Parliamentary Committee after the surrender continued to levy contribution at the same rate, at least for a time, and the first request the corporation made to them on 17 August 1646, was for its abatement.[94]

The fortifications of Worcester in the first Civil War are shown on a contemporary plan of the battle of 1651.[95] The medieval walls were strengthened at various points by bulwarks and by an earthen rampart enclosing the castle on the south-west and extending southwards to include the 'Great Sconce' which gives its name to Fort Royal, where vestiges of it are still traceable. The works were in progress throughout the Royalist occupation and there was a hasty attempt to finish them in July 1646, almost at the end of the siege.[96] Payments for them totalling £303 14s. 4½d. appear in the chamberlains' accounts and the order book contains references to a further £274 8s. mostly raised by fifteenths and special levies, and to £197 10s. charged on the monthly pay which should have borne the whole cost. Repairs to the walls, gates and bridge were done by craftsmen under the governor's direction, as appears from the petition to Prince Maurice in July 1645 that the Mayor and aldermen should choose the workmen to be employed in making the drawbridge at the Severn bridge and that the cost should be shared with the county.[97] The engineer for the new earthwork defences was a Mr Gatten, who received £10 on 22 August 1645,[98] and the work was done either by hired labour, at 8d. a day or by the citizens themselves. The former method was at first adopted when the corporation, on 11 March 1643, voted a levy of 40s. a day for the employment of 60 workmen,[99] a number which Prince Rupert, when he was at Worcester in February 1644, ordered to be increased to 300. The governor, however, Sir Gilbert Gerard, 'for the better convenience and easment of the cittie', imposed instead the system in force at Oxford[100] by which all householders, including strangers and cathedral clergy, were to perform or provide one day's labour a week, and this seems to have continued, more or less effectively, until the siege.

The strategic importance of Worcester and its nearness to Oxford entailed special and unpredictable burdens. In September 1643 the King, at Evesham after abandoning the siege of Gloucester, demanded a loan of £7,000, £4,000 from the city and £3,000 from the county, to pay his army. The corporation appointed assessors for each ward, protesting that they could not raise so large a sum 'in respect of decay of trade of clothing, the weekly burdens and taxes laid on the Inhabitants for making fortifications and scouring the ditches, etc.,' but undertaking if possible to raise £2,000, 'the one half this next weeke, and the other with all speede', for which collectors were appointed on 6 October. The assessments amounted only to £1,500 and at the end of the year a deputation was sent to Oxford to ask that they might be further reduced or cancelled'. At the same meeting the Chamber guaranteed a loan of £200 'for his majestes speedie service'.[101] On 6 June 1644 £200 was voted to the King, 'if he come to this cittie' (in fact he entered it that same night, in the course of the Oxford campaign), half to be subscribed by the Chamber and half by the commoners, either by loan or assessment, and this, apparently, was received in full.[102] On his departure on 12 June he demanded £1,000 'to be suddenly raised in money by to morrowe night' and again assessors were appointed. This was to be a grant and not a loan, though in practice there was little difference between them, and both this and the £2,000 of the previous year were still in arrear at the end of September.[103] In July Charles endeavoured to bring the city's affairs into some order, perhaps at the instance of the corporation, by granting a commission to the Mayor, Aldermen Roger Gough and Richard Heming and others to take accounts of the money that had been received for his service.[104] On 9 May 1645, when he was again in the neighbourhood, £100 was ordered to be sent to him.[105] These details show how unsystematized were the King's finances and how sanguine his expectations. Henrietta Maria, on her way from Yorkshire to join her husband at Edge Hill, was presented, on 10 July 1643 with £100 'in gould and a rich velvett purse'.[106] Similar gifts were made, of 100 marks to Rupert in February 1644 and £50 to Maurice twelve months later, the money in each case being raised by loans on the security of fifteenths.[107]

Gifts to royal and important visitors were traditional, as was much of the hospitality itemised in the chamberlains' accounts. The latter rose markedly during the War and as sharply declined after 1646. Payments for dinners and gifts of wine and sugar loaves, though relatively small in themselves, throw some light on the relations of the Chamber and the citizens with the soldiery, and on the social outlook underlying the Royalist conduct of the War. In 1642–3, £67 17s. 8d. was spent on wine and beer. In December 1645, forty-six gallons of sack and eleven sugar loaves, costing £18 18s. 1d. were distributed as New Year's gifts between the Lord General (Astley), the governor (Colonel Samuel Sandys), Sir Martin Sandys and the Bishop. There were certainly officers who behaved like the Cavaliers of Parliamentary propaganda, such as Lieutenant Colonel David Hide, who defied the governor, Sir William Russell, insulted the Mayor at his New Year's Dinner and was arrested and sent to be court-martialled at Oxford, where, despite his outrageous conduct, he was set at liberty.[108] In March 1644 Martin Sandys and Augustine Irans his servant were accused of the murder of one of his officers, Captain Robert Stayner of Worcester.[109] Quite early in Russell's governorship quarrels, involving mutiny, broke out between him and Colonel Samuel Sandys and other commissioners which led to an inquiry before the Council at Oxford and to his supersession by Sir Gilbert Gerard.[110] The corporation supported Russell with a certificate to the King, 'that wee doe not stand disaffected to his government neither are we diffident of his courage and fidelitie to this cittie' and, soon afterwards by making him an honorary freeman.[111] Much as the city had to endure, personal relations with the Royalist leaders remained, on the whole, friendly. We find Russell dining the Mayor and aldermen and both he and Sir Martin Sandys made presents of bucks for civic feasts. With Gerard, apart from gifts of sack worth £7 1s. 0d. there is no sign of direct social intercourse, possibly because he was not a local man. But of the habits of his successor, Prince Maurice, the details in the accounts give us a vivid picture. On 13 April 1643, the day of his victory over Waller at Ripple, the corporation sent an unusually large present of claret, sack and white wine, costing £16 17s. 10d. to him at Upton-on-Severn. He was afterwards welcomed to Worcester with a hogshead of claret and three sugar loaves (£9 12s. 11d.) and the chamberlains paid £17 9s. 9d. for his provision during his stay. He returned as Lieutenant General of the Associated Counties of Worcester, Hereford, Salop and Stafford and governor of the city in January 1645 and was there intermittently throughout the year, at the Bishop's Palace. The inhabitants had to find the expenses of his table at the rate of £3 15s. 6d. a day.[112] The total of payments on his behalf in the 1644–5 accounts is £325 7s. 2d. of which £67 11s. 2d. for provender for the horses was allowed to be discharged out of the monthly contribution.[113] In addition, the succeeding chamberlains paid £100 15s. 8d. 'for the keepinge of the two princes houses (vide licet) Prince Rupert and Prince Maurice at theire last beinge in Worcester with all manner of provision'. Maurice and his staff were clearly hard drinkers, insistent on the privileges of rank and on maintaining their wonted style of life, regardless of circumstances. Yet he was, on the admission of one of his critics, 'in himselfe cyvyll to all and wel beeloved of

the cytyzens, only too eazye and facyll to the troops of Reformadoes'.[114] The last
Royalist governor was Colonel Henry Washington, a professional soldier and
brother-in-law of a prominent Worcestershire Royalist, Sir John Pakington, who
took over in March 1646 and in July surrendered the city to Rainsborough. The
purchase, for 7s. 4d., of a single gallon of sack to welcome him at the Town Hall
shows to what straits the corporation was by now reduced. Nevertheless, on
29 June they resolved to present him with £100 'whereof £50 ready, for his
especial care and love towards the City, towards the maintenance of his Table,
etc. And' says Townshend 'it is wisely and lovingly done of them. For there was
never Governor more complied with them, And laid less pressure upon them. . . .
Besides it being done freely, it engageth him the more to preserve them.'[115]
Probably it was the only payment that Washington ever received. Meanwhile, on
1 July, the pay of the common soldiers was reduced to 1s. a week.[116]

Rainsborough's triumphal entry three weeks later was greeted in the old style
with a present of a hogshead of claret, fourteen gallons of sack and two sugar
loaves, costing £11 12s. 8d. Soon afterwards, £9 5s. 4d. was spent on sweetmeats,
sturgeon and wine for a banquet to the recorder and the County Committee.
Thereafter, this lavish hospitality practically comes to an end. A few shillings' worth
of wine at business meetings with the Committee, or with the city Members going
to or returning from Parliament; a lamprey pie sent occasionally to London, to the
Members or Cromwell or Chief Baron Wilde; such for the most part, are the items
in the accounts that relieve the austerity of civic life in the 1650s.

Oppressive as their rule was in so many ways, the King's commissioners
interfered far less than their Parliamentary successors in the city's government. On
2 March 1643 five members of the Chamber – Henry Phillips, Edward Elvins,
Thomas Writer, Francis Franks and Fulke Estopp – were certified to Sir William
Russell as having been absent from the city since he had entered it in the previous
November.[117] They were all supporters of Parliament and Estopp, on
3 October 1644, was commissioned as a captain of horse.[118] Yet no action was
taken against any of them before 4 April 1644, when Writer and Estopp were
removed from the Forty-eight.[119] Such interference as there was came rather from
Oxford. It was on the King's orders that, on 16 March 1643, the three aldermen
appointed by Essex were removed – though not from the Chamber – and those
whom they had displaced were restored.[120] Later in the year, the King intervened
in the election of the Mayor, after a series of manoeuvres not easy to disentangle.
On election day, 28 August, Thomas Hacket was chosen Mayor and Thomas
Wilde Sheriff, to be sworn, as usual, within fifteen days of the Monday after
Michaelmas – in that year by 20 October. Meantime, on 18 September, Hacket
was elected Sheriff in place of Wilde and then, on 26 September, re-elected Mayor,
when it was agreed that the present Mayor, Henry Foord, should be removed on 12
October – when his term would, in any case, almost have expired – and Hackett
should be sworn in his place. The corporation, it seems, was trying to resist an

infringement of its privileges, even by the King. By 9 October, royal letters, probably not unexpected, had been received requiring 'in consideracion of these troublesom tymes that some able and expert man that hath borne the office heretofore should be againe elected'. Daniel Tyas was therefore made Mayor and Hacket confirmed as Sheriff for the ensuing year in obedience to the King's command and also on the ground that the two offices 'cannot stand together'.[121] As this must already have been fully realized, the election of 26 September was presumably a piece of face-saving. Tyas, who had been Mayor in 1638–9, was an apothecary with an estate at Powick and had lent £50 to Essex on the Public Faith in 1642. He was induced to accept office by a special allowance of £106 to be subscribed by members of the two companies of the Chamber[122] and he became henceforth the leading Royalist in the corporation. He was knighted when Charles was at Worcester in June 1644. The grounds of objection to Hacket do not appear. As Sheriff, he would normally become Mayor for 1644–5, but when Charles intervened a second time to prevent his election he was successfully resisted. On 20 September 1644, after a special meeting of the common council, with the governor present, a letter was sent to the Secretary of State, Sir Edward Nicholas, affirming Hacket's loyalty and stating that no objections had been raised in the Chamber against him,[123] and the matter was dropped.

Thus the Civil War did not involve, in Worcester, any struggle for power within the corporate body. Known Parliamentarians remained members of it, at least for long periods, as did known Royalists later. There was a reluctance to remove or to accept the resignation of any one who still remained resident in the city. Partly, this was because of a common desire to maintain the chartered rights of self-government against external pressure; and partly because by keeping up the numbers of the common council the heavy financial liabilities that fell upon them could be spread more evenly. Effective resistance against an occupying army was in any case impossible. One grievance, but that not the least of all those from which the citizens suffered, might be remedied by making contact with the enemy; namely, restriction of trade. The King, on 8 December 1642, anxious to show his desire of sparing his subjects as much as possible in a war that had been forced upon him, issued a proclamation forbidding his armies to interfere with persons taking their cloth or other merchandise to London to sell.[124] The Worcester clothiers were particularly vulnerable since their trade was largely with London and much of their stock was held there. Thus in September 1651 the Committee for Compounding ordered that certain Worcester citizens should have their goods in London confiscated until they could clear themselves from the suspicion of having assisted the Scots.[125] The proclamation of December 1642 proved a quite inadequate safeguard and could not, in any case, affect the actions of Parliament. On 17 July 1643 Charles revoked it and forbade any trade to the capital from the parts under his control without special licence.[126] It was, presumably, as a result of this latter order that the corporation sent Thomas

Hacket to Oxford to petition 'for freedom of trade for the cytie to London'.[127] In April 1644 a number of Worcester clothiers paid £29 15s. 0d. by arrangement with the Earl of Denbigh, for free passage of their cloth to London through the Parliamentary armies.[128] A further petition of the inhabitants in the following June, complaining that the loss of their staple trade made them unable to pay their assessments and had caused a great increase in the numbers of poor, induced Charles to relax his ban. But 'being met withall by the King's Forces upon the way, the Carriers had all their Horses and Cloth taken from them: and His Majesties protection made only a Stalking Horse for their Insolencies and Robberies'.[129] It was a situation that could only get worse as the War went on and was probably one of the main reasons for the proposal of petitioning the King to treat for peace that was being discussed at the end of the year. After the establishment of a Parliamentary Committee for Worcestershire in October both sides were raising loans and taxes in the county. The list of persons who lent money on the Propositions of Parliament between December 1644 and the following March includes ten from Worcester, of whom six were clothiers, two carriers and one a skinner.[130] Three of them occur twice, but the total of their subscriptions amounts only to £47 10s. 0d. Only one appears to have been a member of the common council and the three others who can be traced in the Order Books attained no higher civic office than that of constable; suggesting that for the most part they were young men, or at any rate not among the wealthiest citizens. The list is interesting as the only record of active support of Parliament from within the walls. By December 1645, Worcester and Hereford were among the chief remaining royal strongholds and until they could be captured, it was resolved to 'straiten' them by economic blockade. Orders were, therefore, sent by the Committee of both Kingdoms to the governors of fourteen Parliamentary garrisons, from Shrewsbury and Stafford in the north to Bristol, Monmouth and Chepstow in the south and as far east as Northampton that goods consigned to either city should be turned back and should be seized on a second attempt to get them through. This, it was expected, 'would put the people under so great necessity that they would compel the surrender of those places, so as to enjoy their trade again'.[131] It must seriously have weakened the will to resistance and it is surprising that Worcester held out so long as it did. The besiegers in the following summer were confidently expecting help from within if it came to a storm and at the last, according to Townshend, the citizens were threatening to throw the soldiers over the walls or club them if Rainsborough's proffered terms were rejected, 'Being now, as all quiet people are, weary of war, desiring their trading may go on'.[132]

The total cost of the War to the city is impossible to estimate. The chamberlains' accounts, of course, are concerned only with the finance of the corporation and are an imperfect record even of that, since so much, both of revenue and expenditure, did not pass through their hands. But it is worth noting, so far as it goes, that the annual deficit increased in the two years from Michaelmas 1643 from £241 15s. 9d. to £606 14s. 6d. Besides the various *ad hoc* methods of meeting demands that have already been mentioned, there was extensive borrowing of charity monies and loans at 8% were raised which amounted by Michaelmas 1646 to £615.[133] On 22 August 1645 part of the corporation estate was conveyed to Sir Daniel Tyas, Edward Solley and six other members of the Chamber as feoffees in trust for the eventual discharge of the debt;[134] an arrangement which seems to have been on the whole effective and which continued until 1662. It is, in fact, one of several signs about this time that the corporation, faced with so many and growing difficulties, was making efforts at reform. The attempted re-organization of the monthly pay, already noted, is another: and a third is the granting of building leases, a practice common in Elizabethan and Jacobean times[135] and continued under the Commonwealth and Protectorate. Nine such leases were granted between September and December 1645 and the sums to be spent on building by the tenants within three years, which are specified in five of them, total £290.[136] As they are mostly of gardens or open ground, the object seems to have been to relieve the serious wartime overcrowding rather than to repair war damage or, as in many of the later leases, to improve the property.

In 1666 a schedule of 'Disbursements of the city of Worcester in the late wars' was drawn up by four members of the common council.[137] Particular items, many of which can be checked from the order books or the chamberlains' accounts, come to £7,885 13s. 7d. 'Plunder of the city as given in upon oath' is put down at £80,000 and 'Burning the suburbs, hospitals, &c. &c.', at £100,000; besides 'fortifications' at £180 a month and 'Free quarter, contribution, fuel, &c. arising to an immense sum'. Much of this relates to the year 1651, when the city suffered more plunder and destruction in a fortnight than during the whole of the first Civil War. Even so, the £100,000 seems excessive. Losses in the cause of Parliament were, at least in theory, recoverable through the Committee of Accounts: and this estimate may possibly have been made with some idea of compensating loyalty to the King. But it is unlikely that much was ever received.

We can trace throughout the War the gradual deterioration of security and morale. Even at the beginning, administrative muddle and quarrels between the military leaders reflect the essential amateurism of the Cavaliers. But this had no serious effect so long as Worcester was the centre of a Royalist-dominated area. The repulse of Waller in June 1643 no doubt helped to sustain confidence. More ominous signs appeared, early in 1644, in Massey's raids from Gloucester into the south of the county. In August, his troops levied contribution at Powick, only three miles away.[138] By then, threats had developed from Colonel Fox's garrisons at Edgbaston and Hawkesley in the north, and from Colonel Thomas Archer's Warwickshire troops, based on Alcester in the east. The latter surprised the Worcestershire Commissioners at Ombersley and forced them to flee to Hartlebury Castle, 'not daring to make Worcester their sanctuary'. 'Since this action' writes Archer, 'the country, seeing how unable, at least how slow, their Worcester friends have beene in protectinge them, come dayly to us'.[139]

Parliament was now strong enough to establish a Committee for Worcestershire, which was appointed on 23 September,[140] though it had to sit at Warwick until after Massey's storming of Evesham on 26 May 1645. The effect of this move is probably to be seen in the Royalist endeavours for peace at the end of November 1644, when the corporation characteristically resolved to prefer its own petition to the King instead of joining with the county.[141] Henceforth, though the city itself was still not directly threatened, the Worcestershire Royalists were on the defensive. With the loss of Evesham, which cut the direct link with Oxford, the net was drawn still closer. Early in July 1645, the southward advance of Leven and the Scots army offered a chance of reducing Worcester and Prince Maurice prepared for a siege by intensifying work on the fortifications. But the repulse of his reconnoitring party induced Leven to move on to besiege Hereford and the danger, for the present, was over. Some ten weeks later, on 24 September, Anthony Langston, one of the commissioners, wrote a frank account of the state of things within the garrison to Digby, evidently in response to a request for information.[142] Charles had achieved his last success, the relief of Hereford, on 1 September and marched towards Chester in the hope of linking up with Montrose but his dismissal of Rupert on 14 September for surrendering Bristol had added one more to the causes of dissension among the Worcester Royalists. Many of them, says Langston, blame Digby, as Secretary of State, for the King's disasters. The local men are jealous of the favour shown to strangers, and gentlemen of quality residing in the city would leave if they knew where to go. Most of what money can be raised is mis-spent. The quarters are 'narrow and much prest uppon by the enemye, noe defence used agaynst them, some of the cyttyzens beeing taken within sighte of our workes', not always, we may suspect, unwillingly. He concludes his report by saying that 'our hopes from the north keepe us in some lyfe'. Those hopes were shattered on the day that he was writing by the King's defeat at Rowton Heath.

On 6 December 1645 Lord Astley succeeded Prince Maurice as Lieutenant General of the Associated Counties.[143] He was a man of more authority than his predecessor and more mindful of civilian grievances. But, though he was based on Worcester, he was mainly concerned with raising what proved to be Charles's last field army and the affairs of the city could only go from bad to worse. There seems to have been an increasing difficulty in securing attendance at Chamber meetings.[144] When, soon after his arrival, Astley required £70 a month out of the contribution for his Reformadoes, it was resolved to present him with a written statement showing why such a sum could not be raised and to 'desire his favoure therein'. It had become impossible to meet any extra demand for money except by borrowing. By February 1646 the corporation was £1,000 in debt through deficiencies in the monthly pay and yet one more effort had to be made to collect the arrears for the past twelve months.[145] It was a hard winter, with the Severn frozen over and a shortage of coal. In April such was the prevailing distress that

Bishop Prideaux had a special collection for the relief of the poor.[146] Since loyalty to the Church was a scarcely less important source of strength to the royal cause than loyalty to the King, Prideaux may well have played a considerable part in sustaining morale. He was resident at the Palace, with occasional sojourns at Hartlebury, from December 1642 until the end, when he appears as a moderating influence in the stormy scenes between Washington and the Commissioners over the terms of surrender.[147] Regular gifts to him at New Year and at other times suggest that he was on friendly terms with the Chamber and he was, perhaps, none the less acceptable to the citizens for having been, in earlier days, an opponent of Laud.

On New Year's Day 1646 Astley prepared for a siege by issuing orders for the victualling of the city and the putting out of strangers.[148] Having collected 3,000 men he went to join the King at Oxford, but was defeated and surrendered to Brereton, Morgan and Birch at Stow-on-the-Wold on 21 March. Nothing now remained but to capture the King's last garrisons and the victors of Stow summoned Worcester on 26 March. They met with a spirited defiance from Washington, now Governor, and drew off, their combined force of 2,500 being insufficient to invest the place. It could only be a temporary respite. On 30 March Washington burned down the church and hospital of St. Oswald in the northern suburbs and a fortnight later ordered a survey of the householders and of what store of provisions they had.[149] Washington had many of the defects too common among Royalist officers. He was rash, often negligent and subject to violent outbursts of temper. Nevertheless his valour and his 'extreme integrity and faith'[150] seem to have inspired the citizens with something of the courage of despair. On 1 May, the Governor, Commissioners, gentry, Mayor and citizens took an oath promising to 'stick to and be true to' one another and not to agree to the 'surprisal or delivering up' of the city without mutual consent.[151]

V

The final siege began on 20 May and ended on 23 July. Townshend gives a detailed eye-witness account of those last two months,[152] which affords an interesting comparison with Corbet's narrative of the siege of Gloucester three years earlier. Resistance was hopeless from the first. The fall of the smaller Worcestershire garrisons, of Ludlow on 27 May and of Oxford on 24 June released more and more troops for Worcester until the besieging army numbered more than 5,000 men. Small parties of them were quartered up to fifteen miles from the main body and they were able to draw on the greater part of the county for supplies.[153] The defenders had by now lost touch with the King, who had quitted Oxford on 27 April and on 5 May had surrendered to the Scots at Newark. But it was more than a month before the city was completely invested. Until the end of May, Washington's horse were able to forage as far west as

Abberley and Astley. Whalley's and Morgan's lines had at first been drawn in a wide circuit round the east side. They began to close in on the north by occupying Barbourne on 3 June and digging trenches towards the Severn. The arrival of the Ludlow men made possible an advance down the right bank to Hallow and to the suburb of St. John in Bedwardine, at the far end of the Severn bridge, which was seized on 9 June and held against fierce counter-attacks. The bridge of boats, already prepared,[154] could now be thrown across the river. The south side, towards Kempsey, remained open until 23 June, which Townshend notes as the first day that the city was 'surrounded and wholly blocked up'.

Apart from the fighting in St. John's, military operations were somewhat desultory, mainly consisting of intermittent exchanges of artillery fire and 'pickering', 'vapouring' and 'pottering' between parties of horse and foot. There were some spirited sallies by the Royalists, but the besiegers made no attempt at a general assault. It may have been because things were going so slowly that on 8 July Whalley was superseded by Rainsborough, who was sent by Fairfax from Oxford to take command. But it was the repeated summonses to surrender, delivered and answered with all the formalities of seventeenth-century warfare, that protracted the siege more than anything else. Operations began with the presentation by Whalley's trumpeter of a summons from Fairfax at 4 o'clock in the afternoon of 20 May: to which Washington replied that, as the King was said to be in the hands of Parliament, his commands should be obtained for the disposal of the garrison and that 'Till then, I shall make good the trust reposed in me'. A more threatening summons was sent on 24 May by Whalley and the Worcestershire Committee at Evesham, pointing out that after the surrender of Oxford, which was imminent, the besieging forces would be greatly increased and that the citizens, with no further hope of relief, must then yield or expect the worst – 'Our soldiers would fain be trading with you; you will find them but ill Customers. A month's pay to the whole Army both of Horse and Foot will scarce keep them out of your shops and Houses'. The Mayor and aldermen returned a defiant answer, asking leave to send a messenger to the King and, when this was refused, the Mayor, William Evetts, 'himself returned an answer by word to the drummer, that he should forbear bringing any such summons, that he will draw out and fight with them, if they will, and leave men enough to man the City beside'. The deadlock continued so long as Oxford held out. In the absence of news from the outside world the wildest rumours gained currency: now, that the Parliamentary horse at Pershore had mutinied and killed their colonel and now, that the King was marching on London from Newcastle with an army of 80,000 English, Scots and Irish. It was not believed that Oxford had fallen until Fairfax sent Anthony Kempson, Prince Maurice's Secretary, down to confirm it: and then, for the first time, Washington consented to treat. Even so, Kempson was accused of treason and many refused to accept the authenticity of the message which Charles had sent to the two Houses from Newcastle on 10 June with a copy of his warrant to the governors of Oxford, Lichfield, Worcester, Wallingford and his other garrisons commanding them to surrender.[155]

A truce for negotiations was proclaimed from 27 to 30 June. They broke down, however, because the Royalists stood out for better terms than had been offered to Oxford. The forty articles they submitted read less like conditions of surrender than terms of a general peace settlement, taking account of the interests of all the parties – the soldiers, the County Commissioners and gentlemen strangers, the citizens and the clergy – whose representatives had drawn them up. They amount to a statement of a fairly wide cross-section of Royalist opinion at the end of the War, comparable with the Declaration of 1642 at the beginning: and intransigent, even impertinent, as they appear in the military situation, they do, some of them, help to explain the acceptance, a few weeks later, of a new regime. 'Garrison' was defined to comprise everyone within the fortifications. The liberal terms demanded for the troops included a month's pay. All who wished to leave the city should be allowed six months to remove their goods, with a convoy for the northern gentry as far as Darlington. There was to be a complete indemnity, without exceptions, for acts done during the War and neither the Covenant nor any other oath was to be imposed, save for subsequent acts prejudicial to Parliament. All sequestrations were to be taken off and all the Worcestershire garrisons withdrawn: or, if Worcester itself were continued, the contribution for its maintenance was 'to be brought to £1,000 per mensem', which, being levied on the whole county, would mean a great reduction in taxes. Among those to be restored to their houses and estates, special mention was made of Colonel Lygon, a Parliamentary officer whose house at Madresfield had been garrisoned for the King. The corporate privileges of the city were, of course, to be preserved. Excise and monthly pay were to be alternatives, only that with the higher yield being retained. There was to be no taxation of cloth, coal or fuel and the citizens were 'to have free Trade, as formerly'. Arrears of contribution were to be collected only to pay public debts and gentlemen who had spent money on the fortifications were to be reimbursed – apparently by Parliament! – up to a total of £1,200. Perhaps the most remarkable clauses relate to the Church. The Bishop was to be 'continued in his power, His Houses and revenues preserved and restored with arrears', with corresponding assurances to clergy and fellows of colleges in the garrison and the Prayer Book was to be 'continued in this City and County, until it be otherwise ordered by Act of Parliament'. Its use had already been forbidden by ordinance of the two Houses in 1645, but the wording here implies a religious settlement to which the King should be a party. Finally, Fairfax was asked to procure the King's approval of these terms and 'to engage His Honour for an Ordinance of Parliament to confirm what he hath not the power to conclude'.

Fairfax ignored these propositions and hostilities continued for another fortnight, without much incident, but with the effect of the fall of Oxford increasingly felt. The city was now so closely beset, says Townshend, 'that we cannot sally out without hazard of much loss and small benefit'. Rainsborough was disposed to be conciliatory and he could afford to wait. A private letter to the Mayor from a friend, indicating what terms might be granted, was circulated in the city and debated by the Chamber and induced Washington, on 16 July to proclaim another cessation so that a new treaty might be opened. As the suggested terms were especially favourable to the corporation and the citizens the letter had the divisive effect that was doubtless intended. Rainsborough's actual terms, which the corporation accepted on 18 July 'if we may not speedily be assured of better',[156] were mainly concerned with the garrison and, while promising the inhabitants freedom from plunder, omitted the assurance in the letter of indemnity for acts committed against Parliament. A few days of negotiation followed, but it was impossible now to rekindle much spirit of resistance. There was some thought of the garrison's withdrawing from the city to the Great Sconce: but then the townsmen might well assist the enemy against them, many of the soldiers themselves were already enlisting for service overseas and there was only a day's ammunition left to withstand an assault. Washington surrendered on 23 July,[157] on the same day that the King wrote his long-awaited message from Newcastle offering no hope of relief, but urging him, if he could, to hold out for another month.[158]

The motto of the city of Worcester[159] seems to have originated during the siege, when the words 'Civitas Fidelis Deo et Rege' were painted on the drawbridge at the Severn Gate. Only a sense of loyalty could have sustained those who lived there through four years of war, for it was never difficult, until the last few weeks, to move elsewhere. By the summer of 1646, to have been the first city to declare for the King and the last to surrender had become a point of pride and almost to the end there seemed some hope in standing out for better terms. Behind the enmities and confusion increasingly rife during the siege was the question at what point honour might be held to have been satisfied. To begin with, the Governor and the corporation were, ostensibly at least, united in refusing to treat, though the latter were already making independent overtures for peace early in June, when the Mayor, William Evetts, and Edward Solley were described by the Parliamentarians as the leaders of resistance, 'brethren in inquity, men in their cups as fierce as lions'. Evett's verbal defiance of 24 May has been quoted above yet on 16 June he secretly approached the Committee at Evesham to be allowed to take the Covenant and Negative Oath.[160] Though in fact he remained in office until the surrender, when he was imprisoned by Rainsborough, there must have been many actual, unrecorded defections. At a council meeting on 17 June 'some of the Chamber' proposed that the Governor should be urged to treat and others that he should be asked 'what comforts he had received from His Majesty or Oxford for to give them encouragement to hold out': and on the same day the Governor received a body of citizens' wives who appealed to him to preserve the city by seeking honourable terms. At another meeting a month later, when the treaty with Rainsborough began, the draft of a petition to Fairfax was produced which amounted to a surrender on whatever terms he might please to grant. But the Governor and Commissioners persuaded the corporation to tear it up and to take an oath not to divulge that it had ever been considered.[161]

The strains and hardships of that time naturally widened the differences that had always existed between the soldiers and the townsmen. Townshend, a Commissioner of Array, but a civilian, takes a middle viewpoint, critical of 'the soldier and his ranting ways' but critical also of what he considers the apathy of the citizens, 'besotted and stupid concerning their own preservation'. Washington's discipline was certainly bad and the fact that some of his troops were Irish probably did not help to make it better. He failed, even with the promise of payment, to enforce his order that the garrison should collect the tax of provisions due from the neighbouring parishes: while those who seized the countrymen's cattle or broke up outhouses and gentlemen's coaches in the city 'upon pretence of fuel' and sold the wood for liquor went unpunished. In that way, says Townshend, 'most part of the suburbs of St. Peters in Sidbury is defaced' adding that all good christians may insert in their Litany, 'from the plundering of soldiers, their Insolency, Cruelty, Atheism, Blasphemy and Rule over us, *Libera nos Domine*'. The root of the trouble was lack of pay, for which Washington was wholly dependant on the citizens who, with whatever goodwill, were now finding it impossible to raise the full amount. At the beginning of the siege, on 23 May, the corporation made a last effort by voting a weekly tax of £240 for a month to maintain 1,600 soldiers, at 3s. a week, a reduction on the hitherto current rate of 4s. By agreement with the Governor it was to be in lieu of all other taxes, to be repaid out of the country contribution and to cease 'if the enemie remove'.[162] To prevent officers from cheating their men a system was devised by which householders paid each soldier billeted on them on receipt from the captain of a billet or certificate bearing the soldier's name and signed by the Governor. In fact the soldiers received only 2s. 6d. a week until 1 July, when it was reduced for one week to 1s. and only raised to 2s. for the following week 'after long debate and much repining'.[163] At a Council of War on 5 July Washington declared that if he could not honour his promise to the garrison of a week's pay 'He must be enforced to keep his Chamber' and the Mayor and Town Clerk replied that 'the City would lay out no money. And if the City did suffer they could not help it'. A compromise was reached for a week of 1s. in money, 1s. in corn and 6d. in bacon or cheese. Even so, on 16 July when the last cessation began, the weekly rate was further reduced to 8d.[164]

Money for other expenses had still to be raised, though it was now 'desired' and not 'ordered' by the Chamber; a double fifteenth for making up powder, and a levy, agreed to 'with much reluctance' of 4d. a day for a week on each of the Twenty-four, 3d. each on the Forty-eight and 2d. on every commoner to finish the fortifications.[165] The latter, which was for a week's pay in advance, was necessary because the workmen were threatening to strike 'as though there were no siege, nor that their lives and estates were not concerned in it if the city be taken by storm.'[166] The resort to paid labour was probably due to the citizens' neglect of their turns of duty and the two periods of truce, by allowing fraternization, helped to weaken still further the will to resistance. During the second, in the last week of the siege, there were said to be almost as many townspeople in the suburb of St. John's as enemy troops. Indeed the Governor himself had set the example by sending to Colonel Dingley to meet him outside the Foregate 'to talk together, being fellow soldiers in the Low Countries' and remaining there drinking with some of his officers from 5 p.m. till nearly 10 p.m. The incident led to accusations against Washington and to a violent scene in which he completely lost his temper, abused some of the Commissioners, issued a challenge to fight, blamed all the dissensions in the garrison on the Papists, 'that will set all by the ears and will do nothing themselves'[167] and swore that if pay and ammunition could be found for his troops, he would die on the walls. In such an atmosphere, the inevitable outcome must have been attended with general relief.

VI

On the day after Rainborough's entry the corporation re-elected Serjeant Wilde as their recorder. Of the leading Royalist members, Edward Solley, having been in arms as Lieutenant-Colonel of the Militia, was removed on 28 August.[168] William Evetts took the Covenant and Negative Oath on 29 August and continued on the 24 until 4 January 1649 when he was removed, having been absent from the city for eighteen months.[169] Sir Daniel Tyas likewise submitted and remained until his resignation was accepted on 16 February 1649. He was restored in 1660.[170] Both he and Solley continued throughout the Interregnum as trustees of the city lands under the feoffment of August 1645. Evetts compounded for his estate at one-sixth for £359 and Tyas at £270.[171] Compared with the leading county gentry, like Sir William Russell who was fined at one-sixth, £2,071, or Sir John Pakington of Westwood (at one-third, £7,670)[172] they were not wealthy men. Rainsborough became Governor but was soon afterwards followed by the Governor of Evesham, Colonel William Dingley of Hanley Castle,[173] probably in deference to a request of the citizens during the treaty that a local man should be appointed.[174] The Parliamentary Committee was now able to move from Evesham and was established at the Deanery until the Restoration.

During the first twelve or eighteen months after the War there are many signs of a new spirit in the corporation, of a deliberate and energetic policy of reconstruction. The same trend is observable in Oxford[175] and could probably be found in other cities which had suffered severely from the fighting. At Worcester, it can be associated with one man, Edward Elvins, of whom something must be said because he seems to typify that combination of efficiency and zeal which were both a cause and an effect of the Parliamentary victory. By occupation he was probably a clothier.[176] As a member of the Forty-eight, he served, with Daniel Tyas, on the committee of December 1640 to draw up the petition against the Dean and Chapter and as a collector of money for the purchase of ordnance in August 1642.[177] He opposed the Commission of Array and soon afterwards left the county, but returned with Essex and 'did then improve his endeavours to ingage all he could for the Parliament'.[178] He left again when Russell came in and was still absent on 19 February 1644, when a summons to attend the next quarterly meeting on pain of dismissal was left at his house. This was evidently effective, since on 4 March he was elected and sworn an additional constable for St. Peter's Ward. He could not have served long, however, for he was removed from the Forty-eight, having been away from the city for more than a year, on 12 June 1645.[179] For the rest of the war he was active for Parliament in the neighbourhood and in June 1646 appears on the Worcestershire Committee for Taking Accounts of which, during the next three years, he was the most active member.[180] After the fall of Worcester the corporation was without its two chief officers, the Mayor being in prison and the Sheriff, Hugh Greene, having died shortly before.[181] Elvins, who was restored to his place by order of the Parliamentary Committee on 6 August, was elected Sheriff and was persuaded to become Mayor for the following year, 1646–7, 'by the Committee and officers of the Army . . . there being no other that they would confide in'.[182] In September 1647, when his term was almost up, Parliament decided that, notwithstanding charter or custom, he should be continued until further order,[183] though this did not take effect. He was forced to flee a third time before Charles II in 1651 and returned after the battle with Cromwell, on whose persuasion he became Governor, 'not onely to the hazard of his life among the sicke Scottes but alsoe his greate trouble and charge'. He was also, by this time, a member of the County Parliamentary Committee by whom, on 13 April 1653, he was ordered to be paid £10 for 'his charge in solliciting at London the keeping uppe the Colledge Church and continuing it for a publicke meeting place for the service of God':[184] thus it may partly be due to Edward Elvins that Worcester Cathedral is still standing. He was appointed to the Committee of Triers for ejecting scandalous ministers in Worcestershire in 1654[185] and represented Worcester in the first Protectorate Parliament. In the same year he petitioned Cromwell for some compensation for all his losses and was granted £600 out of sequestered estates.[186] He continued an alderman until the Restoration, when he was ejected, and he died in Worcester in 1665.[187]

The most obvious and pressing of the post-war problems with which the corporation was faced was that of finance. Here, the results are striking, though it is not altogether clear how they were achieved. By audit day 1646 the chamberlains' deficit of £606 14s. 6d. had been reduced to £174 16s. 5d. and within the next twelve months was converted into a credit balance of £20 0s. 6d. Receipts from rents rose, 1646–7, from £57 11s. 2d. to £96 12s. 0d. and – still clearer proof of stricter administration – two double-fifteenths, voted in October 1646 and February 1647, were collected in full and paid into the chamberlains' hands. For the future, assessments were to be kept in a book and the collectors were themselves to account at the annual audit. Order was taken for the settlement of long-standing accounts, such as those of the constables, John Nott the gaol-keeper and Alderman Henry Foord, who had spent £139 8s. 4d. of his own money on Sir William Russell's forces during his mayoralty. On 8 April 1647 the constables were directed to take particulars of claims for losses by free quarter. The heaviest wartime burden, the monthly pay, was now controlled by the County Committee and as early as 17 August 1646 efforts were made to secure its reduction, with the result that £80 a month of the arrears of the past sixteen months were cancelled in November.[188] Direct taxation henceforth was both lighter and more centralized. By the Parliamentary ordinance of 23 June 1647 the city was assessed at £43 5s. 6³⁄₄d. a month, a level which was approximately maintained throughout the Interregnum. But arrears still accumulated and the only way of getting them abated in 1653 was to send Elvins with a petition to London.[189]

The Corporation addressed themselves with equal vigour to repairing the damages and removing the traces of war. Expenditure on repairs to property, which had averaged about £4 or £5 annually since 1642, rose during Elvin's year to £101 9s. 8d. The fortifications were slighted, any bricks or stone useable in repairing the bridge and the quay being preserved and the other materials sold.[190] Seven building leases were granted during Elvin's term as Sheriff and Mayor, five of vacant ground and two of houses, and four of them specified the sums to be laid out by the tenants, which total £340. The most important achievement of all was the removal of the soldiers, which the corporation obtained by a petition to Parliament in July 1647.[191]

Besides what the corporation had suffered, almshouses had been destroyed and charitable funds, estimated at £500, had been lost, which could only be made good from some fresh source of capital. This was acquired from the demolition of the 'leaden steeple', a detached belfry in the cathedral churchyard, for which a Parliamentary order was made on 17 February 1648 on the joint petition of the corporation and the County Committee. The sale of the materials realized only £617 4s. 2d. – not much more than half the £1,200 that had been expected – from which £57 had to be deducted for the cost of demolition. £180 was granted for the repair of three churches in the county and the remainder was sufficient to rebuild Inglethorpe's Almhouses and to provide £267 0s. 11d. for the re-endowment of charities.[192]

While the restrictions on outward trade had ceased with the return of peace, the influx of population during the war had given rise to another problem which called for urgent remedy; namely, the infringement of the rights of freedom by foreigners setting up in trade within the city. On 17 September 1644 the corporation had ordered the churchwardens and constables to bring in lists of such persons, and shortly afterwards had opposed the Governor's request that Thomas Devell should be made a freeman because 'he is a man of a great estate and will doe much wrong unto the companie of mercers and other trades if he should be admitted'. On 15 December 1646, an act of the Common Council 'against forraigners and others not free of this cittie' was passed and ordered to be proclaimed whereby a non-freeman retailing any merchandise other than victuals or practising any occupation or handicrafts was to be prosecuted in the name of the chamberlains and fined £4.[193] It is a sign of the importance attached to this order that it is re-copied in full at the beginning of the new order book in 1650:[194] and at the same time it was found necessary to restrain the private suits, unauthorized by the Chamber, that had been commenced in virtue of it.[195] This was a national problem, not peculiar to Worcester, and the importance of the Civil War as a stage in the breakdown of the old guild monopolies might profitably be investigated. On 19 February 1647 two other economic regulations of similar tendency were passed and entered in full in the order book: the one for enforcing of certain old ordinances and of the act of 1563 requiring apprenticeships to be enrolled before the town clerk; and the other, also a recapitulation, for the disfranchisement of freemen who had left the city for more than a year.[196] Not only the right to trade was involved, for freedom entailed burdens to be shared as well as privileges to be enjoyed. Hence the initiative in a petition of 1649 that the cathedral and its precincts should be included in the city boundaries came not from the Chamber but from the commonalty: though nothing was done, evidently because the cost of prosecuting the claim could not be raised by a general subscription.[197]

The post-war inflation and the depression of trade are reflected in the records in a variety of ways: in the reduction, in October 1646, in the rent paid by the wool-weigher for the profits of his place from £3 6s. 8d. to £1 5s. 0d. 'in respect of the troubles of the tyme'; [198] in the table of increased fees due to the town clerk and the serjeants-at-mace for the issue and execution of writs proclaimed by the Mayor and aldermen in November 'by reason of the increase of the rates and values of all manner of sustenance and other things for man's life' and also to prevent the taking of unauthorized and extortionate fees, which had been causing complaint;[199] and in the order of the city Justices at Easter Sessions 1648 fixing the wages of journeymen walkers until Michaelmas at 4s. a week or 8d. a day, working from 5 a.m. till 8 p.m. 'in respect of the deernes of the tymes', a rate which clearly represents an increase.[200]

One of the first concerns of the Worcestershire Committee after the War was ecclesiastical re-organization, which was especially needed in the city because of the poverty of the livings. It was referred to a committee of the corporation to

consider 'the uniting of the parish churches' and their proposals were 'approved
of and much desired' by the Chamber on 24 September 1646. The ten churches
were to be reduced to six; 'Martin and Nicholas, All Hallowes and Clementes,
Hellens and Albons, Peters and Michaells, Swethins of itselfe and Andrew of
itselfe'.[201] This scheme was much modified in practice and it seems unlikely, from
the scanty evidence available, that any settled rearrangement was adopted.
St. Helen's and St. Alban's were united on 21 April 1647 with an augmentation
of £50 a year from the Dean and Chapter lands: but this increase 'contrary to
expectation failing', St. Martin's was added in the following year by order of
Parliament, on the petition of the Mayor and aldermen and the inhabitants of
the three parishes and with the approval of the Assembly of Divines.[202] Yet
St. Martin's was again a separate parish, with Thomas Ince (or Juice) as rector, by
1650 and from 1653 onwards, Richard Fincher combined the livings of All Saints
and St. Nicholas. St. Peter's and St. Michael's, held together with the lectureship
in the Cathedral by Simon Moor is the only other recorded case of a union of
churches during the Interregnum.[203] The problem of clerical stipends was dealt
with from time to time by grants out of the cathedral revenues confiscated under
the Parliamentary Ordinance of 30 April 1649. Thus the Trustees paid £225 for
the remainder of that year to Simon Moor for the use of himself and the other
city ministers.[204] In September 1650 Parliament ordered Lord Chief Baron Wilde
and the rest of the County Committee 'to Inquire of the values of church means
within the City of Worcester', one result of which was the increase of All Saints
rectory to £49 a year:[205] and in 1656 St. Andrew's, which was worth only £6 a
year, received an augmentation of £30, afterwards made up to £50 on the
recommendation of the Trustees for the Maintenance of Ministers.[206] This source
came to an end when the church recovered its lands in 1660. But the
augmentations of vicarages by the restored Dean and Chapter included £48 a
year to St. Peter's.[207]

Under the Parliamentary Ordinance of 1648 the repair of the churches was
supervised by the Mayor and aldermen as Justices of Peace.[208] The civil parishes
remained as separate units, the main duty of the churchwardens now being the
relief of the poor. The importance of the sermon in public worship makes it
perhaps less likely that all the churches were in regular use and the taste for
preaching was further catered for by the visiting ministers who gave the Friday
lectures at St. Swithin's, and whose entertainment, costing some £5 or £6 a year,
was paid for by the chamberlains. An order of Quarter Sessions, made at the
request of the Grand Jury on 11 July 1653, that only one bell should be rung in
any church on the Sabbath is interesting as an example of Puritan austerity and
no less so as implying that the old custom of a full peal was still being observed.

All the incumbents who can be traced were deprived in 1646–7, except for
Richard Fincher at St. Nicholas and Rowland Crosby at St. Swithin's: and
Crosby cannot have survived long, since he preached before Charles II in the

cathedral on 24 August 1651.[209] At All Saints, John Ricketts characteristically records in the register a baptism, 'novo modo', by his successor, Mr Joseph Singe, on 28 July 1646, 'the day after I was confined to the parsonidge house by the Commityes a quibus Deus liberet Ecclesiam'. Singe, who died in 1648, was a Bridgnorth man and a relative, probably a brother, of Edward Singe, who had fled from the Irish rebels in 1641, held the city lectureship, 1643–4, during the Royalist occupation and afterwards returned to Ireland to become a bishop.[210] Of the other Commonwealth clergy, Richard Fincher came of a family of minor Worcestershire gentry, the Finchers of Shell Manor in Himbleton, and Thomas Ince was the son of Richard Ince,[211] clothier, an active member of the corporation throughout the War and until his resignation in 1657. Joseph Baker at St. Andrew's, a native of Stourbridge, was, according to Baxter, 'neither for Prelacy, Presbytery, nor Independency, as then formed into Parties; but for that which was found in all the Parties, and for Concord upon such Catholick terms'.[212] All three were members of Baxter's Worcestershire Association[213] and so may be regarded as moderate Puritans, though they were all ejected in 1661–2. The leading minister in Worcester at this time was Simon Moor, Ince's father-in-law, who represents a more radical Puritanism and is the only one not known to have been educated at either University. He is described in an order of the County Committee as 'a very faythful preacher of God's word and of singular good affection to the government of this Commonwealth', but by Baxter, rather cryptically, as 'an old Independent, who somewhat lost the People's Love, upon Reasons which I here omit'.[214] In 1656 he was one of the signatories of a remonstrance of Gloucestershire clergy to Cromwell against taking the Crown.[215] Moor was a man of importance in the city, employed by the corporation on business in London, in 1647 about the leaden steeple and again in 1650; nominated as one of their referees in 1652 in a dispute with Fulke Estopp, Andrew Yarranton and others over the digging of iron cinders in Little Pitchcroft;[216] and a member, by 1651, of the County Committee.[217] Though he was granted an augmentation of £90 a year on St. Michael's and was master of St. Oswald's hospital, in addition to his two livings and the cathedral lectureship, he was, like all the Worcester clergy, a poor man. The promised augmentation failed, for some reason, and in 1651 he was plundered by the Scots. We find the County Committee making grants towards his maintenance out of the surplus from the sale of lead off the Cathedral roof.[218] He lost his preferments in 1660 and apparently died at a great age in London.

By the end of 1647 much of the impetus of reform seems to have spent itself. Some of the measures undertaken had been only partially successful and others still continued because the same problems still remained, such as the settlement of wartime debts and of the arrears due to the chamberlains. Little could be done to improve the general economic situation and at the beginning of 1648 the 'great extreamitie' of the poor made it necessary to treble the rating assessments.[219] Nevertheless the record of 1646–7 does suggest a planned direction of policy, not very common in seventeenth-century local administration, which offered at least a hope of eventual return to more normal conditions. Though the chamberlains maintained a small, precarious balance on their accounts until 1649–50, the rent receipts sank to a steady average during the next three years of a little over £60. Perhaps the clearest sign of a loosening of control is the recurrence of the old difficulty in collecting taxes: a double-fifteenth voted in October 1647 was still unpaid in February 1649 when new warrants were ordered to be made out to the constables for the speedy collection of the arrears.[220] There is a discernible change: and whatever personal factors may have contributed to it, the main cause lies, no doubt, in the disturbed conditions that heralded the outbreak of the second Civil War. On 25 January 1648 the Mayor and aldermen were 'desired to make choyce of two men in every ward to present the names of such persons . . . that may be thought honest and willing men to be reddy upon all occasions to suppresse any tumult or uproare that shall arise within this cittie', that is, to organize a militia; and the constables were to provide for a watch, day and night, at the gates.[221] Within a month came the Royalist revolt in South Wales. By the end of April there were troops in Worcester, and another detachment of eighty men was expected on the night of 12 May. They were to be quartered at the inns and not, as in the first War, in private houses, though this did not make it any easier to raise the money to pay for them.[222] In April 1649, Alderman Foord, who must have been among the wealthier citizens, advanced £100 'that wee for the present be freed from quarter of the souldiers which otherwise will fall upon us'. And in June the troops had to be called in to assist the constables in the collection.[223] Meanwhile, by an order of 29 April 1648 the County Committee had taken over the raising of a militia for the defence of the city, though deferring to the susceptibilities of the corporation by requesting them to name the officers, the chief of whom, Major Fulke Estopp, had already served in the Parliamentary army and was soon afterwards restored to his place in the Forty-eight.[224] Though there were far fewer troops than in 1642–6, and for shorter periods, their presence was not less resented, for on 7 May 1649 the members of the two companies agreed to subscribe £14 'towardes the reparacion of the damage that was latlie receaved by the souldiers in a tumult made within this cittie'.[225] Early in 1650 there were riots against the Commissioners of Excise both in the county and in the city in which people were killed and which led the Council of State to order the appointment of a new commission.[226] While there is no sign of active Royalism in Worcester, it is significant that when the Engagement 'to be true and faithful to the Commonwealth of England as it is now established without a King or House of Lords' was read in the Chamber on 14 February 1650 only sixteen out of seventy-two members were present.[227]

One result of these events was a closer surveillance of the personnel of the corporation both by the county and the central government. The former had begun, soon after the capture of the city, by scrutinizing the wartime records of some of the corporate officers and assurances had to be given on behalf of the sword-bearer and one of the serjeants-at-mace before they were allowed to retain their places.[228] Persons who had borne arms against Parliament were excluded from all local office by an Ordinance of 9 September 1647 on which, at the end of March 1648 the corporation resolved to seek the Judges' opinion at the next Assizes.[229] Most of the resignations and removals of the next two years are of known Royalists. That they were due to external pressure appears from the entry in several cases that the Twenty-four or the Forty-eight are to have power to elect their successors. Nor was the purge limited to those who had been in arms for the King. On 19 January 1649 George Heming was removed from the Twenty-four by virtue of an order of the Committee of Indemnity at Westminster made in the previous November,[230] a delay which shows the reluctance of the corporation to submit to political interference. Heming was a clothier who had supplied large quantities of cloth for uniforms, to Byron in 1642 and afterwards to Rupert.[231] He had been Sheriff in 1646–7 and it was probably to prevent his succession as Mayor that Parliament had pressed the re-election of Edward Elvins.[232] During the Mayoral years 1648–50 there were fifteen elections to the Forty-eight and nine promotions to the Twenty-four.[233] They include the four militia captains appointed in 1648; another officer, Captain William Scott; Thomas Writer, tanner and maltster, a supporter of Parliament since 1642, who was an excise officer for Worcestershire and in 1652 became Surveyor to the Treason Trustees; and Anthony Carlesse, collector of the monthly assessments for the city.[234] The Chamber was thus acquiring a more definitely political character than it had had during the first Civil War. It was a trend that met with rather more resistance than the better known and more systematic regulation associated with the Clarendon Code, perhaps because Charles II's government in the '60s was stronger in authority and also in public opinion. But the pattern of proscription and monopoly of power that dominated civic life under the later Stuarts had its origin, at least in Worcester, during the Commonwealth.

The likelihood of Royalist risings in the spring of 1651 made the government particularly sensitive to danger from Worcester and orders were given to render the city untenable by slighting the fortifications.[235] That this was done appears from the chamberlains' accounts which show a net profit of some £23 from the sale of materials; though nearly double that amount had to be spent when the works were repaired again in August. At the beginning of that month, Charles and the Scots army crossed the Border and it was soon clear that Worcester would be in their line of advance. Encouraged by Major-General Harrison, who was shadowing their southward march, the Committee had officers determined to hold the city against them. The walls were hastily repaired and 'the well-affected in the city and county' enrolled as volunteers. But on the night of Thursday, 21 August they received a message from the Mayor and Sheriff asking for a meeting to discuss 'the peaceable entry of the enemy into the city'. The request was granted and only three members of the Chamber – Edward Elvins, Major Fulke Estopp and Captain Theophilus Alie – voted for resistance, the majority declaring 'their resolution of delivering the town to the king . . . and that they would not be undone by making resistance in satisfying the wills of three or four men'. This discouragement was offset by the arrival next day of four troops of horse from Harrison's army, and it was only the failure of expected reinforcements from Hereford to materialize that decided the Committee to withdraw to Gloucester on Saturday, 22 August. They had just time to secure the magazine before the Scots entered.[236]

The Mayor, Thomas Licens, formally surrendered the city and proclaimed Charles II. The hope that by submitting to a temporary occupation the horrors of war would be avoided seemed reasonable enough and of Charles's army of 10,000 only 500 entered with him.[237] But in fact, the consequences of resistance could hardly have been worse than what actually happened, culminating in the terrible carnage in the streets on 3 September. The royal troops, after marching 300 miles in three weeks, needed a rest. Whatever might have been his original intention of pressing on, Charles was obliged to establish his headquarters at Worcester, which was therefore bound to become the centre of the approaching campaign. On Sunday, 24 August summonses were issued to the constables of the neighbouring parishes to send their quota of men on the following afternoon to work on the fortifications,[238] which were strengthened, as a Parliamentary observer reports, 'beyond imagination'.[239] Within a week after the battle, the same parishes were to send perhaps some of the same men to level them again on the order of the Parliamentary Commissioners.[240] Recruiting proved more difficult and the *Posse Comitatus*, assembled on Pitchcroft on Tuesday, 26 August was a fiasco.[241] English Royalists would have found the Scots unwelcome allies even in a more hopeful enterprise. To maintain himself and his army the 'King of Scots', as Charles is called in the city records, was wholly dependent on requisition and free quarter. The chamberlains' accounts include daily inventories of supplies for the improvised royal court. The total cost was £187 13s. 2½d. and the provisions sent in on the morning of the battle were 1½ veals, 4 muttons, a couple of hens and a couple of chickens and 7 pounds of bacon, a dozen eggs, a couple of pigeons and 2 pounds of butter, fruit, 9 gallons of sack and 11¼ gallons of claret and half a dozen glasses; altogether £6 4s. 8d. for food and £6 6s. 0d. for wine. Five drapers of the city supplied between them £453 1s. 5d. worth of cloth which was delivered on 2 and 3 September, so that most of it would have arrived too late for making up into uniforms. The last of the drapers' bills was discharged by the chamberlains in 1675.[242]

A few miscellaneous items realistically evoke the scene after the battle was over: such as the payment of 2s. by the chamberlains 'for stonpitch and rosen to perfume the Hall after the Scotts', and payments by the churchwardens of

St. Michael in Bedwardine of 6d. 'for carryage of the litter away which the Scotts lay upon' and of £2 9s. 4d. 'for buryall of the Scotts that were slaine and dyed in our parish, the Pallace, the Colledge, Colledge Greene, Castle Hill. . . . And of divers others that were brought out of the Citty of Worcester and layd in the churchyard'.[243] For the citizens the worst came after Cromwell's victory. The city having been taken by storm, by the rules of war was open to plunder. 'You cannot hear too bad an account of the inhabitants of Worcester' writes Sir Rowland Berkeley, a neighbouring Royalist who had not joined Charles II, 'all houses being ransacked from top to bottom, the very persons of men and women not excepted'.[244] Since the losses were afterwards declared at £80,000 it was a calamity from which it must have taken years to recover. Such was the distress of the poor that the county Quarter Sessions in January 1652 took the very unusual step of making a grant of £500 to set them on work, which was supplemented by a gift of £20 from 'a private Gentleman of Herefordshire'.[245] The prevailing confusion is evident from the gaps in the records. The Order Book gives no meeting in 1651 except on election day, 24 August, but as it seems to have been usual to enter up the minutes some time afterwards, perhaps at the end of the Mayoral year, this may be because the rough drafts were lost when the Treasury was sacked by Cromwell's soldiers.[246] The Mayor and James Bridges, the Sheriff, were taken to London and imprisoned in the Fleet until the following January,[247] which explains Elvins' appointment as Governor. The new officers could not be sworn, as the charter required, within three weeks after Michaelmas and the chamberlains' accounts for 1650–1 were not audited until 1655. Those for 1651–2, 'being the years wherein noe officers were sworne', were kept by Edward Elvins and audited by Francis Franks, Mayor, on 17 January 1653. In 1652 the city Quarter Sessions were held on 16 February before four of the County Commissioners and no Chamber meeting is recorded until 13 August.

The corporation was thus virtually in abeyance for about a year. On 2 March 1652, therefore, the Council of State recommended to the House of Commons the names of persons to be appointed magistrates until further order.[248] Of these, the Mayor, the Sheriff and five aldermen were elected by the Chamber in the usual way for 1652–3. But the nomination as Town Clerk of Thomas Milward of Alvechurch, a member of the County Committee who had commanded a troop of horse under Colonel Lygon, was apparently not accepted, since Francis Street, the former Town Clerk, was continued. Although the election and swearing of officers were held in 1652 it was still nearly a year before the corporation was functioning normally. It must have been much depleted, for only 23 members were present on 6 October 1652 and 31 at the next recorded meeting on 18 July 1653.[249] In the twelve months from Michaelmas 1652, 23 persons were elected to the Forty-eight and 13 promoted to the Twenty-four, so that about half the places had to be filled: and during the same time, there were 12 removals and resignations. These last included Thomas Licens and James Bridges, the Mayor and Sheriff who had delivered the city to Charles II, William Bagnall, clothier, who is said to have assisted his escape by providing him with a horse,[250] and others who seem to have been of Royalist sympathies. Of those elected, Fulke Estopp and Anthony Carlesse were restored to their places, having left the city in 1651. The 13 promotions to the Twenty-four include 2 survivors of the 'Royalist' corporation of the first Civil War and all those, with one exception, who served as Mayor during the remainder of the 1650s. About half the new members – those elected to the Forty-eight – had taken no previous part in civic life and the rest had been constables, but, except for John Greenbank, only since 1646. John Phillips and William Norris had been ward collectors of the money which Charles II had endeavoured to raise from the citizens.[251] There is a curious variety in their subsequent fortunes, so far as they can be traced. James Badham, for instance, who was removed, 'being a sworn fugitive', on 19 June 1660, even before the general purge, is likely to have been a Republican. But John Greenbank and Samuel Matthews were among the four members removed in 1656 for disaffection to the Protectorate government.[252] Both were restored in 1660 and Matthews is described in his epitaph in 1684 as being 'in his religion, orthodox and devout, in his allegiance, constant and hearty'.[253] Altogether, 4 out of the 23 lost their places at the Restoration and others may simply have disappeared from the scene. But some survived and three became Mayors under Charles II.

These elections cannot be regarded as representing a younger generation. Of the 13 members of the Forty-eight and 6 of the Twenty-four during this period whose epitaphs are given in Nash, the average age at election to their respective companies is 43 and 54; a small and random sample but sufficient to indicate how far civic office was from being thought of as a career or as a goal of ambition. If these changes of 1652–3 are, as a whole, rather less political than those of 1648–50, it is because the prime need was to make up the full numbers. In the next reign the same difficulty in filling places was to be a hindrance in many boroughs to the rigid enforcement of the Clarendon Code: and it helps to explain why in James II's charter to Worcester of 1685 the second company was reduced to 32 by providing that no new elections should be made until 17 of the Forty-eight were dead or removed.[254]

VII

The history of Worcester during the Protectorate is relatively uneventful. An order of 23 June 1654 'That the petition now red by Mr Vernon concerning the voting in Parliament shall bee prefered unto the Lord Protectorate his Highnes and his Councell and that the Common Seale shall bee affixed thereto',[255] suggests a political pronouncement unique in the records of the Chamber during these twenty years. But the petition, unfortunately, has not survived. The 'Great

Sconce' and the walls themselves were ordered by the Council of State, in September 1651, soon after the battle, to be demolished, some of the stone being afterwards used 'to quoine the Towne hall'.[256] The garrison, however, was still continued and again the accounts afford glimpses of the unsettled state of the times. In 1655, 5s. was paid for 'fire, beare and tobacco that was spent that night that Mr Mayor watched when the disturbance was in the West', that is, at the time of Penruddock's rising when there was trouble in Worcestershire also.[257] There were similar payments when the Mayor and constables, the Sheriff, Captain Collins the Governor, 'the gentlemen' and others watched for three nights after the death of Oliver Cromwell. When the Major-Generals were established, Worcestershire was at first joined with Cheshire and Derbyshire under Charles Worsley, but was soon afterwards transferred to the command of James Berry. Berry was frequently in Worcester in 1655–6[258] and no doubt was responsible for the attempts to enforce the Ordinance of 1650 for the better observation of the Lord's Day.[259] Four persons were brought before Quarter Sessions by the constables on this charge in August and October 1656, but as none was convicted the city magistrates seem to have administered the law with forbearance. About the same time, the churchwardens of St. Michael in Bedwardine record the receipt of 6s. 8d. for the poor 'beinge levyed on a bargeman for passinge with his vessell on that day'.[260] The regulation of alehouses is another aspect of the moral reformation so characteristic of Cromwell's rule which is much in evidence at Worcester. A list of sixty-six persons 'certified by the inhabitantes of the severall Wards to bee fitting to bee continued inholders and victulars' is entered in the Order Book on 1 September 1654 when they are licensed until the following May.[261] The revival of the waits at the proclamation of Richard Cromwell sounds like the relaxation of Puritan control: though in fact they had been somewhat abruptly 'suppressed from playing of their instruments about the city in the morning' on 17 November 1642, a week after the entry of the King's forces under Sir William Russell.[262]

While the Order Book tends to get rather scanty in the 1650s the Mayor and aldermen are apparently enlarging the scope of their activities as Justices of Peace, mainly because they were the agents of the vigorous policy of the central government in enforcing statutes and ordinances. Besides the poor relief and settlement cases which had hitherto been their chief concern, we find the city Quarter Sessions dealing with Sabbath observance, with swearing (under the Ordinance of 1650),[263] with Popish recusants (under that of 1657),[264] and with forestalling, apprenticeship, suppression of unnecessary maltsters and other economic matters. The main interest of the Chamber records lies in the strenuous endeavours they reveal to cope with a financial situation which the sack of 1651, added to the still-continuing burdens of the first Civil War, must have rendered almost desperate. The prime necessity was for the corporation to establish control of its finances and also of its officers, as evidenced, for example, in the order of 21 December 1655 forbidding the chamberlains to disburse more than £5 without the written consent of the Mayor and the majority of aldermen.[265] A great part of the corporate revenues still remained under the control of the Feoffees appointed for the discharge of the debt in 1645. Their consent, though they had all ceased to be members of the Chamber, was therefore often necessary in the granting of leases and sometimes could only be obtained at the cost of a heavy additional fine on the tenant; hence the repeated orders that the Feoffees should account at the annual audit.[266] From 1655 a Committee of Surveyors of Houses and Lands was appointed,[267] to whose efforts perhaps may be ascribed the marked rise in receipts from rents during the next two years. Besides the improvement of the property by building leases, one of which, in 1656, provided most of the cost of erecting a new gaol,[268] ready money was raised by heavy fines for renewal. An economy of £50 or £60 a year was effected in 1652 by taking over the Sheriff's dues and paying out of them direct the charges for which he had been responsible, the fee farm of the city and the necessary expenses of passing his account in the Exchequer. But an arrangement which deprived the Sheriff of most of the profits of his office made it difficult to find persons willing to serve, even though heavy fines, in one case of £100, might be imposed for refusal. In October 1656, there were five elections before Richard Heming consented to be chosen.[269] Finally there were determined, though apparently not very successful, efforts in 1655–6 to settle outstanding debts including money borrowed by Sir William Russell, Sir Rowland Berkeley and others for Charles I, for which, however, the bonds had been lost: and considerable sums due to charities or to the corporation had to be written off for the same reason or because of the neglect of former officials to sue for them or to renew securities.[270] It is impossible to judge of the effectiveness of these measures as a whole, but clearly they amount to more than a series of expedients. The administrative record of the corporation during these very difficult years must be accounted creditable.

The Protectorate ended with the retirement of Richard Cromwell in May 1659 and the ensuing deadlock between the Army and the Parliament could only be broken by a return to monarchy. In the summer, the threat of a general Royalist rising caused the militia to be embodied throughout the country and to be paid at the same rate as regular troops.[271] By 18 August, when the Chamber at Worcester appointed a committee to settle with the County Commissioners the number of men the city should raise,[272] the danger had been temporarily averted by the defeat and capture of Sir George Booth: and early in September, Major-General Desborough recommended that the militia of Worcestershire and other counties should be paid off. But a week later three companies of the two foot regiments just returned from Flanders were ordered to Worcester which was more or less continuously occupied by militia or regulars for the next two years.[273] The forty-two trained men raised by impressment in the autumn of 1660 were paid at the rate of 1s. a day,[274] more than the New Model had received at the height of its power.

As Worcester was a freeman borough the election of burgesses is some index of changing opinion. In the first two Protectorate Parliaments the members were all active government supporters; in 1654, William Collins and Edward Elvins[275] and in 1656, William Collins and Edmund Gyles. Collins, originally a tanner of King's Norton and now a governor of the city[276] sat also in Richard Cromwell's Parliament, but the second seat was taken by Thomas Street, the well-known lawyer whose judgement against the Crown in Godden v. Hales is the sole and perhaps collusive instance in his career of opposition to the Stuarts. Worcester was unrepresented in the recalled Long Parliament until Alderman John Nash was readmitted with the members excluded by Pride's Purge in February 1660. Thomas Street and Thomas Hall, the Town Clerk, were elected to the Convention in April and with the return of Sir Rowland Berkeley and Thomas Street to the Cavalier Parliament twelve months later the Royalist reaction was complete; though only after a contest which produced a strong poll for a third candidate, John Nanfan, who had been chosen for the county in 1656 but not allowed by Cromwell to take his seat.[277]

When the news came on 3 May that Parliament had accepted the Declaration of Breda and invited the King to return there was 'such a number of bonfires throughout, with ringing of bells, that the City seemed all in a flame most part of the night, every street having at least 4 or 5, Some 12 bonfires, with high and general rejoicings and acclamations'.[278] A week later Charles II was proclaimed with full civic pomp, which Townshend describes in detail, 'and the King's good health with store of wine was drunk freely, never such a concourse of people seen upon so short a notice': and on 3 September there was a thanksgiving service in the cathedral and a 'solemn entertainment' in the Town Hall for 80 of the country gentry and 400 of the 'better sort' of citizens.[279] Such was the dominant mood of 1660. Most of the political changes in the corporation were made more than a year before the Corporation Act became law, beginning with the restoration of Edward Solly on 27 August, when the resolution of 1646, removing him for having been in arms for the King, was rescinded. On 14 September Serjeant Wilde was displaced from the recordership and, at the instance of Lord Windsor, the newly-appointed Lord Lieutenant of Worcestershire, 12 members, including most of the leading Parliamentarians, were removed and 10 former Royalists reinstated. There were 44 present at the first and 39 at the second of these meetings. On 16 October the whole council took the Oaths of Supremacy and Allegiance.[280] Six others, whose names are not recorded, were removed by the Commissioners in August 1662 for not taking the Oath of Non-Resistance and repudiating the Covenant, as the Act required.[281] There were still Parliamentarians who accepted the new regime and who, if they fell into poverty, were relieved by the charity of their colleagues. None had a longer or more active record of service, under both King and Parliament, than Alderman Henry Foord and after he had been removed in January 1662 – whether for political reasons is not stated – he was granted a pension of £10 for the lives of himself and his wife.[282] Similarly in 1666, after his retirement, Richard Vernon was paid £9 'to relieve his necessities'. Francis Frank, one of the most prominent civic figures of the Interregnum, remained on the common council until 1673, when he resigned 'in regard of his low condition of estate' and received £20 'towards his supportance'.[283] The evidence of wills and inventories is too scanty to give any general idea of the financial effects of the Wars on the leading citizens. Some of the principal actors in the struggle, such as Edward Elvins, Theophilus Alie, whose personal estate was valued at £490 13s. 6d., and Thomas Licens,[284] died in comfortable circumstances and bequeathed both freehold and leasehold property in the city. It was sometimes possible to make a fortune out of the Civil War – and generally to lose it at the Restoration – by the purchase of sequestered lands. But such opportunities were rarely open to the inhabitants of a town like Worcester and the picture, as a whole, must be one of impoverishment.

The general rejoicing at the King's return only temporarily allayed the fears and tensions that had rendered necessary the continuing presence of troops in the city and caused the Restoration government, for years after, to be constantly looking over its shoulder at the spectre of sedition in a way that neither Charles's father nor his grandfather, before the Civil War, had felt impelled to do. The disorders at the quay suppressed by the Mayor and constables and the guarding of the passages over the Severn after Venner's Rising of 6 January 1661,[285] are examples of the generally disturbed atmosphere. On Coronation Day, 23 April 1661 'all the trained bands, Horse and foot, were up in arms in several places to prevent Insurrections and tumults of seditious fanatics and schismatics, haters of Monarchy and Episcopacy'. That morning, copies of the following verses, headed 'A seasonable memento', were posted up throughout the city:

> This day it is said the King shall swear once more
> Just contrary to what he swore before.
> Great God, O can thy potent eyes behold
> This height of sin and can thy vengeance hold?
> Nip thou the Bud before the Bloom begins
> And save our Sovereign from presumptuous sins.
> Let him remember, Lord; in mercy grant
> That solemnly he sware the Covenant.[286]

On 28 May, £20 was publicly offered for the discovery of any persons concerned in the libel.[287] But we do not know whether the reward was ever claimed. It was probably about this time that men were set to watch against an expected attempt to dig up the foundations of the Cross,[288] presumably as a desperate demonstration in favour of the Good Old Cause.

Charles II was expected to visit Worcester during 1661. Bishop Morley hoped it might be on 3 September,[289] the tenth anniversary of Cromwell's Crowning Mercy having become, by the turns of fortune, that of His Majesty's Deliverance from His Enemies. In fact, it never took place, but great preparations were made, in repairing the walls and re-erecting the gates, mending the streets and beautifying the Town Hall. The King granted £200 towards the walls and the corporation voted for double-fifteenths, part of which was used to purchase the gates of Gloucester, whose fortifications, like those of Coventry, were ordered to be demolished as a punishment for having resisted Charles I.[290]

Valentine Green, the eighteenth-century historian of Worcester, speaks of the 'truly Roman firmness of support' which the citizens had given to the royal cause;[291] a judgement which, though it had long formed part of popular myth, seems scarcely justified by the foregoing narrative. Such fortitude and such unanimity would be hard to find, during the English Civil Wars, in any part of the country. The city found itself inevitably and closely involved and few places suffered more. Perhaps the most consistent thread in the story, so far as we can piece it together, is the efforts of the corporation to defend their chartered privileges, to assert their independence of the county and to minimize if possible the burdens laid on the inhabitants when they seemed to be past bearing. They were Vigornians first and Cavaliers or Roundheads afterwards. But this deep provincialism, so often emphasised in the writing of Stuart history, conditioned rather than conflicted with the adherence which both sides were able to command from individuals and from the townsmen as a whole at different times. In particular, the history of Worcester bears witness to the existence of a Royalism which was not simply the product of feudal survival or economic backwardness; a feeling often passive, sometimes negative, generally less articulate than that which carried Parliament to victory. Had such a Royalist tradition not been widespread, it would be difficult to explain the Restoration, either in Church or State.

Notes

1. *The Royalist Ordnance papers 1642–1646. Part i*, ed. Ian Roy, Oxfordshire Rec. Soc., vol. xliii (1964), pp. 35–7.

2. Sir Henry Ellis, 'Letters from a subaltern officer in the Earl of Essex's army', *Archaeologia*, vol. xxxv (1853), p. 328.

3. *Diary of Henry Townshend of Elmley Lovett, 1640–1663, vol. i*, ed. J.W. Willis Bund, Worcs. Hist. Soc. (1915), pp. 104–5.

4. Cr. *Dorset hearth tax assessments 1662–1664*, ed. C.A.F. Meekings, Dorset Natural Hist. and Archaeolog. Soc. (1951), App. III, pp. 107–20.

5. For the cloth trade see A.D. Dyer, 'The economy of Tudor Worcester', *U.B.H.J.*, vol. x (1966), pp. 117–36. Dr Dyer's Birmingham University Ph.D. thesis (1966), 'The city of Worcester in the

sixteenth century' deals very fully with the economic and constitutional background, and I am grateful to him for permission to make use of it [before his revised version of it was published in 1973].

6. For a translation of the charter see Valentine Green, *History and antiquities of the city and suburbs of Worcester* (1796), vol. ii, appendix, pp. lxxvi–xcvi.

7. M.F. Keeler, *The Long Parliament, 1640–1641* (1954), p. 144.

8. Ibid., p. 284.

9. For Sandys's navigation see *V.C.H. Warwicks.*, vol. iii, p. 238, and references quoted there; T.S. Willan, *River navigation in England, 1600–1750* (1936), pp. 26–7, 57, 66, 124; *Docquets of letters patent . . . passed under the Great Seal . . . at Oxford*, ed. W.H. Black (1837), pp. 34–5.

10. *The Chamber Order Book of Worcester 1602–1650*, ed. Shelagh Bond, Worcs. Hist. Soc., New ser., vol. viii (1974), p. 299. This volume is hereafter cited as *Bond*.

11. Ibid., p. 343.

12. *Journals of the House of Commons*, vol. ii (1803), p. 71.

13. Penry Williams, *The Council in the Marches of Wales under Elizabeth I* (1958), p. 200.

14. *Journals of the House of Commons*, vol. ii, pp. 191, 210, 216.

15. Ibid., pp. 242, 253; *Bond*, p. 345; Worcester Corporation MSS., Chamberlains' accounts, 1640–1 (not foliated).

16. Chamberlains' accounts, 1640–1, 'to Mr Edward Solley nowe Mayor of this citty that hee expended to one of my lord Presidents gent. to procure a deputacion to the Maior and Aldermen to bee deputy lieftenants for the citty', £2 0s. 0d.

17. *V.C.H. Wilts.*, vol. iii (1956), p. 188; R.V.H. Burne, *Chester cathedral . . . to the accession of Queen Victoria* (1958), pp. 114–16.

18. *Bond*, p. 342.

19. Worcester Cathedral, Dean and Chapter MSS. D. 143, 312.

20. *Journals of the House of Commons*, vol. ii, p. 86.

21. *Bond*, pp. 343, 344, 349.

22. Dean and Chapter MS. D. 312.

23. *Calendar of State Papers Domestic, 1633–4*, pp. 192–3.

24. *The works of . . . William Laud*, ed. W. Scott and J. Bliss, vol. v (1853), pp. 343, 492.

25. P.R.O., S.P. 16/436/60.

26. Dean and Chapter MS. D. 34 (and copy in Bishop Prideaux's register, H.W.R.O., 716.093, box 10 (ii), BA 2648); Worcester Corporation MSS., Quarter Sessions Order Book 1631–55, 10 July 1648 (not foliated); *The Parish Book of St. Helen's Church in Worcester . . .* , ed. J.B. Wilson, vol. ii (1900), p. 131.

27. Chamberlains' accounts, 1640.

28. *Bond*, p. 376.

29. *Archaeologia*, vol. xxxv, pp. 328, 329–30.

30. *Reliquiae Baxterianae*, ed. Matthew Sylvester (1696), lib. I, pp. 40–1.

31. Volume of churchwardens' and overseers' accounts, 1640–99, fols. 40[r–v], 117[v] (deposited with Worcester St. Andrew's parish records), H.W.R.O., b. 850 St. Andrew's, BA 2335/16[b] (v).

32. These customs are first mentioned in 1614 and 1623 respectively, Churchwardens' accounts, 1611–40, fols. 9[v], 81 (H.W.R.O., BA 2335/16[b] (iv)).

33. Churchwardens' and overseers' accounts, 1640–99, fol. 79.

34. Dean and Chapter MS. D. 34.

35. Churchwardens' and overseers' accounts, 1640–99, fols. 79, 83.

36. Ibid., fols. 36[a] 36[b], 82[v], 99[v], 100, 100[v], 110, 123[v], 135[v], 136, 137[v], 139[v], 159, 170. The churchwardens seem to have made a practice of relieving any ejected clergy, wandering through the parish, e.g. (fol. 100) 'Given to a poore minister, a master of artes who came out of Wiltshire (beinge Bishop Thornborough's nephewe)', 1s. (probably Giles Thornborough, rector and patron of Orcheston St. Mary. A.G. Matthews, *Walker Revised* (1948), p. 380); see also fol. 136[v], 'Given to a poore minister's widdow of Shropshire' 17 February 1655. Marston's burial entry, Bodleian, MS. Top. Worcs. d.4, fol. 171 (transcript of St. Michael's parish registers, 1546–1812, by W.H. Challen).

37. Churchwardens' accounts, ut sup., fols. 193[v]–196[v].

38. *Bond*, pp. 335, 337. Chamberlains' accounts, 1639–40, 1640–41.

39. *Bond*, p. 363.

40. S.B., Wheler MS, 1, fol. 101.

41. J.K.G. Taylor, 'The civil government of Gloucester, 1640–6', *Bristol and Glos. Archaeolog. Soc. Trans.*, vol. lxvii (1949), pp. 58–118, especially p. 113. Mr Taylor's study offers many interesting points of comparison with Worcester at this time.

42. Until as recently as 1632, members of the two companies had paid half of all taxes voted by the Chamber, *Bond*, pp. 263–4 [The city's constitution and officers are described ibid., pp. 12–31].

43. Ibid., pp. 343–4.

44. Ibid., p. 350.

45. See the warrant to the petty constable of Salwarpe of 6 July 1642, H.W.R.O., 850 Salwarpe, BA 1054/1, bundle A, no. 53.

46. *A Letter Sent from Mr Sergeant Wilde, and Humphrey Salwey, Esq. . . . To the Honourable William Lentall Esquior, Speaker of the House of Commons . . .* , London, 18 July 1642, H.W.R.O., 899:31, BA 3669/1 (xii).

47. *Three Declarations, . . . Secondly, A declaration and Protestation agreed upon by the Grand Jury at the Assizes held for the County of Worcester, the third day of August 1642 . . .* , ibid., 3669/1 (iv).

48. *Bond*, p. 375.

49. *A List of Officers Claiming to the Sixty Thousands Pounds, & c. Granted by His Sacred Majesty for the Relief of His Truly-Loyal and Indigent Party* (1683), p. 115.

50. P.R.O., S.P. 28/187, accounts of John Beauchamp, Collector, August-November 1646, and Nicholas Lechmere, Treasurer to the County Committee (additional account), 13 December 1647 – 8 April 1648.

51. *Bond*, pp. 449, 447, 457, 446.

52. Worcester Corporation MSS., Chamber Order Books, vol. 3, fol. 10.

53. Ibid., fols. 38, 46.

54. *Diary of Henry Townshend, vol. ii*, ed. J.W. Willis Bund, Worcs. Hist. Soc. (1920), pp. 66–7. The Commissioners' warrant to the high constables is dated at the Talbot 1 August. Sidbury was outside the city's jurisdiction.

55. *Bond*, pp. 353, 355. Cf. *Commons Journals*, vol. ii, pp. 590–1.

56. *Commons Journals*, vol. ii, p. 710.

57. *Diary of Henry Townshend*, vol. ii, pp. 81–2.

58. Ibid., vol. ii, pp. 87–9.

59. Ibid., vol. ii, p. 84.

60. *Commons Journals*, vol. ii, pp., 761. Whether Captain Rea was the Thomas Rea who had signed the Declaration of 3 August does not appear.

61. *Archaeologia*, vol. xxxv, p. 328.

62. *History of the Rebellion and Civil Wars in England*, ed. W.D. Macray (1888), vol. ii, p. 323.

63. *Archaeologia*, vol. xxxv, pp. 326, 328.

64. Churchwardens' and overseers' accounts, 1640–99, fol. 45ᵛ. The payment for ringing on the King's Coronation Day was 1s., and on Bishop Prideaux's first entry into the city, 2s., ibid., fols. 19, 54ᵛ, 79, 45.

65. *Diary of Henry Townshend*, vol. i, p. 180. Cf. John Corbet's observation on Gloucester that 'the King's cause and party were favoured by two extreames in that City; the one the wealthy and powerfull men, the other of the basest and lowest sort, but disgusted by the middle ranke, the true and best citizens' ('The military government of the city of Gloucester' in John Washbourn, *Bibliotheca Gloucestrensis* (1823), p. 14).

66. *Archaeologia*, vol. xxxv, pp. 326–7; J.W. Willis Bund, *The Civil War in Worcestershire 1642–46, and the Scotch invasion of 1651* (1905), pp. 49, 52–3.

67. *Bond*, p. 358. Street was described in his epitaph in St. Andrew's as 'civitatis istius oraculum plane & ocellus ecclesiae Anglicanae filius orthodoxus', J. Nash, *Collections for the history of Worcestershire*, vol. ii (1782), appendix, p. cxxvii.

68. *Bond*, pp. 357–8. Two constables were normally elected each year for six of the seven wards and one for St. Clement's. In 1644, during the Royalist occupation, the number was again doubled for the six wards on 4 March 'by reason of their extraordinarie imployment in collecting of monethlie paie and other duties' (ibid., p. 378), and one additional constable for each of the six wards, 'in respect of their great imployment' was appointed on 8 October (ibid., p. 387).

69. Ibid., pp. 358, 359.

70. *Commons Journals*, vol. ii, p. 791.

71. W. Dugdale, *A short view of the late troubles in England* (1681), pp. 558–9; cf. Thomas Carte, *A collection of original letters and papers concerning the affairs of England from the year 1641 to 1660* (1739), vol. i, p. 15.

72. *Bond*, p. 360; Chamberlains' accounts, 1642–3.

73. Sir Edward Walker, *Historical collections of several important transactions relating to the late Rebellion and Civil Wars of England* (1707), p. 26.

74. *Diary of Henry Townshend,* vol. ii, pp. 123–4.

75. Dean and Chapter MSS., A.28, Treasurer's Book, 1643: 10 November 1643, 'For ringing a peale that day the Governer of our city and Sherief of the county (Sir Wm. Russell) came to reside here, for the guard of both', 2s. 6d.

76. [Cf. P. Styles, 'The Royalist government of Worcester during the Civil War, 1642–6', *Worcs. Archaeol. Soc. Trans.*, 3rd ser., vol. v (1976), pp. 23–39]. For Gloucester see J.K.G. Taylor, loc. cit., pp. 67, 75, and Corbet, loc. cit., p. 41.

77. *Diary of Henry Townshend*, vol. ii, pp. 143, 148–9.

78. B.L., Harleian MS. 6851, fol. 139; *Diary of the marches of the Royal Army during the Great Civil War*

kept by Richard Symonds, ed. C.E. Long, Camden Soc., Old ser., vol. lxxiv (1859), p. 13; *Bond*, p. 393. Captain Martin Sandys was the uncle of Colonel Samuel Sandys of Ombersley (1619–85), the head of the family and a leading Worcestershire Royalist (*Symond's Diary*, p. 13). He appears, from the registers of St. Michael in Bedwardine, to have been living in the Close by 1634 (Bodleian, MS. Top. Worcs. d.4, fol. 92), elected an honorary freeman of the city, 20 January 1643 (*Bond*, p. 361), a colonel by June 1643 (*Townshend's Diary*, vol. ii, p. 123) and was knighted by Charles I, 12 June 1644.

79. *Diary of Henry Townshend*, vol. i, p. 113.

80. *The letter books of Sir Samuel Luke, 1644–45*, ed. H.G. Tibbut, Bedfordshire Hist. Record Soc., vol. xlii (1963), p. 667.

81. *Worcestershire county records, 1591–1643*, ed. J.W. Willis Bund, Worcs. Hist. Soc. (1899–1900), p. 710.

82. *Bond*, p. 362.

83. Ibid., pp. 363–4.

84. B.L., Harleian MS. 6851, fol. 139.

85. *Bond*, p. 365.

86. 16 Charles I, cap. 32.

87. Cf. the schedule of assessments in the Ordinance of 24 February 1643 (*Acts and ordinances of the Interregnum, 1642–1660*, ed. C.H. Firth and R.S. Rait (1911) vol. i, pp. 86–8) with Royalist assessments in *England's memorable accidents*, 21–28 November 1642 (B.L., Thomason Tracts E. 242/28); B.E.G. Warburton, *Memoirs of Prince Rupert and the Cavaliers* (1849), vol. ii, p. 70; B.L., Harleian MS. 6852, fol. 175; M. Coate, *Cornwall in the Great Civil War and Interregnum, 1642–1660* (1933), p. 110.

88. *Bond*, pp. 366–7.

89. Ibid., pp. 392–3, 395, 398.

90. Ibid., pp. 398, 399, 402.

91. Chamberlains' accounts.

92. *Oxford docquets*, ed. W.H. Black, pp. 200–1: commission to Daniel Tyas, Mayor, Edward Solley, alderman, and Anthony Langston, gent., to levy excise within the city of Worcester, 6 May 1644. Fresh commissions were issued on 8 March and 15 December 1645 and 3 April 1646, the last two covering both the county and the city, ibid., pp. 261, 281, 285.

93. *Bond*, p. 404. In view of the general hostility to excise it is surprising that such a request was not made earlier, as it was, e.g., in Somerset on the first appearance of the Commissioners in the previous year, B.L., MS. Harleian 6804, no. 171.

94. *Bond*, p. 415.

95. Engraved by Robert Vaughan, 1662; see M. Corbett and M. Norton, *Engravings in England . . . Part III, the reign of Charles I* (1964), p. 91 and pl. 43. I am indebted for this reference to Dr D.M. Barratt.

96. It is not possible from the items in the accounts to trace the progress of the works with any certainty. The fort or bulwark at the Friars Gate built in 1643 cannot be identified on Vaughan's plan. It may perhaps have been demolished and the southward extension made, from Sidbury to Fort Royal, in May 1646, at the beginning of the siege, cf. *Bond*, p. 411 'That the chamberlaines shall cover the blockhowse at the Friers, and place the stockadoes from the blockhowse unto the poynt of

Mr Wyldes line', Mr Wylde being Robert Wylde of the Commandery. A chain was thrown across the Severn in 1643.

97. *Bond*, p. 397.

98. Ibid., p. 399.

99. Ibid., p. 364

100. Ibid., pp. 377–8. Cf. *Oxford council acts, 1626–65*, ed. M.G. Hobson and H.E. Salter, Oxford Hist. Soc., vol. xcv (1933), p. 379 (9 October 1643). It appears however that paid labour was being used at Oxford by April 1644, ibid., p. 384.

101. *Diary of Henry Townshend*, vol. ii, p. 129; *Bond*, pp. 370–1, 375.

102. *Bond*, p. 380; *Symond's Diary*, p. 8. Cf. Chamberlains' accounts, 1643–4, 'for two purses to putt the £200 in that was by this cytie given and presented to his Majestie', 8d.

103. *Bond*, pp. 381, 385.

104. *Oxford docquets*, pp. 224, 229 (11 July 1643).

105. *Bond*, p. 393.

106. Ibid., p. 368.

107. Ibid., pp. 377, 392. The gift to Rupert is referred to in the Chamberlains' accounts, 1643–4, as £100.

108. J. and T.W. Webb, *Memorials of the Civil War . . . as it affected Herefordshire and the adjacent counties* . . . (1879), vol. i, pp. 219–22.

109. Bodleian, MS. Eng. hist. c.309. In August 1649 he was stated to have been outlawed for the murder and to be in custody in the Gatehouse, awaiting trial in the Upper Bench (*Calendar of State Papers Domestic, 1649–50*, p. 271).

110. MS. Harleian 6851, fol. 135; see *Diary of Henry Townshend*, vol. ii, pp. 131–57.

111. *Bond*, p. 368 (16 July 1643); p. 369 (28 August 1643).

112. *Diary of Henry Townshend*, vol. ii, p. 215.

113. *Bond*, p. 406.

114. P.R.O., S.P. 16/510. Reformadoes were officers whose units had been disbanded or amalgamated with others and who continued to serve as volunteers.

115. *Bond*, p. 412; *Diary of Henry Townshend*, vol. i, p. 160.

116. *Bond*, p. 412; *Townshend*, vol. i, p. 159.

117. *Bond*, p. 361.

118. See his accounts in P.R.O., S.P. 28/188.

119. *Bond*, p. 379.

120. Ibid., pp. 364–5. Cf. p. 297, n. 42 above; the six aldermen, who were also Justices of Peace for the city, were chosen annually from among the Twenty-four and always included the retiring Mayor for the year after his term of office. The majority were generally re-elected, though John Nash, M.P., is the only alderman who served for the whole period, 1640–60.

121. *Bond*, pp. 370, 373–4.

122. P.R.O., S.P. 28/187, Powick parish accounts; *Bond*, p. 373.

123. *Bond*, pp. 383–4.

124. John Rushworth, *Historical collections*, vol. v, (1692), pp. 83–4.

125. *Calendar of the proceedings of the Committee for Compounding*, vol. iv, pp. 286–7.

126. Rushworth, op. cit., vol. v, pp. 343–4.

127. Chamberlains' accounts, 1642–3.

128. P.R.O., S.P. 28/187, accounts of William Collins, April–May 1646.

129. *Weekly account*, no. 44, 26 June–3 July 1644.

130. P.R.O., S.P. 28/187, accóunts of John Fownes, Treasurer of the County Parliamentary Committee, December 1644–April 1645.

131. *Calendar of State Papers Domestic, 1645–7*, p. 258 (10 December 1645).

132. *Diary of Henry Townshend*, vol. i, pp. 120, 182, 190.

133. Chamberlains' accounts, 1645–6.

134. *Bond*, p. 398. The debt is there estimated at £800 'or there aboutes', probably exclusive of loans at interest, the servicing of which was charged on the feoffees by a later order of 3 March 1648, ibid., p. 439.

135. Cf. A.D. Dyer, *The city of Worcester in the sixteenth century* (1973), p. 163.

136. *Bond*, pp. 399–400, 403, 407.

137. Printed in Nash, op. cit., vol. ii, appendix, p. cvi and also in Valentine Green, op. cit., vol. ii, appendix, pp. cliv-clv 'From a MS. in the possession of William Russell Esq. of Powick'.

138. P.R.O., S.P. 28/187, Powick, parish account.

139. *Hist. MSS. Comm., 4th Rep., Appendix* (1874), p. 270.

140. Firth and Rait, op. cit., vol. i, p. 507.

141. *Bond*, pp. 389–390.

142. P.R.O., S.P. 16/510.

143. *Diary of Henry Townshend*, vol. ii, pp. 243–6.

144. Cf. *Bond*, pp. 404–5.

145. Ibid., pp. 407, 408.

146. St. Michael in Bedwardine churchwardens' and overseers' accounts, 1640–99, fol. 92.

147. *Diary of Henry Townshend*, vol. i, pp. 145–6.

148. *Bond*, p. 407.

149. *Townshend's Diary*, vol. i, pp. 100–5.

150. Ibid., p. 150.

151. Ibid., vol. ii, p. 266.

152. The following account of the siege is based on *Townshend's Diary*, vol. ii, pp. 99–197, except where other references are given.

153. Cf. Parish accounts in P.R.O., S.P. 28/187, 188.

154. Ibid., 28/187, William Collins's account, April–May 1646: 28 May, to the bargemen at Holt for bringing down boardes for the bridge, 14s.; 29 May, to the bargemen at the bridge that went over the seaverne, £1 5s.

155. The King's letter and warrant are printed in Rushworth, op. cit., vol. vi, p. 276. All that was received at Worcester was a printed copy, which Kempson had bought off a bookstall. Those opposed to a treaty expected, if not a message from the King himself, at least instructions from his Council at Oxford. Some believed that these had been sent but that Whalley had intercepted them; hence perhaps, the relief in the city when he was superseded by Rainsborough; and hence also the feeling of resentment expressed by Townshend, *Diary*, vol. i, p. 142; 'Never poor Gentlemen and City held out

more loyal and never any so ill-rewarded as being neither remembered, by the King or the Council at Oxford in the Treaty'; cf. also Bond, pp. 411–2.

156. *Bond*, p. 413.

157. Articles of surrender in Rushworth, vol. vi, pp. 286–7.

158. *Calendar of State Papers Domestic, 1645–7*, p. 458.

159. 'Civitas in Bello et Pace Fidelis'.

160. P.R.O., S.P. 23/207.

161. These meetings are not recorded in the Chamber Order Book.

162. *Bond*, p. 410.

163. Cf. ibid., pp. 412–3.

164. Ibid., p. 413.

165. Cf. ibid., p. 413.

166. H.W.R.O., Townshend's MS diary, 899:192, BA 1714, p. 593. Willis Bund omits 'no' in his edition (vol. i, p. 174).

167. The reputation of the city as a refuge for popish recusants during the War was recalled in the House of Commons many years later by Sir Henry Herbert, M.P. for Bewdley: 'knows very well that at Edgehill battle, the late King complained that they did not do their duty and during the War they lay *couchant* at Worcester', Anchitell Grey, *Debates of the House of Commons from . . . 1667 to . . . 1694* (1769), vol. ii, p. 35 (14 February 1673).

168. *Bond*, pp. 414, 416.

169. Ibid., p. 447; P.R.O., S.P. 23/207.

170. *Bond*, p. 448; Worcester Corporation MSS., Chamber Order Books, vol. 3, fol. 37ᵛ.

171. P.R.O., S.P. 23/207; *Calendar of the proceedings of the Committee for Compounding*, vol. ii, p. 1497.

172. *Cal. Committee for Compounding*, vol. iii, pp. 1890–1; vol. ii, pp. 1194–6. Washington's fine at 1s. 6d. amounted to only £34. He complained that his household goods, worth £80, had been taken from him and that the usual allowance of one fifth had not been made to his wife, ibid., vol. iii, p. 1999.

173. The last reference to Rainsborough at Worcester is on 27 September 1646 when he returned thither from London (Chamberlains' accounts, 1645–6). In the following May he was at Portsmouth, about to embark for Jersey. Dingley was put in command of the Fort occupying the Great Sconce on 4 August 1646. (*Commons Journals*, vol. iv, p. 634). He is described as having been Governor of Worcester in his epitaph in Hanley Castle church, which refers also to 'the obligeingness of his Noble Nature to his Endeared Country often by his Ingenious Industry, freed from the Severe and Numerous quarterings both of Horse and Foote'. He died in 1653. Edward Elvins became Governor after the battle in 1651 (see p. 213 above).

174. *Diary of Henry Townshend*, vol. i, p. 81.

175. *Oxford council acts, 1626–65*, pp. ix, xxiii.

176. The Edward Elvins, clothier, who received a loan from Sir Thomas White's charity on 16 October 1646 (*Bond*, p. 419) was probably his eldest son.

177. *Bond*, pp. 342, 355.

178. P.R.O., S.P. 18/71 (Elvin's petition to Cromwell, 1654).

179. *Bond*, pp. 361, 378, 379, 395. His daughter Elizabeth was baptised at St. Helen's on 11 April

1644. (*Parish Book of St. Helen's*, vol. i, p. 71). The statement in his petition that he 'was an Excile from his owne family almost 4 yeares till Worcester was reduced' is not, therefore, strictly accurate.

180. Membership of the Committee is deducible only from the signatures to treasurers', collectors' and officers' accounts in P.R.O., S.P. 28/187, 188, 216. Out of 19 audited accounts, Elvins signs 11 followed by Robert Stirrop, his successor as Mayor of Worcester, who signs 8.

181. 'Hugh Green, Sheriff of this City, died July 12, 1646, aet. 60' (monumental inscription in St. Martin's, quoted Nash, op. cit., vol. ii, appendix, p. cxliv.

182. *Bond*, pp. 414–5; P.R.O., S.P. 18/71.

183. *Commons Journals*, vol. v, pp. 292, 297; *Lords Journals*, vol. ix, pp. 427, 430.

184. P.R.O., S.P. 18/71; Dean and Chapter MSS. D. 223, 224, 605, 606, 607.

185. Firth and Rait, op. cit., vol. ii, p. 976.

186. S.P. 18/71.

187. Buried in St. Nicholas, 8 April 1665, H.W.R.O., Parish register, x850 Worcester St. Nicholas, BA 3790/1(i), vol. 1; and will proved 3 May 1665, ibid., BA 3585, 1665, no. 62.

188. *Bond*, pp. 437, 424, 430, 415, 421.

189. Firth and Rait, op. cit., vol. i, p. 960; Chamber Order Books, vol. 3, fol. 10ᵛ, cf. ibid, fol. 5ᵛ.

190. *Bond*, p. 430.

191. Ibid., p. 432.

192. *Commons Journals*, vol. iv, pp. 343, 466; Bond, p. 433; Chamberlains' accounts, 1646–8, 1649–50; Dean and Chapter MS. D.247.

193. *Bond*, pp. 383, 387–8, 422–4. At Oxford the problem was more drastically dealt with, on 20 November 1646, by ordering the shops of strangers to be shut down (*Oxford council acts, 1626–65*, p. 140); cf. Roger Howell, *Newcastle upon Tyne and the Puritan Revolution* (1967), p. 278.

194. Chamber Order Books, vol. 3, fols. 1ᵛ–2ᵛ.

195. *Bond*, p. 462; for prosecutions under the order of 1646 see ibid., p. 432 and Chamber Order Books, vol. 3, fol. 1ᵛ.

196. *Bond*, pp. 427–8.

197. Ibid., p. 452.

198. Ibid., p. 421. For the following year it was fixed at 30s., ibid., p. 446. For 1653 and 1654, presumably for the same reasons, the rent was remitted altogether, Chamber Order Books, vol. 3, fols, 13, 18.

199. *Bond*, pp. 424–5.

200. Worcester Corporation MSS., Quarter Sessions Order Book, 1631–55 (order of 10 April 1648). In Somerset in 1640 the maximum annual wages of all journeymen was fixed at £3 and in Wiltshire in most trades, including hellers and tuckers, at £3 10s. in 1655. T.G. Barnes, *Somerset, 1625–40* (1961), p. 197n; *Hist. MSS. Comm. MSS. in Various Collections, I* (1901, pp. 169–173. I am indebted to Mr Michael Crowther for these references.

201. *Bond*, p. 417. The deliberate omission of 'St.' is not consistently maintained in the records.

202. *The Parish Book of St. Helen's, Worcester*, vol. i, p. 2.

203. A.G. Matthews, *Calamy Revised* (1934), pp. 303, 196, 354.

204. William A. Shaw, *History of the English Church during the Civil Wars and under the Commonwealth 1640–1660*, vol. ii (1900), p. 549.

205. W.R. Buchanan-Dunlop, 'All Saints Church, Worcester', *Worcs. Archaeolog. Soc. Trans.*, vol. xiii (1936), pp. 22–4.

206. *Reliquiae Baxterianae*, pt. iii, pp. 90–1; *Calendar of State Papers Domestic, 1655–6*, p. 305; Shaw, op. cit., vol. ii, p. 506.

207. Bodleian, MS. Tanner 140, fol. 160.

208. Cf. Worcester Corporation MSS., Quarter Sessions Order Book, 1631–55, orders of 2 April 1649 and 7 January 1650.

209. A.G. Matthews, *Walker Revised* (1948), p. 172.

210. W.R. Buchanan-Dunlop, loc. cit., p. 22n; *Bond*, pp. 363, 383; Chamberlains' accounts, 1642–4; *Dictionary of National Biography*, s.n. Synge, Edward.

211. A.G. Matthews, *Calamy Revised*, pp. 196, 303.

212. Ibid., p. 23; *Reliquiae Baxterianae*, pt. iii, p. 90.

213. Shaw, op. cit., vol. ii, p. 455.

214. Dean and Chapter MS. D. 224; *Reliquiae Baxterianae*, pt. iii, p. 91.

215. A.G. Matthews, *Calamy Revised*, p. 354.

216. *Bond*, p. 433; Chamberlains' accounts, 1646–8, 1649–50; Chamber Order Books, vol. 3, fols. 9, 10. Captain Andrew Yarranton of Astley, a cavalry officer in the Parliamentary army, was the well-known prospector and surveyor and author of *England's improvement by sea and land* (1677–81).

217. H. Cary, *Memorials of the Great Civil War in England from 1646 to 1652* (1842), vol. ii, p. 337; Quarter Sessions Order Book, 1631–55, 16 February 1652.

218. A.G. Matthews, *Calamy Revised*, p. 354; Dean and Chapter MS. D. 224.

219. *Bond*, p. 438.

220. Ibid., pp. 434, 448.

221. Ibid., p. 438.

222. Ibid., pp. 440, 441.

223. Ibid., pp. 449–50, 451.

224. Ibid., pp. 441, 443, 446. The other 'captains' were Theophilus Alie, Richard Cox and William Hughes. Their names were presented to the Committee on 4 August.

225. Ibid., p. 450.

226. *Calendar of State Papers Domestic, 1649–50*, p. 515; ibid., *1650*, p. 12.

227. *Bond*, p. 458.

228. Ibid., pp. 419, 417.

229. Firth and Rait, op. cit., vol. i, p. 1009; *Bond*, p. 440.

230. *Bond*, p. 447.

231. Byron's debt to Heming, of £312, was guaranteed by the bailiff and burgesses of Droitwich and being outstanding in July 1644 was ordered by the King to be discharged out of the profits of the salt works (H.W.R.O., Droitwich Borough MSS., 261.4, BA 1006/34, no. 680, fols. 3–4). The £84 14s. 4d. on Rupert's account was part of the city's debt taken over by the Feoffees in August 1645, when Heming agreed to waive the interest on it for two years (*Bond*, p. 398).

232. Heming was chosen Mayor on election day, 30 August 1647 but on 9 October desired to be excused, no doubt because of the Parliamentary order of 9 September (see n. 183, p. 235 above) and Robert Stirrop was 'suddenly elected' (*Bond*, pp. 433–4).

233. The Order Book gives no attendance lists and records only resignations or removals and, sometimes, restorations and replacements. Normally, the only evidence of election to either company is the payment of the requisite fees entered in the chamberlains' accounts.

234. P.R.O., S.P. 28/187, 188. Carlesse apparently purchased the fee farm of the city in 1651 and was a captain of militia by 1654 (Chamberlains' accounts). With Writer, Fulke Estopp and Theophilus Alie he was among those removed in 1660.

235. *Commons Journals*, vol. vi, p. 550; *Calendar of State Papers Domestic, 1651*, pp. 77, 94, 96.

236. Cary, op. cit., vol. ii, pp. 335–7.

237. Green, op. cit., vol. i, p. 278n.

238. The summons to the constable of Salwarpe survives among the parish documents in H.W.R.O., 850 Salwarpe, BA 1054/1, bundle A. [This document cannot now be traced in this collection of Salwarpe constables' papers, June 1977].

239. Nicholas Lechmere (E.P. Shirley, *Hanley, and the House of Lechmere* (1883), p. 21).

240. H.W.R.O., BA 1054/1, bundle A, no. 34.

241. S.R. Gardiner, *History of the Commonwealth and Protectorate, 1649–1660* (1903), vol. ii, pp. 40–41.

242. The full details of the drapers' bills and the dates at which they were paid are entered in the account book. The Chamber assumed responsibility for these debts on 24 August 1655.

243. Churchwardens' and overseers' accounts, 1640–99, fols. 111, 113^v.

244. *Hist. MSS. Comm., 10th Report*, Appendix 6 (1887), p. 175.

245. Worcester Corporation MSS., Quarter Sessions Order Book, 1631–55, 16 February 1652; St. Michael's in Bedwardine churchwardens' and overseers' accounts, 1640–99, fols. 112^v, 113, 119.

246. Cf. Chamberlains' accounts: 1651–2, 'Payed Stephen Field who had payed to a souldier to regayne some of the records that were taken out of the Treasurie, 5s. 0d.'; 1652–3, 'Paid by Mr Maior's order to a messenger that brought a peece of evidence that concerned the citties land that was taken away in the plunder, 6s. 0d.'

247. *Calendar of State Papers Domestic, 1651*, pp. 421, 422, 423; ibid., 1651–2, pp. 67, 91, 98, 529.

248. Ibid., *1651–2*, p. 166.

249. Chamber Order Books, vol. 3, fol. 9.

250. Nash, op. cit., vol. ii, appendix, p. cxxxviiin.

251. Chamber Order Book 3, fol. 38. An inquiry into the accounts of this collection was ordered on 28 September 1660.

252. Ibid., fols. 37^v, 23^v.

253. Nash, op. cit., vol. ii, appendix, p. cxxxiv.

254. Green, op. cit., vol. ii, appendix, p. xcvi. For similar reductions in the numbers of the second chamber at Gloucester, Shrewsbury and Warwick, see P. Styles, 'The Corporation of Warwick, 1660–1835', *T.B.A.S.* vol. lix (1938), pp. 26–7.

255. Chamber Order Book 3, fol. 13.

256. *Calendar of State Papers Domestic, 1651*, pp. 426, 433, 448.

257. Ibid., *1655*, p. 93.

258. Ibid., *1655*, pp. 275, 378; J. Berry and S.G. Lee, *A Cromwellian Major General* (1938), pp. 119–21, 126–7, 161, 172–3, 186.

259. Firth and Rait, op. cit., vol. ii, pp. 383–7.

260. Churchwardens' and overseers' accounts, 1640–99, fol. 168ᵛ.

261. Chamber Order Book 3, fols. 13ᵛ–14.

262. Chamberlains' accounts, 1657–8; *Bond*, p. 359.

263. Firth and Rait, op. cit., vol. ii, pp. 393–6.

264. Ibid., vol. ii, pp. 1170–80 (26 June 1657). In the autumn of 1657 thirty-two persons were presented as recusants.

265. Chamber Order Book, 3, fol. 21ᵛ.

266. Ibid., fols. 14, 15ᵛ, 18ᵛ, 22ᵛ, 32ᵛ, 34ᵛ.

267. Ibid., fol. 19.

268. Ibid., fols. 22, 28.

269. Ibid., fols. 8ᵛ, 23ᵛ; fols. 12ᵛ, 19ᵛ, 25ᵛ, 26, 27; Chamberlains' accounts, 1656–7.

270. Ibid., fols, 22ᵛ–24ᵛ.

271. *Calendar of State Papers Domestic, 1659–60*, p. 16.

272. Chamber Order Book 3, fol. 36ᵛ.

273. *Calendar of State Papers Domestic, 1659–60*, pp. 176, 195; Chamberlains' accounts, 1659–61.

274. Chamberlains' accounts, 1660–1.

275. An assessment of £40 upon the whole city 'towards the wages of the burgesses that served in the last Parliament' was voted on 23 February 1655 (Chamber Order Book 3, fol. 18ᵛ).

276. *Diary of Henry Townshend*, vol. i, p. 197; Chamberlains' accounts, 1657–8; *Calendar of State Papers Domestic, 1659–60*, pp. 16, 44, 205, 586.

277. *Townshend's Diary*, vol. i, pp. 70, 33.

278. Ibid., vol. i, p. 36.

279. Ibid., vol. i, pp. 38–9, 60.

280. Chamber Order Book 3, fols. 37ᵛ, 38, 40.

281. *Townshend's Diary*, vol. i, p. 93.

282. Chamber Order Book 3, fols. 46, 52 (16 August 1663).

283. Ibid., fol. 65; Chamber Order Books, vol. 4 (1670–1721), p. 33; Frank was reported as absent since Russell's entry, 2 March 1643 (*Bond*, p. 361); he was elected to the Twenty-four, 1645/6, and was Sheriff, 1650/1, Mayor, 1651/2, and alderman, 1653–60 (Chamber Order Book 3, passim); he was a member of the City Militia Committee by 2 December 1648 and a member of the Worcestershire Committee for Scandalous Ministers in 1654 (Firth and Rait, op. cit., vol. i, p. 1245; vol. ii, p. 976).

284. H.W.R.O., wills proved 3 May 1665; 14 February 1679/80; 22 July 1664; BA 3585/255, no. 62; /291, no. 39; /254, no. 88.

285. Chamberlains' accounts, 1659–60; *Townshend's Diary*, vol. i, p. 66.

286. *Townshend's Diary*, vol. i, p. 71.

287. Ibid., vol. i, p. 75.

288. Chamberlains' accounts, 1660–1.

289. Dean and Chapter MS. D. 79ᵃ.

290. Chamber Order Book 3, fols. 42, 42ᵛ.

291. Green, op. cit., vol. i, p. 277.

10

THE ROYALIST NORTH: THE CUMBERLAND AND WESTMORLAND GENTRY, 1642–60

C.B. Phillips*

Here [in Cumberland and Westmorland] the whole gentry are Malignants, Delinquents, Papists, Popish or base Temporisers; Here not ten of the Gentry . . . nay I dare say not so many, have proved Cordiall to the state . . .

(John Musgrave, 1645)[1]

The northern counties were, in the eyes of Parliament, a stronghold of Royalist support in the Civil War: as late as the battle of Naseby the Roundheads had good cause to appreciate the ferocity of the cavalry regiments raised in the area. Dr Blackwood has described in detail the characteristics of the Lancashire Cavaliers; Dr Cliffe has analyzed the allegiance of the Yorkshire gentry, and Dr Holiday has examined the economic fortunes of the Yorkshire Royalists after the Civil War, but no work on the Royalists in the other four northern counties has been published.[2] In an earlier paper on the county committees of Cumberland and Westmorland I showed that very few gentry, and none of any county reputation, were prominent on those committees. *The Calendar of the Committee for Compounding* lists a large number of Cumberland and Westmorland gentry as Royalists, and this would seem to confirm that the two counties were a part of the Royalist North.[3] What was the extent and strength of this support for the King amongst the gentry? And if the counties were overwhelmingly Royalist, then one might expect that their economies, particularly those of the gentry, would suffer from the sequestration and confiscation of estates. On the other hand, Dr Holiday has shown that in Yorkshire, as in south-eastern England, the vast majority of Royalists whose lands were sold by the state regained them, and held on to them for decades. Nevertheless, in an area where most of the gentry were Royalists, and which was subject to the depredations of the Scots besieging Carlisle in 1644–5, and to the Scottish invasions of 1648 and 1651, the effects of war should be the most marked. And Sir John Habakkuk has suggested that the financial strains on Royalists affected their estates into the early eighteenth century, at least in the home counties. Was this the case in Cumberland and Westmorland?

I

In the first Civil War a very small number of Cumberland and Westmorland gentry were active in the King's cause outside the two counties. Sir Richard Graham of Netherby was wounded at Edgehill.[4] Sir Timothy Fetherstonhaugh and Sir William Huddleston were both with Newcastle at York in 1643; Huddleston used his tenants to attempt the relief of Thurland Castle in Lonsdale in that year.[5] Thomas Denton of Warnell-Denton was killed in action in Durham.[6] John Lamplugh of Lamplugh was wounded at Marston Moor.[7] Sir Francis Howard raised a cavalry regiment (of reasonable numbers) which fought outside the North, including the battle of Naseby.[8] The important point about these activists is that they were not involved in events in their own counties, primarily because they were not associated with the peacetime militia which became the Royalist army in the two counties.

We know little about events in Cumberland and Westmorland from the outbreak of the Civil War in June 1642 until the beginning of the siege of Carlisle by the Scottish army in September 1644. But for this period the available evidence suggests little military activity in the two counties. The pamphlet writers of the time make infrequent reference to the area, and the Lords' and Commons' Journals, the State Papers Domestic and the narrative accounts of the period have nothing more to say. Only three local family archives contain significant amounts of material on these years, and, of these, only the correspondence of Sir Philip Musgrave, Bt., of Edenhall, Cumberland, contains any insight into events and motives. The dangers of constructing a narrative of events based on one account are too evident, but we have to rely on Musgrave's letters amplified by occasional references in other documents.

When the Duke of Newcastle was appointed commander-in-chief of the four northern counties on 10 June 1642 he quickly appointed Sir Philip Musgrave to be commander in Cumberland and Westmorland.[9] Musgrave immediately transformed the county militias into a Royalist army. In these two events lay the seeds of inertia which paralyzed the counties for the next two years. Firstly, Newcastle had made the mistake of elevating one of the militia regiment colonels to a primacy over the others which was bound to cause resentment. Secondly, Musgrave assumed that all the militia officers would support the King, and that they would do so actively. In the event only five officers appeared to have favoured an active military policy, while the three most influential colonels in Musgrave's force concerned themselves only with the defence of Cumberland and Westmorland, and with the defence of Cumberland and Westmorland for the King, in that order. So that while Musgrave harnessed to the King's cause the only significant military force in the two counties, he was barely able to use his force inside them, and quite unable to use it outside the counties. Thus the Royalists under Musgrave put down an obscure attempt to take Carlisle for

Parliament in 1643, but simply sat on the Westmorland border and watched the siege of the Royalists in Thurland Castle, without even attempting to help Sir William Huddleston relieve the castle in 1643. Sir Christopher Lowther of Whitehaven, Bt., seems to have been active for the King in west Cumberland, without much reference to Musgrave, but his main interests were doubtless the defence of Whitehaven; John Senhouse of Seascale also acted for the King in this area.[10] The only other military events were skirmishes in Annandale by Scottish loyalists led by the Earl of Annandale and operating from Carlisle.[11]

The major disagreements between Musgrave and his officers were matters of pride and of principle.[12] Musgrave's correspondence suggests that Colonel Sir Henry Fletcher, Bt.'s pride was affronted by Musgrave giving orders to *his* regiment. Thus on 16 December 1643 Fletcher countermanded Musgrave's order for a muster at Penrith, on the grounds that his men were confused by orders from Musgrave, when Fletcher was their colonel. The resultant quarrel was carried to a higher authority outside the two counties, but the breach was not healed before the Scottish invasion in 1644. Fletcher again challenged Musgrave's orders in 1644,[13] in conjunction with Sir John Lowther of Lowther, Bt. Musgrave's letters suggest that Lowther acted for political reasons rather than for the personal prestige which motivated Sir Henry Fletcher. As early as November 1642 when the Westmorland tenants of the Parliamentarian Lord Wharton threatened to form an association to resist the raising of soldiery, it was Lowther to whom they looked for support; other tenants in north Westmorland made it clear that they would not serve outside the county, and south Westmorland tenants and freeholders endorsed this view. Later in that month Lowther opened negotiations with his Parliamentarian cousin John Dodsworth, a captain in John Hotham's regiment in Yorkshire, to convince the Yorkshiremen that Westmorland only wanted to defend itself. Throughout 1643 and 1644 Lowther maintained this neutral stand and in May 1644 took the side of Kendal (where he was recorder) when the town refused to pay for fortifications, lend money for the King's service, and arrest supporters of Parliament within its jurisdiction. It is a tribute to Lowther's weak political support of the Royalist cause that Parliament, although treating him as a compounding Royalist after his surrender in 1644, also appointed him as a justice of the peace for Westmorland.[14] Lowther's influence was at its greatest in north Westmorland. There is no evidence that he collaborated with the few Parliamentarians in the two counties. James Bellingham, Parliament's most influential supporter in the two counties, lived in south Westmorland. His father, Sir Henry Bellingham of Levens was a knight of the shire in the Long Parliament and clearly only a reluctant Royalist. But the exact role of James Bellingham, and the lesser supporters of Parliament in the two counties, is obscure and clearly inactive before 1644. Only one man is known to have been arrested as a supporter of Parliament, and even the men involved in the 1643 attempt to sieze Carlisle were soon released.[15] The emergence of men active in Parliament's cause in the two counties coincides with the siege of Carlisle by the Scots and the county committees which Parliament appointed before that date had no real existence.

A situation in which the supporters of Parliament were inactive, in which most of the peace-time militia was transformed by Musgrave into a Royalist army (or a local defence force if you followed Lowther), and in which there was no military test of allegiance before 1644, makes it difficult to apply the labels 'Royalist' and 'Parliamentarian'. Many of those in Musgrave's command were Royalists in so far as they did not fight for Parliament, rather than because they fought for the King. The country gentry, for instance Colonel Sir Henry Fletcher and his officers, felt they were only filling their usual role in county society, as militia officers. The transformation of that militia into an army which was subsequently adjudged to be Royalist meant that the county gentry thereby became Royalists. But when Musgrave established his command in 1642 not all of his fellow officers saw the force as a Royalist army. His opponents, led by Sir John Lowther, maintained their opposition until 1644, and deserve the label 'neutral' rather than Royalist. But Sir John was a Royalist in Parliament's eyes, like all who served under the commission of array. The two counties were essentially a neutral area in which the Royalists, rather than the Parliamentarians, tried to recruit support.

At the first approach of the Scots to Cumbria the Royalist militia fled. The local men who gathered in Carlisle garrison included the more determined of these troops, and also others such as William Layton of Dalemain, esq., who later claimed merely to be sheltering in the garrison. One or two Cumbrians were prominent in the skirmishes which punctuated this placid siege, but the best Royalist troops were remnants from the Royalist army defeated at Marston Moor, and the garrison commander was Sir Thomas Glemham who was not a Cumbrian. When the garrison surrendered with the honours of war in June 1645 Sir Philip Musgrave led a troop of local gentlemen who continued to fight for the King; ironically, amongst these was Sir Henry Fletcher who was killed at Rowton Heath (Chester) later that summer.[16]

Table 1 summarizes the allegiance of the heads of gentry families, analyzed by social status, in the first war. The neutral families were largely minor gentry. The son of the one neutral knight, Sir Richard Sandford of Howgill, fought for the King. Sandford had been a deputy-lieutenant until the civil war but, possibly because of his age, he played no role thereafter. Little is known of the neutral esquires, but six of them were recusants, which may have decided their actions. Three of these recusants had sons who fought for the King. Five other neutral families acted in local government in the 1650s, and this may just point to their sympathies in the previous decades. Seven of the group of uncertain Royalists may have been neutral rather than Royalist: four of these families were recusants. The other five were Royalists at some time, but there is doubt as to whether they fought in the first, or second, or in both wars. The bulk of the Royalists comprised the county gentry, the baronets, knights and esquires, and relatively few mere gentlemen, and it is this preponderance of titled families that is the sole significant distinction between the Royalists and the other groups.

The Parliamentarian propaganda painted the North as the stronghold of popery: in Cumberland and Westmorland in 1642 thirty-five (19 per cent of the total) of the gentry families contained recusants or Catholics, and in twenty-eight cases the head of the family was a recusant. Fifteen of the recusant heads of family were neutral in the first war; two more were minors, and there is doubt as to whether a further four were neutral or Royalist. Thus only seven recusant heads of family definitely took the Royalist part, and there is doubt as to whether two of these fought in the first, or second war, or in both wars. Counting other male members of the families, a maximum of sixteen recusant families (46 per cent of the recusants) represented by eighteen individuals actively supported the Royalist cause in the first war. Whatever the Parliamentarians thought, Cumberland and Westmorland were not strongholds of papist superstition which filled the ranks of Royalist officers.[17]

Table 1

SOCIAL STATUS AND ALLEGIANCE IN THE FIRST CIVIL WAR
NUMBER OF HEADS OF FAMILIES BY ALLEGIANCE AS DETERMINED IN 1644

Social status of family in 1642	Royalist	Uncertain Royalist	Parl.	Neutral	Other[18]	Total
Baronet	6	–	–	–	–	6
Knight	7	1	1	1	1	11
Esquire	30	6	8	18	5	67
Gentleman	22	5	12	50	7	96
Totals	65	12	21	69	13	180

Including the younger sons discussed above, that group of men with few responsibilities, supposedly eager to grasp the opportunities which war might offer, made small contribution to the Royalist cause.[19] It is often difficult to be sure in which war these younger sons fought, and sometimes there is confusion over names so that certain identification is difficult, and it is usually impossible to assign them to campaigns. Altogether I have identified twenty-eight younger sons who served sometime in the period 1642–51. The head of one of the families concerned was a neutral, and two others were minors, otherwise these younger sons were drawn from families where the head was committed to the Royalist cause. Four eldest sons also joined their fathers in the war, and the eldest sons of three more families took part although their fathers were neutral.

Altogether a maximum of seventy-seven heads of gentry families, seven eldest sons and, at most, twenty-eight younger sons, brothers and uncles, were cavaliers in the first Civil War, involving eighty-three families and a maximum total of 112 men.

The second Civil War began in the North-West with the seizure of Carlisle for the King by Sir Philip Musgrave. The invading Scots army marched through the two counties to defeat in Lancashire, and marched back again. This was a very different war, a more immediate war which involved the gentry personally unless they were away from the area; it was also a war which allowed men to re-think and revise their allegiance in the light of the increasingly extreme political and religious changes taking place in London, and the financial risks now only too apparent for supporters of the King.

Table 2

SOCIAL STATUS AND ALLEGIANCE IN THE SECOND CIVIL WAR
NUMBER OF HEADS OF FAMILIES BY ALLEGIANCE IN 1648

Social status of family in 1642	Royalist	Uncertain Royalist	Parl.	Neutral	Other	Total
Baronet	3	–	–	2	1	6
Knight	6	1	2	2	–	11
Esquire	29	5	6	21	6	67
Gentleman	20	8	10	52	6	96
Totals	58	14	18	77	13	180

Major differences are apparent (Table 2) between the pattern of allegiance of the Cumberland and Westmorland gentry in the two wars. Firstly, only one recusant family, the Salkelds of Whitehall, is known to have been involved in the second war. Secondly, the make-up of the Royalist party changed, as twenty-two heads of families who had been Royalists in the first war kept out of the second. They comprised four baronets, one knight, eight esquires and nine gentlemen; the new recruits to the Royalist cause were only minor families, although they included four leading members of the Westmorland county committee.[20] There is no clear, general explanation for these changes. Some of the feint-hearted Royalists of the first war remained in the King's camp, like Sir Patricius Curwen; but Curwen's colleague in the resistance to Musgrave, Sir John Lowther, remained aloof (he was in Yorkshire at this time). One may surmise that some of the minor gentry were intimidated into the Royalist camp by the soldiery.

Eighteen new Royalist families, together with three eldest sons, raised to 133 the total figure of cavaliers from the two counties, and rendered 101 families liable to sequestration as delinquents.

The third Civil War in 1651 evoked little support from the two counties, although it meant another invasion. Only three heads of families and a few wild younger sons became involved. The two counties were quiet in the 1650s, prominent Royalists were occasionally imprisoned in Carlisle and there were many rumours of plots, but only Sir Philip Musgrave's name is amongst the known plotters. John Lowther, eldest son of Sir John Lowther, and Sir Christopher Musgrave, second son of Sir Philip Musgrave, took part in Sir George Booth's rising of 1659.[21]

II

Parliament's sequestration policy, first sequestering Royalist estates, then allowing Royalists to compound for their estates and, finally, selling the sequestered estates of the most prominent and most obdurate Royalists, developed as the need to support an increasingly expensive domestic policy grew. The Royalists were liable to sequestration from 1643. The sale of sequestered estates was in mind in 1646, but was not decided upon until 1651. It was an obvious exercise for contemporaries in the 1650s and subsequent decades to blame the Civil War for the financial losses and sales of land by Royalist landowners, especially as only those whose estates had been confiscated and sold received any redress at the Restoration.[22] Such a reaction was slow to appear in Cumberland and Westmorland. Sir Thomas Dacre's estates had been confiscated but he had recovered them. His is the only Cumbrian petition to the King in the State Papers Domestic for re-imbursement of losses because of sequestration and his expenditure for the King's army.[23] Sir John Lowther of Lowther spoke in the Convention for the restoration of Crown lands but, pointedly, not those sold privately by Royalists: Lowther had purchased quite a lot of property from such unfortunates.[24] Other comment on the fortunes of Royalist families was muted. In his manuscript description of the three Lakeland counties written in 1671 Sir Daniel Fleming mentioned Royalists who had been killed in the war, but not those who had lost their estates, despite his own suffering in this respect.[25] In 1687, William Gilpin, recorder of Carlisle, claimed that Sir Edward Musgrave, Bt., had sold five manors because of his civil war losses. Gilpin also noted, without comment, the purchase and subsequent forfeiture of ecclesiastical estates by the Parliamentarian William Brisco of Crofton.[26] In the eighteenth century Nicolson and Burn attributed Civil War losses to a number of Royalist families, but made little mention of land transactions by Parliamentarians. What follows is a detailed attempt to assess the impact of sequestration, composition and confiscation.

Sequestration was a relatively simple procedure by which a Royalist lost possession of his estates and could not receive his rents. But in south Westmorland, at least in the early days, the sequestrators thought it easier to let Royalists retain possession, receive their rents and pay an agreed composition as their monies came in; however, south Westmorland soon followed the more usual practice. We know little in detail of the management of sequestered estates, but it is clear that some Royalists leased their own lands from the sequestrators; this was more common before the re-vamping of the county committees in 1648.[27] The length of the period of sequestration and the leasing policy of the sequestrators had important financial consequences for the delinquent, not least when he came to pay his composition fine in order to regain possession of his estates. The method of assessing composition fines, explained by Mrs Green in 1888 and Sir John Habakkuk in 1965, needs no detailed repetition. The fine was based on the confessed annual value of the delinquent's estate, confirmed by the county committee. Allowance could be made for debts and family portions. The annual value was capitalized to give the fine by a multiple which varied according to a delinquent's legal interest in his estate, the speed with which he compounded and the degree of his delinquency – Royalist members of Parliament were the worst delinquents. In theory this method ensured that the worst delinquent paid the most, and gave relief to delinquents who were already in financial difficulty. The aim was to punish but not to destroy delinquent families. In practice the impact of these fines varied according to a number of other factors. Two aspects of the composition procedure tended to reduce the impact of fines. Firstly, the confessed value of an estate could be less than its actual value. Concealment and under-valuation of lands was widespread, and often escaped detection by county committees. Thus a Royalist could raise the fine more quickly. Secondly, after 1648 many delinquents successfully undervalued their estates when appearing before the Northern Committee for Compounding at Newcastle.[28]

Most delinquents, therefore, needed either an accumulation of cash or credit resources with which to pay the first half of their composition fines. Once the first half was paid the delinquent regained possession of his estates, could receive the income and assign it as security for money borrowed. The Cumbrian gentry resorted to several money markets, of which London was the most important but cash was also borrowed locally, and from Manchester and Newcastle merchants. The impact of fines on families was further varied by their individual abilities to raise cash by credit, and, subsequently, to repay such advances. Although allowed for in assessing the fine, pre-war indebtedness and the diversion of income to dowagers and annuitants affected the ability of families to raise and repay loans. Those families whose property sustained war damage were less able to raise money than families who escaped such misfortunes. At least three houses were ransacked and damaged: Sir William Dalston's Smardale Hall, the Rydal Hall property of the Flemings, and Cyprian Hilton's Ormside Hall.[29] In addition Millom Castle and Scaleby Castle,[30] both residential properties, were besieged. Much of the Carlisle area suffered during the 1644–5 siege and from the subsequent depredations of the Scottish garrison; the more widespread ravaging of Hamilton's men in 1648 was notorious.[31] The mere threat of war was enough to make tenants keep rents in their hands. Sir John Lowther (d. 1675) listed unpaid rents from 1642, before his sequestration, among his Civil War losses, and for his Yorkshire estates at least these arrears were uncollected in the 1670s.[32] The non-renewal of crown and church leases reduced the income of a few families in the 1650s, but in general most leases of ecclesiastical estates outlasted the Interregnum or were renewed by the Committee for Plundered Ministers. One example of non-renewal was Alan Bellingham's loss of the tithes of Great Strickland.[33] Increased rent was often the price of a renewed lease. John Dalston of Acorn Bank paid over five times the rent asked by the Dean and Chapter of Carlisle for his lease of Kirkland Rectory taken in 1657.[34] Some delinquents conveyed leases of impropriate rectories and tithes in part payment of their fines. Not all delinquents wished to part with their impropriations, and there were cases of delinquents forced to augment clerical stipends. Usually they were compensated by reduced fines.[35] The impact of such measures was, in general, not great.

Table 3 shows that at least eighty delinquent families were caught in the sequestration process, and had to face the Parliamentary committees, usually without the benefit of counsel in a novel situation where infringements of the committee's procedure, or the Parliamentary ordinance, brought long and costly delays. Sir John Lowther of Lowther spent a year in London over his composition; he was one of the earliest to compound, had influence with the Parliamentarians and had practised as a barrister.[36] Sir Daniel Fleming's attempt to recover his estates, some of which had descended directly from his delinquent father, and some via his father from a recusant-delinquent second cousin, is a good example of the difficulties facing anyone whose case was other than straightforward. Eventually, after nearly two years, Fleming found it quicker, cheaper and surer to purchase one manor from the Treason Trustees, although he had been able to secure the release of the other properties.[37] Four of the fortunate ten families (Table 3) who were not sequestered for delinquency were, however, sequestered for recusancy, the recusant-delinquents amongst them escaping the more severe penalties because their lands were vested in women. There is no explanation for the escape from sequestration of four more of these families, including Joseph Booth, a renegade county committee man in the second war. Two others died early in the war, and their heirs may have escaped notice. This may also explain why the heir of Thomas Stanwix, a sequestered Royalist killed in the second war, was discharged. The infant son of Sir Christopher Lowther of Whitehaven escaped from partial sequestration because his lands were settled on his mother for life. The Eglesfields of Alwarby were sequestered but discharged without compounding after the Cumberland county committee man Richard Tolson intervened on their behalf.[38] They were discharged because their estates were worth less than £200, but many in a like situation were denied discharge. The others who were discharged escaped under the terms of the Act of Oblivion.

Sixty-three heads of families compounded for delinquency, and Table 4 indicates the difficulties which sequestration may have imposed on these families, although no details of their financial situation under sequestration are known. Those in group 1 suffered least. They had all paid the first half of their fine and were freed from sequestration by the end of 1647. They had been sequestered for no more than three years, indeed Sir Richard Graham, Bt., and Sir John Lowther had regained their estates in the autumn of 1646. The fines imposed on this group ranged from between one and four times the agreed net value of their estates, although only Sir George Dalston and his son Sir William, both M.P.s, paid this high level.

Table 3
THE FATE OF DELINQUENTS' ESTATES

	1st war	2nd war	Uncertain	Total
Royalist heads[a] of families	65	18	12	95
Fate unknown	3–		2–	5
	62		10	
Not sequestered	6–	2–	2[b]	10
Total sequestered	56	16	8	80
of whom discharged not fined	6–		3–	9
	50		5	
of whom fined for delinquency	44–	16–	3–	63
Estates sold	5–		2–	7
Estate kept in sequestration	1			1

Table 4
ROYALIST HEADS OF FAMILY FINED IN THE CIVIL WARS

1.	Delinquent in 1st war only: fined once	14
2.	Delinquent in both wars: fined only once	17[c]
3.	Delinquents in both wars: fined twice	13
		44
4.	Delinquents in 2nd war only: fined once	16
5.	Uncertain Royalists	3

[a] Of the eldest sons who fought, two were jointly sequestered with their fathers, three compounded when they inherited, and one compounded for his estates in possession. Only two younger sons were sequestered separately from their family estates: John Philipson of Calgarth (below, p. 252), and Pickering Dalston, whose nephew was head of the family but a minor.

[b] Sequestered only for recusancy.

[c] The estates of Sir Timothy Fetherstonhaugh remained in sequestration after he had been fined (below, p. 249).

The delinquents in the second group comprised seventeen families who were only fined once for their delinquency in both wars. It is not clear why these men escaped. Fourteen were fined at Newcastle, but were also reported to the London committee as not having compounded after the first war: two may have escaped because they were related to county committee men. Sir Timothy Fetherstonhaugh was fined for his first delinquency, but executed after the 1651 invasion and his estates remained in sequestration until at least 1658.[39] Fines in this group, as in others where the Newcastle committee was involved, reached as high as five times the agreed net estate value, but these values were very low.[40] Most of this group were free from sequestration after June 1649 after some six years in the hands of the sequestrators. The third group of delinquents were not necessarily sequestered for so long, as some had paid the first half of their first fine before the second war began, but after the second war they were re-sequestered. They then had to find the second payment of their first fine for the London committee, and pay their second war fine as well, most to Newcastle. The fourth group of delinquents, those who fought only in the second war were also chiefly dealt with at Newcastle. They paid relatively low fines, and were only sequestered for about a year.

The effects of these fines on the delinquents are difficult to detail: three families sold their entire estates, and seven more were financially embarrassed between 1650 and 1700. That five (from group 3) of these ten had paid two fines and been sequestered for long periods suggests that the war was to blame. But amongst these five only the Denton family of Cardew sold their entire estate, and it is clear that their difficulties had begun before the Civil War. During the wardship of George Denton of Cardew who came of age in 1642, his stepfather granted long leases on the estate to his own advantage. The family estates suffered further during the siege of Carlisle. Nevertheless, the fines were a modest £60 10s. 0d. after the first war, and £200 after the second, £90 of which was paid by assigning a lease of tithes valued at £20 a year. George Denton began to mortgage his estates in 1665, and in 1672 he raised £333 2s. 4d. by enfranchising his tenants. In 1677 he sold property specifically to pay debts, and in 1686 and 1688 the remaining two manors were sold off.[41] However, other families recovered from such burdens, and it may well be that George Denton lacked the will and determination to nurse his estates. This was certainly the view some contemporaries took of the other delinquent family forced to sell out, the Duckets of Grayrigg. James Ducket was carefree of the future in twice marrying wives who brought him no portion. His son Anthony Ducket was 'Looked upon as a person that did lessen and not improve his estate and for that reason impaired his repute'.[42] The Duckets lost their estates before 1690.

Two examples from the seven families who overcame their debts are worth giving, the first because it exposes exaggeration, the other because it illustrates the length and complexity of such recoveries. In 1687 William Gilpin claimed that Sir Edward Musgrave had sold five manors as a result of the Civil War. A century later, Nicolson and Burn dramatized the story by alleging that the manors were worth £2,000 a year. In fact Musgrave valued tham at £197 10s. 9d. in his particular, nearly half the total and doubtless an undervaluation, but nearer the truth than £2,000. Musgrave was already, in 1642, committed to raising £1,000 for portions, and his two fines totalling £1,790 19s. 10d. were a heavy but *additional* burden, which the damage to his estate during the war made more difficult to raise. Two manors were sold, in 1652 and 1653, for £990; these sales were no doubt a result of the Civil War. The price and date of sale of the other three manors is unknown, but two were sold before 1671.[43] However, in 1665 Musgrave spent £1,350 on land in Holme Cultram – better property than the manors sold – and refurbished Hayton Castle at an unknown cost. His credit was good for he borrowed £500 from Sir John Lowther, which was repaid in the prescribed period.[44] So it is not proven that Musgrave sold all his manors to finance war debts, and in any case he purchased other property for a substantial sum.

The second example is that of Sir Thomas Strickland of Sizergh, who was forced to sell the Yorkshire manor of East Kilnwick, but retained the rest of his estates through a succession of mortgages which may have continued until 1682.[45] Sir Thomas and his father Sir Robert both fought in the first war, but Sir Robert surrendered on the York articles which saved his estates from sequestration. The Stricklands had a long history of debt, but by 1640 this was under control. Sir Thomas made no claims for debts when he compounded in April 1646. Concealing his reversionary interest in his father's Yorkshire estates, Sir Thomas was fined only £186 on his Westmorland estates in possession. Both he and his father had been active Royalists, raising forces for the King, but there is no indication of how much they spent in this way. Anyway, in June 1647 Sir Thomas mortgaged the manor of Natland for £500. After the second war, Sir Thomas was fined £943 on the reversion of the Yorkshire estates at London, and £308 10s. 0d. at Newcastle on his Westmorland estates, both in June 1649. In that year he borrowed £700 from Humphrey Shalcrosse, to whom he subsequently mortgaged, and did not redeem, East Kilnwick manor. In March 1650 he sold land for £700 and in April 1653 mortgaged the manor of Sizergh for £2,000. This was redeemed on 23 April 1655, but probably by borrowing £2,500 from Sir John Cutler on security of a ninety-nine year lease of the manor of Thornton Bridge, on 20 March 1654[–55]. Further loans of £1,000 by mortgage and £2,000 on a penal bond of £4,000 were raised by the end of 1656 from family friends. It is possible that the last two loans of £1,000 and £2,000 were contracted to repay Sir John Cutler. On this assumption Sir Thomas borrowed a minimum total of £3,500 and raised a further £2,950 by sale of land. There is no indication as to when, or if, the loans from family friends were repaid. Sir Thomas began a second round of heavy borrowing on mortgage from

Sir John Cutler in 1664, which was cleared by 1682 without further sale of land. It is possible that these sums were needed to finance Strickland as a commissioner for prizes, commissioner of the Privy Seal, lessee of salt customs and licensee of the excise on ale for the West Riding of Yorkshire, rather than to repay debts. Strickland also obtained a ten-year lease of confiscated estates in May 1664, and a pension of £400 in 1672.[46] His income was further augmented by the Yorkshire estates after the death of his father in 1670. But his involvement in government finance after the Restoration makes it difficult to assess the level of family debt and to follow the process of recovery.

It is a measure of the confusion surrounding sequestration and composition that of the fourteen Cumberland and Westmorland gentry who appeared in the Acts of Sale, only two, Sir Francis Howard and Sir Philip Musgrave, were prescribed Royalists, although four were recusant-delinquents.[47] Neither Sir Thomas Dacre nor Sir Francis Salkeld, heir of Lancelot Salkeld named in the act, were to lose all their estates, because they were protected by settlements; John Senhouse stood only to lose his Lancashire estate, and that because of administrative confusion; finally, one of Sir Daniel Fleming of Rydal's manors was for sale – a measure of great legal complexity rather than great delinquency. But the entire estates of the others were at risk. Three families compounded for their estates in time to prevent sale, and there is no record of the sale of the estates of John Senhouse, Thomas Wybergh or Simon Musgrave. In 1656 only Musgrave's estate was still under sequestration and the inference is that the others were discharged.[48] The properties eventually sold comprised Fleming's one manor,[49] Sir Philip Musgrave's entire estates (except one manor claimed by a creditor)[50] and the entire confiscated property of six families.

Only two families failed to regain immediate possession of their properties, either in person or through an agent. Sir Philip Musgrave lost the episcopal manor of Bewley Castle, which was sold to Thomas Wharton and Edmund Branthwaite in December 1652; apparently Wharton was not on this occasion acting, as he often did, as an agent. They re-sold it to Robert Braithwaite in 1657, who had previously purchased the fee-simple from the Trustees for the Sale of Bishops' Lands. However, after the Restoration the Bishop of Carlisle re-granted the lease to the Musgrave family.[51] The confiscated third of the manor of Croglin and the other estates of Sir Charles Howard of Croglin and his wife in Northumberland were sold in November 1653. After dispute Lady Howard was provided for out of the proceeds of sale, and re-purchased her North Charlton (Northumberland) estates, which were then sequestered for her recusancy. Her trustees sold this property in 1669.[52] Sir Charles' son never recovered possession of the Croglin estates, for the other two-thirds had been sold privately by Sir Charles in 1649. The other Northumberland properties of Plenmellar and Haltwhistle were in the hands of Robert Cotesworth and William Pearson, respectively, in 1663.[53]

Agents, friends or relatives purchased the remaining properties as they were sold, and the families recovered possession. Subsequently three[54] of these families sold land, and their cases are informative. Sir Philip Musgrave's estates were purchased by his heir, Richard Musgrave, at five years purchase for estates settled by entail, and thirteen years purchase for the rest. The total cost was £7,893 16s. 8d. The manors were then settled on Richard Musgrave in fee-simple in October 1653 to forestall any re-sequestration. Sir Thomas Wharton helped to finance this with a loan of £3,000. Mortgages to secure this and other loans were redeemed in 1662. Sir Philip Musgrave survived these loans and purchases without severe loss. A small parcel of demesne land was sold for £384 in November 1653, and this was never recovered. All the mortgates were repaired in 1662, helped by a gift of money from the crown. In 1666 Sir Philip purchased the manor of Blea Tarn, suggesting that his fortunes were restored.[55]

The history of the estates of Sir Francis Howard of Corby after their sale is neither so simple nor so happy. The Howards retained possession of Corby, Cumberland, until this century; Thornthwaite, in Westmorland, was granted in marriage in the eighteenth century. The difficulty is to elucidate what interest Howard's agent, the notorious Gilbert Crouch, retained in the two manors after he purchased them from the Treason Trustees. In 1657 Howard mortgaged Corby and Thornthwaite to Crouch and Sir Henry Widdrington (a relation of the Howards) for £30,000, and in that year Crouch was described as the lord of Thornthwaite. In 1663 he still had a legal interest in these properties, and when he was paid off is uncertain.[56] The Howards' Durham estates were brought from the Treason Trustees by Sir Thomas Cotton, a relative and friend. In 1655 they were settled, together with the Cumbrian estates, on Cotton in trust for specified uses;[57] within a decade the Durham manor of Neasham was for sale, and Francis Howard was granting rent charges to raise money.[58] But the family's subsequent history, including the landscaping of Corby, c. 1730–1740, demonstrates their survival.

The Philipson of Calgarth family well illustrate the exaggerated tales which these confiscations produced. In the eighteenth century Nicolson and Burn alleged that the family had sold their Yorkshire estates because of the exactions imposed by the Commonwealth, which included the confiscation of the Hollin Howe estate in Westmorland.[59] While these sums no doubt contributed to the family's difficulties the situation was in fact very much more complicated. Although the family was relatively debt free before the war, by the time the Yorkshire property at Melsonby was sold in 1666 two heads of the family had died. Christopher Philipson died in 1654, after a prolonged sequestration and composition case, leaving his wife a dower estate of £50 per annum plus a bequest of £300. His brother John succeeded, and it was his Hollin Howe estate which was sold by the Treason Trustees in September 1654. He recovered it, probably by May 1655. This re-purchase, and his brother's legacies, forced John

Philipson to mortgage part of the estates inherited from his brother. John himself died in 1665. His will mentions mortgages on Hollin Howe, and on the estates inherited from his brother. In addition to these debts John settled the Hollin Howe demesne as dower for his wife, and charged bequests of £406 on his whole estate. A further £600 and £49 per annum were specifically charged on the Yorkshire estate. While the Commonwealth's penalties hindered the raising of such sums, they were not the sole or even the major cause of the sale of Melsonby. Nicolson and Burn's claim overstates and oversimplifies the reason for the sale.

The penalties and taxes of the victors made no marked, lasting impression on the estates of the gentry of Cumberland and Westmorland. No doubt there were other burdens under which these families suffered. Younger sons and daughters found their portions reduced, or payable over long periods because of, as Cyprian Hilton of Burton put it in 1653, 'the great distractions of the times and my sufferings in them I could not make those provisions for them as I desire for the care of my eldest son',[60] and in 1665 Nicholas Fisher blamed his war losses for the meagre provision he made for his younger children.[61] The Royalists also lost their prominent places in county government. In some instances they turned their hands to other matters, and certainly in Cumberland and Westmorland their economic activities, in which the gentry had previously invested, flourished during the 1650s. For those like the Royalist Sir John Lowther of Lowther, with money to invest in land or mortgages, there were many opportunities. Lowther bought land worth more than £1,250 p.a. for £19,495 between 1649 and 1660.[62] The rapidly growing port of Whitehaven which his brother Sir Christopher Lowther founded in the 1630s grew steadily, and in the last four decades of the century this growth accelerated enormously until for a time in the eighteenth century Whitehaven was the second port of the country. The trade in coal and salt which underpinned the Lowther enterprise continued. Other mining ventures developed, and in the 1650s the London Lead Company extended its longstanding interest westward from Alston in the Pennines and established new mines near Cockermouth. Prominent in these arrangements was the Royalist Sir Patricius Curwen of Workington, who had paid two fines totalling at least £3,094.[63] Curwen no doubt wanted to replace his own coal and iron mines which had declined because of flooding and competition from easier workings at Whitehaven and Egremont respectively. Indeed with the resurgence of the Irish iron industry after Cromwell's wars the export of high grade haematite iron ore was a lucrative investment for estate owners.[64] As regards more mundane trade and industry the impression is that normal levels of prosperity were maintained. Moreover, it may be that the ban on imports of Irish stock cattle under the 1664 Irish Cattle act was a greater threat to agriculture than any of the events of the 1640s. Stock farming brought the gentry profits from agistment as well as the cattle trade. Sir Patricius Curwen was anxious to encourage the trade in 1661, and perhaps a quarter of imported Irish cattle came through the Cumbrian ports.[65] All these activities point to a healthy, diversified economy, and while the gentry grumbled about the high taxation of the 1650s, they were no less vociferous against the low rents and poor agricultural profits of the following decades.

III

The split between King and Parliament amongst the gentry of the two counties is an instance which illustrates the limits of the biographical method of analyzing allegiance in the English Civil War.[66] There are no obvious differences between the individual Parliamentarians and Royalists. The Royalists themselves are so diverse a group that such analysis is of little help in understanding the motivation of the Royalists, and the four colonels whose squabbling split the Royalist force are good examples. Sir Philip Musgrave and two of his opponents, Sir Patricius Curwen and Sir John Lowther of Lowther, were much alike; the odd man out was Sir Henry Fletcher, who sided with Curwen and Lowther. The three had extensive experience in local government and in Parliament. All were careful, improving landlords although only Curwen and Lowther are known to have had widely diversified economic interests.[67] Curwen and Musgrave had been to a university, Lowther was a barrister. Surprisingly for so ardent a Royalist, it was Musgrave who had been savaged by the Court of Wards. All were wealthy and came from families of ancient lineage. The closest connection between Fletcher and the others was his sister's marriage to Sir John Lowther. Sir Henry Fletcher's father had been a Cockermouth chapman knighted on progress by James I in 1617. Sir Henry had no higher education, no parliamentary experience and no reputation as an improver of his, undoubtedly large, estates. The diaries and letters which might explain the motives of these men are not extant.

The Royalist group initially led by these men comprised 43 per cent of the Cumberland and Westmorland heads of gentry families in 1644, rising to 53 per cent after the second war. Precise comparisons with the Royalists in other northern counties are impossible,[68] but it is clear that the Cumberland and Westmorland Royalists were unique in that they had virtually no Parliamentarian opposition – only twenty-one mostly insignificant families – whereas in Lancashire and Yorkshire the Royalists faced opponents of more comparable wealth, status and influence. Perhaps the more equal division of allegiance in these counties made local clashes inevitable, while the absence of an opposition in Cumberland and Westmorland led to inertia and dispute. Certainly the militarily insignificant fumbling of the unopposed Cumberland and Westmorland Royalists makes it nonsense to call the counties Royalist because there were 101 nominally Royalist families there. The Catholic gentry in the two counties were a much smaller proportion of the whole than in Lancashire and, less so, in

Yorkshire. One third of the recusant heads of family in Cumberland and Westmorland supported the King compared with a much higher proportion, nearer half, in Yorkshire and (probably) in Lancashire.[69] Insofar as the economic effects of their Royalism were not calamitous, the Cumberland and Westmorland men compare with those of Yorkshire and the south-east where few families effectively lost their confiscated estates. Nevertheles, in the home counties, Sir John Habakkuk found evidence of long-term financial weakness resulting from Civil War (and other) debts; but the legendary deprivations of such as Sir Edward Musgrave prove, in Cumberland and Westmorland, to be part of the myth of the Royalist North.

Notes

*I am grateful to Professor Austin Woolrych for his many kindnesses in supervising my work on the civil war as a research student; and to Mr B.C. Jones, Cumbria County Archivist, and to his staff, who drew my attention to many manuscripts. The responsibility for the views expressed herein is mine.

1. British Library, Thomason Tract Collection, E.318(5): John Musgrave, *A Word to the Wise* (London [n.d.; no printer or publisher given]; endorsed: 26 January 1645[–46]). Musgrave was a Cumbrian; there is no better life than that in *D.N.B.*

2. B.G. Blackwood, 'The Cavalier and Roundhead Gentry of Lancashire', *Transactions of the Lancashire and Cheshire Antiquarian Society* (hereafter *Trans L.C.A.S.*), lxxvii (1977); J.T. Cliffe, *The Yorkshire Gentry from the Reformation to the Civil War* (1969), chap. xv; P.G. Holiday, 'Land sales and re-purchases in Yorkshire after the Civil War, 1650–1670', *Northern History*, v (1970). The definition of the gentry here used includes all men who were consistently called such by their contemporaries, as evidenced by a wide variety of documentary sources; for details see C.B. Phillips, 'The Gentry in Cumberland and Westmorland, 1600–1655', (unpub. Ph.D. thesis, Lancaster Univ. 1973), chap. 1. The present text distinguishes baronets as such only at the first mention of their name; the titles used are those held at a person's death.

3. C.B. Phillips, 'County Committees and Local Government in Cumberland and Westmorland, 1642–1660', *Northern History*, v (1970); *Calendar of the Committee for Compounding etc.* (hereafter *C.C.C.*), ed. M.A.E. Green (5 vols, 1889–1892).

4. P. Young, *Edgehill, 1642* (1967), p. 119.

5. C(umbria County) R(ecord) O(ffice), Carlisle, Musgrave Manuscripts: Civil War letters (hereafter M.C.W.L.), Sir Philip Musgrave to the Westmorland J.P.s, 29 March 1643; *Tracts Relating to Military Proceedings in Lancashire during the Great Civil War etc.*, ed. G. Ormerod (Chetham Society, old series, ii, 1844), pp. 148–50.

6. *Pedigrees recorded at the Heralds' Visitations of the Counties of Cumberland and Westmorland*, ed. J. Foster (1891), p. 33.

7. *C.C.C.*, p. 968. P. Young, *Marston Moor 1644* (Kineton, 1970), pp. 165, 234 suggests that Sir Philip Musgrave, Bt., fought there; but a letter to him at Netherby (north Cumberland) dated 5 July 1644 (M.C.W.L., Savage to Musgrave) giving news of the battle shows he was not there.

8. P. Young, 'The Northern Horse at Naseby', *Journal of the Army Society for Historical Research* (1954), pp. 54–6. Eight of the sons of the gentry also fought outside the two counties.

9. *Life of William Cavendish Duke of Newcastle*, ed. C.H. Firth (1906), p. 10.

10. B. Nightingale, *The Ejected of 1662 in Cumberland and Westmorland* (2 vols, Manchester, 1911), pp. 823–4; *C.C.C.*, p. 1703.

11. C.R.O., Manuscripts of the Dean and Chapter of Carlisle (hereafter D.C.C.), Nithsdale Papers (I am grateful to the Dean and Chapter for permission to consult their archive).

12. I treated Musgrave's efforts to command the army at greater length in Phillips, thesis, pp. 288–95.

13. For the dating of these events from undated draft letters in the M.C.W.L., see Phillips, thesis, p. 292, nn. 3, 4.

14. For Lowther's role see M.C.W.L., passim, especially Rev. Edward Maulever to Sir P. Musgrave, 19 November 1642, and two undated letters, from their contents written in that month; Kendal memo, dated 25 May 1644. H(historical) M(anuscripts) C(ommission), *13th. Report, Appendix I*, p. 186.

15. For a detailed discussion of this event, see Phillips, thesis, pp. 295–6.

16. The best contemporary account of the siege is Isaac Tullie, *A Narrative of the Siege of Carlisle in 1644–45*, ed. S. Jefferson (Carlisle, 1840). The list of voluntary subscriptions to the 'siege fund' there printed is not in Tullie's manuscript; the list is printed in their account of the siege by J. Nicolson and R. Burn, *The History and Antiquities of the Counties of Westmorland and Cumberland* (2 vols, 1777), ii, pp. 234–9, but I have been unable to trace the original manuscript. Clearly a fund which includes contributions from the Parliamentarians is unlikely to be voluntary, and the names on the list raise some puzzles as to its date. For Layton and Fletcher see *C.C.C.*, pp. 1296, 1662. The general context of the siege is outlined in C.V. Wedgwood, *The King's War, 1641–1647* (1958), pp. 442, 468.

17. Statistics from Phillips, thesis, p. 46. For more widespread, corroborative, evidence see K. Lindley, 'The Part Played by the Catholics', in *Politics, Religion and the English Civil War*, ed. B.S. Manning (1973), esp. p. 156; P.R. Newman, 'Catholic Royalist Activists in the North 1642–1646', *Recusant History*, xiv (1977), criticizes Lindley's measurement of Catholic involvement (pp. 26–7); on p. 33 Newman calls the Stricklands of Sizergh Catholics, but Sir Robert Strickland was never convicted of recusancy, and his son Sir Thomas did not openly embrace Catholicism until 1673.

18. Comprising (in this and table 2) the infants and infirm. For the sixteen Parliamentarians on the county committees see Phillips, *Northern History*, v, pp. 40–54; the other families included the Cumberland committee's solicitor, and the Cumberland feodary; two were army officers and one had no official position. New evidence suggests that George Gilpin of Kentmere, esq. (ibid., p. 41) was a Royalist rather than a committee man; he is treated here as an uncertain Royalist. The main sources used to identify Royalists were the Royalist Composition Papers, which include quite detailed proofs of delinquency (P(ublic) R(ecord) O(ffice), London, State Papers, Domestic, S.P.23), the records of the county committees (in P.R.O., Commonwealth Exchequer papers, S.P.28), the M.C.W.L., and the list of Royalist officers (P.R.O., State Papers, Domestic, Charles II, S.P.29/68/19) of 1663.

19. Cf. for Lancashire, Blackwood, *Trans. L.C.A.S.*, lxxvii, p. 81.

20. One of these men, James Bellingham of Levens, was the eldest son of the Royalist Sir Henry Bellingham.

21. For Lowther and Musgrave see *D.N.B.*; David Underdown, *Royalist Conspiracy in England, 1649–1660* (New Haven, Conn., 1960), pp. 46, 69, 87, 108, 114–15, 167.

22. There is a convenient summary of the legislation and administrative methods covering sequestration and composition in *C.C.C.* intro., pts. i and v, and in H.J. Habakkuk, 'Landowners and the Civil War', *Economic History Review*, 2nd ser., xviii (1965), pp. 132–3. Confiscation and sale is covered in Joan Thirsk, 'The Sale of Royalist land during the Interregnum', *Econ. Hist. Rev.* 2nd ser., v (1952), pp. 188–93. For contemporary comments on the effects of this legislation see Habakkuk and Dr Thirsk (above) and also Holiday, *Northern History*, v, pp. 67–8.

23. P.R.O., S.P.29/9/172.

24. R.S. Ferguson, *Cumberland and Westmorland M.P.s* (1871), p. 21.

25. *Fleming-Senhouse Papers*, ed. E. Hughes (Cumberland Record Series, ii [1961]), pp. 3–64.

26. *An Accompt of . . . estates and families in . . . Cumberland*, ed. R.S. Ferguson (Cumberland and Westmorland Antiquarian and Archaeological Society, Tract series, ii, Kendal, 1887), pp. 153, 84–5. Gilpin gives no date for Musgrave's sales and he does not note similar sales by others. Possibly he got Musgrave's explanation via his own father who bought the manor of Scaleby from Musgrave. Sir Daniel Fleming (Hughes, *Fleming-Senhouse Papers*, p. 60) notes this sale but does not comment.

27. P.R.O., S.P.28/216; *C.C.C.*, i, passim.

28. C.B. Phillips, 'The Royalist Composition Papers and the wealth of the gentry: a note of warning from Cumbria', *Northern History*, xiii (1977), p. 170.

29. *C.C.C.*, p. 690; Nicolson and Burn, *History and Antiquities*, i, p. 162; P.R.O., S.P.23/170/623, 628.

30. *Calendar of State Papers, Domestic*, 1644–5, p. 98. Millom belonged to Sir William Huddleston. Scaleby belonged to Sir Edward Musgrave of Hayton, and was besieged in 1644 (H.M.C. *12th. Report, Appendix I*, pp. 185–6. In 1648 it was allegedly burnt (Alnwick Castle, Manuscripts of the Duke of Northumberland, x.ii. 3(7), William Pennington to Hugh Potter, 14 July 1648. I am grateful to his Grace for permission to consult his archive, and to Mr D.P. Graham and the Northumberland County Record Office for their help).

31. *C.C.C.*, pp. 232, 1694; A.H. Woolrych, *Battles of the English Civil War* (1961), pp. 160, 168.

32. C.R.O., Earl of Lonsdale's MSS, D/Lons/L, A1/4, f. 105r.

33. Nightingale, *Ejected*, pp. 1181–2.

34. D.C.C., Registers, vol. vi, pp. 172, 332; Nightingale, *Ejected*, pp. 395–6.

35. For example, Sir John Lowther of Lowther's fine was reduced by £500 for his forced augmentation of Arkengarthdale, *C.C.C.*, p. 1024.

36. C.R.O., D/Lons/L, A1/4, f. 105r.

37. Fleming's ordeal is conveniently summarized in *The Flemings in Oxford*, ed. J.R. Magrath (Oxford Historical Society, xliv, 1903), appendix A, which also refers to notes of fees and gratuities paid by Fleming.

38. *C.C.C.*, p. 1668; P.R.O., S.P.23/88/431, 434, 435.

39. *A discourse of the warr in Lancashire*, ed. William Beaumont (Chetham Society, old series, lxii, 1864), pp. 76–8; *Calendar of the Committee for the advance of Money*, ed. M.A.E. Green (3 vols, 1888), p. 103. A four year lease of Fetherstonhaugh's estate was granted from 15 March 1653/54, P.R.O., S.P.23/171/171.

40. Phillips, *Northern History*, xiii, p. 169.

41. C.R.O., D/Lons/L, Cardew box, bdles 3, 4, 7; Barony of Burgh box, bdle 8; *C.C.C.*, p. 1694; P.R.O., S.P.23/227/783; Nicolson and Burn, *History and Antiquities*, ii, p. 205.

42. P.R.O., Chancery bills and answers, Six clerks series before 1714, Bridges division, C.5/474/8. The Duckets were recusants, but had conformed during the war; there is no evidence that the recusancy fines played a major part in their decline, Phillips, thesis, p. 82.

43. *C.C.C.*, p. 968; P.R.O., S.P.23/179/706–8; S.P.23/227/779–81; Ferguson, *Accompt of Cumberland*, p. 153; Nicolson and Burn, *History and Antiquities*, ii, p. 155. The deeds for the sale of Solport in 1652 for £550 (P.R.O., Chancery, Close Rolls, C.54/3668 m.36) and Rickerby in 1653 for £440 (P.R.O., C.54/3758 m.17) are enrolled in Chancery. Houghton was sold to Arthur Foster before his death in 1670 (*Transactions of the Cumberland and Westmorland Antiquarian and Archaeological Society*, new series, lxi [1961]), p. 171 (hereafter *C.W.2*), and Scaleby to Richard Gilpin by 1671 (Hughes, *Fleming-Senhouse Papers*, p. 60).

44. C.R.O., D/Lons/L, A1/9; C.W.2, xxxii, p. 94; P.R.O., C.54/4163 m.21; N. Pevsner, *The Buildings of England: Cumberland and Westmorland* (1967), p. 136.

45. What follows is based on *C.C.C.*, p. 1130; P.R.O., C.54/3622 m.19; C.54/3516 m.40; C.54/3832 m.20; C.54/4013 m.8 and C.54/4195 m.1; and unlisted deeds in the family archive at Sizergh Castle (I am grateful to the late Col. H. Hornyold-Strickland for permission to examine these documents, and for his kind hospitality). My account amplifies Professor M. Beloff's comments in 'Humphrey Shalcrosse and the Great Civil War', *English Historical Review*, liv (1939), pp. 686 sqq. Professor Beloff calls Sir Thomas a recusant, but a small penalty was incurred for the recusancy of his mother; for pre-war debts and his father's wardship see Phillips, thesis, p. 221.

46. For these posts, pensions and leases see H. Hornyold, *Genealogoical Memoirs of the Stricklands of Sizergh* (Kendal, 1928), pp. 130–1.

47. *Acts and Ordinances of the Interregnum, 1642–1660*, ed. C.H. Firth and R.S. Rait (3 vols, 1911), ii, pp. 520–1, 623–4, 632. There were no Cumberland and Westmorland gentry in the second act.

48. P.R.O., S.P./23/261/1.

49. See above, p. 181. This manor is not noted as sold in Table 3.

50. Musgrave's manor of Soulby was discharged to its mortgagee by the Committee for Compounding in 1651. It passed by process unknown to Musgrave's brother-in-law by September 1654, and two other agents also held it for Musgrave before he redeemed it in March 1662. See Phillips, thesis, p. 330.

51. P.R.O., C.54/3487 m.20; C.54/3932 m.38; Hughes, *Fleming-Senhouse Papers*, p. 24; *C.C.C.*, p. 2308.

52. *C.C.C.*, pp. 2038, 2671; *A History of Northumberland*, ed. E. Bateson (Newcastle-upon-Tyne and London, 1895), ii, p. 296. Sir Charles' son had compounded for the estates but failed to clear them with the Committee for the Removal of Obstructions, and found them sold over his head (*C.C.C.*, p. 2671).

53. *C.C.C.*, p. 2038; P.R.O., Common Pleas, Feet of Fines, C.P.25, Mich. 14 Chas. ii; J. Hodgson, *History of Northumberland*, pt. ii, vol. iii (Newcastle-upon-Tyne, 1740), pp. 115–17, 343–4.

54. For the fourth family, the Flemings of Rydal, see above, p. 247.

55. C.R.O., D/Mus, Court Book, surveys and papers relating to the confiscation; *C.C.C.*, p. 2308;

P.R.O., C.54/3728 m.14; C.54/4094 m.5; G. Burton, *The Life of Sir Philip Musgrave*, ed. S. Jefferson (Carlisle, 1840), pp. 29–30, 41; P.R.O., C.54/3726 m.20; C.54/3764 m.25.

56. *C.C.C.*, p. 2589; P.R.O., C.5/31/69; C.R.O., Lawson of Corby Castle MSS, unlisted deeds; Nicolson and Burn, *History and Antiquities*, i, p. 479.

57. *C.C.C.*, p. 2589. For the position of Sir Thomas Cotton, see G.E.C., *Complete Baronetage*, i, p. 46 and P.R.O., S.P.23/150/199.

58. C.R.O. Lawson MSS, unlisted; C.R.O. D/Lons/L, A1/9; D/Lons/L, letters 14 Dec. 1663; R. Whellan, *Directory of Durham*, states that the Lord St John owned Neasham in 1670.

59. John Philipson was in fact allowed to compound for this estate, but failed to pay the fine in time, (*C.C.C.*, p. 1726). What follows is based on: C.R.O., Kendal, Fleming of Rydal MSS, WD/Ry, original ms. 'R', pp. 115, 118, and will of John Philipson of Calgarth; Nicolson and Burn, *History and Antiquities*, i, p. 183; *The Victoria History of the County of York: North Riding*, ed. W. Page (2 vols, 1914–23), i, p. 106.

60. P.R.O., Prerogative Court of Canterbury, PROB. 11/232, f. 390.

61. C.R.O., Kendal, WD/Ry, will of Nicholas Fisher.

62. Based on C.R.O., D/Lons/L, A1/4 and A1/4a.

63. *C.C.C.*, p. 985; C.R.O., Leconfield MSS, D/Lec, leases, 16/129, 131.

64. C.B. Phillips, 'The Cumbrian Iron Industry in the seventeenth century', in *Trade and Transport. Essays in Economic History in honour of T.S. Willan*, ed. W.H. Chaloner and Barrie M. Ratcliffe (Manchester, 1977), pp. 17–19.

65. *Calendar of State Papers, Ireland*, 1660–62, pp. 626–7; *Calendar of State Papers Domestic*, 1661–62, pp. 340, 596; D.M. Woodward, 'The Anglo-Irish livestock trade of the seventeenth century', *Irish Historical Studies*, xviii (1972–3), p. 497.

66. L. Stone, *The Causes of the English Revolution, 1529–1642* (paperback edn. 1972), p. 32; for a suggestion as to the motivation of the Royalist gentry see L. Stone, 'Prosopography', *Daedalus* (1971), p. 62. There are biographies of Musgrave and Curwen in M.F. Keeler, *The Long Parliament, A Biographical Study of its Members* (Philadelphia, U.S.A., 1954), pp. 148, 283.

67. This difference may be significant if Musgrave *was* only a landowner. But Lowther's brother, Sir Christopher of Whitehaven, another gentleman entrepreneur, was also an ardent Royalist.

68. The definitions of the gentry used by Messrs Cliffe, Blackwood and myself all differ. Dr Cliffe rigidly studied only the armigerous gentry; Dr Blackwood accepts gentleman status in freeholders books as evidence of gentility without question, whereas I regard such books as essentially unreliable for Cumberland and Westmorland (Cliffe, *Yorkshire Gentry*, p. 3; Blackwood, *Trans L.C.A.S.* lxxvii, pp. 77–8; Phillips, thesis, pp. 7–17, esp. p. 16). Thus Cliffe omits many of the minor gentry, Blackwood may include too many; most of them would probably be of undeclared or neutral allegiance. Blackwood (op. cit., pp. 78–80) also appears to 'lose' 126 gentry families in his statistics.

69. Cliffe, *Yorkshire Gentry*, pp. 189, 344–5; Blackwood, *Trans. L.C.A.S.*, lxxvii, pp. 89–90.

11

PARTIES AND ISSUES IN THE CIVIL WAR IN LANCASHIRE AND EAST ANGLIA[1]

B.G. Blackwood

T he purpose of this paper is twofold: to examine the parties in the Civil War in Lancashire and East Anglia (Norfolk and Suffolk), concentrating on the allegiances of the nobility, gentry, townsmen and peasant farmers; and to discuss the main issues in the war – social, local and religious.

I

Seventeenth-century observers believed that there were social differences between the Royalists and Parliamentarians during the Civil War. The Reverend Richard Baxter, a Puritan clergyman, noted that 'a great part of the Lords forsook the Parliament' and that, outside the Home Counties and East Anglia, 'a very great part of the Knights and Gentlemen . . . adhered to the King'. Parliament's support, he said, came from 'the smaller part (as some thought) of the Gentry in most of the Counties, and the greatest part of the Tradesmen and Free-holders and the middle sort of Men'.[2] The Royalist Edward Hyde, Earl of Clarendon, stressed that 'most of the gentry . . . throughout the kingdom' were 'engaged against' Parliament but that 'the common people' were favourable to Parliament.[3] Edward Chamberlayne, writing after the Restoration, named as Parliamentarians 'some of the . . . gentry . . . most of the tradesmen and very many of the peasantry'.[4]

How valid are these interpretations? Were the nobility and gentry predominantly Royalist and the townsfolk and peasantry mainly Parliamentarian? First, what about the nobility or peerage, that is the dukes, marquises, earls, viscounts and barons who sat in the House of Lords? Dr John Adamson considers that, during the period 1643–48, 'of an active peerage (of pre-May 1642 titles), roughly a third were active royalists (commanders or office-holders); roughly another third were actively parliamentarian (serving in the field or on parliamentary committees); and a final third were trimmers in the middle desperately anxious for some moderate settlement and perhaps ready to do business with either side'.[5] In our three counties, however, the nobility were not so evenly divided. In Norfolk all three peers connected with the county were Royalist activists: John Neville, 10th Baron Abergavenny, a Roman Catholic; Edward Sackville, 4th Earl of Dorset; and Henry-Frederick Howard, 'Lord Maltravers', later 15th Earl of Arundel.[6] In Suffolk two peers with local connexions – Thomas Wentworth, 1st Earl of Cleveland, and Thomas Windsor-Hickman, 7th Lord Windsor – were Royalist activists, while one, Francis Willoughby, 5th Baron Willoughby of Parham, a Puritan, was an active Parliamentarian in the first Civil War (1642–46) and an equally active Royalist in the second Civil War (1648).[7] However, those six peers did not play an important part in the history of Norfolk and Suffolk during the Civil War because, although owning land in these counties, they were neither influential nor resident. Here they greatly differed from the nobility in Lancashire. In that northern county the three peers – James Stanley, 7th Earl of Derby; Richard Molyneux, 2nd Viscount of Maryborough in Ireland (RC); and Henry Parker, 13th Baron Morley and Mounteagle (RC) – were not only unanimously and vigorously Royalist, but by their great power and influence raised much support for the King among the gentry and tenant farmers.[8] The Earl of Derby was particularly powerful. However, Clarendon exaggerated when he said that the Earl had 'a greater influence' and 'a more absolute command over the people' in Lancashire and Cheshire 'than any subject in England had in any other quarter of the kingdom'.[9] Indeed, the influence of the Royalist Earl of Derby in Lancashire was probably less than that of the Parliamentarian Earl of Warwick in Essex.[10]

So much for the nobility. What about the gentry, those consistently described in official documents as baronets, knights, esquires and gentlemen and recognized as such by their contemporaries?[11] Were they predominantly Royalist or Parliamentarian? It is hard to say. In some counties, like Berkshire, Lancashire, Norfolk, Suffolk and Warwickshire, the allegiances of a majority of the gentry are unknown, and the bulk of them *may* have been neutral.[12] In other regions, like the Lake Counties and Yorkshire, most gentry did take sides in the Civil War, but very large minorities were neutral.[13] These facts need not surprise us. After all Clarendon remarked that 'the number of those who desired to sit still was greater than of those who desired to engage of either party; so that they were generally inclined to articles of neutrality'.[14] Thus contemporary comment, as well as statistical evidence, suggests that it is perhaps right to emphasize the importance of neutralism in the Civil War.[15]

But what about the gentry who did take sides? Who exactly were the Royalist and Parliamentarian gentry? They were those who, at some time or other between 1642 and 1648, served either the King or Parliament in a military or civil capacity.[16] The Royalists included those in arms, persons 'adhering to' or 'assisting' the King, unspecified 'delinquents', and generally such officials as commissioners of array, commissioners of inquiry into 'Rebellion' and, in Lancashire, members of the Earl of Derby's Council. The Parliamentarians included soldiers, civilian officials like county committeemen, sequestration agents, assessors, collectors and treasurers, and also those voluntarily contributing men or money to their cause. Besides Royalists and Parliamentarians there were a number who changed sides or whose families were politically divided. Leaving this last group aside, how many gentry were Royalists or Parliamentarians? In 1663 Charles Gerard of Halsall, an eminent Lancastrian with nationwide interests and outlook, implied that the combatant gentry were predominantly Royalist in the English Civil War. After commenting that 'very few lawyers . . . adhered to the King', Gerard said that 'the King's cause was truly and constantly maintained by the English gentry'.[17] Table 1 seems to bear out this remark.

Notice in Table 1 that in twelve of these fourteen counties the Royalists outnumbered the Parliamentarians, in ten of them overwhelmingly. Indeed, if we take all fourteen counties together – representing one third of the historic shires – then the Royalist gentry outnumbered the Parliamentarian gentry by nearly two to one. Moreover, Lancashire appears typical and Norfolk and Suffolk seem exceptional regarding gentry allegiance during the Civil War. But is it as simple as that? Let us look at our three shires in detail, beginning with Lancashire.

Table 2 shows that nearly 60 per cent of Lancashire families were neutral or of unknown allegiance, that the divided families and side-changers were statistically insignificant, and that among the combatants the Royalist families had nearly a two to one majority over their Parliamentarian opponents.[18]

To get a full picture of Civil War allegiances it is necessary to classify the gentry on an individual as well as on a family basis because some families sent more of their members into battle than others, while split families did not always divide evenly between the two sides.

Table 3 shows that if we classify the Lancashire gentry on an individual basis, the Royalists had almost exactly a two to one majority over their opponents and that side-changers were statistically negligible.

It is even more important to distinguish between the 'active' and the 'passive' on both sides. The 'active' were those who were prepared to risk their lives and limbs as soldiers and/or who were prepared to undertake much drudgery as civilian officials or as M.P.s. By contrast, the 'passive' tended to be faint-hearted. They usually avoided fighting, even if holding military rank, were content to give or lend small sums of money to their cause and, if nominated as officials, served infrequently, reluctantly or not at all. Table 4 shows that in Lancashire a far larger number of Royalists than of Parliamentarians were passive, but that on both sides the activists were in an overwhelming majority. Moreover, if we concentrate solely on the activists, the Royalists still had nearly a two to one majority over the Parliamentarians.

Tables 2–4 show that the Royalist gentry were numerous *both* in the more arable, lowland parts of Lancashire – West Derby, Leyland and Amounderness

Table 1

CIVIL WAR ALLEGIANCES OF SOME ENGLISH GENTRY[19]

Ref[20]	County	Royalist	Parliamentarian
a	Berkshire	59	20
b	Cheshire[21]	80	66
c	Cumberland and Westmorland	77	21
d	Derbyshire	65	51
e	Kent	500	275
f	Lancashire[22]	192	106
g	Leicestershire	77	31
h	Norfolk	59	106
i	Nottinghamshire[23]	173	40
j	Shropshire[24]	71	43
k	Suffolk	65	112
l	Warwickshire	90	48
m	Yorkshire	242	128
	Total	1,750	1,047

hundreds – and in the pastoral, upland regions of the county: Salford, Blackburn and Lonsdale hundreds. The Parliamentarian gentry, however, were in a minority in every region, except puritanical Salford hundred; but even there they did not greatly outnumber the Royalists.

Let us now look at gentry allegiances in East Anglia, beginning with Suffolk. This county is generally regarded as a Roundhead heartland during the Civil War. Alan Everitt stated that 'probably in no other shire was support for Parliament more widespread' and that 'Suffolk delinquents (Royalists) were so few'. Paul Fincham remarked that 'Suffolk supported Parliament overwhelmingly'.[25] Tables 5–7 seem to support those interpretations.

If we ignore the very large Neutral/Unknown majority and the very few divided families and sidechangers in Table 5, it would seem that, as regards the gentry, Suffolk *did* support Parliament 'overwhelmingly'. Looking at Tables 5–7 it is clear that in Suffolk the Parliamentarian gentry had a two to one majority over the Cavaliers as regards families, a five to three majority as regards individuals and a three to two majority as regards activists. However, this is a somewhat superficial interpretation. If we look closely at the geographical distribution of Parliamentarian and Royalist gentry in Suffolk, we can see that only East Suffolk was a Roundhead heartland. But West Suffolk was almost evenly divided as regards gentry allegiance.

Table 2

CIVIL WAR ALLEGIANCES OF LANCASHIRE GENTRY FAMILIES[26]

Hundred	Royalist families[27]	Parlia- mentarian families	Sidechangers/ Divided families	Neutral/ Unknown families	All families
Salford	**28** (14.3%)	**37** (18.9%)	**11** (5.6%)	**120** (61.2%)	**196** (100%)
Blackburn	**29** (26.4%)	**14** (12.7%)	**2** (1.8%)	**65** (59.1%)	**110** (100%)
West Derby	**57** (28.8%)	**21** (10.6%)	**2** (1.0%)	**118** (59.6%)	**198** (100%)
Leyland	**23** (32.4%)	**5** (7.1%)	**4** (5.6%)	**39** (54.9%)	**71** (100%)
Amounder- ness	**28** (26.1%)	**17** (15.9%)	**2** (1.9%)	**60** (56.1%)	**107** (100%)
Lonsdale	**27** (29.3%)	**12** (13.1%)	**3** (3.3%)	**50** (54.3%)	**92** (100%)
Total	**192** (24.8%)	**106** (13.7%)	**24** (3.1%)	**452** (58.4%)	**774** (100%)

Table 3

CIVIL WAR ALLEGIANCES OF INDIVIDUAL LANCASHIRE GENTRY

Hundred	Royalist[28]	Parliamentarian	Changed sides
Salford	45	53	6
Blackburn	46	26	–
West Derby	87	29	–
Leyland	45	10	–
Amounderness	53	23	–
Lonsdale	38	15	3
Total	314	156	9

Table 4

CIVIL WAR INVOLVEMENT OF INDIVIDUAL LANCASHIRE GENTRY

	THE ACTIVE		THE PASSIVE	
Hundred	Royalists	Parliamentarians	Royalists	Parliamentarians
Salford	38	52	7	1
Blackburn	34	22	12	4
West Derby	65	28	22	1
Leyland	41	10	4	–
Amounderness	39	22	14	1
Lonsdale	33	14	5	1
Total	250	148	64	8

Table 5

CIVIL WAR ALLEGIANCES OF SUFFOLK GENTRY FAMILIES[29]

Region of Suffolk	Parlia- mentarian families	Royalist families	Sidechangers/ Divided families	Neutral/ Unknown families	All families
East	**85** (19.3%)	**42** (9.5%)	**9** (2.0%)	**305** (69.2%)	**441** (100%)
West	**27** (10.9%)	**23** (9.3%)	**4** (1.6%)	**194** (78.2%)	**248** (100%)
Total	**112** (16.3%)	**65** (9.4%)	**13** (1.6%)	**499** (72.4%)	**689** (100%)

Table 6

CIVIL WAR ALLEGIANCES OF INDIVIDUAL SUFFOLK GENTRY

Region of Suffolk	Parliamentarian	Royalist	Changed sides
East	111	53	5
West	41	38	1
Total	152	91	6

What about the Norfolk gentry? Norfolk, too, is generally considered a Roundhead heartland during the Civil War. The late R.W. Ketton-Cremer wrote that in Norfolk 'the majority of gentry in the countryside, and the merchants in the towns, were Parliamentarian in sympathy' and that 'the scattered Royalist elements were easily overawed'.[30] Table 8 suggests that, if we exclude the large Neutral/Unknown majority and the small numbers of divided families and sidechangers, the majority of the Norfolk gentry families *were* Parliamentarian, having a two to one majority over their enemies.

Table 7

CIVIL WAR INVOLVEMENT OF INDIVIDUAL SUFFOLK GENTRY

Region of Suffolk	THE ACTIVE		THE PASSIVE	
	Parliamentarians	Royalists	Parliamentarians	Royalists
East	50	30	61	23
West	27	24	14	14
Total	77	54	75	37

Table 8

CIVIL WAR ALLEGIANCES OF NORFOLK GENTRY FAMILIES[31]

Region	Parliamentarian families	Royalist families	Sidechangers/ Divided families	Neutral/ Unknown families	All families
The Broads	2 (8.3%)	1 (4.2%)	–	21 (87.5%)	24 (100%)
The Fens	5 (27.8%)	2 (11.1%)	–	11 (61.1%)	18 (100%)
Sheep-Corn area	65 (17.3%)	32 (8.5%)	14 (3.7%)	264 (70.5%)	375 (100%)
Wood-Pasture area	23 (13.7%)	18 (10.7%)	6 (3.6%)	121 (72.0%)	168 (100%)
Urban centres	11 (22.9%)	6 (12.5%)	1 (2.1%)	30 (62.5%)	48 (100%)
Total	106 (16.8%)	59 (9.3%)	21 (3.3%)	447 (70.6%)	633 (100%)

However, when we look at individual gentry in Table 9, the Parliamentary majority is not so overwhelming.

Table 9

CIVIL WAR ALLEGIANCES OF INDIVIDUAL NORFOLK GENTRY

Region	Parliamentarian	Royalist	Changed sides
The Broads	2	1	–
The Fens	6	2	–
Sheep-corn area	81	56	7
Wood-pasture area	28	34	4
Urban centres	16	8	–
Total	133	101	11

Moreover, if we concentrate on the activists in Table 10, there is actually a clear Royalist majority.

Table 10

CIVIL WAR INVOLVEMENT OF INDIVIDUAL NORFOLK GENTRY

Region	THE ACTIVE		THE PASSIVE	
	Parliamentarians	Royalists	Parliamentarians	Royalists
The Broads	–	1	2	–
The Fens	2	2	4	–
Sheep-corn area	34	41	47	15
Wood-pasture area	15	22	13	12
Urban centres	8	7	8	1
Total	59	73	74	28

Tables 8–10 show that, unlike in Suffolk, there were not great regional differences between Parliamentarians and Royalists. In Norfolk Parliamentarian gentry families outnumbered the Royalist gentry families in all regions: the Broads, the Fens, the sheep-corn districts, the wood-pasture region and in the main urban centres. As regards individuals, Parliamentarians again had majorities in all these areas, except the wood-pasture region. The strong Royalist presence among the gentry in this region may have been partly a hostile reaction

to the independence of the common people, as it was in other wood-pasture areas (in Derbyshire and north Warwickshire, for example).[32] Finally, as regards the activists, the Royalist gentry outnumbered the Parliamentarian gentry everywhere, except in the Fens and the urban centres of Great Yarmouth, King's Lynn and Norwich.[33]

On the whole, then, the Norfolk gentry, excluding the Neutral/Unknown majority, were fairly evenly divided in their Civil War allegiances, just like the gentry of West Suffolk. It was only the combatant gentry of East Suffolk who were overwhelmingly Parliamentarian, just as the participating gentry of Lancashire were overwhelmingly Royalist.

These statistics of the allegiances of the East Anglian gentry may surprise the modern reader, but they would not have surprised contemporaries. Thomas May, writing in 1647, said of the eastern counties of Cambridgeshire, Norfolk and Suffolk that 'it were certain that many of the chief gentry in these Counties bended in their affections to the King's Commission of Array'. Later on, referring to Cambridgeshire, Essex, Hertfordshire, Huntingdonshire, Norfolk and Suffolk, May said that there was affection to Parliament 'especially among the common people', but by contrast 'a great and considerable number of the Gentry, and those of the highest ranks among them were disaffected to the Parliament; and were not sparing in their utmost indeavours to promote the King's Cause'.[34] Richard Baxter said that 'a very great part of the Knights and Gentlemen of England adhered to the King; except in Middlesex, Essex, Cambridgeshire, Norfolk and Suffolk', but he thought that if the King's army had come to East Anglia 'it's like it would have been there as it was in other places'.[35] In short, the gentry of East Anglia would have been predominantly Royalist, or at least they might have been in Norfolk and West Suffolk.

Let us now turn our attention to the common people, especially the townsfolk and farmers, and then examine the extent of popular Royalism in our three counties. First, a few words about the towns. According to the Hearth Tax returns of 1664, only 11 per cent of the Lancashire people lived in towns of over 1,000 inhabitants.[36] In East Anglia, by contrast, 28 per cent of people did so in the 1670s.[37] Townsmen greatly differed in wealth and status, and it is almost impossible to generalize about them. It is certainly very hard to discover their political outlook. Thus the late Philip Styles wrote: 'When we say that a particular town was Royalist or Parliamentarian in the Civil War we are speaking in terms of military control rather than of opinion'.[38] One modern historian does not share this cautious approach and boldly states that 'the towns and cities, industrial or not, were solidly for Parliament; in fact, it is difficult to call to mind any towns which could be described as "naturally" royalist'.[39] This generalization seems to be almost applicable to East Anglia, but certainly not to Lancashire.

In Lancashire only a slight majority of the eleven towns of over 1,000 inhabitants were Parliamentarian.[40] There were six main textile towns in south-east Lancashire: Blackburn, Bolton, Bury, Manchester, Rochdale and Salford. Bury was very divided and Salford was Royalist. The other four towns were, however, Parliamentarian, especially Bolton, 'the Geneva of Lancashire', which had a very large number of its inhabitants killed by Prince Rupert's forces in the famous siege of 1644. To a certain extent south-east Lancashire resembled the West Country where the 'strength' of the Parliamentarians and Puritans 'was greatest in the clothing districts of north Somerset and Wiltshire'.[41] Lancashire's two main seaports – Liverpool and Lancaster – appear to have been almost Parliamentarian islands in the surrounding area of Royalism. In Dorset, too, 'the port towns went solidly for the Parliament'.[42] The inland towns of Lancashire – Preston, Wigan and Warrington – seem to have been strongly Royalist, like the inland towns of West Dorset and Wiltshire.[43]

In East Anglia there were eighteen towns with over 1,000 inhabitants in 1642,[44] but unfortunately we know the Civil War allegiances of only eight of them. But these eight were overwhelmingly Parliamentarian. In Suffolk the leading textile town, Lavenham, was strongly Parliamentarian. So were the ports of Aldeburgh and Ipswich, though the port of Lowestoft *may* have been Royalist in sympathy. Bury St Edmunds, a declining industrial town but not yet a gentry leisure centre, was, like Bury in Lancashire, politically divided.[45] In Norfolk the three main towns – Norwich, Great Yarmouth and King's Lynn – seem to have supported Parliament during the Civil War. In the textile city of Norwich 'the Parliamentary-Puritans' had 'a clear majority in the (large) freeman electorate and, by the outbreak of war in 1642, in the magistracy'.[46] According to a contemporary tract Cavaliers (150 horse and 300 foot soldiers) were roaming the outskirts of Norwich in mid-August 1642, but there were more than 2,000 armed men in the city ready to 'live and die in the defence of Parliament'.[47] However, in April 1648 many of the citizens were hostile to Parliament and a pro-Royalist mob numbered between 500 and 600.[48] Nevertheless, there was more support for Parliament in 1642 than there was for the King in 1648. In the port of Great Yarmouth there was 'little Royalist sympathy' and when 'money and plate were to be collected for the defence of King and Parliament, the people . . . responded generously to the call'.[49] As is well-known, the port of King's Lynn was turned into a Royalist garrison in 1643 by Sir Hamon L'Estrange. But Dr Morrill may be right in saying that the townsmen were largely Parliamentarian,[50] because King's Lynn was one of only twenty-two places in England which raised volunteers for Parliament *before* the raising of the royal standard at Nottingham on 22 August 1642.[51] Indeed, King's Lynn seems a good example of a town that was Royalist in terms of military occupation but Parliamentarian in terms of opinion.

So much for the townsmen. What about the countrymen? As previously stated, Edward Chamberlayne named as Parliamentarians 'very many of the peasantry'. In Lancashire the peasantry were largely tenant farmers and as such many were pressurized by the Earl of Derby and other powerful landlords into fighting for the King.[52] Other tenants obediently followed their Parliamentarian landlords into battle.[53] However, let us not exaggerate those 'feudal' influences. There was also much voluntary support for Parliament among the Lancashire peasantry, though it cannot be quantified. The Reverend Adam Martindale, a Puritan minister, recorded that 'many yeomen's sonnes' fled to the Parliamentarian garrison at Bolton to escape being forced to serve in the Earl of Derby's Royalist regiments, 'and tooke up armes there' for the Parliament. 'The young youths, farmers' sons' around Chowbent, near Atherton, fought vigorously against the Earl of Derby's forces. The 'club men in Middleton, Ouldham and Rachdall' came to the aid of Bolton when it was besieged by the Royalists. The term 'club men' almost certainly refers to the peasantry.[54] A number of tenants supported Parliament against their Royalist landlords, including the Earl of Derby, and most of them must have been peasant farmers. Some of those who rose for Parliament were tenants of the Crown, like the 'sturdy churls in the two forests of Pendle and Rossendale'.[55]

In East Anglia, too, there seems to have been much voluntary support for Parliament among the farmers. Thomas May believed that 'the Freeholders and Yeomen' in Norfolk, Suffolk and Cambridgeshire 'in general adhered to the Parliament'. John Rushworth noted that 'many of the Chief Gentry of those Counties', together with those of Kent, Sussex, Surrey and Middlesex, 'were for paying obedience to his Majesty's Commission of Array', and he contrasted them with 'the Freeholders and Yeomen' who were 'generally of the other (Parliamentarian) side'.[56] That there was considerable support for Parliament among the peasant farmers is suggested by the generous contributions to the Propositions for raising money and horses in 1642. A total of £995 raised in Wangford hundred in north-east Suffolk for the Parliamentary cause included sums of over £100 from quite small villages like Mettingham and South Elmham All Saints and St Nicholas.[57] Villages in West Suffolk, like Alpheton, Cockfield and Shimpling, also supplied plenty of men, money and muskets for the Parliamentary cause.[58]

An impressionistic survey, then, suggests that there was much popular urban and rural support for Parliament in both Lancashire and East Anglia. What about popular support for the royal cause? There seems to have been plenty in the former but little in the latter. To assess – at least partially – the extent of the popular Royalism we need to use, very cautiously, the maimed soldiers' petitions among the Quarter Sessions order books and the lists of 'Royalist' suspects drawn up in 1656. Regarding the former source, an Act of 1662 required justices of the peace to pay small pensions to maimed or indigent former Royalist soldiers or their widows. Unfortunately the petitions seldom give the status or occupations of the petitioners, but they do relate mostly to common soldiers and N.C.O.s and thus give a good indication of the extent of plebeian Royalism during the 1640s.

David Underdown studied the maimed soldiers' petitions for 1662–67 and found as many as 815 former Royalist soldiers in Dorset and 327 in Wiltshire.[59] Mr G.M. Brightman[60] has examined these petitions for Lancashire for the whole of Charles II's reign and found over 500 former plebeian or non-gentry Royalist soldiers. I have studied the Quarter Sessions order books for the same period[61] and found only fifty ex-Royalist maimed soldiers in Suffolk[62] and, incredibly, just seven in Norfolk.[63]

The lists of 'Royalist' suspects tell a similar story. These were drawn up in 1656 by Oliver Cromwell's Major-Generals after Penruddock's rising in 1655. The Major-Generals were instructed to take security for good behaviour from all suspected Royalists. These returns give the names of people believed to have Royalist sympathies, and in most cases the domiciles, status and occupations of the 'Royalist' suspects are mentioned. Professor Underdown has studied the 1656 list for Dorset, Somerset and Wiltshire and shown that plebeians formed over 90 per cent and the 'middling sort' (traders, craftsmen, yeomen) well over 40 per cent of all suspects in his three counties.[64] The numbers and social composition of 'Royalist' suspects in Lancashire, Suffolk and Norfolk are given in Table 11.

Table 11 shows that in Lancashire, as in the West Country, there was a huge number of suspects. Also, as in western England, over 40 per cent of suspects belonged to the 'middle sort', a group generally regarded as Parliamentarian in sympathy. But whereas in Underdown's counties the traders and craftsmen were the most conspicuous middling group with yeomen poorly represented, in Lancashire yeomen were almost as numerous as traders and artisans. Moreover, the proportion of gentry was much greater among the Lancashire than among the western suspects; even so, plebeians comprised over 80 per cent of those under suspicion.

What about East Anglia? Here a completely different picture emerges. Table 11 suggests that popular support for the Stuarts was minimal. Only six plebeian 'Royalists' are named in Norfolk and a mere five in Suffolk. Other eastern counties tell a similar story. In Hertfordshire only sixteen plebeian 'Royalist' suspects are listed, in Buckinghamshire fifteen suspects, and in Cambridgeshire just three plebeian suspects are named.[65] Of course, the very small numbers of 'Royalist' suspects recorded in East Anglia may well have been partly due to administrative factors. Charles Fleetwood, Major-General for the eastern counties, being a member of Cromwell's Council, was unable to be active in obtaining names of 'Royalist' suspects because he had to leave his work to (lazy?) deputies. By contrast, Charles Worsley, Major-General in Lancashire, Cheshire and Staffordshire, and John Desborough, Major-General in the south-western counties, were particularly energetic administrators, hence the large numbers of plebeian 'Royalist' suspects recorded in their areas. However, personalities cannot entirely explain the difference. The fact is that, as regards the common people, East Anglia was a Parliamentarian stronghold, hence popular Royalism

Table 11
STATUS AND OCCUPATION OF 'ROYALIST' SUSPECTS IN 1656[66]

Status or occupation	Lancashire	Suffolk	Norfolk
Gentry	**200** (19.6%)	**19** (67.8%)	**19** (76.0%)
Clergy, professionals	**3** (0.3%)	**4** (14.3%)	–
Traders and craftsmen	**217** (21.2%)	**4** (14.3%)	**3** (12.0%)
Yeomen	**211** (20.6%)	–	**3** (12.0%)
Husbandmen	**346** (33.8%)	–	–
Labourers	**14** (1.4%)	–	–
Unknown	**32** (3.1%)	**1** (3.6%)	–
Total	**1,023** (100%)	**28** (100%)	**25** (100%)

appears to have been very weak in the region – except in Bury St Edmunds and Norwich in 1648.

To sum up, Lancashire, like the West Country, gave strong popular support both to the royal cause and to Parliament, but East Anglia mostly to Parliament. Was East Anglia typical of south-eastern England, and were Lancashire and Underdown's counties typical of the outlying regions? Only further research will answer that question.

II

We have noted that among the combatant gentry the Royalists outnumbered the Parliamentarians in most areas. Was this Royalist majority caused by fear of the populace? Professor Manning has in fact suggested that popular hostility towards the upper classes was an important reason for the growth of the Royalist party in 1642.[67] Indeed, Clarendon wrote of the

> fury and license of the common people, who were in all places grown to that barbarity and rage against the nobility and gentry (under the style of *Cavaliers*)

that it was not safe for any to live at their houses who were taken notice of as no votaries to the Parliament.[68]

If the common people were anti-gentry and pro-Parliament, why was this? Historians have suggested that in Lancashire it was due to popular hostility to the 7th Earl of Derby and agrarian discontent. I have argued elsewhere[69] that hatred of the Earl of Derby has been greatly exaggerated, especially by biased commentators like Clarendon, and that local records repeatedly testify to his popularity. Even the Parliamentarian Edward Robinson of Euxton admitted that the Earl was well loved in his country, hence the 'great cheerfulness' with which '3,000 countrie people' of the Kirkham area came to his assistance in 1643 against the Parliamentarians. But if the Earl of Derby was so popular, why did many of his tenants in the Liverpool and Bury areas support Parliament during the Civil War? It does not seem to have been because of agrarian discontent. In the case of the Bury tenants it may have been for religious reasons.[70] But it was not because the Earl had oppressed them. This he only seems to have done after the Civil War, apparently because they had served 'the Parliament ffaithfully'. Other Royalist landlords in Lancashire and Cheshire besides the Earl of Derby seem to have victimized their Roundhead tenants after the Civil War. In general, the exploitation of the tenantry in Lancashire appears to have been the *result* rather than the *cause* of their Parliamentarianism.[71]

In East Anglia social and agrarian discontent seems to have been even less important than in Lancashire. However, Professor Manning refers to popular hostility in August 1642 towards upper-class Papists or suspected Papists in the Stour valley, a wood-pasture area.[72] Mobs attacked and plundered the houses of the Countess of Rivers at St Osyth in Essex and at Long Melford in Suffolk. The house of another Papist, Sir Francis Mannock at Stoke-by-Nayland in Suffolk, was also raided. Later the mob got out of hand and plundered 'as well protestants as papists'. Recently John Walter has implied that these riots were inspired by fear of Roman Catholics rather than by hatred of the upper classes.[73] But whether expressions of anti-Catholicism or of class hatred, those attacks, far from driving large numbers of Suffolk gentry into the arms of the King, drove many into the arms of Parliament. In Professor Ashton's words, 'fear of popular disorder was likely to work in favour of the King's opponents who in some areas appeared as the only effective guardians of public order'.[74] However, the fact that in West Suffolk – where the riots took place – the Royalist gentry were almost as numerous as the Parliamentarian gentry suggests that there may be at least some truth in Professor Manning's thesis.

If social and agrarian issues were not of paramount importance in the Civil War in Lancashire and East Anglia, what about local issues? It was once fashionable to interpret the English Civil War in terms of 'localism'.[75] Professor Ivan Roots succinctly defined this as 'a priority given to the apparent needs of a community smaller and more intimate than the state or nation'. Hence 'in Dorset, Somerset and Lancashire, it was local rather than national politics that men revelled in', and 'Rebellions, including the Great Rebellion itself, were emphatically local movements'.[76] There is indeed a *prima facie* case for emphasizing the parochialism and localism of our seventeenth-century ancestors. Local feelings and local loyalties were bound to be strong among all social groups in an age when transport facilities and communications were poor and when a journey from Manchester to London might take anything up to a week.

However, in Lancashire and East Anglia local issues only seem to have been of moderate importance. There are certainly some good examples of localism. In Lancashire the town of Salford seems to have supported the King because of its local rivalry with neighbouring Manchester, which was strongly Parliamentarian. It is possible that Liverpool supported Parliament against the Royalist Molyneuxes of Sefton simply to gain control of the town windmill and ferry boats.[77] In East Anglia the likely Royalism of Lowestoft would have been due less to its love of the King's cause than to its traditional fishing rivalry with nearby Great Yarmouth, which was 'wholly committed to the Parliament'.[78] Indeed, it is not too fanciful to suggest that, had Yarmouth been Royalist, Lowestoft might well have been Parliamentarian through local cussedness.

Nevertheless, we must not exaggerate the importance of local disputes in deciding political allegiances. The Civil War in our three counties was not just the result of 'little local difficulties', important though these sometimes were. In Lancashire the Cavaliers were much concerned with national problems. This is partly suggested by the fact that at least 99 of the 218 Royalist gentry soldiers fought outside Lancashire at some time or other during the Civil War.[79] Some historians have stressed that localism was shown by a reluctance to fight outside one's own county.[80] But Lancashire Royalists fought in thirty-one English and Welsh counties and also in Ireland.[81] Several of the Royalist gentry fought outside Lancashire in some of the more famous Civil War battles, like Edgehill, first and second Newbury, Marston Moor and Naseby.[82] The non-local outlook of Lancashire Royalists is further shown by the fact that they served as officers in twenty-seven non-Lancashire regiments as well as in the twenty-six regiments raised in the county.[83]

East Anglian Royalists were also non-local in outlook. Of the sixty-seven Royalist gentry soldiers of Norfolk, at least forty-two fought outside their native county. Of the fifty-eight Royalist gentry soldiers of Suffolk, at least forty-three fought outside their own county. East Anglian Royalist gentlemen saw military action at Alresford, Ashby-de-la-Zouch, Auburn Chase, Basing House, Bridport (Dorset), Bristol, Burleigh House (near Stamford), Burton-on-Trent, Carlisle, Colchester, Copredy Bridge, Edgehill, Exeter, Faringdon, Gainsborough, Gloucester, Gosworth Bridge (Kent), Langport, Leicester, Lincoln, Lostwithiel, Marston Moor, Naseby, Newark, first and second Newbury, Oxford, Pontefract,

Reading, Rowton Moor, South Wales, Stow-on-the-Wold, Taunton, Tewkesbury, Truro, Wallingford, Wetherby, Winchester, Woodstock, Worcester and York.[84]

Some Parliamentarians also demonstrated their non-local outlook by crossing county boundaries. Of the forty Parliamentary gentry soldiers of Suffolk, nineteen fought outside their native county. The Norfolk Roundheads were, however, more localist. Of the forty-four gentry soldiers, only fourteen definitely served outside Norfolk.[85] At first sight the Lancashire Roundheads appear to have been more localist than their Norfolk counterparts, since of the ninety Parliamentarian gentry soldiers, only twenty-two apparently fought outside the palatinate.[86] Yet Lancashire Parliamentarians were far from being parochial in outlook. In Manchester during the siege of 1642 the local Parliamentarians clearly subordinated local and personal issues to national ones. A contemporary Parliamentarian said that 'private and particular interests are wrapped up in the Publique, not so much publique in private'. He went on to say that 'the remembrance of Parliament ingagement, and an honourable esteem of the Publique Faith did no little availe'.[87]

Localism and local issues in Lancashire and East Anglia, then, do not appear to have been of major significance. So what was the most important single issue in the Civil War in our three counties? It is now as fashionable to emphasize religion as a Civil War issue as it was to stress localism in the 1960s and '70s. Professor Fletcher has said that what 'distinguished the two armies' – and presumably the two sides – in the Civil War was 'the sharp contrast between their religious attitudes'. Dr Morrill has called the English Civil War 'the last of the Wars of Religion'. Recently Conrad Russell has said that 'many people, and very many of the first activists, did fight for religion'.[88] My work on Lancashire and Suffolk would confirm these interpretations, but my researches on Norfolk would only partially do so – at least as regards the gentry. But first let us be clear about the religious groups to which we are referring.

During the Civil War period observers generally spoke of three religious parties: Papist, Protestant and Puritan, though 'Papist' was becoming synonymous with 'Romane Catholicke' and 'Protestant' with 'Anglican'.[89] The least difficult group to identify are the Roman Catholics or 'popish recusants'.[90] They are to be found in the recusant rolls, lay subsidy rolls, state papers and various miscellaneous sources. Puritans, however, are much harder to identify and enumerate. Contemporaries vaguely called them 'the hotter sort of protestants'.[91] Nevertheless, during the Civil War period we may perhaps safely regard the following as Puritans: those appointing or financially assisting Puritan ministers;[92] dedicatees of Puritan works; builders of chapels used for Puritan worship; members of puritanical religious committees; elders of Presbyterian classical assemblies; (the very few) members of Independent congregations; and, finally, those shown to be Puritans by their wills,[93] correspondence or the opinions of their contemporaries. Anglicans, nominally the vast majority, are the hardest of all to identify, but Dr New has aptly called them 'those generally satisfied with the Church (of England's) doctrine, organization and ceremonial'.[94]

Table 12 shows how much support these three religious parties obtained from the gentry of Lancashire and indicates that over half the Lancashire gentry were Anglicans, but how many were devout and how many were indifferent cannot be quantified. Puritanism was embraced by only one in seven gentry families, though it was strong in Salford hundred.[95] Roman Catholicism was the religion of only three in ten gentry families. Yet Lancashire had a higher proportion of Roman Catholics than any other shire, except perhaps Monmouth, so we are probably justified in calling Lancashire an Anglican county with a strong Catholic presence. The statistics certainly suggest that religion was a vital issue to the combatants in the Civil War. Among the Parliamentary gentry families Puritans formed a large majority. The Puritan author of *Discourse of the Warr in Lancashire* was indeed correct in saying that 'of those that first put themselves into Armes (for Parliament) were men of the best affection to Religion'.[96] Among the Royalist gentry families Papists formed the vast majority. Moreover, Mr Gratton has shown that among 214 Lancashire Royalist gentry army officers, 124 were Roman Catholic.[97] The strong Catholic support for the King is hardly surprising. An anonymous correspondent wrote in 1642 that 'the Catholiques in this Kingdome give all lost, if . . . this Parliament be not subdued'.[98]

Table 13 (see p. 279) shows that in Suffolk, as in Lancashire, the gentry were deeply divided during the Civil War period. It also shows that the Anglican/Indifferent group was considerably stronger among the Suffolk than among the Lancashire gentry. Not only did Anglicans form the vast majority of the Royalist and Neutral/Unknown families, but also a substantial minority of the Parliamentarian families. Not surprisingly, however, and in contrast to Lancashire, gentry support for Roman Catholicism in Suffolk was negligible, among Royalist and Neutral/Unknown families alike. Very surprisingly, though, is the fact that the proportion of gentry families who were Puritan was no greater in Suffolk than in Lancashire. Moreover, just a small majority of the Parliamentary gentry families were Puritan. Yet we are probably justified in describing Suffolk as an Anglican county with a strong Puritan presence because if we concentrate on the individual Roundhead *activists*, the link between Puritanism and Parliamentarianism is close. Of the seventy-seven active individual Parliamentary gentlemen, fifty-one were Puritan. Among the hyperactive, the twenty Parliamentarians who vigorously served *both* as soldiers and officials, all save three were Puritan.

Table 14 (see p. 279) shows the religious situation among the Norfolk gentry during the Civil War period. It indicates that the Anglicans or the Indifferent were in an overwhelming majority among all political groups of Norfolk gentry. As in Suffolk and unlike in Lancashire, the proportion of Roman Catholic gentry families was negligible. Again as in Suffolk and unlike in Lancashire, Catholic

Neutrals outnumbered Catholic Royalists. But the most interesting discovery about the Norfolk gentry is the tiny proportion of families who were Puritan – only one in fourteen.[99] Moreover, only one-third of the Norfolk Parliamentarian families were Puritan. Even among the fifty-nine individual Parliamentary activists, only a minority – twenty-seven – were Puritan. However, Table 14 shows that while most Parliamentary gentry were not Puritan, most Puritan gentry were Parliamentarian, and these included several leading Roundheads such as Sir John Hobart of Blickling, Sir John Holland of Quidenham, Sir John Potts of Mannington and Major-General Philip Skippon. So the evidence suggests that even in Norfolk religious issues mattered during the Civil War, though not as much as in Lancashire and Suffolk.

Table 12

RELIGION AND CIVIL WAR ALLEGIANCES OF LANCASHIRE GENTRY FAMILIES[100]

	Royalist families	Parlia-mentarian families	Sidechangers/ Divided families	Neutral/ Unknown families	All families
Roman Catholic[101]	**132** (68.8%)	–	**5** (20.8%)	**89** (19.7%)	**226** (29.2%)
Puritan	**7** (3.6%)	**75** (70.8%)	**11** (45.8%)	**21** (4.6%)	**114** (14.7%)
Anglican/ Indifferent	**53** (27.6%)	**31** (29.2%)	**8** (33.4%)	**342** (75.7%)	**434** (56.1%)
Total	**192** (100%)	**106** (100%)	**24** (100%)	**452** (100%)	**774** (100%)

III

Let us now sum up, beginning with Civil War allegiances. The nobility in our three counties were almost entirely Royalist. Nationwide, however, the peers were more evenly divided. The combatant gentry were predominantly Royalist in twelve English counties, including Lancashire, fairly evenly divided in Norfolk and West Suffolk, and largely Parliamentarian only in East Suffolk. Did the gentry elsewhere in England also have strong Royalist predilections? The towns of known allegiance

Table 13

RELIGION AND CIVIL WAR ALLEGIANCES OF SUFFOLK GENTRY
FAMILIES[102]

	Parlia-mentarian families	Royalist families	Sidechangers/ Divided families	Neutral/ Unknown families	All families
Roman Catholic	–	**6** (9.2%)	–	**28** (5.6%)	**34** (4.9%)
Puritan	**60** (53.6%)	**5** (7.7%)	**9** (69.2%)	**26** (5.2%)	**100** (14.5%)
Anglican/ Indifferent	**52** (46.4%)	**54** (83.1%)	**4** (30.8%)	**445** (89.2%)	**555** (80.6%)
Total	**112** (100%)	**65** (100%)	**13** (100%)	**499** (100%)	**689** (100%)

Table 14

RELIGION AND CIVIL WAR ALLEGIANCES OF NORFOLK GENTRY
FAMILIES[103]

	Parlia-mentarian families	Royalist families	Sidechangers/ Divided families	Neutral/ Unknown families	All families
Roman Catholic	–	**11** (18.6%)	–	**18** (4.0%)	**29** (4.6%)
Puritan	**36** (34.0%)	**2** (3.4%)	**7** (33.3%)	**3** (0.7%)	**48** (7.6%)
Anglican/ Indifferent	**70** (66.0%)	**46** (78.0%)	**14** (66.7%)	**426** (95.3%)	**556** (87.8%)
Total	**106** (100%)	**59** (100%)	**21** (100%)	**447** (100%)	**633** (100%)

showed a slight majority for Parliament in Lancashire, but an overwhelming one in East Anglia. The peasant farmers in Lancashire and particularly East Anglia also seem to have had Parliamentarian tendencies. Popular Royalism varied regionally, being strong in Lancashire – as in the West Country – but weak in East Anglia.

Although political divisions roughly coincided with social divisions, the Civil War in our three counties was not a class conflict, perhaps not even in West Suffolk. Nor were local issues of major importance, as in Kent. The Civil War in Lancashire and Suffolk was largely a 'war of religion', but in Norfolk religious issues seem much less important. In this respect was Norfolk an exception among English counties, or were Lancashire and Suffolk the exceptions? It is hard to say until *all* counties have been thoroughly investigated.

Notes

1. This paper owes much to discussions with Dr J.S. Morrill, Mr G.M. Brightman, Miss Gwenyth Dyke, Mr Malcolm Gratton and the late Brigadier Peter Young. Any remaining errors are mine.

2. Richard Baxter, *Reliquiae Baxteriana*, ed. M. Sylvester, (1696), p. 30.

3. Edward, Earl of Clarendon, *The History of the Rebellion and Civil Wars in England*, ed. W.D. Macray, 6 vols (Oxford, 1888), ii, p. 318; iii, p. 80.

4. Edward Chamberlayne, *Anglia Notitia* (1669), p. 59.

5. Communication of 28 January 1992 from Dr J.S.A. Adamson, Peterhouse, Cambridge. Dr Adamson excludes from his calculations peers abroad, peers disqualified from participation in politics and peers under age.

6. On the Norfolk peers see R.H. Mason, *The History of Norfolk* (1884), pp. 315, 318; R.W. Ketton-Cremer, *Norfolk in the Civil War*, 2nd edn (Norwich, 1985), pp. 137, 145, 148–49, 288.

7. On the Suffolk peers see P.R. Newman, *Royalist Officers in England and Wales 1642–1660: A Biographical Dictionary* (New York, 1981), pp. 403, 418; Clive Holmes, *Seventeenth-century Lincolnshire* (Lincoln, 1980), pp. 146–50, 155–59, 161, 164, 168–69, 171–72, 182–85, 187, 203, 217.

8. B.G. Blackwood, *The Lancashire Gentry and the Great Rebellion, 1640–60*, Chetham Society, 3rd ser. xxv (1978), 47–48, 52; idem, 'Parties and Issues in the Civil War in Lancashire', *Transactions of the Historic Society of Lancashire and Cheshire*, cxxxii (1983), 103–4; E. Broxap, *The Great Civil War in Lancashire 1642–51*, 2nd edn (Manchester, 1973), p. 21.

9. Clarendon, *Rebellion*, ii, 469.

10. Robert Rich, 2nd Earl of Warwick, possessed sixty-four manors in Essex in 1630, while the 7th Earl of Derby owned only twenty-six in Lancashire in 1642: William Hunt, *The Puritan Moment* (1983), p. 15; Blackwood, *Lancs. Gentry*, p. 131. Manors were of course an index of power rather than of wealth. For a balanced, authoritative account of the power of the 7th Earl of Derby see Barry Coward, *The Stanleys, Lords Stanley and Earls of Derby, 1385–1672*, Chetham Soc., 3rd ser. xxx (1983).

11. For a fuller discussion of the term 'gentry' see Blackwood, *Lancs. Gentry*, pp. 4–5.

12. G.C. Durston, 'Berkshire and its County Gentry' (2 vols, unpub. Ph.D. thesis, Reading Univ., 1977), i, 37–38, 212–13, 217; Ann Hughes, *Politics, Society and Civil War in Warwickshire, 1620–1660* (Cambridge, 1987), p. 162. For Lancashire, Suffolk and Norfolk see Tables 2, 5 and 8 below.

13. C.B. Phillips, 'The Royalist North: the Cumberland and Westmorland Gentry, 1642–60',

N(orthern) H(istory), xiv (1978), 175–76; J.T. Cliffe, *The Yorkshire Gentry: From the Reformation to the Civil War* (1969), p. 336.

14. Clarendon, *Rebellion*, ii, 469.

15. For a discussion of neutralism in Lancashire see Blackwood, *Lancs. Gentry*, pp. 38, 48–50; idem, *THSLC*, cxxxii, 104–5.

16. These dates are justifiable because 'the Second Civil War, in 1648, was . . . the perpetuation of ideological and political conflict which, since 1642, had divided Royalist and Parliamentarian': Brian Lyndon, 'Essex and the King's Cause in 1648', *Historical Journal*, xxix (1986), 19. See also idem, 'The South and the Start of the Second Civil War, 1648', *History* lxxi (1986), 393–407. For a contrary view see J.S. Morrill, 'The Northern Gentry and the Great Rebellion', *NH*, xv (1979), 81; idem, *The Revolt of the Provinces*, 2nd edn. (1980), pp. 126–31.

17. *Crosby Records: A Cavalier's Note Book*, ed. T.E. Gibson (1880), p. 264. I owe this reference to Dr P.R. Newman.

18. For statistical purposes the family unit includes the head of the family, his wife and children, his younger brothers and unmarried sisters, and the widow of any previous head of the family. However, where the head and younger brother both had adult sons, these have been counted as two separate families.

19. Statistics in this table refer to families in all counties except Berkshire, Derbyshire, Kent and Nottinghamshire, where the data concern individuals. I have answered objections to the statistical approach to Civil War allegiances in Blackwood, *THSLC*, cxxxii, 105, 121 fn. 17.

20. References are (a) Durston, thesis, pp. 37–38, 212–13, 217; (b) M.D.G. Wanklyn, 'Landed Society and Allegiance in Cheshire and Shropshire in the First Civil War' (unpub. Ph.D. thesis, Manchester Univ., 1976), p. 272; (c) Phillips, *NH*, xiv, 175; (d) J.T. Brighton, *Royalists and Roundheads in Derbyshire* (Bakewell & District Historical Society, 1981), pp. 52, 54; (e) A.M. Everitt, *The Community of Kent and the Great Rebellion 1640–60* (Leicester, 1966), p. 34 n.; (f) see fn. 26; (g) David Fleming, 'Faction and Civil War in Leicestershire', *Leicestershire Archaeological and Historical Society Transactions*, lvii (1981–82), 32; (h) Gordon Blackwood, 'The Gentry of Norfolk during the Civil War', *Historical Atlas of Norfolk* (Norwich, 1993), p. 106 (hereafter *Norfolk Atlas*); (i) A.C. Wood, *Nottinghamshire in the Civil War* (repr. East Ardsley, 1971), pp. 217–24; (j) Wanklyn, thesis, p. 272; (k) Gordon Blackwood, 'Parties and Issues in the Civil War in Suffolk', *Suffolk Review*, new series, xviii (Spring, 1992), 2; (l) Hughes, *Warwickshire*, pp. 161–62; (m) Cliffe, *Yorkshire Gentry*, p. 336.

21. Dr Wanklyn has tables of four categories of Royalists and Parliamentarians, based mainly on landed wealth. But in my calculations I have ignored category D which, he tells me, refers mostly to non-gentry. See Wanklyn, thesis, p. 272.

22. These figures supersede those I have given elsewhere. The following families may be added to those named on the maps in my *Lancs Gentry*, pp. 39–45: *Royalist*: Bradshaw of Haigh (Roman Catholic), Croston of Bury, Holden of Crawshaw (RC), Holden of Holden, Holland of Pilkington, Hothersall of Hothersall (RC), Knipe of Rampside (RC), Lance of Abram (RC), Lathom of Mossborough (RC), Shireburn of Ribbleton (RC), Shireburn of Wolfhouse (RC), Thornborough of Hampsfield (RC), Walmesley of Dunkenhalgh (RC), Walton of Walton (RC), Whitacre of Simonstone. *Parliamentarian*: Barnard of Alkincotes, Blackhurst of Preston, Bradshaw of Aspull (Puritan), Crombock of Clarkhill, Crompton of Breightmet (P), Cubban of Bickerstaffe (P), Deane of Salford,

Edge of Holt (P), Edge of Lower Darwen, Gellibrand of Ramsgrave (P), Lomax of Middleton, Risley of Risley (P), Sephton of Skelmersdale (P), Taylor of Sankey, Willoughby of Horwich (P).

23. I have subtracted peers and aldermen from the list of Royalists and Roundheads in Wood, *Nottinghamshire*, pp. 217–24.

24. See fn. 21.

25. *Suffolk and the Great Rebellion, 1640–1660*, ed. A.M. Everitt, Suffolk Records Society, iii (1960), 11, 21 fn. 1; P. Fincham, *The Suffolk we live in* (Norwich, 1976), p. 47.

26. For a critical discussion of the sources see my *Lancs. Gentry*, p. 66 fn. 11. The names of the extra Royalist families and individuals have been gleaned mainly from *The Royal Martyrs* (1663); *A Catalogue of the Lords, Knights and Gentlemen (of the Catholick Religion) that were Slain in the late Warr* (1660); Stuart Reid, *Officers and Regiments of the Royalist Army*, 5 vols (Leigh-on-Sea, n.d.); Newman, *Royalist Officers*. The extra Parliamentarian families and individuals are from P(ublic) R(ecord) O(ffice), State Papers Domestic, Commonwealth Exchequer Papers, SP 28/252;/253 B;/255;/256;/257; Exchequer, King's Remembrancer, Bills and Answers of defaulting accountants, E 113/9; *The Letter Books of Sir William Brereton*, ed. R.N. Dore, 2 vols, Record Society of Lancashire & Cheshire, cxxiii, cxxviii (1984, 1990), hereafter *Brereton Letter Books*.

27. The numbers are conservatively estimated. The papers of the Committee for Compounding (PRO, SP23), Thomas Dring, *Catalogue of the Lords, Knights and Gentlemen who have compounded for their Estates* (1655) and M.G.W. Peacock, *Index of . . . Royalists whose estates were confiscated during the Commonwealth* (Index Society, ii, 1878) give another thirty 'delinquents' of borderline gentility. If these were added, the total number of Royalist families and individuals would be 222 and 344 respectively.

28. See fn. 27.

29. For sources see Blackwood, *Suffolk Rev.* n.s. xviii, 12 fn. 9. Uncited information on Suffolk in this paper comes from these sources.

30. R.W. Ketton-Cremer, 'The Human Background: Social, Political and Religious', *Norwich and its Region*, British Association for the Advancement of Science, 2nd edn. (Norwich, 1961), p. 109.

31. For sources see bibliography in Blackwood, *Norfolk Atlas*, p. 194. Uncited information on Norfolk in this paper comes from these sources.

32. Hughes, *Warwickshire*, esp. pp. 4–6, 151, 157.

33. For further details of geographical distribution see map in Blackwood, *Norfolk Atlas*, p. 107.

34. Thomas May, *The History of the Parliament of England* (1647), Book ii, 108; iii, 78.

35. Baxter, *Reliquiae*, p. 30.

36. Blackwood, *THSLC*, cxxxii, 109, 122 fn. 32.

37. John Patten, 'Population distribution in Norfolk and Suffolk during the sixteenth and seventeenth centuries', *Pre-industrial England: Geographical Essays*, ed. J. Patten (Folkestone, 1979), pp. 74–75.

38. P. Styles, 'The Royalist Government of Worcestershire during the Civil War, 1642–6', *Transactions of the Worcestershire Archaeological Society*, 3rd ser. v (1976), 24.

39. John Kenyon, *The Civil Wars of England* (1988), p. 38.

40. For details and documentation see Blackwood, *THSLC*, cxxxii, 110–11, 123 fns 39–56.

41. David Underdown, *Revel, Riot, and Rebellion: Popular Politics and Culture in England 1603–1660* (Oxford, 1985), pp. 165, 276.

42. Ibid., pp. 170–71.

43. Ibid., p. 197.

44. Patten, *Pre-industrial England*, p. 75.

45. For details and documentation see Blackwood, *Suffolk Review*, n.s. xviii, 4–6, 13 fn. 17–24 & 28.

46. John T. Evans, *Seventeenth Century Norwich* (Oxford, 1979), p. 135.

47. *Newes from the Citie of Norwich*, 26 August 1642, B(ritish) L(ibrary), Thomason Tracts, E. 114(15).

48. Evans, *Norwich*, p. 175 & fn. 6.

49. Ketton-Cremer, *Norfolk*, pp. 156–57.

50. Morrill, *Revolt*, p. 97.

51. Conrad Russell, *The Causes of the English Civil War* (1990), pp. 21–22, 226.

52. Blackwood, *Lancs. Gentry*, pp. 51–52; Joyce L. Malcolm, 'A King in Search of Soldiers: Charles I in 1642', *HJ*, xxi (1978), 268; *The Farington Papers*, ed. S.M. ffarington, Chetham Soc. o.s. xxxix (1856), 88–89; *Discourse of the Warr in Lancashire*, ed. E. Beamont, Chetham Soc. o.s., lxii (1864), 19–20; *Lancashire Civil War Tracts*, ed. G. Ormerod, Chetham Soc. o.s. ii (1844), 56.

53. Blackwood, *Lancs. Gentry*, pp. 51–52.

54. In a Lancashire context the term 'club men' does not mean armed neutrals.

55. For details and documentation of this paragraph see Blackwood, *THSLC*, cxxxii, 112–13, 124 fns 65–71.

56. May, *Hist. Parliament*, Book ii, 108; John Rushworth, *Historical Collections*, 8 vols (1721–22), iv, 680.

57. S(uffolk) R(ecord) O(ffice) I(pswich branch), Borough and Parish records, HD 224/1, fol. 8r.

58. Bodleian Library, Tanner MS.284, fols 42, 45–47.

59. Underdown, *Revel*, pp. 192, 295–96.

60. His Cambridge University Ph.D. thesis on popular allegiances in Lancashire is nearing completion.

61. Unfortunately the Quarter Sessions rolls for Suffolk do not begin until 1682. Those for Norfolk from 1660 to 1680 appear to have no references to ex-Royalist maimed soldiers.

62. Four of them were gentry, the rest plebeians. See SRO1, Quarter Sessions Order Books, 1658–83, B 105/2/5; 2/7; 2/10.

63. One pensioner was a gentleman-officer and one was the widow of a clergyman. The rest were plebeians. See Norwich Record Office, Sessions Order Books, 1657–81, C/S/2; S/3.

64. *Revel*, pp. 200–1, 296.

65. BL, Additional MS. 34,013 (Major-Generals' returns), fols 5–6, 8, 16, 19, 22, 28–29, 32, 36–37, 40, 43, 47, 51.

66. Ibid., fols 1–55. There is little doubt that some of the people listed were unjustly accused of Royalist sympathies and that others had never served the King in the Civil War. Yet independent evidence tentatively suggests that a majority of suspects may have been Royalists in the 1640s. In Lancashire, of the 200 gentry suspects, 146 (73 per cent) persons or their relatives had served Charles I. In Norfolk seventeen (68 per cent) of all twenty-five suspects, and in Suffolk *at least* fifteen (54 per cent) of all twenty-eight suspects, had likewise supported the martyred king.

67. Brian Manning, *The English People and the English Revolution 1640–9*, 2nd edn (1991), passim.

68. Clarendon, *Rebellion*, ii, 318.

69. Blackwood, *THSLC*, cxxxii, 113–14.

70. Coward, *The Stanleys*, pp. 175, 185 fn. 53.

71. For details and documentation see Blackwood, *THSLC*, cxxxii, 113–15, 124 fns 74–83.

72. Manning, *English People*, pp. 244, 252–59.

73. J. Walter, 'The impact on society: A world turned upside down?', in *The Impact of the English Civil War*, ed. John Morrill (1991), pp. 109–10.

74. Robert Ashton, *The English Civil War*, 2nd edn (1989), p. 152.

75. See especially Everitt, *Community of Kent*; idem, *The Local Community and the Great Rebellion*, Historical Association Pamphlet G.70 (1969); idem, *Change in the Provinces*, Univ. of Leicester, Dept. of English Local History, Occasional Papers, 2nd series, I (1969); J.S. Morrill, *Cheshire 1630–1660* (Oxford, 1974); idem, *Revolt*. For brilliant critiques of the local interpretation of the Civil War see esp. C. Holmes, 'The "County Community" in Stuart Historiography', *Journal of British Studies*, xix (1980), 54–73; Ann Hughes, 'Local History and the Origins of the Civil War', *Conflict in Early Stuart England*, ed. Richard Cust and Ann Hughes (1989), pp. 224–49.

76. I. Roots, 'The Central Government and the Local Community', in *The English Revolution, 1600–1660*, ed. E.W. Ives (1968), pp. 37, 40.

77. Blackwood, *THSLC*, cxxxii, 110–11, 115.

78. Ketton-Cremer, *Norfolk*, p. 179.

79. For sources see Blackwood, *Lancs. Gentry*, p. 66 fn. 11; fn. 26 above; B.G. Blackwood, 'The Lancashire Gentry, 1625–1660: A Social and Economic Study' (unpub. D.Phil. thesis, Oxford Univ., 1973), Appendix IV, pp. 344–50.

80. Anthony Fletcher, *The Outbreak of the English Civil War* (1981), pp. 327, 380–81; G.M. Trevelyan, *England under the Stuarts*, 19th edn (1947), p. 209.

81. Information supplied by Mr Malcolm Gratton, engaged on a Manchester University Ph.D. thesis on 'The War Effort in Lancashire, 1642–51'.

82. Blackwood, thesis, App. IV, pp. 344–50.

83. Ex inf. Mr M. Gratton.

84. For sources see Blackwood, *Suffolk Rev.* n.s. xviii, 12 fn. 9; idem, *Norfolk Atlas*, p. 194.

85. Ibid.

86. Fourteen of these are listed in Blackwood, thesis, App. IV, pp. 342–43. For the other eight – Ralph Assheton of Middleton, junior, John Bradshaw of Bradshaw, Edward Hulton of Hulton, Gerrard Markland of Wigan, James Schofield of Schofield, Alexander Standish of Duxbury, Ralph Taylor of Sankey and Thomas Willoughby of Horwich – see *Brereton Letter Books*, i, 188–89, 487, 529; ii, 168, 302, 382, 385–86, 409–10, 438.

87. Ormerod, *Civil War Tracts*, p. 119.

88. Fletcher, *Outbreak*, p. 346; John Morrill, 'The religious context of the English Civil War', *Transactions of the Royal Historical Society*, 5th ser. xxxiv (1984), 178; Russell, *Causes*, p. 62.

89. Thomas H. Clancy, 'Papist – Protestant – Puritan: English Religious Taxonomy 1565–1665', *Recusant History*, xiii (1976), 227–53; John Morrill, 'The Church of England, 1642–9', in *Reactions to the English Civil War 1642–49*, ed. John Morrill (1982), p. 231 fn. 2.

90. By 1641 'Church-Papists were a virtually extinct race'. John Bossy, *The English Catholic Community 1570–1850* (1975), p. 187.

91. As did Percival Wiburn in 1581. See P. Collinson, *The Elizabethan Puritan Movement* (1967), pp. 26–27. The differences between Puritans and Anglicans, Collinson writes, 'were differences of degree, of theological temperature . . . rather than of fundamental principle'. Until the Civil War Puritans were mostly members of the Established Church, albeit the more radical members.

92. The evidence of presentations generally needs to be corroborated by other information.

93. Wills must, of course, be used cautiously, since they sometimes reflect the views of the scribe rather than of the testator.

94. J.F.H. New, *Anglican and Puritan: The basis of their opposition 1558–1640* (1964), p. 2.

95. Blackwood, *Lancs. Gentry*, p. 28.

96. Beamont, *Discourse*, p. 19.

97. M.J. Gratton, 'The Earl of Derby's catholic army', *THSLC*, cxxxvii (1988), 40.

98. Sir George Duckett, 'Civil War Proceedings in Yorkshire', *Yorkshire Archaeological and Topographical Journal*, vii (1881–2), 74. The writer was not just concerned with Yorkshire but also with 'other Countyes' (ibid., p. 75).

99. This is not surprising for 'in Norfolk . . . Puritanism was predominantly an urban phenomenon', being largely confined to Norwich, Great Yarmouth and King's Lynn. C. Holmes, *The Eastern Association in the English Civil War* (Cambridge, 1974), pp. 17–18.

100. This and Tables 13 and 14 refer to heads of families. For sources regarding religion see Blackwood, *Lancs. Gentry*, p. 36 fn. 196–97.

101. The following families, erroneously considered Anglican in my *Lancs. Gentry*, have now been established as Roman Catholic: Baylton of Barnacre, Girlington of Thurland, Middleton of Leighton, Mort of Preston, Robinson of Old Laund.

102. For sources regarding religion see Blackwood, *Suffolk Rev.* n.s. xviii, 14 fns 42 & 44.

103. Main sources for names of Puritans are J.T. Cliffe, *Puritans in Conflict* (1988); K.W. Shipps, 'Lay Patronage of East Anglian Puritan clerics in Pre-Revolutionary England' (unpub. Ph.D. thesis, Yale Univ., 1971); *Journal of House of Commons*, ii. pp. 52, 54, 165, 437–38; *A Collection of all the public Orders, Ordinances and Declarations of both Houses of Parliament*, ed. Edward Husband (1646), pp. 129, 133. For names of Roman Catholics see PRO, Exchequer, Lord Treasurer's Remembrancer, Recusant Rolls, Pipe Office Series, E 377/49, fols 128–29; King's Remembrancer, Lay Subsidy Rolls, 1641, E 179/153/617;/153/619; BL, Additional MS.5508 (Accounts and papers relating to sequestered estates 1642–8); *Calendar of Proceedings of Committee for Compounding*, 5 vols (1889–92), supplemented where necessary by original records in PRO, SP 23. For both Puritans and Catholics see Ketton-Cremer, *Norfolk*, passim.

12

LAND SALES AND REPURCHASES IN YORKSHIRE AFTER THE CIVIL WARS, 1650–70

P.G. Holiday

T he years immediately following the second civil war saw the country almost swamped by a wave of land sales unparalleled since the dissolution of the monasteries. The victorious parliament sold off all the property it had confiscated in a vain attempt to achieve solvency and settle its mounting debts.[1] First the estates of church and crown were put up for sale and knocked down to the highest bidders. Such a move had not been totally unexpected – what did surprise many contemporaries was the subsequent confiscation and sale, in the early 1650s, of the estates of well over 700 royalists, many of whom were minor landowners of no political significance whatever, whose sole crime was in most cases that of combining Catholicism with delinquency.[2]

These confiscations and sales were condemned in no uncertain manner by the cavalier propagandists. Royalist pamphleteers related how parliamentary profiteers, speculators and 'carpetbaggers' had acquired the confiscated estates, often making quick profits by reselling the lands, whilst the delinquent ex-owners starved. They pictured the dispossessed royalists being forced by economic pressures to surrender their legitimate titles to the new landowners in return for a pittance on which to live.

The 1660 Restoration settlement was equally attacked for its failure to redress the situation. Estates were not merely handed back to their pre-war owners – the royalists had to prove their titles at law. Some had, under duress, surrendered this equity of redemption; others could not afford the legal expenses involved, whilst those who did eventually recover their estates were often financially crippled as a result of their Interregnum losses and had to resell their property almost immediately.

This, then, was the gloomy picture of the middle decades of the seventeenth century painted by the royalist historians – one of parliamentary speculators retaining their ill-gotten gains and stepping to profit and power over the economic corpses of their late opponents:

There were in Yorkshire a hundred families extinct or undone, so that none of them could appear again as gentlemen. Death, plunder, sales and sequestrations sent them to another world or beggar's bush, and so all – or most shires. I verily believe that, in the quarrel of the Two Roses, there was never half as many gentlemen slain, and so many base men, by the others loss and slaughter, made gentlemen.

and

From pardons which extend to woods,
Entitle thieves to keep our goods,
Forgive our rents as well as bloods,
God bless, etc.

From judges who awared that none
Of our oppressours should attone
(The losses sure were not their own),
God bless, etc.

From duresse, and their dolefull tale,
Who, famisht by a lawless sale,
Compounded it for cakes and ale,
God bless, etc.[3]

For many years this interpretation was accepted by the majority of historians: for example, John Lingard, writing in the early nineteenth century, described the situation in these words:

Since the year 1642, a considerable portion of the landed property in every county had passed from the hands of the original owners into the possession of new claimants . . .[4]

The records of the Committee for Compounding,[5] calendared towards the end of the nineteenth century, seemed to endorse this analysis of the situation. H.E. Chesney examined the sales of confiscated royalist land listed in the Committee's files, and noted the frequency with which the same names appeared over and over again as purchasers: he concluded, not unreasonably, that a number of prominent speculators were at work.[6] He paid less attention to the land settlement at the Restoration, which he saw as 'a triumph for the "new men" – . . . business men who had thriven under the Commonwealth'. Nevertheless Chesney calculated, from the evidence then available, that 'the returns of Crown lands up to 1667 would seem to indicate that many [of the confiscated royalist estates] were not returned'.[7]

Dr Joan Thirsk was the first to challenge this analysis of the problem in any detail. From a thorough study of the situation in the south-east, she pieced together the histories of fifty cavalier families and showed that, whereas on the one hand approximately 25 per cent of the royalists recovered their estates within a few months of confiscation and sale (generally by direct repurchase from the Trustees,[8] through intermediaries), the ultimate recovery of confiscated property at the Restoration, though by no means a foregone conclusion, was usually achieved, although it could be a very costly and long-drawn-out affair.[9]

Dr Thirsk's findings have emphasized the need for further detailed regional investigations into the whole land situation during and after the Interregnum. This article describes the fortunes of the 61 members of the Yorkshire royalist gentry whose estates were confiscated and sold in the years following the civil wars, and attempts to show to what extent the fate of the Yorkshire gentry can be compared with that of their royalist brethren in the south.

The idea of the confiscation of royalist property was not a new one. The Committee for Compounding had suggested it in 1644 as the punishment for all those delinquents who neglected to surrender to parliament and compound for their delinquency. Compounding involved the payment of a heavy fine: royalist estates were seized and only returned to their original owners when half the fine had been paid and sufficient security given for the remainder. In this way parliament hoped to pay for the war with money levied from its erstwhile enemies.

But 2 types of royalist were not permitted to compound – certain named cavaliers who had been the king's principal military and political advisors[10] and the Catholic royalists. The estates of these delinquents remained sequestered (administered by parliament) and their revenues were paid into the central treasury at Haberdashers' Hall.

Despite parliament's expectations, the punitive fines extracted from the royalists proved wholly inadequate as a means of settling the government's mounting debts, especially when these were alarmingly increased with the expenditure resulting from the second civil war.[11] The pressing demands of the government's creditors became more and more urgent as the bonds issued as security for state loans (public faith bills) spiralled down in value on the open market. Eventually parliament was forced to realize some of its capital assets, and its considerable reserves of confiscated property were sold to meet immediate financial needs. From 1649 to 1651 the market was flooded with land as the capitular, royal, crown and ecclesiastical estates were disposed of. When this had been accomplished, parliament turned to the still-sequestered estates of the delinquents: after a few months grace during which the royalists who had not yet paid all their fines were allowed to do so, the estates of the remaining cavaliers still in government hands were confiscated and thrown on the market.

Three acts were passed authorizing the confiscation and sale of these lands – the first one on 16 July 1651, a second on 4 August 1652 and the third on 18 November 1652. They listed 71, 29 and 680 names respectively.[12] The first 2 acts were mainly concerned with the estates of the more prominent cavaliers:

the third act, however, indiscriminately confiscated the lands of hundreds of minor royalists. The vast majority of the victims of this final proscription were Catholic delinquents – those who would normally have been permitted to compound had it not been for their religion – together with a handful of royalists who had been unable (or unwilling) to pay their composition fines. Many of these cavaliers were men of no political or economic significance. The government was thus faced with the problem of disposing of a multitude of minor estates scattered all over the country (although the majority lay in the north and west: of the 680 people named in the third act, 407 lived in the 6 northern counties and a further 77 in the 4 counties of the south-west).[13]

The sales were controlled by seven trustees, sitting at Drury House. They nominated surveyors, who were to appraise the size and value of the confiscated properties. When their reports had been checked and registered, a copy of the survey (but not the valuation) was posted publicly, and after the 30 days' pre-emption granted to tenants by the acts of sale, contracts were made with the highest bidder, subject to the bid meeting the minimum purchase price established by parliament. This was originally set at 10 years' purchase, although it fluctuated to some extent according to the state of the market.

The machinery set up to administer the sale of royalist lands worked fairly smoothly, for by 1651 the government had acquired considerable experience in the disposal of confiscated estates.[14] Prospective purchasers were guaranteed a secure title by parliament, and to prevent any subsequent disputes over the property, a body called the Committee for Removing Obstructions was made responsible for hearing all claims. If it was satisfied as to their validity, the allowances (whether to dependents, creditors or heirs) were paid either from the receipts of the sale or by granting part of the estate to the claimant in full satisfaction of his claim. Although such matters were normally settled before the estate was put on to the market, there were instances where the property was sold still charged with liabilities, due allowance being made for these in the purchase price: for example, the manor of Marricke was sold for £2,126 13s. 1d. on condition that the purchasers adopted £4,277 19s. 6½d. worth of debts on the property.[15]

In several cases the sales of estates were delayed due to the difficulty in sorting out the various claims and counter-claims of creditors, heirs and relations. Even after this had been completed, the trustees still had to disentangle the estates which could be sold from those which could not (by no means an easy task when estates held in many different forms of tenure had long been administered as a single unit). For example, rectories and impropriate church properties were excluded from the sales, being transferred to the Committee for Plundered Ministers in a laudable attempt to increase incumbents' salaries.[16] Some estates were reserved for various officials or were granted away as rewards for war services or in lieu of salary.[17] Other provisions in the acts of sale safeguarded the rights of the royalists' families: entailed property could only be sold for the lifetime of the delinquent concerned, and reverted to his heirs upon his death.[18] And (although not specifically mentioned in any of the acts) it appears that copyhold land was also excluded from the sales.[19]

Despite the difficulties in settling the claims and counterclaims of creditors, dependents and others, the Drury House trustees were usually able to offer the estates for sale within a few months. But before the land could be put on the open market, the acts of sale required that the sitting tenants should be allowed thirty days' pre-emption in which to purchase the property. The third act extended this facility further: in order to expedite the disposal of the multitude of small estates, parliament, with its own novel mixture of opportunism and social justice, allowed the delinquents themselves to compound for their forfeited lands at one-third of their capital value – in other words, at 6 years' purchase. (A Commons' resolution granted the same terms to the victims of the second act of sale, but it is not certain whether this was put into effect.) The majority of the delinquents were therefore granted the opportunity of regaining their estates at a cost which, though considerable, was certainly substantially less than the minimum purchase price established by the acts of sale.[20]

This article is concerned with the fate of those members of the Yorkshire gentry who suffered from the acts of sale: 61 cavaliers, representing 54 families. 50 of these gentlemen were Catholics, royalists who had been disabled from compounding solely because of their religion.[21] Between them, these 61 cavaliers owned 211 estates – 103 manors and 108 other parcels of land. These holdings varied in size from the great domains of men like Sir Henry Slingsby (who owned 8 manors and at least 4 other properties) to insignificant estates, such as the few acres in Ripon belonging to Miles Newton. Irrespective of the size or importance of their patrimonies, however, virtually all the royalists (like their brethren in other counties) endeavoured to recover their property as soon as possible.

Because the royalists refused to accept the confiscations passively, it is extremely difficult to analyze the sales of land without discussing the question of recovery in parallel – the two were often part of the same operation. Indeed, many cavaliers opened their campaign for the recovery of their lands even before the sales took effect; the Committee for Removing Obstructions was inundated with claims from wives, children and other relations pleading entails, dowers, reversions and countless other special reasons why their property should not be confiscated and sold. As a result, only 185 of the 211 estates were eventually marked for sale. 12 estates – 3 manors and 9 other parcels of land – were completely discharged as their owners had died leaving entailed estates, and 14 other properties (5 of which were manors) were not sold because of the form of tenure by which they were held; although not discharged absolutely, the royalist ex-owner was permitted to remain a tenant of the still-sequestered lands and was not otherwise disturbed.[22]

Perhaps more significant is the fact that nearly half of the cavaliers whose lands were confiscated (29 out of the 61) had some type of reversionary claim recognized on their property. The estates of 15 were entailed, 7 had jointures settled on their lands, 5 more had large debts or mortgages and 2 were completely discharged because of various settlements. Of the 185 properties actually marked for sale, reversionary claims were allowed on 68 (35 manors and 33 other parcels of land) by the Committee for Removing Obstructions: such estates could therefore only be sold for the lifetime of the present owner, which obviously limited the value of the property in the eyes of an outside buyer.[23]

The majority of these entailed properties tended to be grouped in the hands of a few rich delinquents. For example, the Middletons' 7 manors were entailed, as were 7 out of Sir Henry Slingsby's 8, all 5 of Sir Philip Constable's and Thomas Tankard's 3. This fact made it all the easier for such royalists to take part in the sales and ensure that their lands would not be lost by the family.

The first move towards the wholesale recovery of confiscated property was taken during the 30 days' pre-emption period following the third act of sale. 13 royalists came forward to 'compound' for all their property, and 5 more compounded in part. As a result 13 manors and 16 other parcels of land passed straight back into the hands of their original owners on the payment of a fine equal to 6 times the annual value of the property.

It is significant that all but two of the above estates were held in fee simple and could thus have been sold in perpetuity. The exceptions were the dower of Mrs Frank from her first husband (which had been confiscated for the delinquency of her second) and the Constables' estates in Holderness, held under some complicated form of entail since the days of Henry VIII.[24]

Theoretically, those compounders who were recusants had to sell their recently-recovered estates within a year, or they became liable to the full weight of the new recusancy laws.[25] These demanded the sequestration of two-thirds of the recusant's estate: coming immediately after composition, such an act would simply bankrupt the unfortunate royalist. In actual fact, this regulation was never fully put into effect, and not one of the compounders was resequestered for his recusancy (although all but one were Catholics). Only 2 were ever proceeded against: their fines, recorded in the traditional manner on the Recusancy Rolls, were ridiculous undervaluations, and were apparently never paid.[26] Only one person sold his estate – John Constable of Kirkby Knowle, who (already heavily in debt) had been ruined by the cost of compounding.[27]

The case of Charles Thimelby of Snydal presents a typical example of composition in action. Within five months of his £2,084 fine having been set, the royalist was fully discharged. Soon afterwards he conveyed his whole estate in trust to John Wolstenholme and Thomas Stringer (close neighbours and friends and, incidentally, also ex-royalists), both to secure the debt incurred in paying the fine and to prevent any further resequestration. Thimelby received the incomes from his lands during the Interregnum, and also farmed his still-sequestered tithes in Snydal, Carlton and Tanshelf from the local commissioners for £54 a year. According to the 1655 Recusancy Roll, he was charged with popery and ordered to pay two-thirds of his income: this was estimated at £35 a year, less than a seventh of the correct amount. Thimelby's economic position was soon strengthened by careful estate management and the exploitation of all resources, and by 1660 he was well on the way to regaining his pre-war financial position.[28]

The 30-day pre-emption period for tenants and ex-owners was utilized almost exclusively by the royalists themselves. There were only three instances where a tenant took advantage of his pre-emptive rights. In each case the tenant had already purchased the property in question from its delinquent owner during the wars, and was merely securing his title (as uncompounded delinquents were theoretically not permitted to sell or transfer property).[29]

With the expiry of the pre-emptive period, those estates which had not been discharged or recovered by composition were offered for sale – 156 properties were involved (82 manors and 74 non-manors) belonging to 45 members of the gentry. Because of reversions, 42 per cent of these estates (35 manors and 31 other parcels of land) could only be sold for the lifetime of their late owners; this lessened their attractiveness as an investment, as prospective purchasers would indeed be gambling with fate in the hope of making a profit.

During the interim period between the confiscations and the actual sale of their lands, the cavaliers had not been idle. Many had made arrangements with friends, relations or lawyers for the repurchase of their property. Lord Fauconberg urged Sir Henry Slingsby to take such precautions:

> You are in the greate booke of selling Estates & manie frends your name had when it was voted against you, therefore let not your Estate be ruinated, nor your woods felled, etc.: but cum vp & sollicit it your selfe, & I am assured by one of your frends that yet it may be saved yf you came in time. Once againe let me desire you to cum vp spedily . . . [30]

When these estates were put on the market, therefore, there was an immediate rush of purchasers – not as speculators, but as agents and trustees for the late owners. Gilbert Crouch, John Rushworth, John Wildman, Robert Thorpe, John Fullerton, John Blount, Thomas Wharton: these and others came to the aid of the defeated royalists. Some of the agents specialized in property in one particular area of the country: for example, John Rushworth, a Northumbrian, acquired 21 properties in Yorkshire, Lincolnshire and Northumberland, whilst Gilbert Crouch, also of northern origin, purchased 38 estates in the North (31 of which were in Yorkshire and the north-east). John Wildman, however, acquired over 40 properties, large and small, scattered throughout 24 counties, and

Samuel Foxley was equally unselective, his 29 purchases representing 13 counties. Almost every major agent dealt with some lands in the North, for well over half of the confiscated estates lay in this region of the country.[31]

Chesney saw these men as speculators, making substantial profits from the waves of land sales;[32] in fact, they were doing exactly the opposite – they were *preventing* a land revolution by enabling the cavaliers to recover their property. Altogether, speculators played a surprisingly small part in the Yorkshire sales: they were at a distinct disadvantage, in that the ex-owners, having an intimate knowledge of the estates, knew the exact value of the property and the scope for improvement. It was only in cases where the royalist was unwilling or unable to bid for his own estate that speculators and outside buyers were able to acquire land.

In all, 105 properties (56 manors and 49 non-manors) were regained immediately through the services of friends, relations or agents. This figure represents over 67 per cent of all the land finally sold – a staggering proportion.

It is significant that these direct repurchases involved the entire estates of 24 delinquents and part of the lands of a further 4. In other words, recovery by trust purchase was not an unco-ordinated attempt by the royalists to save scattered parts of estates, but was a carefully planned exercise by which those who could raise the necessary money regained all their property in one single manoeuvre. The price involved – 10 years' purchase or more – was certainly high, but by retrenchment, careful estate management and the forcing up of rents the majority of the cavaliers seem to have been able to repay the debts and mortgages incurred as a result of repurchase.

The majority of such estates were recovered through agents, usually London lawyers and merchants, men who had connections with the London money market and who were well placed to negotiate with the Drury House trustees. Crouch, Rushworth, Wildman, Foxley: the same people feature again and again in the records of the sales. Crouch and Rushworth played a very prominent part in the Yorkshire sales, purchasing 53 properties either separately or in conjunction with other agents. Altogether these London buyers were responsible for the recovery of 81 properties.

A further 21 estates were regained through the activities of local people: it is interesting to note that 7 of the 12 purchasers involved were ex-royalists! Three more properties were recovered by the son of the delinquent concerned.

There is little doubt that contemporaries realized what was happening – for instance, Lucy Hutchinson arraigned Wildman as ' . . . a great manager of papists' interests'.[33] Parliament was content to accept the situation as it existed, and made no attempt to prevent the purchase of confiscated lands by agents. The Drury House trustees were most likely well aware that they would have faced great difficulties in disposing of many of the smaller estates, especially those which were entailed, had not the royalists (or their representatives) been able to come forward as purchasers. In any case, parliament had already conceded the principle by permitting some of the royalists to compound for their lands in the thirty days immediately following confiscation.

The success of these trust purchases naturally depended upon the financial stability of the estate in question, for it was the delinquent ex-owner who had to raise the purchase price, usually by a mortgage on his property. It appears that a considerable proportion of the money received by the Drury House trustees was in the form of 'doubled bills'.[34] This may well account for the absence of speculators and City financiers from the sales of northern estates;[35] they could make substantial (and probably equally lucrative) profits by lending money to the delinquents (especially if the money was partly in the form of public faith bills, acquired on the black market at deflated rates) without tying up their credit in a questionable title.

One family which apparently paid part of the cost of repurchasing land in these government securities was the Slingsbys of Scriven. Sir Henry's lands were nearly all entailed, and could therefore be sold for his life only. They were repurchased by his nephew, the republican merchant Slingsby Bethell, acting in conjunction with Robert Stapleton. Bethell wrote to his uncle that the estate ' . . . cost six yeres purchase, and . . . the whole as contracted for with the State amounts to £11,220 16s. 7d., which I reckon is money £6,400'. In other words, the rest of the purchase price would be paid in public faith bills. As half the money had to be paid before the estate could be handed over, several purchasers settled their accounts as quickly as possible in order to gain the Lady Day rents. Here again we meet the able financier Slingsby Bethell: 'We haue for payment eight weekes for the first halfe, and six moneths after for the second moyety, But because it is our design to saue lady-dayes rents, and if wee will doe that wee must pay in our first payment before the 25th Mche, I haue therfore made use of my credit . . . '.[36] Other purchasers adopted the same system – during 1653 there was a significant rise in the number of settlements made immediately prior to each rent day.[37]

Not all the cavaliers who attempted to recover their lands saw their efforts crowned with success; their failure was generally the result of financial difficulties. Robert Doleman of Badsworth engaged John Rushworth to purchase his forfeited property, but found himself unable to raise the necessary money. In order to regain part of his estate, he surrendered his title to the rest: Rushworth still acted as purchaser, but merely transferred his allegiance to John Bright of Carbrook, an up-and-coming parliamentarian who bought the title from Doleman, and subsequently acquired the lands themselves from the trustees through Rushworth's services.[38]

But most of the royalists who recovered their estates through trust purchase succeeded in holding on to their lands. Sir Philip Constable of Everingham, who had already recovered some land in Holderness through composition, raised a loan of £12,488 on the security of his estates to cover both the purchase price of his confiscated lands (over £7,500) and his own personal debts. Most of the money was borrowed from London merchants, a large part apparently in public faith bills. Once the estate had been recovered, Rushworth (the Constables' agent) acting as manager, 'improved' the property: the income from some of the lands rose by as much as 40 per cent in the next few years. Part of the huge debt was translated into personal annuities, either for life or for a specific term of years. For 20 years the Constable estates were saddled with mortgages (it was only in the 1670s that the debts and annuities were finally discharged), but all this was achieved without the sale of more than one small piece of land.[39]

The remainder of the confiscated estates – 51 in all, belonging to thirteen delinquents – were not immediately redeemed, but fell into the hands of parliamentary grantees (5 properties), creditors (18) or independent purchasers (28 estates). The grantees were all loyal parliamentarians who received property as compensation for their sufferings during the war. 16 of the estates which fell to creditors were so heavily indebted that nothing remained to be sold after the claimants had been satisfied (and in the case of Sir George Ratcliffe's lands, the property was insufficient to meet all the claims). The 2 remaining properties which devolved upon creditors were bought from the Drury House trustees by the mortgagees, who had their debt allowed for in the purchase price.

Few of the independent purchasers seem to have been large-scale buyers or speculators, although 2 had previously been involved in the purchase of confiscated church property.[40] 13 estates went to Yorkshire buyers, 11 to Londoners and the remainder to non-local provincial gentry. It is impossible to generalize on the motives of these purchasers – some may have been minor speculators, but the majority appear to have been acquiring land as a personal investment or as an appendage to their existing estates.

It is interesting to compare the results of the sales in Yorkshire with those in the South-East. Over 67 per cent of the 156 Yorkshire estates actually sold by parliament were immediately recovered, nearly 12 per cent went to creditors, 3 per cent to parliamentary grantees, 8 per cent to local buyers and just under 10 per cent to non-local purchasers. In the area covered by Dr Thirsk's survey, however, only 25 per cent of the lands were immediately recovered, whereas 11 per cent went to creditors, 11 per cent to grantees, 36 per cent to local purchasers and 17 per cent to non-local people.[41]

There were several factors which may have contributed to this difference in the proportion of estates recovered by the cavaliers. The South-East had been fairly loyal to parliament, whilst Yorkshire was essentially royalist (there were several instances where ties of blood, transcending party loyalties, mitigated the worst effects of the parliamentary legislation). A number of the royalists examined by Dr Thirsk were prominent people who were in exile, with therefore limited opportunities to contract for their property. Lands near to the capital also offered a much more attractive bargain to prospective London speculators than scattered estates in the provinces. And it must be noted that Dr Thirsk's survey includes a substantial amount of land in London, where tenants of individual properties were quick to exercise their pre-emptive rights.[42]

We must now turn to the fate of those royalists who had been unable to retrieve their estates directly from the Drury House trustees. Faced with the loss of their lands to a creditor or independent purchaser, some cavaliers simply gave up the struggle. 5 delinquents surrendered the title of all or part of their estates to the new owner: thus 10 properties passed irrevocably into the hands of their commonwealth purchasers. Such settlements, though made under the pressure of acute financial distress, were regarded as being legally 'voluntary'; thus, at the Restoration, the property in question remained in the hands of its new landlords.

But one family had the good fortune to repurchase the majority of its lands from their commonwealth buyers. The Plumpton family estates had all fallen to creditors (1 estate) or independent purchasers (2 properties), but the delinquent's grand-daughter, Jane, still held the title to the 7-year leases issued in 1652.[43] The income from these leases (which was all that the commonwealth purchasers would receive until their expiry in 1659) was considerably less than the 1653 valuation on which the sale had been based, so that the new owners found that they had no immediate opportunity to recoup the considerable outlay involved in purchasing the estates.

Old Sir Edward Plumpton took full advantage of this situation; he placed the management of the estates in the hands of William Worthington, whose son was soon to marry the eldest of the Plumpton children. Worthington gradually repurchased all the family estates, although the property which had fallen to creditors was soon resold to pay pre-war debts. By 1660 the whole of the family domains had been recovered, but only by raising huge loans, the interest on which swallowed up most of the annual revenue. Slowly the estate recovered, a process which took over 30 years, and which was no doubt helped by the entail drawn up by Robert Plumpton, under the terms of which anyone attempting to sell any part of the property immediately forfeited all interest in the estates.[44]

The months prior to the Restoration saw a period of considerable doubt and confusion, made all the more chaotic by the rapid decline in the powers of the local committees after mid-1659. Dispossessed royalists and parliamentary purchasers alike squabbled over disputed estates, the one trying to gain control of the property and the other attempting to acquire a secure title. The royalists clamoured for compensation for their losses, sometimes using force to recover their lands. Such disturbances eventually led the king to urge all claimants to observe the *status quo* 'till Our Parliament shall take Order therein, or an Eviction be had by due Course of Law'.[45]

But the settlement of the land question proved to be much easier to promise than to perform. Clearly no one simple formula could reconcile the rival parties and procure an equitable solution. The confiscations could of course be legally reversed, but some of the forfeited estates had already been resold by their original purchasers, so that any general restoration of land would penalize innocent people who had acquired the property in good faith, whilst leaving the original commonwealth purchasers with a handsome profit.[46] Nor would such a solution help those cavaliers who had voluntarily sold their title, or who had been able to recover their property only as a result of extensive borrowing leading to a crushing mortgage. There was also the problem of how voluntary sales (sales not directly the result of confiscation) could be reversed, for some of those who had amassed a fortune in land by purchasing property from bankrupt royalists were in fact royalists themselves.[47]

The problem of devising a comprehensive formula to settle the land question defied the efforts of parliament, and the eventual solution was a compromise. The acts of the Interregnum governments (and thus the confiscations and sales) were invalidated, although transactions entered into voluntarily by 2 people were recognized as legitimate. Dispossessed cavaliers could therefore retrieve their patrimony through the due processes of law, provided they had not alienated their title and could afford the legal and other expenses involved.[48]

This settlement severely penalized 2 groups of royalists – those who had relinquished their equity of redemption without ever having recovered their lands and the delinquents who, after recovery, had been so embarrassed by debts that they had been compelled to resell their property almost immediately. 5 cavaliers (10 estates) came into the former category and 4 more (4 estates) into the latter. In the words of a Restoration ballad, they had sacrificed all future hope of regaining their lands 'for cakes and ale'. In general, these sufferers were the poorer cavaliers who, already in debt, had been ruined by the extra expenses attendant upon the civil wars. Unfortunately they were also the people who were least likely to benefit from the royal bounty after 1660.

Fortunately for Yorkshire, the land situation at the Restoration presented less of a problem than in many other counties. The fate of only about 30 per cent of the confiscated estates remained to be settled, for of the 185 properties marked for sale (i.e., not discharged prior to sale or composition), 29 had been compounded for, 105 repurchased at first hand, and 3 at second hand. Thus the future of a mere 48 properties remained undecided – although in 10 of these cases the full title had been relinquished by the former owner and thus, according to the terms of the Restoration settlement, the estate could not be recovered.[49]

Much of the litigation involving land in the early 1660s was therefore of a formal nature, as the complicated legal fictions which had protected estates in the past decade were unscrambled. For those who had retrieved their estates through agents, few problems arose. The ex-owner merely took over the legal possession of his property, and acknowledged the debts owing to those who had advanced money for the original repurchase. A few such estates were indeed resold due to heavy debts: for example, the lands of Marmaduke Cholmley and Sir Marmaduke Langdale prior to the Restoration, and those of William Bulmer and Laurence Sayer after 1660.[50] Such sales were, however, the exception rather than the rule.

Estates recovered by composition were equally secure. The guise of a 'sale' (to avoid resequestration) could now be abandoned, and the original owners took upon themselves the legal, as well as the *de facto* ownership of the property.

Some cavaliers were very fortunate, in that their estates reverted to them almost automatically. Grants of impropriate rectories and other church properties were negatived, and such estates returned to their former owners.[51] Property granted by parliament to the regicides and principal parliamentary leaders was also generally (though not always) returned to its ex-owner; in this way Sir Marmaduke Langdale recovered his 4 manors of Holme, Pigehills, Molscroft and Gatenby within 2 years of the Restoration.[52] These 4 had all been granted to leading parliamentarians; the fifth Yorkshire estate which had been granted away – that of Matthew Boynton of Barmston – cannot be traced after 1660.

In general, however, it was only in cases where the confiscated estates had been purchased by an agent or friend of the royalist that the post-Restoration transfer was accomplished in peace and harmony. Where the property was still in the hands of a creditor or independent purchaser (as happened in 43 cases) the invariable result was a lawsuit even where the royalist had already forfeited his equity of redemption.[53]

There were eighteen estates granted by the Committee for Removing Obstructions to creditors in settlement of their debts.[54] Here the chance of recovery depended upon the influence of the delinquent and his relations with the mortgagees. For the latter had generally acquired the property at a considerable undervaluation: the Drury House trustees sold an estate at between ten and fifteen years' purchase (for fee simple), whereas the normal estimate of the capital value of land was at least 20 times its annual revenue. Thus there was every incentive for the creditor to keep hold of the property he had acquired, by dubious means if necessary.

These 18 estates belonged to 6 delinquents; half of them were the property of one man, Cuthbert Morley of Seamer. In general, they were not recovered or, if they were, had to be resold soon afterwards to meet outstanding debts. All 6 cavaliers attempted to regain their estates – there was always the possibility that the Court of Chancery would rule that the interim profits (from 1653 to 1660) could be counted towards the repayment of the mortgage (as actually happened on one occasion). But the incidence of permanent recovery was not high; the 2 smallest landowners never redeemed their estates, 2 more succeeded in doing so and retained possession, whilst the remaining 2 cavaliers – Robert Plumpton and Cuthbert Morley – also recovered their patrimony, but had to resell almost immediately because of heavy debts (which, in the case of Morley, had been substantially increased by the costs of an 11-year lawsuit).[55] Of the 18 estates which went to creditors, only 8 remained in the hands of their original owners after the 1680s.

Where the confiscated estate had fallen to an independent purchaser, there were no guaranteed debts or other charges to complicate the recovery. Of the 28 properties which had originally been acquired by outside buyers, 2 (part of the Plumpton estates) had been recovered before 1660 and the title to 9 more had been surrendered by the lawful owner prior to the Restoration.[56] Unfortunately only 6 of the remaining 17 parcels of land can be traced: 4 were regained in 1660 and 2 were not redeemed: all of the former were later sold to pay the outstanding debts of their royalist owners.

Recovery was not merely an automatic operation, however. In many cases the royalist had to fight hard for his rights. There is no doubt that, in the early months of 1660, when the old forms of law and order were crumbling in the face of the impending Restoration, coercion was used as a means of re-occupying a lost estate. With a sympathetic county administration, the enterprising royalist could achieve much. No examples of the use of brute force have been recorded in Yorkshire, but the fact that the king had to condemn such practices shows that they were fairly widespread.[57]

Sometimes, no doubt, a tacit agreement was reached between the royalist claimant and the *de facto* owner or tenant. Cuthbert Morley's manor of Hawnby, bought during the Interregnum by Robert Dowker and Henry Pounall, was recovered in 1660, although the 2 commonwealth purchasers appear as tenants ten years later – a strong suggestion that an advantageous lease was offered in return for peaceful possession.[58]

When coercion was banned by royal edict, and where no settlement could be reached between the 2 (or more) claimants, recourse had to be made to the law. The royalist claimant could sue out a writ of trespass and ejectment, alleging that the present owner had gained possession by illegal means. As the confiscation and sales were now no longer recognized as legal, judgement would normally be for the plaintiff.

Cuthbert Morley attempted to retrieve his lands in Hawnby, Lackenby and Normanby in this way. He obtained a favourable judgement in the first 2 cases but John Hill, a lawyer who held the manor of Normanby, succeeded in delaying proceedings; this encouraged the tenants of the other 2 estates to sue out writs of error. It took Morley several months and a considerable amount of money before he redeemed his estates.[59]

In cases where the common law proved to be ineffective, the royalist could turn to Chancery or, in the last resort, to the House of Lords. The Court of Chancery had an added attraction in that it was empowered, in cases of this kind, to rule that the profits from the estate during the Interregnum should be awarded to the royalist ex-owner. But the law could be a very long and expensive method of recovering property, and more than one cavalier was left destitute and landless as a result of the clever manoeuvrings of his opponent.

Some of the more influential cavaliers by-passed the courts of law and gained immediate recovery by means of a private act of parliament. Although expensive and out of the reach of most royalists, it was far simpler (from the point of view of the large landholder) than suing many small purchasers or tenants in turn. As parliament was the highest court in the land, it also removed the danger of time and money being wasted on successive appeals.

The king, alarmed at the number of private acts before parliament, urged that 'the good old rules of law are the best security';[60] few bills were presented to parliament after this warning, one reason being that most of the richer and more influential royalists had already gained satisfaction. Only one Yorkshire gentleman recovered his estate through legislation – Thomas Radcliffe (son and heir of the late Sir George), whose bill was passed at the second attempt in 1661.[61]

The various cases cited above illustrate the difficulties involved in the redemption of confiscated property after the Restoration. The commonwealth purchaser often tried to delay a final settlement by legal manoeuvring, hoping that circumstances would force the impecunious royalist to surrender his title. Even where the property was recovered, legal expenses, added to debts accumulated during the civil wars and Interregnum, could have a very serious effect: of the estates actually recovered at second-hand from their commonwealth owners (either from creditors or from independent purchasers), 50 per cent were sold within ten years of the Restoration. In contrast, only 3½ per cent of the compounded lands and 16 per cent of those regained by direct repurchase had been resold by 1670. Thus the delinquents who had neither the resources nor the ingenuity to recover their property at once (and who had thus to suffer during the Interregnum in straitened financial circumstances) were far more likely to sink into economic decline than their most enterprising brethren.

The history of these 61 cavaliers illustrates the tenacity and financial resilience of the Yorkshire royalist gentry. 185 estates were confiscated and put up for sale; 134 were recovered within a few months. Of the remaining 51 properties, 5 fell to grantees and 18 to creditors (the royalists could not have recovered these directly in any case) and only 28 were lost through lack of initiative or a shortage of capital.[62] Even so, the vast majority of these 51 estates were eventually recovered by their ex-owners – only 15 of those which can be traced were lost for good. 10 were never redeemed because the title had been sold by the

LAND SALES AND REPURCHASES IN YORKSHIRE AFTER THE CIVIL WARS, 1650–1670

a Nature of sale (or repurchase) and to whom sold	b No. of estates involved	c No. of estates where title sold by owner prior to 1660, and therefore estate never recovered	d No. of estates recovered by the original owners prior to 1660	e No. of estates in cols. (d) which were later sold privately before 1660	f No. of estates recovered by the original owners after 1660	g No. of estates in cols. (d) and (f) which were sold privately after 1660	h No. of estates never recovered (excl. those listed in col. (c))	j No. of estates where the fate of the property is unknown
COMPOSITION	29	–	29	1	–	–	–	–
TRUST PURCHASE	102	–	102	2	–	14	–	–
DIRECT REPURCHASE (by royalist's family)	3	–	3	1	–	–	–	–
AWARDED TO GRANTEES	5	–	–	–	4	–	–	1
SOLD OR AWARDED TO CREDITORS	18	1	1	–	13	6	3	–
SOLD TO OTHER PURCHASERS	28	9	2	–	4	4	2	11
TOTALS	185	10	137	4	21	24	5	12

impoverished cavaliers, 3 remained in the hands of the creditors to whom they had been awarded and the remaining 2 fell to the step-sister of the original owner as the result of a family quarrel. The fact that several royalist estates changed hands was by no means due to the permanence of the commonwealth sales; rather was it caused by the after-effects of recovery: the burden of mortgages raised in order to repurchase the estate, heavy debts incurred as a result of living on credit during the Interregnum, lawsuits, and even such causes as riotous living and gambling! The royalists who suffered in this way were generally those who had been in an insecure economic position in 1642, or who had neglected to economize and improve their estates after the Restoration.

An example of the side effects of the confiscations is afforded by Robert Gale of Acomb Grange near York. A Catholic delinquent, he was not in a very healthy financial position on the eve of the civil wars. His estate was confiscated in the third act of sale, but Gale recovered it at the Restoration. However, the cost of recovery, when added to his pre-war debts, reduced him to the level of a pauper. He decided to sell his patrimony rather than mortgage heavily 'for ther is small pleasure in paying every halfe years rent for that which was my owne inheritance . . .'.[63]

Even some of those who regained their property immediately through the agencies of trustees occasionally failed to survive after 1660. The high cost of repurchasing land, when added to pre-war debts (and often post-war extravagance) terminated the landowning careers of several gentlemen. But such economic collapses were rarely attributable to the after-effects of the sale alone – there were usually other contributory causes, such as gifts to the king, high taxation, war damage, etc. The number of landowners who were ruined by the composition fines or land-repurchase charges *alone* was relatively small. The expense of recovering his estate proved to be the final blow to Laurence Sayer, who had 'bin totally ruined in his Estate for adhering unto his maj^te during the late Rebellion & being indebted unto severall *p*sons in severall greate & considerable somes of mony . . . ';[64] despite the accumulated effects of war damage, pre-war debts, and substantial monetary presents to Charles I, it was eighteen years before indebtedness finally forced Sayer to sell!

Of the 185 Yorkshire properties marked for sale, 158 were recovered, 15 were lost and 12 cannot be traced. These findings can be compared with Dr Thirsk's discoveries in south-eastern England. There, only 130 out of 179 properties can be identified; but 126 of these – 97 per cent – were recovered before or after the Restoration. In the case of Yorkshire the percentage is slightly less spectacular – 87 per cent of the identifiable estates were regained by the delinquents or their heirs.[65] But the result was the same in each case: the vast majority of the royalists redeemed their lands, even if some of them did have to sell their property soon afterwards.

The price of recovery could be extremely high: for those who compounded it was 6 years' purchase; for those who bought their lands through agents it was almost twice as much (and could be even higher), whilst recovery after 1660 could be equally expensive. The recovery of forfeited estates often resulted in heavy debts and liabilities. Only 15 properties were unredeemed, but 28 of those recovered had been resold by 1670. Nevertheless, approximately three-quarters of the confiscated estates were redeemed and remained in the hands of the families of their original owners well into the 1680s. The royalist gentry were a remarkably resilient group, and firmly resisted the adverse economic pressures of the time for as long as possible – with considerable success.

Notes

1. It had been parliament's original intention to use the profits from confiscated property as regular revenue – sale was only a final expedient forced on an unwilling government by its pressing creditors, and by the practical difficulties of administering scattered estates profitably. (At the same time, many royalists were also selling property in order to pay their composition fines.)

2. i.e., royalism. Most delinquents expected that a distinction would be drawn between property held by institutions (e.g., crown and church lands) and estates belonging to private individuals.

3. *A Royalist's Notebook. The Commonplace Book of Sir John Oglander*, ed. F. Bamford (London, 1936), p. 109, quoted by H.J. Habakkuk, 'Landowners and the Civil War', in *Economic History Review*, 2nd series, xviii (1965), p. 131. 'The Cavaleers Litany' (25 March 1660), in *The Cavalier Songs and Ballads of England from 1624 to 1684*, ed. C. Mackay (London, 1863), pp. 205–6. Other contemporaries, by no means all of them royalists, painted a similar picture.

4. J. Lingard, *History of England*, vii (London, 1829), p. 358.

5. *Calendar of the Committee for Compounding with Delinquents, 1643–1660*, 5 parts, ed. M.A.E. Green (London, 1889–92). This Committee, originally set up to raise money for the war, gradually developed as the authority which exacted the fines that the defeated royalists had to pay in order to recover their estates. It also informed the local authorities of the sales of confiscated royalist property, so that the lands in question could be desequestered and duly handed over to their new owners.

6. H.E. Chesney, *The Sequestration of Estates, 1643–60* (unpublished Ph.D. thesis, University of Sheffield, 1928), ch. viii, passim; Chesney, 'The Transference of Lands in England, 1640–60', *Transactions of the Royal Historical Society*, 4th series, xv (1932), pp. 190–7.

7. Chesney, *T.R.H.S.*, 4th ser., xv, p. 210. Chesney guessed that some purchases were made on behalf of the royalist ex-owners, but greatly underestimated the extent of these negotiations.

8. The Drury House Trustees, also called the Treason Trustees, were the 7 men responsible for handling the sale of confiscated royalist property.

9. I. Joan Thirsk, *The Sale of Delinquents' Estates during the Interregnum and the Land Settlement at the Restoration* (unpublished Ph.D. thesis, University of London, 1950); Thirsk, 'The Sales of Royalist Lands during the Interregnum', *Ec.H.R.*, 2nd ser., v (1953), pp. 188–207; Thirsk, 'The Restoration Land Settlement', *Journal of Modern History*, xxvi (1954), pp. 315–28.

10. These people had been excluded from the several 'peace treaties' presented to the king during the latter months of the war – for example, the Propositions of Uxbridge and of Newcastle. See *The*

Constitutional Documents of the Puritan Revolution, 1625–60, ed. S.R. Gardiner (London, 1958), pp. 275–86, 290–306.

11. The fines and the extent of their effect on the delinquents are discussed by H.J. Habakkuk, 'Landowners and the Civil War', *Ec. H.R.*, 2nd ser., xviii (1965), pp. 130–51, and by P.G. Holiday, *Royalist Composition Fines and Land Sales in Yorkshire, 1645–65* (unpublished Ph.D. thesis, University of Leeds, 1966), chapters 2, 3, and 7.

12. *Acts and Ordinances of the Interregnum, 1642–60*, ed. C.H. Firth and R.S. Rait (London, 1911), ii, pp. 520 sqq., 591 sqq., 623 sqq. Most authorities, whilst citing Firth and Rait, incorrectly give the numbers as 73, 29 and 678.

13. Lancashire = 213; Yorkshire = 118; Northumberland = 30; Durham = 20; Cumberland = 15; Westmorland = 11. In the south-west, Somerset = 34; Devon = 20; Dorset = 13; Cornwall = 10. The 680 names do not actually represent 680 people: the names are listed by county, and duplication occurs where a royalist held land in more than one county. It is unfortunately impossible to cross-check each name and arrive at an authentic total.

14. A detailed description of the organization and prosecution of the sales is given in Thirsk, *Ec.H.R.*, 2nd ser., v, pp. 188–207. See also the terms of the individual acts (fn. 12 above).

15. Sale of 13 July 1654, Public Record Office, Chancery, Close Roll C.54/3785 no. 40.

16. Firth and Rait, *Acts and Ordinances*, ii, p. 524.

17. For example, Laurence Maidwell received half of the Morley estates; Firth and Rait, *Acts and Ordinances*, ii, pp. 540–1.

18. Such settlements had to have been made prior to 20 May 1642 in order to be recognized by the Committee for Removing Obstructions; Firth and Rait, *Acts and Ordinances*, ii, pp. 593, 643.

19. Legal advice on the position of copyhold property to Sir Henry Slingsby; Yorkshire Archaeological Society, Slingsby MSS, DD 56/107.

20. *The Parliamentary or Constitutional History of England*, xx (London, 1763), p. 91; *Journals of the House of Commons*, vii, p. 156; Firth and Rait, *Acts and Ordinances*, ii, pp. 644–7.

21. Although in the early 1650s the government actively considered allowing Catholic delinquents permission to compound (and some even had their fines set), the harsher policy of confiscation and sale finally prevailed. All proceedings before the Committee for Compounding involving Catholics were simply discontinued, and thus these royalists, as uncompounded delinquents, were swept into the wide net cast by the third act of sale.

22. P.R.O. Index, 17349, f. 72; P.R.O. State Papers Supplementary, S.P. 46/107, Book i, pp. 192, 194.

23. For statistical purposes, I have only regarded an estate as having a valid entail or reversionary charge in cases where such a claim was actually allowed by the Committee for Removing Obstructions; in some cases, the Committee's decision is not recorded, and I have therefore assumed that no discharge was made. Thus the percentage of entails and claims is, if anything, an underestimate rather than an overestimate. A list of claims appears in P.R.O. Index, 17349, passim.

24. Frank: *Royalist Composition Papers*, ii, ed. J.W. Clay (Yorkshire Archaeological Society Record Series, xx, 1896), pp. 69–70; P.R.O. Index, 17349, f. 36. Constable: *Royalist Composition Papers*, iii, p. 88; Dom H. Aveling, 'Catholics and Parliamentary Sequestrations', *Ampleforth Journal* (June, 1959), p. 111.

25. According to the terms of the third act of sale.

26. P.R.O. Recusancy Roll, E.377/61. The debts are marked unpaid in 1660, yet the account books of the various local committees do not show the lands as having been sequestered in the meantime.

27. *Royalist Composition Papers*, iii, p. 60; *Victoria History of the County of York*, ed. W. Page, ii (London, 1912), p. 46; P.R.O., Feet of Fines, C.P. 25(2)/Bundle 614, Trinity 1654.

28. *Royalist Composition Papers*, iii, p. 59; leases in P.R.O. Commonwealth Exchequer Papers, S.P. 28/215; survey of estate – P.R.O. S.P. 23/G58, p. 48.

29. P.R.O., S.P. 23/G58, p. 11; P.R.O., C.54/3755, no. 6; *Cal. Committee for Compounding*, p. 1749.

30. Lord Fauconberg to Sir Henry Slingsby, 12 January 1650, in *Diary of Sir Henry Slingsby*, ed. Rev. D. Parsons (London, 1836), p. 343.

31. *Cal. Committee for Compounding*, passim. These 4 were the largest agents. Other less prolific buyers included Thomas Wharton of Grays Inn (related to the Whartons of Gilling, Yorkshire), who acquired 20 properties, all but 2 in the north, and Colonel Robert Thorpe, with 12 purchases. The remaining agents worked on a smaller scale, and did not specialize in any particular area of the country. It should be noted that, in this paragraph, the statistics refer to *purchases of whole estates* (which varied in size from one house to several manors) and not, as in the rest of the article, to individual manors or parcels of land.

32. Chesney, *T.R.H.S.*, 4th ser., xv, pp. 196–7.

33. Lucy Hutchinson, *Memoirs of the Life of Colonel Hutchinson*, ed. C.H. Firth (London, 1906), p. 282. 'Wildman's lack of any violent religious convictions enabled him to act, without worrying, in several business deals as an agent for Roman Catholic families'. (M. Ashley, *John Wildman, Plotter and Postmaster* (London, 1947), p. 72).

34. The government allowed the holders of public faith bills (debentures issued as security for loans to parliament), on payment of a sum equal to the original loan plus accumulated interest, to charge the whole amount against purchases of confiscated property. Habakkuk has calculated that a considerable portion of the government's income from the sale of confiscated royalist estates was in the form of doubled bills. See H.J. Habakkuk, 'Public Finance and the Sale of Confiscated Property during the Interregnum', *Ec.H.R.*, 2nd ser., xv (1962), pp. 71–4.

35. None of the independent purchasers, grantees or creditors involved in the purchase of Yorkshire estates seem to have acquired much confiscated property (either royalist, crown or ecclesiastical) on their own behalf. Edward Greene of Mattherne is the only person who can be regarded as a land profiteer – he also bought church estates. Greene acquired the Plumpton patrimony, but sold it soon afterwards.

36. Slingsby Bethell to Sir Henry Slingsby, 13 March 1651/2, in W. Wheater, *Knaresburgh and its rulers* (Leeds, 1907), p. 243.

37. See the list of the contracts for the sale of confiscated lands, and the dates on which the first halves of the purchase price were paid: P.R.O. S.P. 46/107.

38. P.R.O. C. 54/3748, no. 39 and C. 54/3663, no. 3; Sheffield Central Library, Bright MSS, BR 185 (b) v/112.

39. Aveling, *Ampleforth Journal* (June, 1959), pp. 111 sqq.; East Riding Record Office, Constable of Everingham MSS, DDEV/50/44, 48a.

40. Edward Greene of Mattherne and Thomas Redshawe of Ripon. Redshawe seems to have been related to a minor royalist family, but the actual link is uncertain.

41. Thirsk, *The Sale of Delinquents' Estates*, table iv, p. 130.

42. Thirsk, *The Sale of Delinquents' Estates*, chapter iii, passim.

43. P.R.O. S.P. 28/215 (list of seven-year leases from 25 Mar. 1652). Normally 7-year leases held by delinquents became null and void when the estate was confiscated, but the Plumpton leases were held by Jane (who was not a delinquent), and were therefore continued.

44. P.R.O. C. 54/3835, no. 31; 3832, no. 33; 3834, no. 14; 3841, no. 33; and 3965, no. 8; Leeds Archives Department, Gascoigne MSS, GC/E 10/1 (Plumpton Account Book), ff. 23, 29–30, 48, 51 sqq.; Borthwick Institute of Historical Research, York: Registered copies of wills, vol. 50, f. 211 (will of Robert Plumpton).

45. 29 May 1660, *Journals of the House of Lords*, xi, p. 46.

46. There does not appear to have been much traffic in confiscated property in Yorkshire, although an appreciable amount occurred in the South-East – Thirsk, *The Sale of Delinquents' Estates*, table of purchases at second and third hand, p. 168.

47. For example, the Wentworths of Woolley, loyal supporters of the king, made their fortune by acquiring lands from the Aldburghs, Brettons and Wheatleys, all cavalier families who had been severely hit by the civil wars and composition fines: Y.A.S. Wentworth MSS, DD 57/d/Old Deeds, ii, no. 361; *Yorkshire Archaeological Journal*, xii (1893), p. 162.

48. Detailed accounts of the protracted negotiations leading up to the Restoration settlement are given by Thirsk in *The Sale of Delinquents' Estates*, chapter vi, and in Thirsk, *Journal of Modern History*, xxvi, pp. 315–28.

49. This fact did not prevent the royalists from trying to retrieve their property. The 48 estates whose fate had yet to be decided comprised 5 which had been awarded to grantees, 17 which had fallen to creditors and 26 which were in the hands of independent purchasers. (The other 3 estates which had not been immediately recovered by their ex-owners – 1 of which had gone to a creditor and 2 to independent purchasers – were the Plumpton estates which had been regained at second hand prior to the Restoration.) Unfortunately, 12 of these 48 properties cannot be traced after 1660.

50. In all, 4 estates were sold prior to 1660 and 14 after that date, nearly all of them belonging to families who had been impoverished, were in a delicate financial position, or had had scarcely any capital resources in 1642.

51. *Journals of the House of Lords*, xi, p. 472 (19 May 1662); *Statutes of the Realm*, v (London, 1819), p. 420.

52. F.H. Sunderland, *Marmaduke, Lord Langdale* (London, 1926), p. 231; *V.C.H. Yorkshire, North Riding*, i, pp. 359–60; East Riding Record Office, Miscellaneous MSS, DDX/85/3. All the recipients of grants of confiscated property in Yorkshire were prominent parliamentarians whose estates were confiscated at (or soon after) the Restoration; this fact made it all the more straightforward for the ex-owners to retrieve their property.

53. Lawsuits even followed in cases where the equity of redemption had been voluntarily surrendered – e.g., the Chancery case of Richard Vincent, who claimed extenuating circumstances: *Cal. Committee for Compounding*, pp. 1291–2; P.R.O. Index, 17349, f. 76; P.R.O. C.54/3894, no. 4; P.R.O. Chancery petition, Whittington, C. 10/492/157.

54. 16 estates had been granted in full payment of debts; 2 more properties (late belonging to Marmaduke Frank of Knighton) had been bought by creditors, who had had their debts allowed against the purchase price. (One of these estates – that of Robert Plumpton – had already been recovered prior to 1660.)

55. Holiday, *Royalist Composition Fines and Land Sales*, pp. 364–71.

56. The tenth property, the title to which had been surrendered by the royalist ex-owner, was the estate of Richard Vincent which had fallen to a creditor, rather than an independent purchaser.

57. See above note 45.

58. P.R.O. C.54/3894, no. 5; *V.C.H. Yorkshire North Riding*, ii, p. 33; hearth tax returns for 1662/3 and 1670: P.R.O. E.179/215/451, E.179/216/461.

59. Historical Manuscript Commission, *Report*, vii, *House of Lords*, p. 147.

60. E. Hyde, *The Life of Edward, Earl of Clarendon*, i (Oxford, 1857), p. 576.

61. *Journals of the House of Lords*, xi, p. 188; *Journals of the House of Commons*, viii, pp. 269, 288; H.M.C. *Report*, vii, p. 135; *Statutes of the Realm*, v, pp. 319–20.

62. There is strong evidence to suggest that the principal reason why royalists failed to recover their property by composition or direct repurchase was a financial one. Of the 28 properties sold, 6 were very minor estates, 11 belonged to impoverished delinquents with no capital resources and little chance of raising a substantial loan, 3 to royalists who lacked the opportunity to recover their lands, whilst 2 fell to a relative who advanced a better claim at law.

63. Letter to Robert Shireburne at Everingham, 1661: East Riding Record Office, Constable of Everingham MSS, DDEV/1/36. Gale negotiated with Shireburne because both men were Catholics: 'I have a desire to bargain with you rather then any other in respect of being Catholicks'.

64. North Riding Record Office, *Meynell Calendar 'A'*, passim; P.R.O. C.54/3804, no. 19, 3781, no. 4; P.R.O. Chancery petitions, Hamilton division, C. 7/179/117; Bridges division, C.5/551/77; Collins division, C.6/51/80.

65. This excludes the estates recovered by composition, so that a direct comparison can be made with the lands covered by Thirsk's survey. If the compounded lands are included, the percentage of confiscated estates recovered in Yorkshire rises to over 91%.

NEWCASTLE AND THE NATION: THE SEVENTEENTH-CENTURY EXPERIENCE

Roger Howell, Jr.

T he interaction of local community and central government is one of the pervasive themes of the history of early modern England; it is also, from the standpoint of historical analysis, one of the most perplexing. While never wholly neglected, even by those historians whose focus was on broad national issues of constitutional or religious conflict, local history and the sense of local perspective have increasingly drawn the attention of those investigating the development of politics and political structures in Stuart England. The results have been stimulating and refreshing, and yet some key problems of interpretation remain. From a view of historical development that stressed the centrality of the court and parliament, there has been a marked shift of interest to the local political perspective, to the realization of the importance of local issues for the vast bulk of the political nation, and towards the view that political attitudes and actions were shaped more by local perceptions of developments than they were by abstract and general concerns with issues of economic, political, or religious liberty so beloved by an earlier generation of historians.[1] The change of emphasis has no doubt served as a healthy corrective, but what has not yet emerged is a satisfactory working model of the interaction of the two perspectives. If a history of seventeenth-century England written from the vantage point of Westminster distorts and exaggerates the picture, the replacement of it by a history written solely from the vantage point of the parish pump does little better. What one needs to know is the manner in which the local issues, local perceptions, and local problems shaped and informed the national perspective as they were expressed and generalized, for example, in parliament, and conversely how that sense of generality, which is so integral a part of the national perspective, was transferred and perhaps translated back into the framework and language of local politics.[2] That the flow of influence was not unidirectional seems obvious enough; conflict, for example, over a particular local clergyman influenced in major ways the locality's view of national religious policy, but in equally significant fashion a sense of national religious policy informed the locality's interpretation of its own particular situation.[3]

Newcastle in the seventeenth century provides a useful case study of the interaction of local community aspirations and perceptions with the broader issues agitating state and church throughout the century. The pattern of interaction was far from tidy or clear-cut; there were times when the interests of Newcastle coincided closely enough with the intentions of central policy to make a close working partnership seem appropriate and orderly, but equally there were occasions when the divergence became so marked as to raise questions not only about the specific application of policy to Newcastle, but also about the general nature of the policy itself. If there are threads to be found that run consistently through the whole story, they can perhaps be reduced to two. On the one hand, Newcastle, given its sizeable population and its obvious political, economic, and strategic importance, was always a natural area of concern for the central government, whether that government were king and parliament, king acting alone, parliament acting alone, or parliament and lord protector. On the other hand, the Newcastle reactions to such forms of solicitous attention were highly likely to be conditioned by local perceptions of the extent to which they reinforced or diminished the town's cherished sense of liberty and local authority. The stronger the impression of diminution of local liberty and authority, the greater was the possibility that specific local grievance would be translated into a generalized rejection of governmental policy, or, put in another way, the more likely it was that discussion of issues would rise above exclusively local concerns and begin to embrace the characteristics of the 'national' issues that dominate histories written from the perspective of the central government. While the consecutive history of the interaction of local and national affairs is beyond the scope of a single paper, a series of case studies drawn from one of the areas where the potential for conflict was high, namely the structure and functioning of local government including the election of members of parliament, can effectively illustrate the general nature of these relationships for the period between the accession of James I and the Glorious Revolution.[4]

The latter part of the sixteenth century had witnessed an intense struggle in Newcastle over issues related to the structure of local government. That struggle was basically the result of the increasing dominance in local affairs exercised by a small and exclusive clique of powerful merchants. Almost entirely composed of mercers and coal traders, the inner ring, or 'lords of coal'[5] as they were dubbed at the time, were already in a dominating position by the mid-Elizabethan period, well before their control was legitimated and firmly established by charters from the crown; in the period between 1581 and 1591, each of the major coal traders served a term as mayor of the town, eight of those so serving being directly involved in the management of the Grand Lease.[6] This process, by which power in the world of trade was extended directly to the political sphere, was not unresisted, and there was something in the way of a reform group in the 1590s which sought to preserve the rights of the general body of freemen in town government and to rescue what was conceived as the burgesses' share in the

Grand Lease from the private interests of the grand lessees. Though the reform movement succeeded in capturing the mayoralty in 1593, its success was neither impressive nor sustained.[7]

Two factors account, in the main, for the limited success of the reform group, and each has a bearing on the complex interaction of central and local government. On the one hand, the reformers were themselves in an ambiguous position. Hardly classifiable among the economically disinherited of Newcastle, they did not seek the destruction of a system of privilege and monopoly; their aim was the far more limited one of widening the inner ring to a slight degree to include others from the upper levels of town life. Yet as allies they could only expect aid from interests which sought a wider destruction of the privileges of the town; the Bishop of Durham and the Lord Mayor and chief traders of London were allies of precisely this stamp. It is not unreasonable to conclude that support of this kind probably did as much to curtail the activities and enthusiasm of the reformers as any overt opposition on the part of the inner ring itself.[8] On the other hand, the reform movement was also faced by a powerful coalition of interests in support of the growing stranglehold of the inner ring on Newcastle politics, for the aspirations of the lords of coal meshed closely with the drift of national policy. Generally speaking, both the Tudor and Stuart monarchs sought to obtain control of the governing bodies of the boroughs, and the most obvious way in which to pursue this policy was to remove the choice of those governing bodies as far as possible from the hands of the whole community of citizens.[9] Thus, at the start of the seventeenth century, crown policy and the desires of the dominant political group in Newcastle were in apparently total agreement. Local circumstances had led to the increasingly powerful position of a ring of related families with interests in the coal trade. They provided exactly the sort of tight and potentially dependent oligarchy that the crown was seeking, a dependency moreover that could be intensified by royal action to support the monopoly position of the Hostmen. The result of this close community of interest is to be found in the charters of Elizabeth I and James I to the town and to the Hostmen.[10]

The pattern of government thus established was to remain the political framework for seventeenth-century Newcastle, and political debate was to revolve around its preservation from change, either as the result of local initiatives to widen the base of power or as the result of royal desires to tighten the element of control even further. To forestall the first threat, the inner ring could call on royal support, since the crown had as substantial an interest in maintaining the tight monopoly control as the town oligarchs did; the problem was that recourse to such support from the central government raised the potential for increased royal interference in town affairs. What was, in its origins, a nice conjunction of interests could under stress become something quite different, and that realization obviously influenced in profound ways the interaction of Newcastle government with central government throughout the seventeenth century.

That the stranglehold of the inner ring on town government was the norm for the seventeenth century is graphically revealed by an analysis of town office holding. Such an analysis also reveals clearly that the key to the inner ring was simultaneous position of strength in both the Merchant Adventurers (particularly the Mercers) and the Hostmen, rather than a base in the Hostmen alone.[11] The latter company, it should be remembered, was accessible to any free burgess 'of any free mystery' by the charter of James I; the very fact that entry was 'open' in this manner meant that the company could not, by itself, serve as the screen that filtered membership into the inner ring.[12] On the other hand, the combination of membership in the Merchant Adventurers and the Hostmen was a striking feature of those who ruled the town throughout the seventeenth century.[13] Between 1600 and 1640, 28 different people held the office of mayor; of these 18 were both Mercers and Hostmen, and 8 others were members of other branches of the Merchant Adventurers and the Hostmen. The remaining two holders of the office were both Merchant Adventurers. Between the Restoration and the Glorious Revolution, 29 different men held the office of mayor; of these 27 were definitely members of the Merchant Adventurers, and at least 20 and probably 22 were also members of the Hostmen at the same time. The same sort of preponderance is seen in other aspects of office-holding as well; those who became sheriffs, both before the Civil War and after the Restoration, reflect the same affiliations, as do members of parliament for the town. It is striking, for example, that of the 8 different men who served Newcastle as a member of parliament from 1600 to the summoning of the Long Parliament, all were both Merchant Adventurers and Hostmen, and only one was not a Mercer.[14]

The omission of the years 1640–60 from the above analysis was both deliberate and significant. In the confused years of the Civil War and Interregnum, the pattern of inner-ring dominance was profoundly challenged. But if the overall nature of the interaction of central government and local government is to be appreciated fully, it must be recognized that there were other occasions outside those chaotic decades when challenges were raised in equally clear fashion. It should not be thought, for example, that the chartered establishment of inner-ring control shut off the sort of protest that had characterized town politics in the 1590s; instead it tended to intensify the cleavages that had marked that decade by making the successors of the reform group of the 1590s a dissident element within the corporation.

The Shrove Tuesday riot of apprentices in the town in 1633 reveals this clearly and also casts some useful light on the central problem under investigation, the interaction of the locality and the central government.[15] Ostensibly the riot had been caused by the construction of a lime kiln on the town drying ground by one Christopher Reasley, a non-freeman who had connections with the inner ring. It is clear, however, that Reasley was the pretext rather than the cause of the troubles, and it is striking that the representatives of the central government suspected this before the town authorities were willing to admit it was the case. Secretary Coke was already referring to the events as 'the late seditious riot' before the true circumstances surfaced.[16] What was actually at stake, as Coke shrewdly surmised, was the monopoly of the inner ring and the continuing desire of a reform element in the town to modify it. The surviving evidence suggests that the town authorities felt themselves to be in a somewhat ambiguous position with respect to the central government's interest in the affair. While they welcomed support of their position, they were reluctant to see that support extended to too close an enquiry into their affairs, and the mayor, at least, was clearly less than happy with Coke's suggestions that he should have taken more forceful immediate action; if nothing else, such reprimands appear to have suggested to those in Newcastle a lack of understanding on the part of governmental authorities of the nuances of the local situation.[17] When the real issues surfaced in June 1633 in the form of a petition from 700 or more burgesses to the King,[18] the inner ring was no doubt grateful for the support it received for its position from Charles I, although it seems that, from the perspective of the central government, the events looked rather more sinister than they did from the local perspective. In retrospect, it appears that the petitioners were well within the reform tradition that had been established in the 1590s. In that sense, they were, of course, of considerable concern to the inner ring. But crown authorities saw a deeper significance in the events, drawing attention to a growing population of mariners, colliers, keelmen, watermen and those of mean condition 'who are apt to turn everye pretence and colour of greivance into uproare and seditious muntinye'.[19]

Although the evidence is by no means unambiguous on this point, it appears that the town authorities, while desirous of royal support for their position, were concerned about the form that support might take in the deteriorating political conditions of the 1630s. The reform group was limited in their manoeuvring by essentially the same concern, for they too had no interest in lessening the independent privileges of the town, yet this is precisely what increasing reliance on the support of the central government might be thought to lead to. What was happening was that the politics of the town were increasingly complicated by the development of national politics as it became clear that opposition to the inner ring and opposition to the policies of Charles I did not always go hand in hand. This point can be illustrated by a number of circumstances. Opposition to the imposition of ship money, for example, tended to pull inner ring and reformers together; resistance appears to have been widespread, with the general body of burgesses rallying behind the inner ring in a determined effort to avoid payment after the first two levies.[20] Attempts by the crown to influence local elections were likewise sternly resisted. In 1639 the King expressly warned the town 'that they should be very careful in choosing the mayor for this next succeeding year and by no means admit any factious or seditiously affected person to that place'.[21] It is clear that his message was intended to forestall the election of Robert Bewick, a Puritan against whom he had been specifically warned.[22] Yet Bewick was elected and no trace of local discontent about the choice is to be found. That he did not owe his election exclusively to his Puritan opposition to the crown is obvious enough; he was a Hostman and Mercer, a previous holder of the mayoralty, and a member of the inner ring, but that he was elected against the express wishes of the crown is an equally obvious indication of the limits of inner-ring subservience to the crown, even at a time of apparently increased agitation over their position.

The municipal and parliamentary elections held within a short time of each other in 1640 provide further examples of the extent to which national politics and local political traditions interacted.[23] The swing in the municipal elections against Puritanism can be attributed to external factors, but not to the machinations of the crown, however helpful the results were for the crown's purposes. The Scottish invasion and occupation had been the critical factor, and the feeling had clearly grown up that Puritan religious sympathies with the Scots had been at least partially responsible for the occupation of the town.[24] The elections to the Long Parliament remain somewhat obscure, but one clear fact does emerge, and that is the widespread support for men of local connection. Of the three candidates who stood in the election, only one was thoroughly typical of inner-ring politics, Sir Henry Anderson, and he was returned unopposed. The other seat was contested between John Blakiston, whose close local connections were counterbalanced by the fact that he was not a powerful and wealthy Hostman and the knowledge that he was prominently identified with the Puritan movement, and Sir John Melton, a total outsider to town politics, Secretary to the Council of the North, and a pronounced Straffordian. If powerful external backing was sufficient for Melton to be elected on one return, it should be remembered that the proceedings in the election were under investigation for corrupt practices by the Committee for Privileges when Melton died and that it was subsequently decided simply to amend the return in Blakiston's favour, rather than hold a new election, a strong indication of the popularity of his candidacy in the original election. That an outsider to the inner ring and a Puritan to boot could achieve this level of support in a climate that was clearly anti-Puritan, while a court backer with powerful connections could not attract more significant support, even though aided by the fear that parliamentary reformers would assault the privileged position of the Hostmen, is a telling illustration of the power of local identification in the politics of the period.

The years of the civil wars and Interregnum were to see the pattern of Newcastle politics altered, at times by the application of external pressures.[25] On two occasions in those years, the rights of election of mayor were over-ridden by outside authority. In October 1642 Sir John Marley was elected by mandamus from the king; in 1645 he was removed from office by an ordinance of parliament and Henry Warmouth substituted in his place.[26] There were, in addition to these actions, various purgings of the town corporation reflecting the shifting fortunes of the war. In April 1643 Henry Warmouth was removed from his aldermancy for neglect of duty,[27] while the following September thirty-five freemen were disfranchised.[28] Following the reduction of the town to parliament, the chief royalists such as Marley and Sir Nicholas Cole were ordered purged by parliament.[29] Such interference in the normal life of the corporation is hardly surprising, given the conditions of the time, but it is not easy to come by evidence concerning the town's reactions to such exterior pressures, which they clearly would have resented and resisted under normal circumstances. What evidence there is, however, suggests that the existing structures of the town showed remarkable resiliency in the face of such pressures, and that, where changes did occur, they were at least in part the result of anticipatory changes stemming from town initiative rather than wholly imposed alterations from outside.[30]

The existence of a substantial and important core of town office holders who not only survived all changes in government but co-operated with each in turn is a case in point. Men whose roots were firmly fixed in the pre-Civil War corporate exclusiveness of the town continued to serve as active members of the corporation while Newcastle was held for the King, reduced by the Scots, subjected to parliamentary control and ultimately the control of the Lord Protector, and then returned to what was essentially its pre-war political condition at the Restoration.[31] The loyalties of such men might well seem baffling, both to the more zealous partisans of their own age and to subsequent generations of historians because, in a real sense, they had no fixed loyalties with respect to the large and complex questions that were agitating national politics. At the worst, they can be pictured as secular vicars of Bray; looked at in a more positive light, they are men whose concerns for the stability and smooth functioning of traditional local arrangements were paramount.

An analysis of the changes which actually were made during the period reinforces the impression of the persistence of local structures and rivalries, even in the face of intense pressures from outside, a persistence that is frequently disguised at first glance because of the patterns by which the labels of the 'national' struggle – royalist versus parliamentarian, presbyterian versus independent – were taken up by the participants themselves and super-imposed on the 'local' struggle. One certain result of the reduction of Newcastle to parliament was an alteration, extending throughout the Interregnum, in the old inner-ring control of town government. The new governing clique, led by Thomas Bonner and the Dawson family, appears to have established an impressive hold on the mayoralty;[32] in 1656 it was alleged that the Dawsons in collusion with Bonner had managed the election for mayor as they pleased for some years past,[33] and the results of elections seem to validate the allegation. But while the Dawsons had, in effect, ridden to power on the back of the parliamentary victory, they did not represent a totally new impulse in the politics of the town. They could trace their roots to the reform movement of the 1630s, and their behaviour in office was completely consistent with that line of descent. They had no interest in destroying the privileges of the town; their concern was to broaden the base of monopoly control only slightly to include themselves and their most immediate supporters. In practice they proved as uncompromising in their opposition to genuine reformers and as staunchly defensive of the charter rights and independence of the town as any of the older oligarchs they had for the moment displaced.[34]

Between the establishment of the parliamentary corporation in 1645 and the reshaping of town government in the aftermath of the Restoration, two aldermen were removed from office, and the circumstances surrounding their removals can be taken as further evidence for the persistence of local issues disguised in the terminology of national issues. The first to be removed was John Cosins in 1647,[35] although there is some ambiguity about the circumstances of his removal, the chief issue seems to have been the newly created ascendancy of the Dawson group. If Cosins was not a member of the inner ring, his repeated recourse to the town charter as the core of his attack on the Dawsons suggests that he was arguing the case of the inner ring or at least a case with which they could readily identify. Following Cosins' removal, his affairs became much entangled with broader national issues. Cosins himself was a conservative Presbyterian parliamentarian and in the context of a growing split between the Presbyterians and the Independents, exacerbated by disturbances in the army, his report that there was danger the town might be secured against the present government received excited attention in London.[36] But it should not be thought that the issues thus raised were the ones which had led to his expulsion, for it was not until the beginning of July, more than three months after his expulsion, that the Newcastle authorities raised the argument that Cosins intended to bring the Scots back into England, embroiling the nation once more in civil strife.[37] The impression that the root of the trouble was local and connected with inner-ring resistance to the Bonner-Dawson clique is further heightened by the minor riot following Bonner's election as mayor the next year; it was triggered off by the actions of Edmond Marshall, a servant and apprentice of Cosins, and appears to have had no connection with broader issues of national politics.[38]

The second alderman removed was Leonard Carr, and his case even more clearly reflects the general pattern which has been suggested. Carr was an established figure in the town and in most ways, other than his origins in Yorkshire, a person typical of inner-ring politics; he had become an alderman by 1642, had served as steward and governor of the Hostmen before the Civil War, and had been assistant and governor of the Merchant Adventurers in addition.[39] He had admittedly participated in the defence of the town in 1644,[40] but it is striking that no question of his loyalty appears to have been raised on the occasions of royalist scares in 1648, 1651, and 1655. But in 1657 articles accusing him of royalist sympathies were presented to the Council of State.[41] On close examination, the charges now appear to have been fabrications,[42] but they were sufficient to convince the Council of State; that body directed the mayor and Common Council to remove Carr, which was done on 28th December 1657.[43] The spurious nature of the charges against him and the fact that he was a sick man over eighty years old at the time of his removal suggest that this is something other than the case of an active and loyal corporation reporting on and with the help of the Council of State removing a dangerous royalist. When one realizes that Carr had been an outspoken opponent of the Bonner-Dawson clique,[44] questioning their management of elections and accusing them of extensive abuses of power, all the while continuing to hold an aldermancy and preventing the election to it of one of their own supporters, the whole episode assumes a quite different character and become an excuse to eliminate a person who was a problem in local affairs and to the Dawsons rather than in national affairs and to Cromwell. The election of a close supporter of the Bonner-Dawson clique, Ambrose Barnes, to fill the vacancy would seem to complete the picture.[45]

One final observation about the politics of Newcastle in the aftermath of the parliamentary victory needs to be made: despite a clear recognition on the part of parliament that the town corporation should be reshaped to serve new purposes and new loyalties, the overall form which that reshaping took appears to have been generated as much from below as from above. It is suggestive, for example, that there was a sizable time lag between parliament's naming of delinquents to be removed in March 1645 and the local enactment of their disfranchisement in late September 1645.[46] What is even more telling is the evidence which suggests that the parliamentary ordinance for settling the government of Newcastle confirmed an existing situation rather than created a new one. Details of how the town government functioned between the reduction of the town and the parliamentary ordinance are scanty.[47] Part of the resulting obscurity concerns the critical entry into aldermanic office of Henry Dawson and Thomas Bonner, but there is no doubt that they were occupying such places a month or more before parliament named them.[48] Likewise, one of the aldermen named in the parliamentary ordinance does not appear in the first list of the new corporation, nor for that matter in any subsequent list of town office holders, and it is surely more than coincidence that his place was assumed by a relative of Henry Dawson.[49] Bulstrode Whitelocke was later to assert that the House of Commons took order for settling the magistrates of Newcastle in violation of their charter;[50] on one level that observation was valid, but on another it was misleading. If the breaking of inner-ring control and the rise of the Bonner-Dawson clique constituted something in the way of civic revolution, it was a revolution which in key ways had been engineered from within Newcastle itself and the parliamentary role can more accurately be described as a confirmation of a situation already existing in the town.

The restoration of the monarchy in 1660 and the consequent purging of the corporation in 1662 allowed for the re-establishment of inner-ring control. But again, the process by which that control was established must be observed carefully if the delicate interaction of town affairs and central government actions is to be rightly understood. The task of investigation is complicated by the fact that no complete list of members of the town government exists for 1660–61 and thus tracing the changes in membership between 1659 and 1662 is difficult. But the only signed order for the mayoral year of John Emerson shows that at least one of the old inner-ring oligarchs, Sir John Marley, who had been purged in the 1640s, had re-established himself in the town government before the actual purging under the terms of the Corporation Act,[51] and there is some additional evidence to suggest that others in this category, Sir Nicholas Cole and Sir Francis Bowes among them, had done the same.[52] The actual purge of 1662 was a relatively limited affair, and again there must be a sizable suspicion that the impetus for the precise changes made came from within the town rather than from without. Five aldermen were removed, all clearly associated with the Bonner-Dawson group; five members of the old inner ring of pre-Civil War days replaced them.[53] Those whose early careers and family connections had cut them out for inner-ring politics survived, their activity in the Commonwealth and Protectorate corporation notwithstanding.

The Restoration, then, returned Newcastle politics to its normal seventeenth-century stance. The inner ring dominated, grateful no doubt for the general support of the monarchy, but anxious, as before, that this solicitous concern should not interfere in local rights and privileges under the guise of solidifying that support. The increasingly aggressive stance of the later Stuart monarchs towards the issue of royal control of boroughs made that sort of partnership in the long run impossible. The fine line between support and control had always made such conflict a potentiality; the policies of Charles II and James II made it a reality.

For the initial part of the reign of Charles II, the political situation in Newcastle appears to have been relatively settled, even though the activities and agitation of dissenters became a prominent part of the scene and inevitably had political overtones.[54] The town had been quick to make a loyal address to the restored monarch, expressing the hope that he would be the instrument to unite a divided church, compose a distracted kingdom, and ease an oppressed people.[55] In the heady atmosphere of the Restoration itself, aggressively overt royalism became the order of the day; at the parliamentary elections a health was drunk to the King and confusion to Zion,[56] while a number of tracts were locally published to stress the deep and continuing loyalty of the town.[57] For his part, the King in February 1664 by a charter of inspeximus confirmed the charters of Elizabeth I and James I with their ancient privileges.[58] As late as 1682, John March, the vicar of Newcastle, could express in a sermon the confident feeling that the magistrates of Newcastle and the monarchy were still working in a pattern of close co-operation, despite the many distractions that plagued national affairs.[59]

'This famous Town, over which you preside, has always been esteemed a place of very great importance . . . Now a Town of this importance, as it well deserves, so in such times of distraction as we live in, it may justly challenge the greatest care and vigilance of those that are intrusted with the Government of it. And I do heartily rejoice, that I need not fear the least imputation of flattery, whilest I proclaim to the world that as there is not any Town which can equal it for Trade, Populousness, and wealth, so there is none that doe Surpass it, and but very few that equal it in point of Loyalty and Conformity.

This Happiness and Glory we owe in great measure to that Loyalty and Conformity which shine forth in your own Examples; partly also to that great encouragement you give unto the Loyal and Orthodox Clergy of the place, but chiefly to the due exercise of your Authority, in surpressing Conventicles, those notorious Seminaries of Popery, Schism, and Rebellion.'

Despite these hopeful comments, a crisis was at hand in the relations between Newcastle and the central government. In the last years of his reign, as he sought to rule without parliament, Charles II escalated the pressure exerted by the monarchy on the boroughs, and Newcastle was one of the targets of that pressure. The precise nature of the intrigue and in-fighting that ensued escapes us at some key points, but the general outcome of the pressure was clear enough. The attempt to enforce confusing and ultimately unpopular royal policies through the manipulation of the corporation in defiance of its chartered rights led to a repudiation of the Stuart monarchy which the corporation had long claimed to support.

The first act in the unfolding crisis appears to have passed off with surprisingly little overt negative reaction. Early in 1684, Charles II signified to the corporation that he expected a surrender of their charter, 'which was to be renewed on condition that the mayor, recorder, sheriff, and town clerk might always be in the King's power to appoint or confirm'.[60] While the surrender was not enrolled, the King granted a new charter in 1685, in it constituting several new aldermen and reserving to himself the power to displace the mayor and aldermen at his pleasure.[61] The charter itself did not reach Newcastle until after the death of the King; the proclamation of James II and the arrival of the charter fell within two days of each other. A contemporary tract recalled the two events as being the cause of great celebration:[62]

Bells rang, Minstrills play'd, and Cannon did Thunder . . .
Pikes, Muskets and Drums, and mony gay Fellowes
The King's Health was Drunk at ilk Tavern and Ale-house
Instead of fair water their Fountains sprang Clarret.

The tract labelled the new King 'the justest Man on Earth',[63] and referred to the charter as 'their Rule, their Light, and their Guide'.[64]

As the unhappy mayoralty of Sir Henry Brabant revealed, the actual situation was far from as stable as these observations might suggest.[65] Brabant himself was a confirmed loyalist, one who, as Richardson observed in the nineteenth century, 'carried his attachment to the sovereign to an extent bordering on monomaniacism'.[66] His administration appears to have been the source of contention from the very beginning, though it is unclear whether his attitude towards the crown or his rivalry with other town political figures, especially Sir William Blackett, was the root cause of the difficulty. In any case, the clash led to efforts by both sides to the controversy to invoke the aid of the crown in support of their position. The election of the sheriff and Common Council had been suspended by Brabant because of an effort to elect his opponents; he wrote to the Earl of Sunderland to seek royal support and appears to have received it, for he summoned the electors, told them he had the King's support, and asked if they had any reason why the Common Council as named by him should not be sworn. He recalled that Sir William Blackett, speaking for the dissident group, 'dissatisfiedly said they had nothing to do, since your Majesty took the power from them, and so departed before the said Common Council could be all sworn'.[67]

In an apparent attempt to solidify his position, Brabant called a meeting of all the freemen of the town to explain the nature of the King's interference. According to his account, the meeting was awkward since his opponents 'did most wickedly disperse and spread abroad that the Mayor called a Gill [*sic*] in order to give up their Charter, which made the Mobile much more numerous at and about the Town Court that day than ever was seen before'. This uneasiness about the charter suggests that the picture of happy acceptance of Charles II's new charter may be somewhat overdrawn. Despite the obstruction of a significant number of aldermen, Brabant was able to calm the crowd by assuring them there was no further action contemplated with respect to the charter. 'They unanimously gave a great shout of "God bless the King"' and were dismissed without any disorder. 'All things', he noted, 'looked very serene and peaceable amongst the Commons, of which the far greater number are very loyall, but of late years much disheartened by the overawe of the Magistrates, who make a great many act against their inclinations'.[69]

The next stage in the crisis came by an unexpected route. Sir William Blackett, utilizing his position as a member of parliament, appears to have been able to persuade the crown to purge the corporation under the terms of Charles II's charter, in order to reduce Brabant's forces to a minority. Given the fervent loyalty of Brabant himself, the action of the crown at this juncture is difficult to explain, unless it is assumed that Blackett's true intentions and feelings were deliberately misrepresented, as Brabant claimed.[70] Even more puzzling is the failure of the crown to make any reply to Brabant's impassioned petition that the situation be rectified and the ascendancy of the Blackett group curtailed by a royal order continuing Brabant in his mayoralty for an additional year.[71]

The tenseness of the situation and the interaction of local rivalries with national issues was well illustrated in the celebrated struggle during Brabant's mayoralty to erect a statue of James II in Newcastle.[72] It is clear that Brabant himself was the moving force behind the decision to erect the statue, but the Blackett group entered strong objection to the scheme and refused to sign an order for it until Brabant threatened to send a list of those who would not sign directly to the King. At this point, he noted, they agreed, 'more out of fear than love'.[73] If the opposition to Brabant had its origins in local rivalries, it was by now clearly intertwined with national concerns as well. Blackett may not have hesitated to use the King to purge the corporation, but when it came to erecting a statue to him, his supporters were not slow to declare publicly that 'the erecting of the said statue looked like Popery'.[74]

In the succeeding municipal elections, the Blackett group had its way. Brabant was not continued in office, and the Blackett-backed candidate Nicholas Cole was elected mayor. Although Cole's mayoralty passed without undue intensification of the growing rift between crown and community, two events falling within it were disturbing pointers to the continuation of crisis. At the end of May the King sent a mandate to the corporation instructing them to admit Sir William Creagh, a notorious papist, to his freedom and he was duly admitted a month later.[75] In September, an address, signed by Cole as Mayor, was sent to the King; though couched in terms of formal loyalty, it clearly expressed deep concern about a growing pattern of interference with civic privileges and overt support of Catholics in the process. It thanked the King for his 'repeated acts of grace and bounty vouchsafed to this your ancient corporation' but then added the significant qualification that the thanks were being extended for those acts 'not only in the free enjoyment of our liberties and priviledges, but more especially in the full exercise of the professed religion of the Church of England, whereof we are true members, true loyalty being inseparable from the principles of that church'.[76]

In the months that followed, the intertwining of local grievance with general national policy was intensified. There is every reason to suspect that Newcastle's antagonism towards the King would have markedly increased even had they conceived the interference with local conditions to be directed against the corporation alone; when they could see it as part of a broader policy, their sense of grievance in like manner broadened. Newcastle's experience in the last years of James II was far from unique; that unhappy monarch was busily unravelling the complex web of support for the monarchy that his brother had so patiently created, and his hand fell clumsily on many corporations and institutions.[77] In Newcastle the net result of his machinations was the alienation of the older governing elite by his interference with the charter, the alienation of the nonconformists by his papist policy, and the eventual restoration of inner-ring control in reaction to both these developments.

In 1687 John Squire was elected mayor in succession to Nicholas Cole; as a Merchant Adventurer and Hostman, he was a typical inner-ring candidate. At the end of December, James II, acting under the terms of the new charter, moved to reconstruct the corporation into a more pliant instrument of his will. By mandate he displaced the mayor, six aldermen, the sheriff, the deputy recorder, and fifteen of the Common Council. In addition he commanded the electors to choose the recently intruded Sir William Creagh as mayor, along with a carefully selected new set of officials to replace those he had removed.[78] Apparently the electors refused to elect them on the grounds that they were 'papists and persons not qualified' but this action had no effect, for Creagh and his colleagues assumed office notwithstanding.[79] Within a month the new corporation had drafted what was described as 'a remarkably fulsome address'[80] to the King, but it was not sent, a majority of the Common Council over-ruling it. Despite that setback, the adherents of royal policy appear to have believed that they had succeeded in controlling the corporation for James II. In a sermon preached before the mayor on 29th January 1688, a Jesuit Philip Metcalfe remarked that on the basis of 'universal applause' he could only conclude that Creagh 'commanded the hearts of all'.[81] If Metcalfe was apparently blind to the tension created by royal interference in the town's politics, he did sense that Creagh's religion was a source of contention: 'our Prince is pleased with your constant Loyalty; the famous Town of Newcastle with your prudent Government; good Christians with your exemplary life; I wish your Religion were in the same esteem with many as your Person is'.[82] Given the consistently anti-Catholic stance of the Newcastle clergy in the years preceeding 1688, the latter point was hardly surprising.[83] Even Vicar March, who could not accept the Glorious Revolution in good conscience, had never been able to tolerate the slightest sympathy for the religion of his royal master.

In fact, both religious and political concerns were present. If the traditional elite had been disturbed by the issue of a new charter and the use made of it to date, their concern must have been immeasurably heightened by a further breach of the privileges carried out with the connivance of Creagh and his subservient colleagues.[84] In February a *quo warranto* was served on the mayor; the closeness of the date to that of the failure to carry the loyal address to the King is suggestive. At the beginning of March Creagh and his colleagues surrendered the charter of Charles II, although once again the surrender was not enrolled. Sometime after 9th June and before 22nd September James II granted a further new charter to the town 'whereby the ancient custom of electing the mayor &c and burgesses for parliament were changed and the same in great measure put into the power of the mayor and aldermen', a power being 'reserved in the King to place or displace'.[85] The most plausible reconstruction that can be made of the ensuing municipal elections is that a combination of dissenters who opposed the Catholicism of Creagh and his colleague and traditional Newcastle political figures who were horrified by the manipulation of the town's charter combined to thwart the continuation of the Creagh group. The design of the latter was to secure the election of Catholics as both mayor and sheriff; the result was a victory for two protestants, William Hutchinson and Matthew Partis. It is certain that Ambrose Barnes played a critical role in organizing the opposition and securing the result, but it is worth remembering that his biographer was at pains to stress that this was no 'clandestine election of Dissenters' but rather that many who co-operated 'were known to be zealously affected to the Church of England'.[86]

The royal policy with respect to Newcastle was clearly in disarray. Even a corporation already reshaped in the royal interest could not be coerced into the desired results in 1688. The last desperate gamble of reversing the policy of charter interference in October did nothing to alter the situation from the royal point of view. All it allowed was a quiet transition back to inner-ring control following the repudiation of the new charters of Charles II and James II.[87] On 5th November Hutchinson and Partis relinquished their offices, to be replaced by Nicholas Ridley, the sheriff of 1682, and Matthew White, both typical inner-ring figures; as James Clephan put it, 'corporate life had flowed back to its old channels'.[88] It was coincidental but appropriate that the soon-to-be William III landed on the same day.

To use the terminology of modern political discussion, one could argue that the political consciousness of Newcastle had been considerably, if perhaps temporarily, raised in the events that culminated in the Glorious Revolution. It had been raised in that familiar progression by which specific grievance was generalized and then elevated to the level of ideological opposition. In describing these events with specific reference to Newcastle in the following year, James Welwood noted, 'The Acession of a Popish Prince to the throne, the barefac'd Invasion of Liberty and Property, the palpable Incroachments on Laws and Fundamental Constitutions . . . were Events too great and important not to awaken England out of a Lethargy the reiterated Promises of preserving the Protestant Religion as by Law establish'd had cast her into'.[89] His analysis is substantially correct. A corporation whose general stance was in favour of the crown because of the support the crown could give to its own peculiar forms of monopoly was turned to opposition when support was replaced by control; a dissenting element excluded from town political life was not long deceived about the true import of James II's interest in toleration and not willing to continue their support at the price demanded. In December 1688 Lord Lumley entered Newcastle declaring 'for the protestant religion and a free parliament'[90] and in May of the following year the statue of James II was pulled down by an unruly mob incited to action by the garrison soldiers.[91]

Not everyone in Newcastle accepted the Glorious Revolution without question. A sermon by Thomas Knaggs preached in June 1689 struck a strongly protestant and loyal note and asked for a blessing on the forces of William and Mary in the war against the French; in his preface to the printed version, Knaggs noted 'A few hot, inconsiderable men among us were very angry after I preach'd it'.[92] Vicar March, though remaining strong in his denunciation of papacy, could not reconcile his view of monarchy with the events of 1688; in July 1690 he was warned by the Common Council that his salary would be stopped unless he would pray for William and Mary by name.[93] But for the bulk of the population, the outcome of these stirring events meant the return to life as normal, at least so far as political life was concerned. At various points throughout the century local and national politics had intersected in ways that intensified the nature of political debate. Local grievances became the medium through which many national concerns were perceived, while the issues and labels of national debate were used to clothe the continuing local political struggles. The two perspectives were deeply intertwined. If local issues or the local interpretation of issues continued to be predominant and concern for the town's chartered privileges remained to the fore, both were touched, influenced, and informed by the constant concern of the national government for the secure allegiance and peaceful governance of such a populous and economically important town.

Notes

1. For a general discussion of this tendency with respect to the years of the English Revolution, see R.C. Richardson, *The Debate on the English Revolution* (London, 1977), chap. 7. R. Howell, *Newcastle upon Tyne and the Puritan Revolution* (Oxford, 1967), was an early attempt to apply this perspective. J.S. Morrill, *The Revolt of the Provinces* (London, 1976), is an excellent recent study informed by this perspective.

2. This critical point is raised, briefly discussed, but not wholly resolved in R. Ashton, *The English Civil War: Conservatism and Revolution 1603–1649* (London, 1978), chap. 3, esp. pp. 67–70.

3. This situation is amply reflected in the case of Newcastle in the period of the English Revolution. See Howell, *Newcastle and the Puritan Revolution*, chaps. 3 and 6.

4. The interaction of local and national perspectives was hardly confined, of course, to the political sphere, and given the relations of political, religious, and social factors, the isolation of the political element for study here has some aspects of artificiality. This paper is not intended to minimize the importance of the other forms of interaction but rather to offer some suggestions about the manner in which the process of interaction worked by examining its specific manifestation within the political sphere.

5. B.L. Lansdowne MSS 66, no. 86.

6. R. Welford, *History of Newcastle and Gateshead* (Newcastle, 1884–7), 3:420. C.H. Hunter Blair, *The Mayors and Lord Mayors of Newcastle upon Tyne 1216–1940 and the Sheriffs of the County of Newcastle upon Tyne 1399–1940* (Newcastle, 1940), pp. 44–6. The grand lessees holding office were William Johnson, William Riddell, Henry Anderson, Henry Mitford, Henry Chapman, Roger Nicholson, William Selby and George Farnaby.

7. Lionel Maddison was the mayor in 1593; he was said to be in sympathy with the reformers and to have 'proved the Townes interest in the grannde lease'. B.L. Lansdowne MSS 81, no. 41.

8. The Lord Mayor of London noted in January 1596 that the prominent reformer Henry Sanderson refused to act in any way to the prejudice of the Newcastle corporation and would only testify on behalf of London if the suit were directed solely against the co-partners of the Grand Lease. J.U. Nef, *The Rise of the British Coal Industry* (London, 1932), 2:124. The general difficulties of the reform group over this point are usefully discussed, *ibid.*, 2:121–25.

9. For a brief discussion of this point, see J.H. Sacret, 'The Restoration Government and Municipal Corporations', *EHR*, vol. 14 (1930), pp. 232–59 and B.L.K. Henderson, 'The Commonwealth Charters', *TRHS*, 3rd Series, vi (1912), pp. 129–62.

10. On the charters and the nature of town government, see Howell, *Newcastle and the Puritan Revolution*, pp. 42 ff.

11. For a more detailed discussion of this point, see *ibid.*, pp. 46–7. In any case it is clear that the Hostmen did not exactly usurp power from the older merchant gilds as some have asserted. For an example of this sort of view, see *A Short View of the Rights of the Freemen of Newcastle upon Tyne in the Town Moor* (Newcastle, 1962).

12. F.W. Dendy, ed., *Extracts from the Records of the Company of Hostmen of Newcastle upon Tyne* (Durham, 1901). Surtees Soc., vol. 105, p. xli; J.F. Gibson, *The Newcastle upon Tyne Improvement Acts. . . . with an Introductory Historical Sketch* (London, 1881), p. xxxvi. While the Hostmen argued that this provision did not include the 15 bye-trades, this point was not consistently enforced; for example, Thomas Turner, a barber surgeon, was admitted on 17th January 1604. Dendy, *Records of the Hostmen*, p. 267.

13. Statistics on the mayors and sheriffs are compiled from Blair, *Mayors and Sheriffs of Newcastle*; M.H. Dodds, ed., *The Register of Freemen of Newcastle upon Tyne* (Newcastle, 1923): and the records of the Hostmen and Merchant Adventurers.

14. Statistics on M.P.s are compiled from C.H. Hunter Blair, 'Members of Parliament for Northumberland and Newcastle upon Tyne 1559–1831', *AA*[4], xxiii (1945); Dodds, *Register of Freemen*; and the records of the Hostmen and Merchant Adventurers.

15. For a detailed discussion of the riot, see Howell, *Newcastle and the Puritan Revolution*, pp. 53 ff.

16. *Cal. S.P. Dom., 1625–49 Addenda*, p. 453.

17. For Coke's criticisms see *ibid*. For the mayor's despondent response see *Cal. S.P. Dom.*, 1631–33, p. 585.

18. PRO SP/16/240/27. The text of the grievances is printed in Welford, *History of Newcastle*, 3:313–15.

19. PRO SP 16/245/32. The Council of the North noted that it had decided to look more fully into the matter because they realized the significance of the town to the King. *Ibid.*

20. M.H. Dodds, 'Ship Money', *Newcastle Citizen*, vol. 1 (1930), pp. 68–70. Cf. also *Cal. S.P. Dom., 1638–9*, pp. 4–5, 80, 105, 321, 325; *Cal. S.P. Dom., 1639–40*, p. 460; *Cal. S.P. Dom., 1640*, p. 133.

21. *Cal. S.P. Dom., 1639*, p. 480.

22. *Ibid.*, pp. 450–51; the informant was Sir John Marley.

23. For a detailed discussion of these elections, see Howell, *Newcastle and the Puritan Revolution*, pp. 124 ff. The discussion of the elections to the Long Parliament should be supplemented by R. Howell, 'The Elections to the Long Parliament in Newcastle: Some New Evidence', *AA*, xlvi (1968), pp. 225–7.

24. For an example of the reaction against the Scots, see *A Letre from an Alderman of Newcastle Shewing in Part the Grievances There* in M.A. Richardson, ed., *Reprints of Rare Tracts* (Newcastle, 1847), vol. I. This letter appears to have been circulated in manuscript form. There are copies in PRO SP 16/466/89; Bodleian Library Tanner MSS 65, ff. 110–11v; B.L. Harleian MSS 1576, ff. 312–13 v; William Trumbull MSS, xx, f. 48 (Berkshire Record Office).

25. For a detailed discussion of political life in Newcastle in this period, see Howell, *Newcastle and the Puritan Revolution*, chaps. 4 and 5.

26. A.M. Oliver, *The Mayoralty of Newcastle upon Tyne* (Newcastle, 1910), pp. 21–2.

27. M.H. Dodds, ed., *Extracts from the Newcastle upon Tyne Council Minute Book 1639–1656* (Newcastle, 1920), p. 24.

28. *Ibid.*, pp. 27–8. The order was confirmed at the beginning of October. *Ibid.*, pp. 29–30.

29. They were named in an act of 24th March 1644/5. Newcastle Common Council Book 1645–50, Tyne and Wear County Archives, f. 25. They were also named in the ordinance for the government of Newcastle, 26th May 1644/5. *L.J.*, 7:395.

30. The pattern is not unusual to Newcastle. I have discussed this point in more general terms in R. Howell, 'The Structure of Urban Politics in the English Civil War', *Albion*, vol. 11, no. 2 (1979), pp. 111–27.

31. Examples among the aldermen would include Robert Shafto, Mark Milbank and John Emerson. Again, the existence of this middle group, which successfully sought accommodation with successive and conflicting regimes, would seem to be a general feature of urban politics in the period rather than a peculiar Newcastle feature. Cf. Howell, 'Structure of Urban Politics', pp. 116–19, 122–3.

32. For a detailed discussion of the Bonner-Dawson clique, see Howell, *Newcastle and the Puritan Revolution*, chap. 5.

33. Newcastle Common Council Book 1650–9. Tyne and Wear County Archives, f. 406.

34. This was revealed clearly, for example, in their struggle with Ralph Gardner. If anything, Gardner seems to have fared less well under the parliamentary corporation than he had when the inner ring predominated. See R. Howell, *Monopoly on the Tyne 1650–58: Papers Relating to Ralph Gardner* (Newcastle, 1978).

35. The effective order for his removal was dated 24th March 1647. Dodds, *Council Minute Book*, pp. 68–9. An order to remove him had been signed as early as 18th February. Newcastle Common Council Book 1645–50, Tyne and Wear County Archives, f. 110. It is interesting to note that Cosins invoked both a 'local' and a 'national' argument against his removal. On the one hand, he relied on the charter for his position; on the other, he argued he could not be removed since he was brought in by parliamentary ordinance. *Ibid.*, ff. 124–6.

36. *C.J.*, 5:208. Cosins was not alone in commenting on this subject. Cf. the two letters from Skippon, the parliamentary governor of Newcastle, printed in H. Cary, *Memorials of the Great Civil War 1642–1652* (London, 1842), 1:229–32.

37. *C.J.*, 5:229.

38. Dodds, *Council Minute Book*, pp. 102–4.

39. *Ibid.*, p. 21; MSS Hostmen, Old Book, ff. 185, 187, 188; MSS Merchant Adventurers, Order Book, ff. 1, 18, 26.

40. Cf. E33 (17), *A True Relation of the Late Proceedings of the Scottish Army* (London, 1644), pp. 11–13; *Kingdomes Weekly Intelligencer*, no. 69, 21–7 August 1644, pp. 556–7; E16(5), *A Particular Relation of the Taking of Newcastle* (London, 1644), pp. 12–13, 9 (2nd pagination).

41. *Cal. S.P. Dom.*, 1656–7, p. 272.

42. On the falsity of the charges, see Howell, *Newcastle and the Puritan Revolution*, pp. 180–81.

43. *Cal. S.P. Dom., 1656–7*, pp. 226–7; Newcastle Common Council Book 1656–1722, Tyne and Wear County Archives, f. 12v.

44. Cf. Newcastle Common Council Book 1650–9, Tyne and Wear County Archives, f. 406.

45. It is perhaps suggestive that George Blakiston, a younger generation member of an old-style Newcastle political family, resigned from the Common Council in protest at the election. *Ibid.*, f. 467. But it may be that the objection was simply to Barnes's youth. Cf. W.H.D. Longstaffe, ed., *Memoirs of the Life of Mr. Ambrose Barnes* (Durham, 1867), Surtees Soc., vol. 50, p. 99.

46. Newcastle Common Council Book 1645–50, Tyne and Wear County Archives, f. 25.

47. No records of meetings of the Common Council were kept until 28th March 1645. Dodds, *Council Minute Book*, p. 25. The financial machinery of the town appears to have been reestablished more quickly. Receipts were kept from 22nd November 1644 and payments from the fourth week of October. Newcastle Chamberlains' Accounts 1642–5., Tyne and Wear County Archives, ff. 58, 190v.

48. They are among the signatories of a letter to Speaker Lenthall a month before the first official notice of their appointment. *C.J.*, 3:714.

49. The alderman so named was Henry Lawson, the fifth senior member of the Common Council. Dodds, *Council Minute Book*, p. 21. William Dawson appears in his place in the earliest list of the parliamentary corporation which dates from the audit of accounts, 4th October 1645. Newcastle Chamberlains' Accounts 1642–5, Tyne and Wear County Archives, f. 167.

50. B. Whitelocke, *Memorials of the English Affairs from the Beginning of the Reign of Charles I to the Happy Restoration of King Charles II* (Oxford, 1853), 1:348.

51. Newcastle Common Council Book 1656–1722, Tyne and Wear County Archives, f. 43.

52. *Ibid.*, f. 44.

53. Those removed were George Dawson, Christopher Nicholson, Henry Rawlings, William Johnson, and Peter Sanderson. Seated in their stead were Sir James Clavering, Sir Francis Anderson, Sir Francis Liddell, Henry Maddison, and Cuthbert Carr. Predictably, the middle group represented by Robert Shafto, Mark Milbank, and John Emerson survived.

54. Concern about the dissenters is widely reflected in the literature emanating from the Newcastle clergy in the later Stuart period. Cf. for example, J. March, *The False Prophet Unmaskt* (London, 1683); J. March, *A Sermon Preached before the Right Worshipful the Mayor, Recorder, Aldermen, Sheriff &c of . . . Newcastle* (London, 1677); J. Rawlet, *A Dialogue betwixt Two Protestants* (London, 1685); and J. Shaw, *No Reformation of the Established Reformation* (London, 1685). When Thomas Story visited a conventicle at Newcastle he was most impressed by the political overtones. 'Expecting to hear something like Doctrine from so noted a Man among them', he was disappointed that the message was substantially 'suggestions of Jealousy and Dislike against the Government'. *A Journal of the Life of Thomas Story* (Newcastle, 1747), p. 3.

55. *Cal. S.P. Dom., 1660–1*, p. 4.

56. E1038 (8) *The Lords Loud Call to England* (London, 1660), p. 19.

57. R. Astell, *Vota Non Bella* (Gateshead, 1660): R. Hooke, *The Bishops' Appeale or an Address to the Brethren of the Presbyteriall Judgment* (Newcastle, 1661); R. Thomson, *The Loyall Subject* (Newcastle, 1660 and 1662).

58. J. Brand, *The History and Antiquities of the Town and County of the Town of Newcastle upon Tyne* (London, 1789), 2:193.

59. J. March, *Th' Encaenia of St. Ann's Chappel in Sandgate* (London, 1682), sig. A3–A3v.

60. Brand, *History of Newcastle*, 2:194.

61. Longstaffe, *Memoirs of Barnes*, p. 176 n.

62. G. Stuart, *A Joco-Serious Discourse in Two Dialogues* (London and Newcastle, 1686), pp. 1–2.

63. *Ibid.*, sig. A4.

64. *Ibid.*, p. 3.

65. The following account of events in the mayoralty of Brabant is drawn substantially from *The Eve of the Revolution in Newcastle upon Tyne* in M.A. Richardson, ed., *Reprints of Rare Tracts* (Newcastle, 1847), vol. iv.

66. *Ibid.*, p. 15. The biographer of Barnes recorded that Brabant once declared 'if the king should command him to kill a man in cold blood, he took himself bound in conscience and duty to execute his command'. Longstaffe, *Memoirs of Barnes*, p. 193.

67. *Eve of the Revolution in Newcastle*, p. 8.

68. *Ibid.*, p. 9.

69. *Ibid.*, pp. 9–10.

70. *Ibid.*, p. 10.

71. *Ibid.*, pp. 13–14.

72. On the statue see M.R. Toynbee, 'Fresh Light on William Larson's Statue of James II at Newcastle upon Tyne', *AA*[4], xxix (1951), pp. 108–17; M.R. Toynbee, 'A Further Note on William Larson's Statue of James II at Newcastle upon Tyne', *AA*[4], xxxiv (1956), p. 91.

73. *Eve of the Revolution in Newcastle*, p. 13.

74. *Ibid.*

75. Longstaffe, *Memoirs of Barnes*, p. 176 n.

76. *Ibid.*

77. M. Ashley, *James II* (Minneapolis, 1977) and J. Miller, *James II: A study in Kingship* (London, 1977), *passim*.

78. Longstaffe, *Memoirs of Barnes*, p. 176 n.

79. *Ibid.*

80. *Ibid.*

81. P. Metcalfe, *A Sermon Preached before the Right Worshipful the Mayor of the Town & County of Newcastle upon Tyne* (London, 1688), sig. A2.

82. *Ibid.*, sig. A2v.

83. For examples of this anti-Catholicism, cf. J. March, *A Sermon Preached before the Mayor*; J. March, *Sermons Preach'd on Several Occasions* (London, 1699); J. Rawlet, *A Dialogue betwixt Two Protestants*; J. Rawlet, *An Explication of the Creed, the Ten Commandments, and the Lords Prayer* (London, 1679); J. Shaw, *No Reformation of the Established Reformation*; J. Shaw, *Origo Protestantium or an Answer to a Popish Manuscript* (London, 1679); J. Shaw, *The Pourtraicture of the Primitive Saints* (Newcastle, 1652). For the imporance of

anti-Catholicism in the period, see J. Miller, *Popery and Politics in England 1660–1688* (Cambridge, 1973).

84. Longstaffe, *Memoirs of Barnes*, p. 176 n.

85. *Ibid.* Oliver gives the date of 24th July for the new charter. Oliver, *Mayoralty of Newcastle*, p. 25.

86. Longstaffe, *Memoirs of Barnes*, pp. 176 n, 177–8.

87. Blair, *Mayors and Sheriffs of Newcastle*, p. 79.

88. J. Clephan, 'William Hutchinson Merchant Adventurer', off-print from *AA*, 1880, p. 16.

89. *Vindication of the Present Great Revolution in England in Five Letters Pass'd betwixt James Welwood M.D. and Mr. John March* (London, 1689), sig. A2.

90. *Universal Intelligencer*, no. 1, 11 Dec., 1688, quoted in *Destruction of the Statue of James the Second at Newcastle* in M.A. Richardson, ed., *Reprints of Rare Tracts* (Newcastle, 1847), vol. iv, p. 8.

91. *Ibid.*, pp. 9–17. The frequently repeated statement of Bourne that the statue was torn down in 1688 is clearly erroneous. H. Bourne, *The History of Newcastle upon Tyne* (Newcastle, 1736), p. 131.

92. Longstaffe, *Memoirs of Barnes*, p. 436.

93 *Ibid.*, p. 438. *Vindication of the Present Great Rebellion in England*, p. 25 accuses March of labelling the actions of the Prince of Orange 'with the infamous Names of Rebellion, Damnation and the like'. March himself asserted that passive obedience was 'a Principle founded in the Word of God'. *Ibid.*, p. 5.

INDEX